Karl Moore's Visual Basic .NET: The Tutorials

KARL MOORE

Apress™

Karl Moore's Visual Basic .NET: The Tutorials
Copyright © 2002 by Karl Moore

ISBN (pbk): 1-59059-021-X

Printed and bound in the United States of America 12345678910
Trademarked names may appear in this book. Rather than use a trademark symbol with every occurrence of a trademarked name, we use the names only in an editorial fashion and to the benefit of the trademark owner, with no intention of infringement of the trademark.

Technical Reviewers: Patricia Moore, Richard Costall, Ray Ellison, Erik Giggey, Donald Carter
Editorial Directors: Dan Appleman, Peter Blackburn, Gary Cornell, Jason Gilmore, Karen Watterson, John Zukowski
Managing Editor: Grace Wong
Project Manager: Alexa Stuart
Copy Editor: Tom Gillen
Production Editors: Janet Vail and Grace Wong
Compositor: Impressions Book and Journal Services, Inc.
Indexer: Ann Rogers
Cover Designer: Tom Debolski
Marketing Manager: Stephanie Rodriguez

Distributed to the book trade in the United States by Springer-Verlag New York, Inc., 175 Fifth Avenue, New York, NY, 10010
and outside the United States by Springer-Verlag GmbH & Co. KG, Tiergartenstr. 17, 69112 Heidelberg, Germany.
In the United States, phone 1-800-SPRINGER, email orders@springer-ny.com, or visit http://www.springer-ny.com.
Outside the United States, fax +49 6221 345229, email orders@springer.de, or visit http://www.springer.de.

For information on translations, please contact Apress directly at 2560 Ninth St., Suite 219, Berkeley, CA 94710.
Phone: 510-549-5903, Fax: 510-549-5933, Email: info@apress.com, Web site: http://www.apress.com

The information in this book is distributed on an "as is" basis, without warranty. Although every precaution has been taken in the preparation of this work, neither the author nor Apress shall have any liability to any person or entity with respect to any loss or damage caused or alleged to be caused directly or indirectly by the information contained in this work.

The source code for this book is available to readers at http://www.apress.com in the Downloads section. You will need to answer questions pertaining to this book in order to successfully download the code.

Dedicated to my loving family: David, Patricia, and Jo-Anne.

Oh, and my brain—without whom none of this would've been possible.

Brief Contents

v

Contents

Tutorial 5 Using Objects *367*

5.1 Why Objects Are Important *369*

5.2 Objects in Real Life, Class Libraries, and More *391*

Tutorial 6 Services Rendered *417*

6.1 Introducing the World of Web Services *419*

8.2 Intermediate Tips and Techniques 487

8.3 Advanced Tips and Techniques 505

Foreword

"The man who has no imagination has no wings."—Muhammad Ali

NOT EVERYTHING IN LIFE IS EASY.

Nuclear physics. Advanced trigonometry. The Welsh language. Pushing a twenty-ton truck up a hill using your left pinkie. That's not easy.

But some things definitely are. Like *programming*, say.

The problem is, if you've ever tried to learn how to program, you'll know most of the books out there are about as exciting as Bill Gates' cardigan collection. They're full of annoying acronyms and confusing concepts. On every other page, they stick whopping great big tables containing "keywords to remember."

Yeah, like that's going to happen.

When I decided to teach programming online some years ago, I decided to go against the flow. I decided to use what I knew about the learning process to help my readers understand concepts quicker and to actually *enjoy* the whole process.

I wrote in plain English. I constantly linked new concepts back to stuff each reader already knew. I presented the big picture and kept asking questions. I regularly presented review sheets. I explained geek speak. I held the users' hands at first, pointed out potential pitfalls, then let each individual fly.

It worked, and the response blew me away.

Thankfully, I managed to catch a plane back—and began writing the book you're holding right now, all about the new .NET technologies. And this baby works in just the same way as my online tutorials, only better.

My mum is *so* proud.

This book is split into eight separate tutorials, each of which teaches a real-to-life area of programming. From databases to the Web, it's all here, and each tutorial will turn you into a real guru, with suggestions as to how you can take your knowledge *even further*.

So, let's prepare to enter the nerd world. Grow a beard and apply a little BO—and remember, don't worry and don't memorize. Just play and have fun!

Thank you for learning with me.

Karl Moore, April 2002

About the Author

KARL MOORE IS A TECHNOLOGY AUTHOR living in Yorkshire, England. He runs his own consultancy group, White Cliff Computing Ltd., and is senior editor behind the popular development site, VB-World. When he's not writing for magazines, speaking at conferences, or making embarrassing mistakes on live radio, Karl enjoys a complete lack of a social life.

Karl says his life goals include climbing out of bed, reaching the high notes in "Loving You", and learning to speak in hieroglyphics.

You can visit Karl on the Web at `www.karlmoore.com` or email him at `karl@karlmoore.com`.

Acknowledgments

When I first plotted this book on a train home from Cardiff Central last year, I hadn't planned on including an Acknowledgments section. In fact, I'd only planned on three individual tutorials, one that never made it, and six extra that did.

But Acknowledgments? Hah, it was just me and my trusty fake-leather organizer.

How very wrong I was. I've learned in the past months that writing a book is a true culmination of efforts—and to all the people who have helped, I'd like to extend my sincere thanks.

First and foremost, thanks go to Tricia Moore, a family member and technical reviewer, for her patience and coordination skills—and for being one of the few people who didn't mind knocking me off my horse when things didn't work. Big appreciation also goes to project manager Alexa Stuart, who always managed to get me back on it.

Thanks to Tom Gillen, my editor, for recognizing that most of my best jokes were libelous and removing them before the lawyers did. Kudos to you, intelligent man. Also, my appreciation goes out to Grace Wong, who encountered all those last-minute typesetting hurdles—and survived. Plus I raise my hat to the best marketing queen of all, Stephanie Rodriguez.

Of course, the Apress editorial directors also need mentioning, not as a matter of course, but because they're real people. First and foremost, Dan Appleman, who kept me entertained with readers' stories in London and has since regretted ever giving me his e-mail address; Gary Cornell, whom I shared an ice cream with in Barcelona and who convinced me that VB6 books were a dying breed back in the year 2000; and Karen Watterson, who provided much-needed moral support and now has her electricity back.

A big thanks also goes out to Mark and Katrina, the BBC pals who constantly remind me sleep is actually good for you. Also, the team behind my own company, White Cliff, deserves a round of applause for their initiative and bright thinking—they're the people who continued to earn me a salary during the months I couldn't.

And, of course, the people who actually inspired the book: those who read my online scribblings and prompted me to go one step further. From the African King with an interest in programming, to the recently released Australian convict taking a long overdue career move, to Jenny in Auckland who has just passed her programming class with flying colors—you are the people who kept me burning the candle well into the midnight hours. Thank you.

Finally, to the most important people of all: Mum, Dad, and Jo-Anne. It is to these three I owe my life.

About This Book

THIS BOOK IS SPLIT INTO EIGHT SEPARATE TUTORIALS, each designed to get you up to speed with a different area of the .NET world:

Tutorial 1, "Beginning VB .NET": Who puts the *fun* into programming fundamentals? If you're new to VB .NET, this is your starting block. This five-chapter tutorial will provide you with a thorough grounding in programming with your soon-to-be favorite language. Covering everything from painting a form to error handling.

Tutorial 2, "Doing Databases": In the real world, databases are essential. This five-chapter tutorial is your ultimate survival guide, covering everything from creating your own simple Access database through to writing your own transactional SQL Server-powered transactional Web application. Corr blimey, missus.

Tutorial 3, "Working the Web": No matter how little Internet experience you have, this three-chapter ASP.NET tutorial will show you how to create your own fully interactive, advanced Web sites in minutes. Covering everything from Web controls to user authentication.

Tutorial 4, "Going Mobile": Fancy writing applications that can run on anything from your cell phone to that wired microwave? Get your VB .NET code talking in the language of mobile devices, with the free Mobile Internet Toolkit and this two-chapter lifesaver. A real eye-opener.

Tutorial 5, "Using Objects": Create better, more-maintainable, bug-free applications, quicker, by using object-oriented programming techniques. This two-chapter tutorial gives you the full lowdown on how using classes can really improve both your code and salary.

Tutorial 6, "Services Rendered": It's DCOM on a longer wire, it's a groovy way of getting computers talking to each other, it's a cross-platform XML-based communication method. It's cool, it's Web Services, and this single-chapter tutorial shows you how to get your own up and running within half an hour.

Tutorial 7, "From VB6 to .NET": If you've just moved to the world of .NET from Visual Basic 6, you need to get your head around a few changes. This one-chapter overview provides a quick rundown of the differences, plus advice on where to go from here.

Tutorial 8, "Tips and Techniques": Split into Beginner, Intermediate, and Advanced chapters, this part provides reams of ready-to-run solutions to some of the most common .NET programming tasks. Whether you want to print from your program or generate OLE DB strings with ease, this nifty collection is a complete must-read for all developers.

Appendixes: Installing Visual Studio .NET, Project Defaults, Standard Naming Conventions, Windows Form Controls, VB .NET Data Types, and SQL Server Data Types.

If you're new to programming, it's recommended that you start with Tutorial 1, "Beginning VB .NET", and then read through each tutorial sequentially. Every chapter builds upon the knowledge you acquired in the last. Also, ensure that you read the Review Sheets at the end of each chapter to help solidify your knowledge base.

If you have programmed in a previous version of Visual Basic, start with Tutorial 7, "From VB6 to .NET", which should give you a grasp of changes in the new programming platform. After this, read the Review Sheets at the end of each chapter in Tutorial 1 "Beginning VB .NET", to ensure that you really grasp the key concepts. Once you've gotten an overview of the differences, start selectively reading the tutorials that interest you. Each includes special references for those coming from VB6.

Users of all levels will find it enormously beneficial to spend time browsing all the code samples in the three chapters of Tutorial 8, "Tips and Techniques". They demonstrate real code in action and should help you grasp many of the techniques shown throughout the book.

Good luck!

TUTORIAL 1

Beginning VB .NET

Programming, Visual Basic, and Everything

"Technology, like art, is a soaring exercise of the human imagination."
—Daniel Bell

HAVE YOU EVER WANTED TO PROGRAM—but couldn't be bothered with all that technical jargon? Ever seen a nerdy bookshelf—and felt slightly overwhelmed by the mass of 1,500-page code books written by socially inept types with beards and BO? Ever wanted to ditch your current job for a hilariously high salary as a Silicon Valley developer?

Well, hello sailor! Welcome to the solution! I'm your host, Karl Moore, and you're reading the very first tutorial here in *Karl Moore's Visual Basic .NET: The Tutorials*. This is where your journey begins—the start of a five-chapter roller coaster that'll teach you all the essentials and infinitely more.

Hmm, roller coaster? Okay, maybe not. It's just a shorter programming guide with a couple of cheap puns. But it works and it will be fun. I promise.

Don't worry if you're new to all this; I won't be drowning you in weird or confusing acronyms. Neither will I be teaching you how to double-click. Or launch the Help feature. Or plug your computer in. You're not a dummy, and you shouldn't buy books that say you are *<hint, hint>*. This is just straight talk from a curvy guy.

So, what's on the agenda today? Well, we'll start by learning exactly what VB .NET is all about and how it fits into the big picture. Then we'll be getting our hands dirty by knocking together our very first application.

After that? Oh, basically, you'll read a few more tutorials and become all knowledgeable, clever, and completely in-the-know. In two month's time, you'll turn into a fire-blazing industry leader and leave me to clean the toilets in Aberdeen for the rest of my years.

Ready to begin? Without further ado, let's start today by asking ourselves: *What exactly is this VB .NET lark all about?*

What Is VB .NET?

So, what's this VB .NET thing all about?

Well, unless you accidentally thought this was a guide to geraniums, you've probably already got a fair idea. But let's clarify.

We've all heard of the Windows success story. It's an operating system used on zillions of computers throughout the world and possibly beyond. But, back in the early days, Billy Boy Gates and his gang of merry geeks needed to drum up interest. So they had an idea: why not create one big easy-to-use Windows program that you can use to create other Windows programs?

Heck, why not? It'd increase the popularity of Windows, the number of programs on the market, and Bill's bank balance. So they did, and, on my birthday, May 20, 1991, it was officially christened *Visual Basic 1*. Everyone say *ahhhh.* . . .

The plan had just one slight flaw: Visual Basic was about as technologically advanced as a broken abacus. It was deemed an industry play tool, and anyone wanting to push it further had to delve into the advanced help file, which held a minimum entry requirement of two Oxford degrees.

Thankfully, times changed and Visual Basic rapidly matured through the years. People began using the language to create programs for the business world, to create games for the players, to create Web sites for the surfers, to create huge whopping bank balances for themselves. Life was good, and, by the time version six hit the stores, VB was the most popular programming language in the entire world, ever.

By this time, Gates was getting pretty darn bored. Already richer than a million manufacturers of Monopoly money, his job no longer gave him the thrill it presented when he released the first version of Windows or Visual Basic. Oh, and programmers were complaining that the old tools were starting to wear and that they were unable to keep up with the fast-moving technology market.

So, he decided to do it all over again.

Nine years later, in the year 2000, Gates and his now slightly older gang of geeks unveiled something called the .NET strategy. The strategy was essentially a big revamping operation, a chance to splutter the market with brand spanking new technology tools (and earn Bill even more money).

So all the programmers got back to work, and, in the first quarter of 2002, Microsoft officially unveiled a whole bunch of new tools to cover this new strategy thing.

First off, they knocked out the .NET Framework, which is something you'll hear a lot of hype about in the programming world. Well, ignore all that rubbish. The truth is it's essentially a Windows upgrade that works for .NET programs. It "runs" .NET applications, it handles program memory, and it provides a common base of functionality for programmers to use. It does all the boring plumbing stuff you really don't care about. Ladies and gentlemen, the .NET Framework.

At the same time, they also unveiled Visual Studio .NET, a package that allows you to create programs that run on top of that .NET Framework. (See Figure 1-1 for a basic diagram.) And you can write those programs in languages such as Visual C#, Visual C++, and *<drum roll>* Visual Basic.

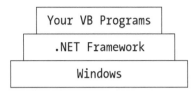

Figure 1-1. How It All Fits Together, and other bedtime stories

This new version of Visual Basic was christened *VB .NET*, which leaves us just where we are today: sitting with these super new tools in front of us. They're the result of years of behind-the-scenes work, and they sport a whole wad of mega-cool, crème-de-la-crème features that developers have been dreaming about for decades.

Here, we'll be learning to take advantage of all these new wizzy what-nots. You'll learn how to create programs that your customers can use to simplify their lives, and earn yourself a big chunk of cash in the process. (Donations accepted with thanks.) The road to programming magician won't be immediate, but bear with me, and everything will start falling into place quicker than you'd believe.

But, first, as is typically a precursor to getting stuck into VB .NET, we need to actually install it. So, if you don't yet have Visual Studio .NET on your machine, head over to Appendix I to figure out how you can get it up-and-running.

If, however, you already have the package installed, it's time to move on. We've got some idea as to what this VB .NET lark is all about now and how the .NET Framework and Visual Studio .NET fit into the picture. Next, it's time to see it all in action.

All aboard for the VB .NET lightning tour. Ding ding!

Creating Your First Program

So, you've slapped VB .NET on your machine and you're ready to rumble. Great stuff. Let's dive straight into the deep end with a little hands-on:

1. Launch Visual Studio .NET via the Start menu: Start ➤ Programs ➤ Microsoft Visual Studio. NET ➤ Microsoft Visual Studio. NET.

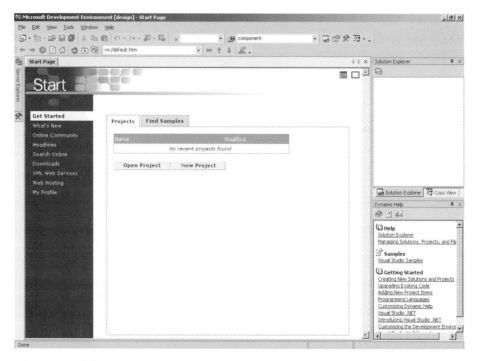

Figure 1-2. Welcome to your new home!

After a mass of whizzing and whirring, the screen shown in Figure 1-2 should pop up.

This is Visual Studio .NET, the place where programmers spend their time designing screens and writing code, regardless of whether they're using Visual Basic or Visual C#.

2.   Click on the New Project button.

Now you get to choose the sort of project you want to create in Visual Studio .NET. (See Figure 1-3.)

We're concerned with only Visual Basic projects in this book, and, specifically for this tutorial, only the Windows application project, which allows you to create a regular desktop program to run under Windows.

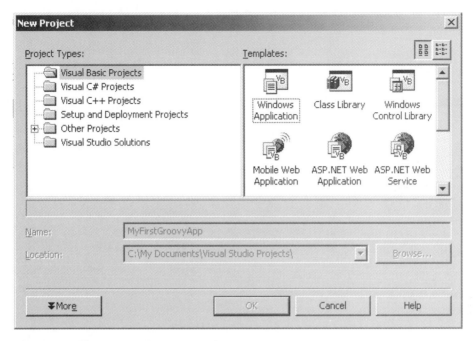

Figure 1-3. Choose a project, any project.

What are the other options? Well, you could create an ASP.NET Web service here, which allows you to make certain chunks of information available to other programs through the Internet or a network. You can also create an ASP.NET Web application if you're interested in throwing together a full-blown interactive Web site in just a couple of lines of code.

We'll be looking at all of these in later tutorials, but for now:

3.   Select the Windows Application icon.

4.   In the Name box, type "MyFirstGroovyApp".

Cast your eyes down to the Location box here. This is where all the files used in your project will be stored, including your final program itself. You're fine to stick with the default, but just remember what it is.

5.   Click on the OK button when finished.

Then, fifteen seconds of churning later, you should have something like
Figure 1-4 pop up.

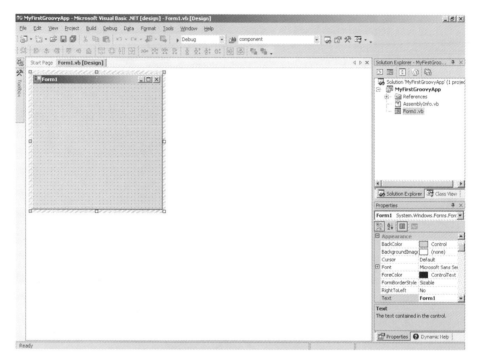

Figure 1-4. The development environment

Supercool! This is where you actually slap together your application. That
thing called Form1 in the middle is what users will see when they eventually run
your program.

Now, imagine that you're actually Vincent Van Gogh. Actually, you're better:
you have two ears and no sunflower fetish. I hope. Now, if you say that Form1 is
your canvas, it'd be fair to call the toolbox on the left your palette. It holds all the
mega-cool widgets you can paint onto your form to make a great program.

> **TOP TIP**   *If you can't see the toolbox, select View ➤ Toolbox from the menu, or click the hammer icon to the left of your screen. To stop the toolbox from automatically hiding itself, click its small tack icon.*

Have a quick scroll up and down, looking at the names and pictures. Recognize anything?

> **TOP TIP**   *They may look cool, but all those items in the toolbox are offi-cially called* .NET Framework components. *How incredibly uncool. However, in the real world, most programmers simply call them* controls. *Remember that; it'll gain you Brownie points in the nerd world.*

So, don that beret, yell "oh-la-la" every ten seconds, and let's do a little program-painting ourselves:

6.   Click on the Button control (Figure 1-5) in the toolbox, then click any-where on your form.

Figure 1-5. The Button control

Now, the Button control is actually, yes, a button. This control is one of those clicky OK-Apply-Cancel-type things you find all over the place. They're a little like McDonalds: completely overused, found everywhere, but you just can't live without 'em.

So, you've added your button and your form looks a little like that shown in Figure 1-6.

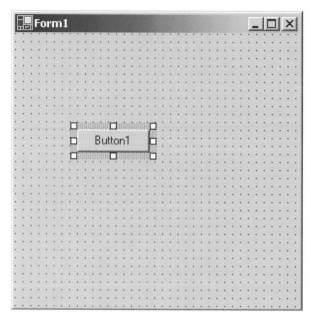

Figure 1-6. Move over, Van Gogh!

Hmm, not very impressive for something bearing the title ".NET Framework Component," is it? And, to be frank, if you were imitating Van Gogh, I've a gut feeling you'd be spotted as a fraud. But this is still the beginning. (At least, I hope it is. Otherwise, this'll be an incredibly short book.)

7. Resize your button by dragging it out using the eight white boxes surrounding it.

Now, move your eyes down to the bottom right of your screen. Notice the Properties window? The Properties window allows you to change how your control looks and works. You might want to change its color, its text, its font, or whatever. Simply enter a new value in the control property you want to change, and the control will be altered.

Spend a couple of minutes perusing the available properties. Play around. Change them. You won't break anything. (Much.)

8. Click on your button so its properties appear in the Properties window. (It should say Button1.)

9. Change its Text property to "Click Me Quick!"

10. Change the Font property to something wacky.

Figure 1-7. My final form

My form currently looks a little something like Figure 1-7.

You know, I'm sure I could've gone into design. Anyway, we've started creating our application, so let's get a feel for how it would work in the real world.

11. Click on the Start button on the menu. (It looks like Play on your VCR.)

This runs your program, ready for you to play with it. It puts it into what is known as *runtime*.

TOP TIP *You'll often hear programming nerds talking about* runtime *and* design time. *Runtime is when your program is actually running, either when you click on the Start button or when you actually run the final executable file. Design time is just the opposite: the time when you're actually painting your forms or writing code (the time when you're designing your program).*

You'll hear a bit of chugging as your hard disk suffers some sort of coronary attack, then your program should pop up. Start playing around here: try clicking your button and playing with the various buttons at the top right of your form.

12. After experimenting, click on the small X in the top right-hand corner of your form to close it.

Okay, so maybe it ain't Microsoft Office just yet, but this tutorial still has another four-and-a-half chapters to go!

Let's Code, Geek to Geek

You may have noticed a slight flaw in that last exercise. When you actually clicked the button, nothing happened. And typically, in a sensible application, something would. Well, you make that something happen by adding code.

Think of code as the glue that binds your whole program together. You might write code that displays a message and then adds some information to a file somewhere. Or you may change how your form looks and then print out a document.

VB .NET and the .NET Framework have dozens of features to help you code. To start, we're going to learn how to display a message box.

1. Double-click on your button.

You'll be taken straight to the coding window (as seen in Figure 1-8), the home to many a nerd for many an hour. I promise it really isn't as scary as it looks.

Everything you see right now is code. Looks a bit complex, doesn't it? Think of it as a very naked version of your actual form. Let me try to explain.

It all starts off with `Public Class Form1` and finishes with `End Class`. This is saying that this is a class (a code object you work with) that is public (can be seen by other parts of your program) and that is called Form1.

The second line here—`Inherits System.Windows.Forms.Form`—says that this class actually "inherits" all the regular functionality of a standard Windows form, as determined by the .NET Framework.

Next, you find the grayed-out line `Windows Form Designer generated code`. If you're feeling sadomasochistic, try double-clicking on it. It'll expand to reveal all the awful code that actually tells Windows how it should organize the bits of your form; change the title, move that button over there, put that picture just next to it. No, a little more to the right.

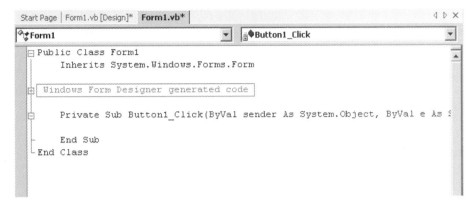

Figure 1-8. The code window, home to many a nerd for many an hour

> **TOP TIP**   *In VB .NET, whole chunks of code can be expanded and collapsed like this, making it all look a lot neater. To collapse a region such as this, simply click on the minus sign next to its* #Region *line.*

So, all the code we've stumbled across so far simply describes our form—and it's all been automatically generated. The only bit we still have left to explain is:

```
Private Sub Button1_Click(ByVal sender As System.Object, ByVal e As
System.EventArgs) Handles Button1.Click
End Sub
```

This was also automatically created when you double-clicked on your button. It's called a *subroutine*, a chunk of supporting code. Here, our subroutine is called Button1_Click and it handles the "click event" of Button1. When you click on your Button1, any code inside this subroutine runs. Simple dimple.

Ready to add some code?

2. Between the lines Private Sub Button1_Click and End Sub, type the following:

    ```
    MessageBox.Show("Hey, hey - that tickles!")
    ```

Now, this MessageBox.Show (Figure 1-9) is part of the .NET Framework, a function that displays a message box. We're calling that function here, passing it the message to display in the box.

> **TOP TIP**   *So, why do we put our message in quotation marks? Well, if you just typed it out, VB .NET might think it's another function that it needs to run. What if I wanted to display the text "MessageBox.Show"? VB .NET might think it needs to display another box! Therefore, VB .NET makes you enclose strings of text like this in quotation marks to avoid confusion.*

> **ANOTHER TOP TIP**   *So, why do we use those brackets here? Well, if we don't insert those brackets, VB .NET would do it for us. Basically, our message is what is known as a parameter (sometimes called an argument) of the message box function. And VB .NET likes to put those in brackets, to make it all look neat and nonconfusing.*

```
Public Class Form1
    Inherits System.Windows.Forms.Form

Windows Form Designer generated code

    Private Sub Button1_Click(ByVal sender As System.Object, ByVal e As
        MessageBox.Show("Hey, hey - that tickles!")
    End Sub
End Class
```

Figure 1-9. Our MessageBox code

Righto, that's our simple line of code added. Let's now return to our form and test our application so far.

Glance up at the top right of your screen. Do you see the Solution Explorer (as shown in Figure 1-10)?

This is the one window we haven't really looked at yet. But, trust me, it's about as simple as I am. And I'm pretty darn simple. Basically, this bit keeps track

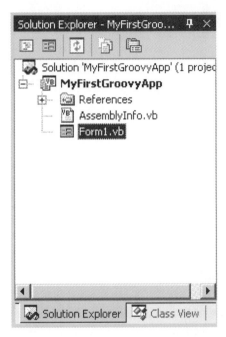

Figure 1-10. Reader, meet Solution Explorer. Solution Explorer, this is Reader.

of your project and all the files you use in it. It's like Windows Explorer for your forms and code.

> **TOP TIP**   *If you want to find out what files are added by default to any VB .NET project and exactly what they do, check out Appendix B.*

3. Right-click on Form1.vb in the Solution Explorer.

4. Click on the View Designer option.

TOP TIP *If you want to rename a particular form file, right-click on it in the Solution Explorer and select Rename.*

Smashing. You should now have your form back up in front of you. So, ready to rumble? Let's strut our stuff.

5. Click on the Start button in VB .NET once again.

TOP TIP *Instead of constantly clicking on the Start button to run your application, you can also press F5 at any time. It does the same thing.*

After a few seconds, your form should display.

6. Click on your button.

Your message box should appear, along with a little *ping*! If so, hurrah and hujjah with frilly lace and curly knobs! If not, well, you're about as lucky as Herbie the Hedgehog. That's Herbie the I-Like-Hibernating-on-Route-66 Hedgehog. Poor guy.

Now, just imagine that this is all your users want. They've actually asked for an application that simply gripes about you clicking it. Hey, it's possible. So, what's next? You couldn't just give them your code! No, you need to "compile" your program into something your users can run. And we'll find out just how to do that, next.

Compiling Your Program

Before I start rambling off in this section, a big congratulations on getting this far! I'm really pleased you're sticking with the tutorial. You're obviously one of the few people that truly aren't offended by my smell.

Now, here, we're going to compile our application, which means that we'll ask VB .NET to take all the stuff we've done so far—our form, our control, our code—and slap it all together into one juicy, ready-to-run executable file.

Let's do that now.

1. From the menu, select Build ➤ Build.

You'll see a dozen lines fly past in the Output window at the bottom of your screen and, finally (one hopes) a message saying something like "Done – I succeeded". Well, that's good news; it means your program is now sitting in EXE form somewhere on your machine (while all the original source code still remains completely intact).

2. Using Windows Explorer, navigate to the folder you stored your project files in.

> **TOP TIP**   *You probably made a note of the location folder earlier, didn't you? You didn't? That's okay; it's not a problem. It's most likely that your files will be stored in the My Documents/Visual Studio Projects/MyGroovyFirstApp folder. Check it out!*

3. Open the Bin subfolder.

(Here in England, a bin is where you store all the rubbish or trash. In America, it's where you store valuable computer files. Go figure.)

Now, in that folder you should find MyFirstGroovyApp.exe, your very own executable file. When VB .NET builds this file, it fills it with MSIL (Microsoft Intermediate Language) code, which is basically a very raw version of your code ready to run direct on the .NET Framework.

4. Double-click on the MyFirstGroovyApp.exe program. (See Figure 1-11.)

Figure 1-11. Your final EXE file at runtime—oh, I'm so proud!

The first time your program is run on a machine, the MSIL code gets fully compiled, optimized for that particular machine and processor, and then cached away for its next use. This is all handled automatically by a part of the .NET Framework called the Common Language Runtime (CLR), and you don't really need to worry about it. I just thought I'd mention it because MSIL is one of those terms mega-geeks like to thrash about so it's only fair to warn you.

You should be able to see your finished program right now. Does it look familiar? Try experimenting with it all once again: play with the form, check out the message box, and so on. Everything should work exactly the same.

Now, after you've compiled (or "built") your application, all you need to do is to copy and paste it straight over to another machine that contains the .NET Framework—and Bob's your uncle! (Actually, he's mine, but that's irrelevant.)

Later, we'll be looking at how we can actually package our EXE file into a neat setup package that's ready to run on any machine. Before that, however, we'll spend time getting a real grasp on all the essentials to turn you into a top-notch developer. All that, coming up.

But, for now: a big well done on compiling your very first program! Open the champagne, smile, and let's wrap up the evening.

CONCLUSION

A huge well-done and mega-hug on finishing the first chapter of Tutorial 1, "Beginning VB .NET"!

Today, we took a whirlwind tour of the VB .NET programming world. We looked at how Visual Basic fits into the big picture, then went on to paint our own first program, with a sneak geek peek at forms, controls, properties, and even code! Finally, we compiled and tested our final program.

If you get a few minutes, try exploring a few more of those controls in your toolbox. Which do you think are the most important?

In the next chapter, we'll be finding out just that, with a listing of the top ten. We'll also be learning more about things called *methods* and *events*. After that, we'll look at writing some pretty impressive decision-making code, and even dip into "debugging" our application. So get that Fly Killer handy; it's all seriously groovy stuff and it's all happening, next time.

But until then, this is your host, Karl Moore, signing off for today, wishing you all a very pleasant evening, wherever you are in the world. Goodnight!

CHAPTER 1.1

PROGAMMING, VISUAL BASIC, AND EVERYTHING REVIEW SHEET

- At the heart of Microsoft's .NET strategy is the .NET Framework. This is essentially a Windows upgrade that runs .NET programs and provides common functionality, plus manages much of the standard "plumbing" as well.

- Microsoft Visual Studio .NET is a product that allows you to create programs to run on the .NET Framework. Among the languages you can use in Visual Studio .NET, we find Visual C#, Visual C++, and Visual Basic.

- You can create many different types of projects in Visual Studio. Currently, the most common is a Windows application, which is a standard Windows desktop program.

- To create a regular Windows application project, you typically: draw controls onto your form(s), change control properties using the Properties window, and add code to stick it all together.

- Compiling your application consists of selecting Build from the Build menu. This generates an executable file (with the .exe extension) in your project's Bin folder. This program will run on any machine containing the .NET Framework.

- Compiled executable files produced by Visual Studio actually contain raw MSIL (Microsoft Intermediate Language) and metadata (descriptive information about your code). When an EXE file is run for the first time on a machine, this MSIL code is optimized for the computer, fully compiled, and then locally cached.

- Having the MSIL and metadata helps the .NET Framework analyze your application and automatically handle memory and provide all the plumbing options it does. However, this is all automatic, and so it isn't something you must know about before building .NET applications.

Exploring Controls and Making Decisions

"I think there is a world market for maybe five computers."
—Thomas Watson, IBM Chairman, 1943

YOU'VE LEARNED THE BASICS, and now you're hungry for more. And in this section, you'll learn it. Over the next hour, we'll be taking your programming knowledge right to the next level.

We'll start this chapter by learning more about how you can really use the hidden power of the VB .NET controls in your applications. We'll also review the top ten widgets in your toolbox. Then, it's five minutes for coffee and croissants before we're off for another grueling visit to the code window, where you'll learn how to write your very own groovy if/then decision makers.

Trust me, you'll love it. And, if you don't, I'll eat my hat. And, if you do, I'll eat this great big chunk of Cadbury's chocolate neatly perched in front of my keyboard.

Too late. Gone. You'd better enjoy it!

So, grab your jumper and don those Coke-bottle spectacles. It's time to reenter the programmatic world of VB .NET.

Exploring Controls

Controls, controls, controls.

To say we've already experienced our fair share of controls would be rather like saying that you've sampled the entire cross section of American cuisine after stuffing two burgers and a pretzel into your mouth.

Actually, you probably have, but the point I'm trying to make is that we've only looked at the Button control so far, which won't win you an awful amount in the application design stakes. There's a lot more to discover. So, what else is available? Which are the best controls to use right now?

We'll be finding the answer to that very question in just a few moments, but first we need a more solid understanding of controls—with a quick look at properties in code, methods, and functions, plus reacting to events. Let's see what I mean:

1. Launch Visual Studio. NET.

2. Create a new Windows application.

Now, although we've already seen the Button control once, let's quickly run over it again.

3. Add a button to Form1.

Before continuing, have a quick play around in the Properties window. Try altering the Font property. What about the ForeColor, too? Also, try changing the FlatStyle property to Flat, and then test your application by pressing F5. See what happens? What if you add two flat buttons? Notice how you can tab between them?

There is life beyond the button, though. Let's try the text box, for example.

4. Add a text box to Form1.

The TextBox control allows you to accept input from the user. You've seen it before. Now, quickly, try changing its PasswordChar property to an asterisk (*). Run the application by pressing F5 and see what happens when you try to type something into the text box. What about altering the MultiLine property? What does that do? Also, try looking at the ScrollBars property. Can you imagine creating your own mini word processor with this control? (Please say yes. *Pretty please?*)

Talking to Controls in Code

Now, there's one property that every control has that we haven't yet looked at: Name.

Have a look at the Name property for your text box. It's probably TextBox1 right now. Go and check the Name property of your button, too. Call me a psychic mushroom, but it's Button1, right?

Now, when programming, you often need to refer to your controls in code. And you do that in just the same way as you'd refer to a person in a real life: by using his or her name. Let's christen our TextBox control now, in the name of our VB father, Bill Gates:

1. Change the Name property of your text box to "txtPhone", as shown in Figure 2-1.

Figure 2-1. Christening our control

> **TOP TIP**   *In the programming world, it's deemed supercool practice to fol-low naming conventions. That means if you have a TextBox control, you prefix its name with "txt". (A three-character code is usually used to repre-sent the control.) This helps keep any code you write nice and clear. You can find a full list of standard prefixes in Appendix III. Also, note that, unlike names in real life, you can't have spaces, hyphens, or apostrophes in control names. Cardinal sin, that.*

2. Clear the Text property of your text box to remove its default text.

3. Double-click on your Button1 to open the code window.

4. Type the following unfinished line of code into the window:

```
txtPhone.
```

Notice how a list appears when you hit that period key? Some of these are properties that your control supports, as you saw in the Properties window. These are represented by the icon of a blue pointing finger. You can usually read and write properties in code. Let's test that now.

5. Complete that line of code behind the click event of Button1, as follows:

```
txtPhone.Text = "555-555-5555"
```

Here, we're setting the Text property of our txtPhone TextBox control equal to 555-555-5555. We enclose our string of text here in quotation marks, so VB .NET doesn't try to interpret it as some sort of command. *We're setting a property.*

> **TOP TIP** *With this sort of property, we're setting a string. However, some other properties work with other types of data, such as the values True or False, a date, or even a predefined list of values. We'll see examples of these later today.*

6. Press the F5 key to test your application.

7. Click on your button and close when finished.

What happens? How about if you change the contents of the text box and try clicking on the button again?

So, that's how we can set a property in code. Now what about reading?

8. Change the code behind the click event of Button1 to

```
MessageBox.Show(txtPhone.Text)
```

Here, we're passing the Text property of our txtPhone text box to the MessageBox.Show function to display. We're just treating the property like a regular piece of text. What do you think should happen?

9. Press the F5 key and test your application.

Tested it? Good. Did it work as expected? What happens if you enter nothing in your text box and click the button? You could even try entering something such as a "MessageBox.Show" statement into your text box and clicking the button. What happens? Nothing. It's just treated as regular text, not an actual command. That's *reading a property.*

So that's how to set and read properties in code. No problemo, simple enough. Now, you also have these mega-exciting control beasts called *methods* and *functions*, which are represented in that Intellisense list by some sort of purple diamond icon thing. (Don't ask me.)

Let's check out one of these—a method—right now.

10. Change the code behind the click event of Button1 to

```
txtPhone.Clear()
```

11. Press the F5 button and test your application.

Try running your application, entering a few words into txtPhone and clicking on your button. See what happens? What other methods are available? Why not try out `.Undo` or `.SelectAll`?

So, that's a method. You run the command, and it performs an action. Oh, the power! But it's still about as exciting as the Pope's left pinkie.

Now, what about those things called *functions*? Actually, these aren't overly common in controls, but they basically work like read-only properties in that they just return a value. TextBox control examples include `.ToString` and `.Contains`. You'll find functions of more use when you actually learn how to create your own, which we'll look at in more depth with Chapter 1.4.

Let's move on, shall we?

Responding to Events

So, you know how to change how controls behave at runtime using a couple o' lines of code. But sometimes you want to respond when something happens to that control.

For example, you might want to respond when someone clicks on your button (you've already done that), or you may want to run some code when the user types something in your text box, or you could perhaps update a database when someone selects a new value from your list.

You do this using events. With the button so far, we've responded to its click event: when someone clicks the button, it runs our Button1_Click subroutine, which handles that event. Let's explore a couple of others:

1. Open the code window, by right-clicking your form in the Solution Explorer, then selecting View Code.

At the top of the code window, you should see two amazingly boring dropdown boxes: Class Name and Method Name.

2. Select your txtPhone TextBox control from the first box, as shown in Figure 2-2.

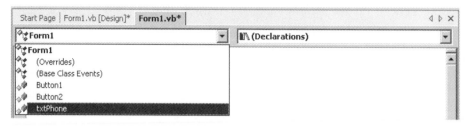

Figure 2-2. Selecting our control from the amazingly boring drop-down box

The Method Name box will now be filtered down to display all the events for txtPhone. Have a browse through the list. All the events should have a small, yellow lightning "action" symbol next to them.

Here, you have the click event, which would run when someone clicks the control. The enter event occurs when someone enters the control, and the TextChanged event runs after the contents of your text box have changed.

> **TOP TIP** *You can get a full list of events supported by any particular control by selecting it on your form and then pressing the F1 key.*

Let's check out that TextChanged event now.

3.   Select the TextChanged event from the second box.

A subroutine will be generated, as it is automatically when you double-click on a Button control. Pull up your pew and look closely at this one. Can you tell how VB .NET knows this should respond to the TextChanged event of the txtPhone control?

4.   Enter the following code behind the TextChanged event of your text box:

```
MessageBox.Show("So far, you've typed: " & txtPhone.Text)
```

Now let's test it.

5.   Press F5 to test your application. (See Figure 2-3.)

What happens when you type something into your TextBox control, as in Figure 2-3? When could you use this? What other events here could be useful? Go check out the "Creating a Number-Only Text Box" tip in Chapter 8-1 "Beginner Tips and Techniques" for inspiration. See the "parameters" in use with the event there? What do you think now?

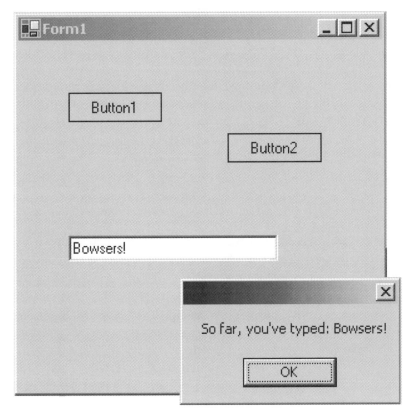

Figure 2-3. Our application in action

Here's another little gem of knowledge: your form also has events you can react to. Try selecting "(Base Class Events)" from the Class Name drop-down and browsing the available events. What here could help you build a better, more intelligent program?

The Top Ten Controls

Yes, you are now officially a complete expert and stunningly cool nerd on all things button and text box. But, unless you have an incredibly undemanding employer, that really isn't going to get you a job. Anywhere. Ever.

The problem is that there's a complete mass of controls bundled with VB .NET, and learning all about every single one of them sounds about as fun as the Children's Book of Nuclear Physics. Translated into a foreign tongue.

Still, you'll find some information regarding all those controls in Appendix D, just in case that insomnia kicks in again. But, for the rest of us, how are you supposed to know which controls you need? And which properties, methods, functions, and events are the most useful?

No problem, matey! Just read on, as we prepare our supercool lineup of the top ten most fashionable controls!

Now, as each of these steps down the catwalk to strut its programmatic stuffs, I want you to add one to your form and play with all the features I suggest. Try figuring out which of the features I mention are also common to most controls. Go on; give it a go. And if you don't, well, I'll cry.

So, let's bring out the first number: the Label control!

The Label Control

The Label control (Figure 2-4) displays a chunk of text, and that's about it, really. Still, you'll find it used all over the place, most typically for descriptions or to display output.

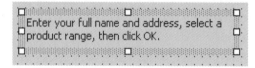

Figure 2-4. The Label control

- *Key properties*: Text, Font, ForeColor, TextAlign

- *Key methods and functions*: BringToFront

- *Key events to play with*: Click, MouseMove

- *Sample code*:

```
lblWelcome.Text = "Welcome, User!"
```

The LinkLabel Control

Is it a bird? Is it a plane? Is it a bowl of soup? No, it's the LinkLabel control (Figure 2-5), and it has the look and feel of one of those hyperlinks you'd find on a Web page. But this link doesn't simply take you to a site. Instead, clicking it will run a chunk of code in your program.

Figure 2-5. The LinkLabel control

- *Key properties*: ActiveLinkColor, Cursor, LinkColor, Text, LinkBehavior

- *Key methods and functions*: Show, Hide

- *Key events to play with*: LinkClicked

- *Sample code*:

```
lnkCompanySite.LinkBehavior = LinkBehavior.HoverUnderline
```

> **COMPLETELY RANDOM TOP TIP** *Need to add a menu to your application? You're looking for the MainMenu control. But don't worry about this just yet; we'll cover it all in Chapter 1.4.*

The Button Control

Okay, so you've seen this one before, but I'm feeling repetitive. Repetitive. Repetitive. What, not even a sympathy laugh? Sheesh. That's the thanks you get. Anyway, it's a button. (See Figure 2-6.) You click it; it does stuff. Whoop-de-doo.

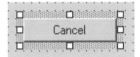

Figure 2-6. The Button control

- *Key properties*: FlatStyle, Image, Text, TextAlign, Image, ImageAlign

- *Key methods and functions*: PerformClick, Focus

- *Key events to play with*: Click, MouseMove

- *Sample code*:

```
btnOK.PerformClick()
```

The TextBox Control

Now, if this isn't about as essential as hot water and Pop-Tarts, I seriously don't know what is. It's a box that holds text—hence, the ingenious name—and it does it all rather well. The TextBox control (Figure 2-7) can display information, hold data that the user types in, plus even look like a password dialog box. Pretty groovy.

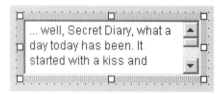

Figure 2-7. The TextBox control

- *Key properties*: ScrollBars, Font, Text, MaxLength, MultiLine, PasswordChar, and TextAlign

- *Key methods and functions*: SelectAll, Clear, Undo, ClearUndo, AppendText, Focus, Cut, Copy, and Paste

- *Key events to play with*: TextChanged, Enter, KeyDown, KeyPress, KeyUp, and Leave

- *Sample code*:

```
txtData.AppendText("My Text ")
```

The CheckBox Control

Yes or no? No or yes? With this control, it's all choices, choices, choices. It's a checkbox, and you can check it or not check it. It's as simple as that, and it's great for getting the user to give you a yes or no answer. (See Figure 2-8.)

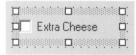

Figure 2-8. The CheckBox control

- *Key properties*: CheckState, Text

- *Key methods and functions*: SendToBack

- *Key events to play with*: CheckedChanged

- *Sample code*:

```
chkSex.SendToBack()
```

The RadioButton Control

When you need to give the user a short list to choose from, radio buttons are a heaven-send. Add as many as you like, but remember that only one can be selected at a time. (To use multiple sets of RadioButton controls on a form, put each set inside its own GroupBox, as described later.) They have nothing to do with radios though, and they don't look much like buttons either. (See Figure 2-9.)

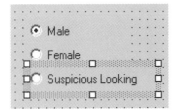

Figure 2-9. The RadioButton control

- *Key properties*: Checked, Text

- *Key methods and functions*: PerformClick

- *Key events to play with*: CheckedChanged

- *Sample code*:

```
radOption1.Checked = True
```

The GroupBox Control

This control brings you the latest in modern borders. It's slick, stylish, contempo-rary . . . uhm, it's actually just a box with a caption somewhere at the top. You can also put other controls inside the box and they stick with it when moved about. Cool or what? Okay, so it's *what*. (See Figure 2-10.)

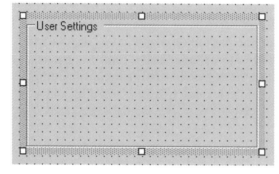

Figure 2-10. The GroupBox control

- *Key properties*: BackgroundImage, Text, Visible

- *Key methods and functions*: Show, Hide

- *Key events to play with*: MouseMove

- *Sample code*:

```
grpDetails.Visible = False
```

The PictureBox Control

Now this is a real teaser. As its name absolutely does *not* suggest, this is a box that holds a picture (like half of my mug). And that lovely big white bit. Still, in the real world it really is surprisingly useful for holding logos . . . and logos . . . and pictures of me. Ahem. (See Figure 2-11.)

Figure 2-11. The PictureBox control

- *Key properties*: Image

- *Key methods and functions*: BringToFront

- *Key events to play with*: Click

- *Sample code*:

```
picAuthor.BringToFront()
```

The ListBox Control

You will have undoubtedly seen the ListBox control (Figure 2-12) hanging about before. It typically displays a short bunch of items, ready for the user to select one. If you change the right properties, you can allow the user to select multiple items from the same list. It's great for holding, uh, lists and so on. (Come on, I'm trying.)

Figure 2-12. The ListBox control

- *Key properties*: MultiColumn, SelectionMode, Sorted, Items

- *Key methods and functions*: ClearSelected, FindString, FindStringExact

- *Key events to play with*: SelectedIndexChanged, SelectedValueChanged, TextChanged

- *Sample code*:

```
lstItems.ClearSelected()
```

The ComboBox Control

You absolutely can't live without this baby. When you need to display a longer bunch of items for the user to select from, this control steps onto the scene. It presents a drop-down box of items for the user to peruse and select from. It's great for holding, uh, longer lists and so on. (Come on, I'm *still* trying.) (See Figure 2-13.)

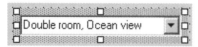

Figure 2-13. The ComboBox control

- *Key properties*: DropDownStyle, Text, MaxDropDownItems, Sorted, Items, SelectedText

- *Key methods and functions*: BeginUpdate, EndUpdate, ResetText

- *Key events to play with*: SelectedIndexChanged, SelectedValueChanged, TextChanged

- *Sample code*:

```
cboUsers.ResetText()
```

The MonthCalendar Control

Need the user to provide you with a date? Fancy adding a mini calendar to your program? Hey, have *we* got a treat for you. Yes, it's a calendar, and you can move about, select dates and ranges, plus . . . oh, that's about it, actually. (See Figure 2-14.)

Figure 2-14. The MonthCalendar control

- *Key properties*: FirstDayOfWeek, MaxDate, SelectionRange, ShowToday, ShowTodayCircle, ShowWeekNumbers

- *Key methods and functions*: AddAnnuallyBoldedDate, AddBoldedDate

- *Key events to play with*: AddMonthlyBoldedDate, RemoveBoldedDate, SetDate, SetSelectionRange

- *Sample code*:

```
calDate.AddBoldedDate(#5/20/2002#)
```

> **TOP TIP**   *When typing dates directly into the Visual Basic code window, you need to enter them in the American style (m/d/yyyy) and surround them with hash marks to ensure VB .NET doesn't confuse the numbers with a calculation.*

Counting our controls again, it totals eleven, not ten. Tsk, what can I say? Either I can't count or "The Top Eleven Controls" as a section title doesn't sound awfully cool. Uhm, you decide.

Bringing It All Together

Are you sick of playing with silly samples that are about as pointless as size 12 shoes in Munchkin Land?

Have no fear. In this section, we're going to bring together all the knowledge we've gained so far to make a genuinely useful application. That is, if you've ever wanted to view pictures.

Why? Because it's a picture viewer: your user will select an image from his or her computer and it'll be displayed in your supercool program. We'll also be touching upon a few neat interface tricks too, just to keep you ahead of the crowd.

Getting excited? What's that? Oh. Well, let's get going anyway.

1.   Create a new Windows application in VB .NET.

2.   Change the Name property of your form to "frmMain".

3.   Change the Text property of your form to "Picture Viewer".

4.   Select your form and, using the resize boxes, enlarge it so that it fills your screen.

5.   Using the Solution Explorer, rename Form1.vb to "frmMain.vb".

Designing Our Interface

There's a certain dynamic that goes on when the user first launches your program. It needs to be love at first sight. In other words, it needs to have a sexy interface. Let's work on that now. We'll start by adding a title to our application, along with a little blurb.

1. Add a label to the top of your form, changing its properties as follows:

    - *Name*: "lblTitle"

    - *Text*: "Wizzy World Picture Viewer"

    - *Font*: Tahoma, bold, size 16

2. Add another label just under the main header, changing its properties to:

    - *Name*: "lblDescription"

    - *Text*: "To get started, click on the Choose Picture button to select an image. You can resize this form using the controls to your upper left. Enjoy!"

    - *Font*: Tahoma, size 8

Next, we'll add that Choose Picture button we talked about. (See Figure 2-15.)

3. Add a button under your labels, changing the properties as follows:

    - *Name*: "btnChoose"

    - *Text*: "Choose Picture"

    - *FlatStyle*: Flat

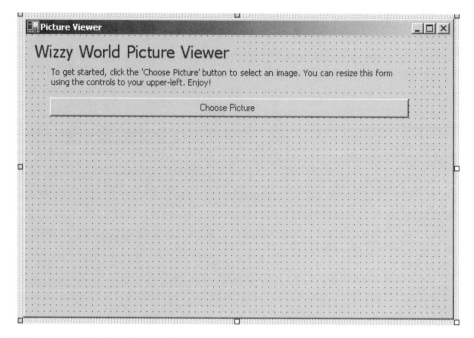

Figure 2-15. The interface so far . . .

And now? Well, there's always the actual PictureBox control, which will actually hold the selected image.

4. Covering the rest of the form, draw out a PictureBox control, changing its properties to:

    - *Name:* "picImage"

    - *SizeMode:* StretchImage

We're also going to change the Anchor property of our PictureBox control. We've not seen this before, but with VB .NET you can "anchor" a control to certain sides of a form, meaning that, if the form is resized, the control gets stretched out and resized for you. Let's change the property now and see it in action later.

5. Change the Anchor property of picImage so it anchors top, bottom, left, and right.

One final thing we need to add is the OpenFileDialog control. It's invisible, yes, but you use it in code just like a regular control.

6.   Drag an OpenFileDialog control onto your form, changing its Name
      property to ofdImage.

Sticking It Together with Code

So, that's our user interface sorted, and, if I say so myself, it's looking smarter
than Albert Einstein on Ginkgo Biloba. Next, let's think about adding a little code:

1.   Enter the following code to respond to the click event of btnChoose:

```
ofdImage.Filter = "Picture Files|*.bmp;*.jpg;*.jpeg;*.gif;*.ico"
ofdImage.ShowDialog()
```

Here, we're setting up our OpenFileDialog control. We start by saying the
Open dialog box should display only picture files whose filenames end with
.bmp, .jpg, .jpeg, .gif, or .ico extensions. Next, we're running the ShowDialog
method of our control, which prompts the user for the actual file. This doesn't
actually do anything, however; it simply collects a filename for us to use later.

> **TOP TIP**   *Here, we're filtering only for picture files. However, you can also
> have multiple filters, just by separating each set using the pipe symbol
> (|). Check out the help files for more information. Here's a more
> complex filter string that accepts files created using the Office suite:*
> ```
> Excel Spreadsheets|*.xls|Word Documents|*.doc;*.txt|Access
> Databases|*.mdb |All|*.*
> ```

By this point, our user will have been prompted for a filename and hopefully
will have selected something. Next, we need to take that image and load it into
the PictureBox control. How do we do this?

2.   Add the following code to the click event of btnChoose:

```
picImage.Image = New Bitmap(ofdImage.FileName)
```

Here, we're setting the Image property of our PictureBox control to a new
Bitmap object, passing this object the FileName property from the
OpenFileDialog control.
      It may seem a little confusing at first, but basically our Image property needs
you to set it to a particular type of object (anything that talks the "language" of
System.Drawing.Image in the .NET Framework).

Enter stage left, the Bitmap object, which is best for this job and talks that language. So here we create a new Bitmap object, passing in the filename. This then returns a picture that the Image property can understand.

Confused? You won't be.

Basically, this is just one part of the .NET Framework, and it's simply how the objects within this bit work. Your form is an object, and it can work in many different ways. Just as you can write code that can perform hundreds of different, strange actions, the .NET Framework holds objects that likewise work in different manners.

You simply need to stay eager, learn a few techniques, and the rest will start fitting together. For everything else, you always have the Help feature. Actually, that's how I found out how to do this bit. But I didn't want to tell you 'cause you'd think I was a . . . *d'oh*!

> **TOP TIP** *If you ever need to know how to manipulate a particular property—such as the Image property of the PictureBox control—simply type out and highlight that property in the code window and press F1. You should be given a code example as to how you can use it in your program. That's how I found out how to use the Image property.*

Testing Your Program

Congratulations on getting this far! You've finished building your application, and it's time to test.

1. Press the F5 button to test run your application.

If Visual Studio .NET complains that there is no startup object, give it a big slap. When we changed the name of our form, it lost track of which object to show when your application launches. Try right-clicking on your project in the Solution Explorer and selecting Properties, changing the Startup Object to frmMain, clicking on OK, and trying again.

2. Click on your Choose Picture button.

Notice how flat the button looks and how it darkens as you hover over it? How could you change the colors used here? An Open file dialog box should appear after you click the button. (See Figure 2-16.)

3. Select an image from your computer.

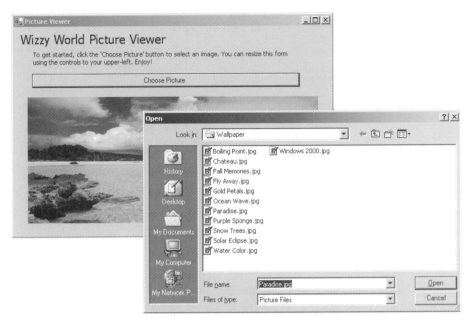

Figure 2-16. Ladies and gentlemen, the Open file dialog box!

The image you choose should display itself in your PictureBox control.

4. Maximize your form so that it fills the entire screen.

Notice what happens? Compare how the PictureBox anchors to the sides, as opposed to the button (with which we stuck to the default Anchor setting).

5. Close your form.

Next, let's step through our code line by line so you can see exactly how it all fits together.

6. In your code window, click anywhere on the first line of your subroutine that reacts to the click event of btnChoose.

7. Press the F9 key. The line should become highlighted in red as shown in Figure 2-17.

```
Private Sub Button1_Click(ByVal sender As System.Object, ByVal e As System.EventArgs) Ha
    ofdImage.Filter = "Picture Files|*.bmp;*.jpg;*.jpeg;*.gif;*.ico"
    ofdImage.ShowDialog()
    picImage.Image = New Bitmap(ofdImage.FileName)

    End Sub
End Class
```

Figure 2-17. Debugging: On

Debugging is now active. When this line of code is encountered in your application, you'll be returned to the code window and allowed to step through it all line by line. Imagine it as virtual swatting, a tool to help you catch the bugs. Or maybe I'm just trying to make it sound exciting.

8. Press the F5 key and test your application once more, using the F8 key to step through each line of code.

See how it all runs? What do you think? What happens when you hover your mouse over the properties you use in code? Could this be useful in helping to weed out problems in your code, especially larger applications?

Any ideas as to how you could improve the interface? Does all the code make sense to you? Also, here's an experiment: restart your application, then (in debugging mode) try clicking on your Choose Picture button and then canceling the dialog box. What happens? Where does the error occur, and can you figure out how to fix it?

If you have time, why not think about making your own mini word processor using the techniques we've learned today? You might also want to learn how to read and write files, using the "Reading and Writing Files" tip in Chapter 8-2 "Intermediate Tips and Techniques".

Making Decisions

Well, we've still got two minutes before the end of this chapter, so how about I quickly introduce the If statement and we'll see whether you can pick it up. (Actually, I know you'll be fine; it's slow divvy teacher-types like me who have problems.)

When it comes to making decisions, some programming languages—and, specifically, VB .NET—use something called an *If statement*. Let's take a quick sneak geek peek at one of these now:

```
If txtPassword.Text = "secret" Then MessageBox.Show("Access Granted!")
```

Here, we're just checking the Text property of our TextBox control. If it's equal to "secret", then a message box is displayed. Lovely jubbly. Go try this out for yourself. But this is an easy example, and sometimes you might want to run whole blocks of code for an If statement, like this:

```
If txtPassword.Text = "secret" Then
    MessageBox.Show("Access Granted!")
    Application.Exit
End If
```

In this chunk of code, if the password is equal to "secret", all the code through to our End If is run. That means we'll get a message box and then the program will close due to the Application.Exit command . . . now *there's* a new one for us.

1. Save your Picture Viewer from the last exercise. We'll need it again later.

2. Create a new VB .NET Windows application and experiment with all the following If statements, adding controls as necessary.

Let's get a little more complex now:

```
If txtPassword.Text = "secret" Then
    MessageBox.Show("Access Granted!")
ElseIf txtPassword.Text = "password" Then
    MessageBox.Show("What do you think this is? X-Files?")
Else
    MessageBox.Show("Take a hike, hacker face...")
End If
```

Here, we're using the extra ElseIf and Else statements. What would happen if I entered a password of "secret"? How about if I entered "Babylon"? And what if I tried "secrets" on my third attempt? How about "Password"? "SECRET"?

TOP TIP *Visual Basic .NET is case sensitive, which means that, by default, "secret" does not equal "SECRET". To convert a string of text to upper- or lowercase, use the ToLower or ToUpper properties of its Text property, like so:*

```
MessageBox.Show(txtPassword.Text.ToUpper)
```

You can get even more complicated with If statements, too, by using greater-than (>), less-than (<) and not-equal-to (<>) symbols, along with multiple If statements. Let's look at another example:

```
If txtPassword.Text <> "this" And txtPassword.Text <> "that" Then
    txtPassword.Text = "the other!"
End If
```

Is this vaguely understandable? Run over all these examples again in your head. It's important that you grasp what these chunks of code are up to because the If statement is a really hot building block for all your future programming what-nots.

Check out the "Tips and Techniques" section of this book (Tutorial 8) and browse some of the samples to get a feel for it in action. Go on, do it now. Dog-ear this page and explore away. I'll still be here when you get back.

And, to help you really understand this beast, let's return to our picture viewer example. Remember that if you clicked on Cancel in the Open file dialog box, you received an error? Why? Because the ofdImage.FileName property was blank. Do you think you could fix that now? Could you perhaps check it, then display the image only if one has been selected?

Here's a small project for you: using an If statement, stop the picture viewer error from occurring when a user cancels the Open file dialog box.

It's a challenge, but I know you can do it.

CONCLUSION

Well, hurrah and hujjah on coming this far! *(Hey, publisher people, can't we put that to music?)*

In this mammoth second chapter, we've covered more than I could ever hope for, which is probably because we've overrun the page count again—and all because I just love getting slapped silly by my editor.

So, what did we do today? Well, we opened with a look at controls, exploring the concepts behind properties, methods, functions, and events. Then, we cut out all the rubbish and played with the top ten (eleven) controls, figuring out exactly what each is particularly good at.

Next up, we put everything we've learned so far into practice, with a super-cool picture viewer. Oh, and finally, we spent a few minutes learning about the If statement and how it can help you make decisions in code. We also tried to fix one of our picture viewer's bugs using that newfound knowledge.

Wow. Now that's a lot of work, and, if I keep treating you so cruel, you're going to go out, buy a whole mound of competitors' books, and cuss me on the newsgroups.

That's why the very next chapter will be jam-packed with wizzy fun stuff. You'll spend your time finding out about all the really interesting features, learning about functionality that you truly need in a great application.

Hmm, got a spare few minutes before the next session? Keep playing with all the controls you find in VB .NET, incorporating them into If statements. And, if you need help with any particular feature, don't forget to just highlight it and press F1.

And that's all from me for today, so goodnight, God bless, and go safely. Ciao for now!

EXPLORING CONTROLS AND MAKING DECISIONS REVIEW SHEET

- Every control you add to a form has a Name property, which is how you refer to it in code.

- Most controls include a mixture of methods, functions, and properties. A method is a command that typically performs an action, such as TextBox1.Clear. A function is a command that "returns" a value, such as TextBox1.Contains. A property is a value that can usually be both read and set, such as TextBox1.Visible.

- Typing the name of a control, followed by a period, in the code window behind your form displays a list of available methods, functions, properties, and events.

- Certain controls don't have a visible form side to them. However, you can still change their properties and access them in code by referencing their name. Invisible controls appear in a control bar underneath your form. Examples of such controls include OpenFileDialog and Timer.

- Your form itself can be treated as a regular control and contains its own methods, functions, and properties. To refer to your own form in code, type "Me".

- Most controls—and your form itself—support events. These allow you to add code in a subroutine that runs whenever a particular event occurs, such as a click or selection change.

- The most common way to enter code to respond to an event is to select a Class and Method name using the drop-down boxes in the code window. To enter code to respond to a form event, you need to select "(Base Class Events)" as the Class entry.

- You make decisions in code using the If statement. Here are some examples of its use:

```
If TextBox1.Text = "password" Then
        MessageBox.Show("Access Granted!")
End If


If chkPartner.Checked = True And _
            txtPartnerName.Text.Length < 1 Then
   MessageBox.Show("You have a partner with no name?")
End If
```

Variables
and the Coolest Code

"Computers in the future may have only one thousand vacuums and perhaps weigh less than one-and-a-half tons"—Popular Mechanics, 1949

WE'RE STARTING THE THIRD CHAPTER, and you've still not been put off. Wow, this really is a record. And to reward you for all this dedication, today is going to be one exciting, adrenaline-packed session.

Trust me, I'm a programmer.

We'll start by taking a sneak geek peek at the world of variables, cool code widgets that can help give your application a little added intelligence. Then, we'll be positioning those shades and slapping on the beeswax as we go all cool in an exploration of the top five grooviest chunks of .NET functionality you simply won't be able to live without.

Seriously, though, you won't have had this much fun since you last picked your nose.

Well, with the tone suitably set, it's time to launch back into the world of VB .NET for another dozen pages. So, are you sitting comfortably? Then I'll begin.

Using Variables

When I started in the programming world, my science professors told me about the RIRO theory: you get from a computer what you put into it (rubbish in, rubbish out). This apparently explained why I held the university record for the highest recorded number of application crashes over my five terms. Still, my report card wasn't too negative. At least it praised me for being consistent.

The problem is that my applications weren't very intelligent. However, if I would've read my manuals and figured out what variables were all about, at least I'd have been able to make it look as though my programs had a little more brain power.

So just what are variables then?

You can imagine variables as being invisible text boxes. You create them in code and they hold data for you, whether it's a number, a string of text, or a date. You can then change them in code whenever you want.

Simple as an amoeba? You bet your bottom dollar, kiddo, but they're also incredibly useful and can make your app seem rather clever. Let's get down-and-dirty.

1. Create a new Windows application in Visual Studio .NET.

2. Draw out a button onto your form.

First off, let's create—or "declare"—a variable. It's not too difficult and won't cost you a nickel. Here, we're going to create a variable that holds a string of text.

3. Behind the click event of your button, add the following code:

```
Dim MyNameVariable As String
```

Here, we're declaring a variable—an "invisible text box"—called MyNameVariable to hold a string of text. Next, let's change the value of that variable, then display it in a message box. Remember, we just treat the variable like a property or a regular piece of text. Here goes:

4. Add the following code under your variable declaration:

```
MyNameVariable = "Karl"
MessageBox.Show("Your name is " & MyNameVariable)
```

Understand? Let's give it a test run:

5. Press the F5 key and test your application.

What happens when you click on the button, as in Figure 3-1? What gets displayed in the message box?

Figure 3-1. Anything to declare?

Hmm, what's that? You'd have to be about as thick as the Las Vegas marriage register to think that was intelligent? Think you're right, actually, but at least we're moving forward. Let's change our example slightly to use an InputBox.

6. Amend the code behind the click event of your button so that it reads as follows:

```
Dim MyNameVariable As String
MyNameVariable = InputBox("What is your name?")
MessageBox.Show("Your name is " & MyNameVariable)
```

Here, we're using the InputBox function, which is another great little Visual Basic feature. It'll pop up a standard box that allows the user to type something. It then "returns a result"—the definition of a function—which we place in our variable. The variable value then gets displayed in our message box.

7. Press the F5 key and test your new code.

See what happens? What do you think? Figure 3-2 shows my own application in mid-action.

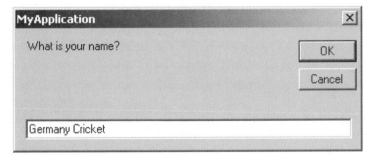

Figure 3-2. Everyone, it's the InputBox!

Can you understand how all this code works? How do you think variables could be useful?

Getting More Complex

There's just one slight problem with normal variables: they're a bit like my Grandma. No, they don't wear curlers, play bingo, or enjoy afternoon naps. Rather, they're ever-so-slightly forgetful.

You see, after the subroutine that handles your button click event finishes, that's it. Visual Basic .NET forgets all about the MyNameVariable, unless it gets created again. It only "remembers" the variables in its current scope.

This means that, if you declare a variable in your particular subroutine, it will only be available in that subroutine. Sometimes this can be really useful, and other times it can be a pain in the proverbial.

To stop your variable disappearing out of scope, you need to declare it somewhere else—somewhere that your subroutines can "see." In other words, you need to move the declaration from your subroutine to your form.

Let's check it out.

1. Create a new Windows application in Visual Studio .NET, naming the solution "CountClick".

First off, let's declare our variable. We're going to do this at the top of our form so that all of our subroutines can still see it. If we put it inside one of the subroutines, only that subroutine will be able to see it. (See Figure 3-3.)

2. In the code behind your form, under the `Public Class` and `Inherits` lines, add the following line:

```
Dim shtCountClick As Short
```

```
Public Class frmMain
      Inherits System.Windows.Forms.Form
      Dim shtCountClick As Short

   ⊞  Windows Form Designer generated code

   End Class
```

Figure 3-3. Declaring a form-level variable

Here, we're "declaring in memory" (*Dim*-ing) another variable. It's called shtCountClick, and, instead of it holding a string of text, it's holding what is known as a *Short*, which is basically just a data type that can hold a number up to approximately 32,000.

> **TOP TIP** *In your code, you'll use just a few really important data types:* String, *which holds regular text;* Short, *which will hold a whole number up to 32,767;* Boolean, *which holds a True or False value; and* Date, *which can hold both a date and time. Just like controls, it's good practice to prefix each of these with a three-character identifier, too—like "sht" for a Short. You can find a full list of data types in Appendix E, along with suggested prefixes in Appendix C.*

Next, let's add code so that a value of 1 is added to this variable each time the user clicks a button. We'll then display that number in a message box:

3. Draw a button onto your form.

4. Add the following code behind the click event of your button.

```
shtCountClick = shtCountClick + 1
MessageBox.Show("Ooh, you've clicked me " & shtCountClick & " times! PERV!")
```

Here, we're simply taking the current value of shtCountClick and adding 1 to it. Then, we're displaying the result in a message box.

> **TOP TIP** *Is your code underlined with a blue squiggly line? This indicates an error, and it always occurs to me when I teach this example. It's usually the result of a rather embarrassing typo, particular when dealing with variables so sensitively christened as "shtCountClick". If this occurs to you, hover your mouse over the squiggly to check the problem, then fix it!*

5. Press the F5 key to test your application.

Try clicking your button a few times. What happens? Does the number keep incrementing? What if you restart your program? Is the variable wiped clean?

The very first time you click on the button, it should say something like, "You've clicked me 1 times." How could you use an If statement so that on the first click, it says "You've clicked me 1 *time*" (in the grammatically correct singular, instead of plural)? Give it a go.

And, if you just decide to change it to, "You've clicked me *N* time(s)," then you *are* the Weakest Link. *Goodbye!*

Do you have a solid idea now of where "local" subroutine variables could be useful, and how they differ from form-level variables? Think about it. What about the advantages and disadvantages of both methods? We'll be dealing with variables more later today and you'll soon start to see how very useful they can be.

Move on when you're ready.

Time for a Test

Congratulations on coming this far!

Next up, we're going to create an application that brings together everything you've learned so far. Actually, *you're* going to create an application that brings together everything you've learned so far; *I'm* just going to be a cruel author with an evil laugh and bushy eyebrows.

What is this application? Well, before we dive into all that cool stuff in the next section, I want you to create a password program. It needs a login screen that accepts a username and password. When the user clicks on OK, the username and password should be checked. If the correct details are entered, an "Access Granted!" message should be displayed.

However, if the username and password combination are incorrect, you need to deny access. More than that, if the user successively enters an incorrect password three times, you need to display a message telling them to shove off (or words to that effect) and then end the program.

How could you do this? Well, you'll probably need If statements to check the password, plus a form-level variable to hold the number of logon attempts. And, to end the program, remember that `Application.Exit` command.

Righto, give it a go! I did it. (See Figure 3-4.) If you succeed, I promise you a huge massive great whopping reward in the next section. And, if you don't, I promise you a bowl of minestrone soup. It's your call.

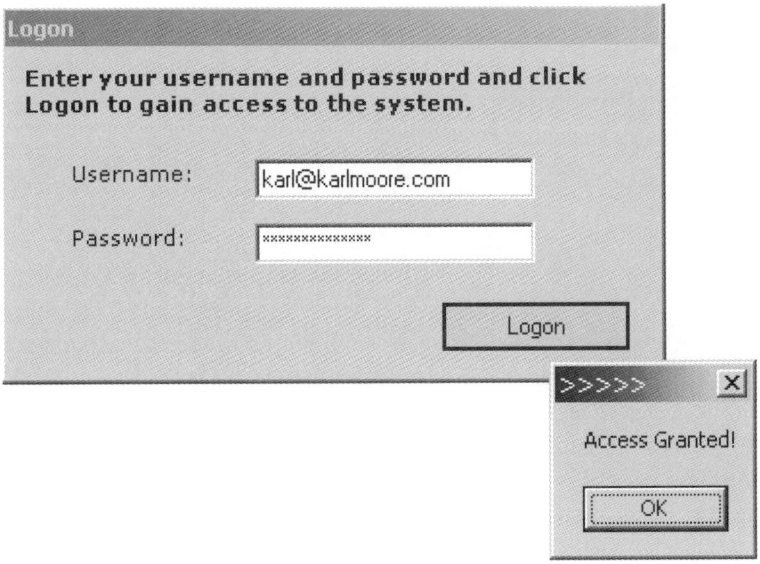

Figure 3-4. My final login application—where's yours?

And Now, the Cool Stuff!

We've talked about the .NET framework before. It automatically handles program memory, it runs our .NET applications, and it packs a bundle of "base classes," which is common functionality that you can use in your own applications.

You know that, and, if you don't, you do now.

So, how do we tap into all that cool functionality? Well, the first thing you need to know is that all such functionality is categorized into what's known as *namespaces*. (This is just a groovy name for the way in which it's all organized, like a high-tech name for a filing cabinet.)

Let's see what I mean.

1. Create a new Windows application in Visual Studio .NET.

2. Add a button to your form and double-click on it to enter the code window.

We're going to explore one of these namespaces right now.

Microsoft.V

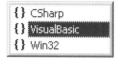

Figure 3-5. Exploring the Microsoft namespace

3.   Type "Microsoft" and press the period key, as in Figure 3-5.

Here, we're accessing the Microsoft cabinet, the Microsoft namespace. Inside, you should be able to see a few subfolders: C#, Visual Basic, and Win32. Each of these subfolders contains their own individual chunks of functionality.

The Microsoft Visual Basic namespace, for example, holds all the older functions you may have been used to working with in Visual Basic 6, such as MsgBox. Let's check it out.

4.   Finish typing your line of code, as follows:

```
Microsoft.VisualBasic.MsgBox("Welcome!")
```

5.   Press F5 and test your application.

So, that's one sample namespace (one provided by Microsoft to offer backward compatibility with older versions of the language). This Microsoft namespace is automatically distributed with the .NET framework for Windows.

But that's not the only namespace. There is, of course, the most important one. The Godfather of Namespace Land. The one they call . . . *System.*

6.   Remove the line of code behind your button.

7.   In its place, type "System" and then press the period key.

Wow! You should see a list longer than Bill Crosby's filmography, and just about as exciting. These are all chunks of functionality that are available to us under the main entry point to the .NET framework base classes—the System namespace.

For example, all the code objects you need to access data in SQL Server can be found in the System.Data.SqlClient namespace, whereas objects for working with XML can be uncovered in System.Xml.

How do you use them all? Well, that's a little like asking Einstein, "So, what's this relativity all about?" There's a lot of intricate detail you really don't need to know about here (like how to set the pixel offset mode when coding imagery, or why ISecurityEncodable is inherited by the CodeAccessPermission class under OleDb . . . and all that rubbish).

During the course of these tutorials, I'll be teaching you all the most important what-nots, cutting out the excess rubbish that Bill Gates probably just put in for laughs.

Tsk, the things they do to pad out a programming language.

Still, if there's something you specifically want to do, you'll always find reference to it in the help files, which will give you a pointer as to which namespace provides just the functionality you require, usually along with full code samples too.

> **TOP TIP** *Do you really want to learn about all the functionality behind the System namespace? Either press the F2 key to browse the namespace objects (and then press F1 on any item of interest), or nab one of the new books attempting to explain away all the key objects. Be warned however: this is serious bedtime material. Choose a night when your partner has a headache. Oh, and tell him or her to bring an aspirin for you, too . . . just in case.*

So, there we have namespaces for you. They're a digital filing cabinet for functionality, and, for the rest of this section, we're going to explore five top features from within the .NET framework, chunks of functionality that I think you'll really find useful in your applications. And we begin with the MessageBox. But, haven't we already . . . ?

Baby, you ain't seen nothing yet.

Going Further with the MessageBox

You've seen MessageBox.Show in action already. It displays a message, in a box, and hence the cunning name.

But it's actually a function, like InputBox, which means that it returns a value. We've been using it only to display simple OK messages so far, but, if we were asking users whether they wanted to continue, they might choose Yes, No, or Cancel. And how could we tell what they pressed? By looking at what value the function returns.

Let's check out an example.

1. In your open VB .NET application, change the code behind your button click event to:

```
MessageBox.Show("Continue?", "KarlOS", _
    MessageBoxButtons.YesNoCancel, MessageBoxIcon.Question)
```

This tells the function to display a message box with the title of "KarlOS", asking whether our user wants to continue. The box should display Yes, No and Cancel buttons, with a Question icon.

> **TOP TIP**   *Think our MessageBox line of code looks a little weird here? I agree. We're using the continuation character—an underscore—at the end of the first line. It allows you to carry long chunks of code over to the next line. You'll find these used throughout this entire book. For more information, look up "Using Special Code Characters" in Chapter 8.1, "Beginner Tips and Techniques".*

If you didn't notice the first time round, try retyping this MessageBox line. Look at how each of the arguments is named and described so we know what to specify here—it's the same with almost every feature in the .NET framework. Also, did you notice how the options for the buttons and icon styles automatically appeared in a list for us? No difficult looking-up for me!

But still, this is pretty useless. If I go and run the application, I get the desired message box—but I'm still not using the information our function returns. Let's amend our code:

2.   Change the code to:

```
If MessageBox.Show("Continue?", "KarlOS", MessageBoxButtons.YesNoCancel, _
    MessageBoxIcon.Question) = DialogResult.Cancel Then
    MessageBox.Show("Operation aborted!")
End If
```

3.   Press F5 and test your application.

See what happens? Try playing around with the `MessageBox.Show` function, exploring its capabilities. (See Figure 3-6.) What other button options can you display?

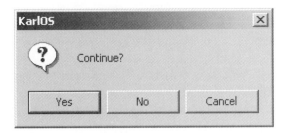

Figure 3-6. The MessageBox in full-swing

It's worth noting that the `MessageBox.Show` function returns a result of the type `DialogResult` (do you see that?). That means we can also declare a variable of the type `DialogResult`, return the result into that variable, then analyze it from there—useful if you want to check the result at multiple points, not just in one If statement. Here's what I mean:

```
Dim MyResult As DialogResult
MyResult = MessageBox.Show("Continue?", "KarlOS", _
    MessageBoxButtons.YesNoCancel, MessageBoxIcon.Question)
If MyResult = DialogResult.Cancel Then MessageBox.Show("Operation aborted!")
If MyResult = DialogResult.Yes Then MessageBox.Show("Operation accepted!")
```

Check out this code and make sure you play around yourself! Tsk, what a funky function. But this is just the beginning—let's start making some real noise!

Open That Thing!

Want to launch something? Whether it's a file, an Internet address or a Titan rocket from the Kennedy Space Center, the Start function is for you. (Okay, so I was lying about the Titan thing). It's located in the System.Diagnostics.Process namespace, accepts a filename or Internet address, and fires it off for you.

Let's see some action.

1. In your open VB .NET application, change the code behind your button click event to:

    ```
    If MessageBox.Show("Do you want to open the site?", "KarlMoore.com", _
        MessageBoxButtons.YesNo) = DialogResult.Yes Then
        Process.Start("http://www.karlmoore.com/")
    End If
    ```

2. Press the F5 key and test your code.

> **TOP TIP** *You can access the Start function by typing "System.Diagnostics.Process.Start". But here, we're only typing "Process.Start" because the .NET framework's System.Diagnostics namespace is "imported" (referenced) by default in a Windows Application project. You can see what I mean by opening your Project Properties (right-click on your project title in the Solution Explorer and select Properties), then exploring the standard entries in the Imports section. It's for this same reason you can run the MessageBox function without referencing its direct namespace of System.Windows.Forms.*

So, what else can you pass to this Start function? How about a program, such as Microsoft Word? A file created in Notepad? An FTP site address? Go push those capabilities.

Writing to Files

Want to create your own mini word processor? All you need is love, la-la-la-la-la. Oh, a TextBox control and a few lines of code wouldn't go amiss either.

Now, you manipulate files using code objects in the System.IO (In/Out) namespace, and you'll be pleased to hear that creating and writing to files is actually pretty simple. You just create a FileStream object to access the file and then use a StreamWriter object to put information into that FileStream.

These new object names sound a bit weird—and it's all certainly different from previous versions of Visual Basic—but why don't we spend a few minutes checking it out?

1. Create a new Windows application in VB .NET.

2. Draw out a TextBox control onto your form, setting the Name, Anchor, MultiLine, and ScrollBars properties as you deem fit.

3. Add a Save button to your form.

4. Using the following code as a template, add code behind your button to save the contents of your TextBox control to disc:

```
Dim MyStream As New IO.FileStream("c:\test.txt", IO.FileMode.Create)
Dim MyWriter As New IO.StreamWriter(MyStream)
MyWriter.Write("Welcome to my great file!")
MyWriter.Close()
MyStream.Close()
```

Finished? What do you think? Have you tried it yet? Does it work? (My offering is shown in Figure 3-7.)

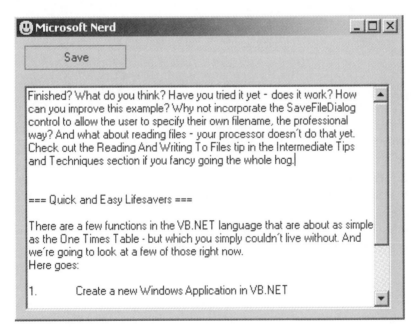

Figure 3-7. My final application—Move over, Microsoft Word!

How can you improve this example? Why not incorporate the SaveFileDialog control to allow users to specify their own filename, the professional way? And what about reading files? Your processor doesn't do that yet. Check out the "Reading and Writing Files" tip in Chapter 8.2, "Intermediate Tips and Techniques" if you fancy going the whole hog.

Quick and Easy Lifesavers

The VB .NET language has a few functions that are about as simple as the 1 times table but which you simply couldn't live without. And we're going to look at a few of those right now.

1. Create a new Windows application in VB .NET.

2. Add a button and then insert the following code behind its click event:

    ```
    Dim MyVariable As String
    MyVariable = InputBox("Enter something, anything:")

    MessageBox.Show("Is your entry numeric? " & IsNumeric(MyVariable))
    MessageBox.Show("Is your entry a date? " & IsDate(MyVariable))
    MessageBox.Show("The Val of your entry is: " & Val(MyVariable))
    ```

    Here, we're demonstrating three new functions. The first is IsNumeric, which returns a True if the item you pass it is a number. Then we have IsDate, which returns a True if the item you pass it represents a valid date. And, finally, we have the slightly different Val, which returns the first numeric portion of a string, if it exists, shaving off any excess.

3. Press the F5 key and test your application with the following entries: Karl, 20/05/1975, 05/20/1975, 1990, 5023, -502.21952, 40-yrs, K25.

    What do you think? Do you think these could be useful for checking inputs in your application? How could you use them with an If statement?

Going Random

The marketing department is on the phone again. What on earth could they want? You've delivered that high-tech publishing program, you've fine-tuned their extranet so they can easily share in-house resources with suppliers, and you've written full application user guides so they should never have problems ever, *ever* again.

Then they say they're coming downstairs to meet you. Right now. With a box of Turkish Delight in hand. But why you ask? They want you to create a program to handle their office lottery pool.

Who said random numbers were useless? Not if you have a fetish for Turkish Delight, they ain't. And the .NET framework includes its own Random class that allows you to generate your own random numbers at the tap of a key. Sounds like just the ticket.

Let's look at a code sample:

```
Dim objRandom As New System.Random()
MessageBox.Show(objRandom.Next(6))
```

Here, we're creating a new instance of our Random class, then running the Next function, which generates a new random number. We're passing it the number 6 as the maximum value parameter; the function will then choose a random value from a range starting at 0 and going up to, but not including, your maximum value. In other words, it will return a number from 0 to 5.

And there, ladies and gentlemen, we have our own mini die, in just two lines of code! (Okay, so dice don't have a 0 and do include a 6, but you catch my drift).

But the marketing department wants you to do this six times, generating six numbers between 1 and 49 for them to use on the lotto. Save all that nonsense about picking lucky numbers from birthdates and house numbers.

Yes, you could just write that second line of code six times, but there's a smarter way. You simply use a loop. Nope, don't look at me: these are *computer* loops and are actually quite easy. How do they work? Let's explore the new loop concept and a little random-number code, all in a final sample application.

1. Create a new Windows application in VB .NET.

2. Draw a ListBox control onto your form, changing its Name property to "lstLotto".

3. Add a button to your form, changing its Text property to "Go Lotto!" (See Figure 3-8.)

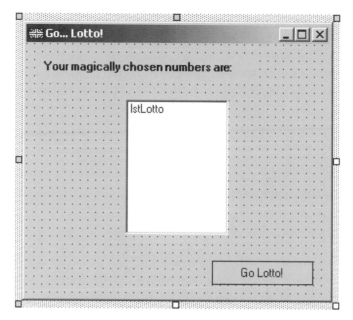

Figure 3-8. It's time to play Go Lotto!

4. Behind the click event of your button, add the following code:

```
Dim objRandom As New System.Random()
Dim shtLoopCount As Short

lstLotto.Items.Clear()

For shtLoopCount = 1 To 6
    lstLotto.Items.Add(objRandom.Next(49) + 1)
    MessageBox.Show("Added entry number " & shtLoopCount)
Next
```

What's happening here? Well, first off, we're creating a new instance of our Random class, called objRandom. Then, we're simply declaring a short to be used in our loop, plus clearing all items currently in our ListBox control.

After that, we begin the loop with our For statement. We're saying that this is a chunk of code that should loop one to six times, and, with each loop, it should put its current loop number in the shtLoopCount variable. When it reaches the Next line, it will start again and increment its loop number until finished.

Inside the loop, we're just adding an entry containing the returned random number (plus one) to our ListBox and then displaying the loop number in a message box.

5. Add a break point to the first line of code here, by moving to that line and pressing the F9 key.

6. When you're ready to run it, press F5 and test your application, stepping through each line of code using F8.

See what happens? Notice how the loop fires off exactly six times? Try hovering your mouse over our shtLoopCount variable as you move about in debug mode. Notice it increment?

Loops are incredibly popular and have many, many uses in programming. Can you think of any right now? Any ideas how this technique can help you develop smarter applications? Check out examples of loops in the "Tips and Techniques" section for a little divine inspiration.

A quick aside: imagine you have a program wherein the user needs to tell you how many times they want to loop around before doing so. In other words, you aren't hard-coding the numbers 1 to 6, as we are here. Any idea how you could do that? Using variables?

CONCLUSION

Well done on finishing the third chapter in the "Beginning VB .NET" tutorial!

Today, we started by looking at variables and how we can use them to build intelligent applications, programs that can "keep track." Then, we created our own mini password program, and we explored some of the most useful features hidden inside the .NET framework classes.

Oh, and I cunningly slipped in a whole section about the world of loops, in the hope that you wouldn't really notice. But you did and I'm sorry and I'll try harder next time.

Anyway, fancy a little homework? No? Excellent. Well, just keep exploring those classes! Get yourself onto the VB .NET Web sites. Explore this book's "Tips and Techniques" sections. Open up those samples distributed with Visual Studio .NET. Use the F2 key to figure out which namespaces hold the most valuable features. And remain curious, the true sign of a great programmer.

Or whatever.

In the next chapter, we'll be looking at how you can expand your groovy applications by learning a bundle of supercool development techniques. I'm talking about slapping together your own menus, methods, modules, and multiple forms. And I'll even show you how to have multiple forms. Truly amazing.

So join us then. But, for now, this is Karl Moore wishing you all a very pleasant evening. Goodnight!

CHAPTER 1.3

VARIABLES AND THE COOLEST CODE REVIEW SHEET

- Variables are like invisible text boxes: you create them in code and they hold data for you.

- When you declare (*dim*) a variable, you specify what sort of data it should hold. Popular data types include String (text), Short (whole numbers up to 32,767), Boolean (true/false), and Date (date/time).

- It's also advisable to use one of the standard three-character prefixes when declaring variables. Doing so makes your code more understandable. The following examples demonstrate the proper form:

```
Dim blnSex As Boolean
Dim strUsername As String
Dim datAppointment As Date
Dim shtAge As Short
```

- You can set the value of a variable as you declare it, using this syntax:

```
Dim strUsername As String = "Karl"
```

- Namespaces are a logical way of organizing functionality. You can liken a namespace to a digital filing cabinet for functions. You can even "build your own" application namespaces if you wish.

- The most important namespace you'll find in the .NET framework is System, which links to objects dealing with everything from accessing an SQL Server database to manipulating files.

- The Microsoft.VisualBasic namespace contains a lot of the functions familiar to Visual Basic 6 programmers and is distributed with the .NET framework.

- Loops are a great way of running chunks of code more than once. Here is an example of a For-Next loop:

```
For shtLoopCount = 1 To 10
    MessageBox.Show("Loop Number: " & shtLoopCount)
Next
```

- You also have a Do-Until loop, which—although not covered in this chapter—works in a similar way:

```
Do Until lstRubbish.Items.Count > 10
    lstRubbish.Items.Add("Another Entry")
Loop
```

Menus, Methods, Modules, and Multiple Forms

"There is no reason for any individual to have a computer in their home."
—Ken Olson, President of Digital Equipment Corporation, 1977

IT'S A VERY SPECIAL FOURTH CHAPTER TODAY. I mean, boy, have we got a lineup for you. Actually, we haven't. But if we had, boy, would it be good.

Instead, I've got a handful of ideas I scribbled on the back of a cigarette packet this morning. So tell me, how does this sound: today, I'd like to talk about *expanding your application*. I'm talking about making it larger, moving it on up, getting yourself in with those big boys.

Erm, let me rephrase that. I'm talking about building your program, adding menus, using multiple forms, exploring methods and functions, figuring out modules, and other, completely clean stuff.

In this chapter, we've got five mini sections dedicated to expanding your application development techniques—simple quickies that will demonstrate some very important principles. Ready to join me? Strap yourself in as we shoot off into the coding world once more. Or as you turn the page.

Listen, just don't say that I don't *try* to make it sound interesting.

Expanding with Menus

Menus are jolly useful tools.

Whether you're in a first-class restaurant or coding on that dodgy 286, they're a real gem. But people are so used to them in programs now that, if your application doesn't have them, ol' Mr. User is likely to get rather confused.

And bearing in mind that the IQ of our average user actually dips into the red, trust me—they're a real essential. And adding a menu or two to your amazingly groovy program is exactly what I'd like to teach you how to do, here in this first section. Let's start:

1. Create a new Windows application in VB .NET, naming it "MyExpansion".

2. From your toolbox, drag a MainMenu control onto your form, as shown in Figure 4-1.

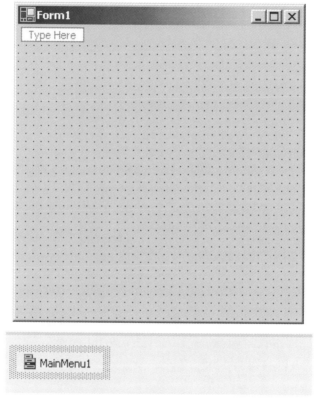

Figure 4-1. Adding the MainMenu control

The MainMenu control allows you to visually design your menu. The top of your form should turn gray, in anticipation of a menu, with a little Type Here box appearing in the top left-hand corner.

3. Click on the Type Here box and type "&File". (Yes, that's right: there's an ampersand before the "File" there.)

4. Press Enter when finished.

See what happens after you press Enter? The "F" becomes underlined, turning it into the hot key for that menu item. Let's carry on.

5. Add the following entries under the File heading:

   • &New

   • &Open

   • –

   • E&xit

See what happens when you add that third item (the dash)? Notice what it turns into? We could continue and add further menus and submenus at this point, simply by following the Type Here signs, but we'll keep it simple for now. My brain is already starting to overheat.

6. Select Exit on our menu.

If you glance over to the Properties window (Figure 4-2), you'll notice that every item on the menu is actually a separate MenuItem control, which each sit on top of that MainMenu control. The Exit item is probably something like MenuItem5.

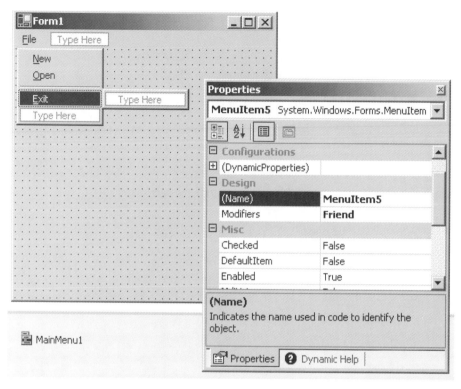

Figure 4-2. The properties for our MenuItem control

Look through the list of available properties for one menu item. See what you can change, such as the name, for a start, plus whether the menu item can be checked? Another great little feature is the Shortcut property.

TOP TIP   *Looking for an Image property? Hah, weren't we all! I'm afraid that you still can't add images to standard Visual Basic menus. Instead, you'll have to head down to a company such as ComponentSource and pick yourself a third-party component to do the job. I just feel sorry for your wallet.*

Let's try a couple of these properties out.

7. Change the Name property of your Exit menu item to "mnuFileExit".

8. Change the shortcut of your Exit menu item to "CtrlX".

This means that, whenever a user presses the key combination Ctrl and X while in this form, the code behind this particular menu item will run. Oh, except we haven't actually added any yet, which is perhaps a slight flaw in the plan. Let's fix that now.

9. Double-click on your Exit menu item.

10. Add the following code to respond to its click event:

```
Application.Exit()
```

Not too in-depth, that code. But will it work as we expect?

11. Press F5 and test your application.

What does your menu look like? What happens when you click on the New menu item? And the Exit item? Try pressing Ctrl+X, too.

Now, one thing that was always a bit problem in the golden olden days of Visual Basic was figuring out when the user was actually playing with the menus.

You know how some applications give you descriptions of what individual menu items do as you hover over each of them? Well, certain smart Visual Basic 5/6 types wanted to do this, too. The problem was that it usually resulted in around two tons of subclassing code that was about as puzzling as the world's largest Rubik's cube.

In VB .NET, however, each MenuItem control has its own select event, which runs as you move your mouse over the individual menu item. Fancy checking that out?

12. Add a label to your form.

13. Behind the select event of each of your MenuItem controls, add code to change the Text property of the label to a description of what that menu item does.

14. Press F5 to test your application when finished. (My effort is shown in Figure 4-3.)

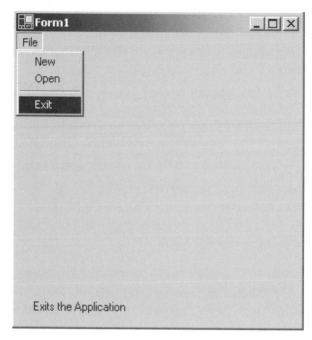

Figure 4-3. My menu, strutting its programmatic stuff

TOP TIP   *Want to know when the user has started browsing the entire menu and when they've finished? Check out the MenuStart and MenuComplete events of your form.*

And that's pretty much menus in a nutshell. They're a really neat way of expanding your application. After you've learned the basics, it's all pretty routine, ma'am.

Erm, so I guess that means it's time to move onward, Sailor—through to figuring out how we can host multiple forms in our applications.

TOP TIP   *Wondering how you can have multiple forms open inside one big container form, then have your menu list the individual windows? You simply need to change the MdiList property of your MenuItem to True. Check out "Creating an MDI Application" in Chapter 8.2, "Intermediate Tips and Techniques" for more information.*

Expanding with Forms

"Hello World!" programs.

Yes, they're fun. Yes, they demonstrate you can type at least one line of code. Yes, that loving greeting truly exhumes vibes of a quintessential humanitarian sort hidden somewhere inside of you.

But it's a bit simple, isn't it?

I mean, don't get me wrong; I can appreciate simple. Simple is my thing. But a one-form Hello World just ain't going to crack it in the real world. Now if you had *two* forms . . . well, that same world is your rather clichéd oyster.

Erm, but just how do you do that? No, not cliché an oyster—I'm no Julia Child. Rather, I'm asking how you can add multiple forms to your application. Well, listen closely:

1. From the menu in your existing project, select Project ➢ Add Windows Form.

2. Change the name of the form to "Calculator". (See Figure 4-4.)

3. Click on Open.

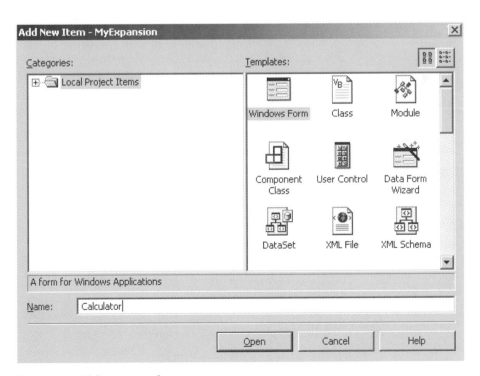

Figure 4-4. Adding a new form

And there we have it! You've just added a separate form to your application, and didn't feel a thing. Next, we just design and code this new calculator form as usual. There's nothing special here.

The real problem, however, is getting from one form to the next. When your application launches, only the one main form spouts up. How do you open that second form?

4. Back on your main form, add another menu item next to File. Change the text of this one to "Launch Calculator".

Note that there are no submenus here; it's just a "root" menu item all on its own. Hokily dokily, programmer people, let's move on.

5. Behind the click event of this Launch Calculator menu item, add the following code:

```
Dim MyCalc As New Calculator()
MyCalc.Show()
```

Here, we're declaring a new instance of your calculator form, calling it MyCalc. We're then running the .Show method inherited by all Windows forms.

> **TOP TIP**   *In this code, we're treating our calculator form just as you have treated classes in the .NET framework. Now, if you cast your mind right back to the very first chapter, you may remember exploring the code behind a form—and we saw that a form is in fact just that—a class, an object you work with in code. Is this making sense, or do you still think I'm a complete nut?*

And that's that. To display a form, you simply add one, then design and code it as usual. Next up, you link between forms using code similar to the preceding lines.

6. Press F5 and test your application.

What happens when you click your button? Does the calculator form show itself? (My own application is shown in Figure 4-5.)

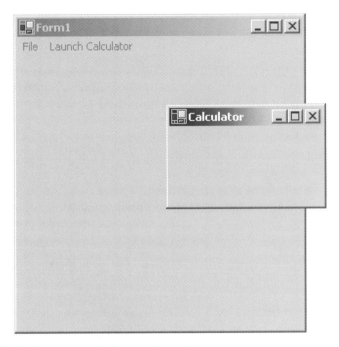

Figure 4-5. Displaying your new form using code

Notice how the form stays open and functional even after the code has finished running.

Instances Galore

How about if you go back to the first form now and click the button again? What happens? And again? With each click, another new instance of your calculator form appears, just as your code instructs it too. Hmm, problem or opportunity?

Think about programs such as Word or Paint Shop Pro, which may have multiple forms open at any one time. These programs need to run code like this over and over. But some programmers hate it: it's one form and they want it to appear only once!

And sometimes that's the best thing. For example, you may be dealing with a logon screen or settings form or some such. And you don't want those blighters littering the screen.

So, how do you stop the multiple instances from occurring? Well, let's think about what's happening here: your button can be clicked multiple times and a new instance created over and over, all because its `As New` code is running over and over again.

The best solution, therefore, is to stop that code running by taking the `As New` statement out of your subroutine and putting it "behind your form," as though you were declaring a form-level variable.

If it's declared `As New` only once there, it'll never keep running and creating new, unwanted instances. Move closer and let me show you what I mean:

1. Move the line of code where you declare a new instance of your form, from your subroutine to the form-level Declarations area (that is, just under the `Public Class` and `Inherits` lines).

2. When finished, press F5 and test your application.

What happens? Does it all make sense? Also, can you now access that form instance from any subroutine on your form? Check it out.

> **TOP TIP**   *Another great idea is to declare a new instance of a form in something called a* module, *which we'll explore later today. Putting it inside a module, you'll be able to access that one instance of the form from anywhere in your application. I'll demonstrate exactly what I mean shortly.*

And so, my fluffy friends, that's how to expand your application with multiple forms. Interesting stuff. You can tell why I get so many dates.

Talking of all things romantic, can I interest you in a special preview session of my up-and-coming movie, *What Women Don't Want*?

Expanding with Methods

So, you want to expand your application with methods, huh? Oh, well that's lucky. Because that's exactly what this section is all about, and, once you start using them, you'll find these little chunks of code incredibly useful.

Just what is a method? Well, you've seen them before: we've already run `.Clear` on a TextBox control and `.Show` on a form. It's something you run that performs an action. And, oh, what action!

Well, you can also create your own methods, but why would you want to?

Let's imagine that you've finished development of your supercool application, F2K (the Finger2Keyboard suite, renamed shortly after "Finger Under Keyboard" was ruled a decidedly risqué title). It's essentially a Word takeoff that you hope will make it big in the processor stakes. Ha—move over Bill Gates!

However, when your user finishes tapping away on your application, you want to thank them for their continued support and adding an extra $30 to your bank account. How could you do that?

Well, if they exited the program via the Close item on the menu, you could put the code there. But what if they just close the form? Or how about if they just clicked the Logout button, ready for another user to enter? You'd still want them to see the message.

Now you could put that same bit of code behind the Close menu item, some form Unload event, and the Logout button. But that'd get awfully repetitive, and what if you ever needed to change it? Plus, let's imagine that you were writing the username and date details to a security log as well. You really wouldn't want to replicate that code over and over again. Well, I suppose you could, but it'd get messier than a Freddy Krueger flick.

And that's where methods can help out. They provide a groovy way to package chunks of code up into nice ready-to-run blocks. Let's explore.

1. In your existing Windows application, open the calculator form.

2. In the lower left-hand corner of your screen, add a Logout button.

3. Add a menu to this form, with a Close menu item on it. (See Figure 4-6.)

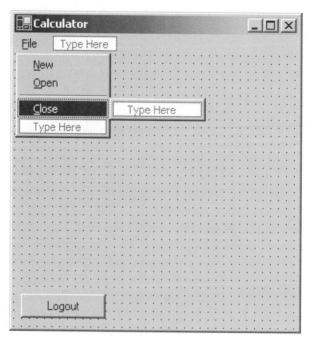

Figure 4-6. Our sample F2K application so far

This will be a relatively simple example. We have two points here at which we want to run the same chunk of code: behind our menu item and behind our button. Let's code that:

4. Somewhere inside your calculator form class, add the following code (just not inside another subroutine!):

```
Sub Goodbye()
    MessageBox.Show("Thank you for using F2K and " & _
        "taking my bank balance to new heights!")
    Me.Close()
End Sub
```

Here, we've created our own subroutine—our own method—called Goodbye. When it runs, it'll display a message box and then close the current form. What do you think? Simple dimple or about as understandable as a Stephen Hawking bestseller?

Let's fire off this chunk of code now, when our menu item is pressed and when our button is clicked.

5. Behind the click event of both your button and menu item, add the following code:

```
Goodbye()
```

When VB .NET stumbles across this line, it realizes it should go run all the code behind that particular method and then return. Let's test it out:

6. Press F5 to run your application.

From your main form, open your calculator form. Try clicking on the Logout button. What happens? Next, reopen the form and test out your Close menu item. Does the same occur?

Okay, so it's a simple example, and there are probably better ways of handling the situation, but it's getting late and I'm getting desperate. No change there, then.

7. Close your application when finished.

So, methods are chunks of code that perform an action. Where could they be useful in your applications? How could you expand on our application here? Just imagine that this method actually contained a whole load of code that actually went and stored user values in the registry, or tracked program activity in some sort of security log. That would save you time and duplicated code, and it'd make development easier as well.

It's all possible—by expanding your application with methods.

Oh, and with parameters, too. After all, if you're going to store user values in the registry, you need to tell the method what those user values are. And you do that using parameters. You can see an example of a method with parameters on today's Review Sheet—or you can just sit tight as we encounter them in the next section when dealing with functions.

Functions?

Expanding with Functions

"Yes, what?" you grunt down the line. It's the accounting department again. They called last February and are already way over their technical support quota.

Actually, it's the manager, and he's making a request. He needs a number-adding program. Apparently, they're running low on calculators and the temps have yet to figure out basic arithmetic.

"Whatever!" you yell and slam down the receiver.

Now, you could just ignore the call and go back to that game of Solitaire, but I hear you're one of those conscientious types who actually quite likes the idea of a monthly paycheck.

So, a number-adding program. Not rocket science, I'm sure you'll agree. However, there was one peculiar request: the head number-crunching bloke asked specifically for four mini calculators on one screen.

Which leads us onto functions.

You've already played with functions. You've seen MessageBox.Show and tinkered with that eternally useful InputBox. Functions are basically like methods, except they can *return* a value.

When I was first taught about these function beasts, in some dodgy back-street training joint in downtown Leeds, well, to say I was completely befuddled would be an understatement. I just didn't have a clue (and neither did the lecturer, which really didn't help).

Let's see if I can do a better job. This, my friends, is a sample function:

```
Function GetUsername() As String
    GetUsername = "Karl Moore"
End Function
```

Admittedly, it isn't a very useful function, but it should demonstrate the principle. Here, we have a function called GetUserName that returns a string. The code inside it here does very little: it sets the return value of GetUsername to the "Karl Moore" string.

Understand the code so far? We might call a groovy function like this from our code, as so:

```
MessageBox.Show(GetUsername())
```

We just treat it like a regular string or variable. The function name here gets replaced by the return value of the function and is displayed in a message box. And that's not all—you can also have arguments with functions. No, not literally (you'd look a bit strange), but instead like this:

```
Function Login(ByVal Username As String, ByVal Password As String) As Boolean
    If Username = "Karl" And Password = "BEDKNOBS" Then
        Login = True
    End If
End Function
```

There we go: a login function with parameters (which are often referred to as *arguments*). It takes username and password values and returns a Boolean (True/False) value. The code here simply checks the username and password values, and returns a True if valid.

> **TOP TIP** *Just in case you were wondering, by default a Boolean is set to False. You can see why I'm so popular at cocktail parties, can't you?*

> **ANOTHER TOP TIP** *The ByVal keywords in the function here were inserted automatically by VB .NET. ByVal means that this parameter is being passed "by value," its default behavior. However, you can also change this to ByRef, which means that, if your program passes a variable in as a parameter and your function changes the value of that parameter, the original variable changes also. In other words, the original variable is passed by reference. There's more about this in the FAQ of "Doing Objects" (which can be found in Chapter 2.5). Lovely.*

So how could we call a function, like Login, in code? Let's think about it:

```
Dim blnValidLogon As Boolean
blnValidLogon = Login("Karl", "BEDKNOBS")

If blnValidLogon = True Then
    MessageBox.Show("You successfully logged on!")
End If
```

Make sense? My fingers are crossed that you're nodding. Okay, let's step back a couple of pages to the accounts department and that number-adding program they wanted. Fancy creating it now?

1. Open your calculator form.

2. Draw out four sets of two TextBox controls, one label and one button, as shown in Figure 4-7.

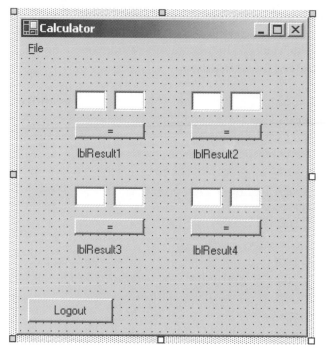

Figure 4-7. Trust me; this will all make sense soon.

Each of these four sets of controls will take a couple of numbers. When the user clicks on the button, a result appears in the Label control. Now, we could just put code to add each value together under each and every button.

And that would be fine, if I wasn't so completely idle. Oh, and it's pretty bad programming practice, too. Not very flexible in case of future changes, you know.

Instead, we'll create one function to do the actual addition and have it return the value to put in our label. Let's go:

3. Add the following function to your form.

```
Function Add(ByVal Number1 As Short, ByVal Number2 As Short) As Short
    Add = Number1 + Number2
End Function
```

Here, we have a function called Add that very simply accepts two parameters, adds them up, and returns the result. Do you understand what's happening here? Make sure you fully understand the concept before continuing. Let's actually add code to call the function now.

4. Using the following line of code as a template, call the Add function from the Click event behind each of your four button controls.

```
lblResult.Text = Add(txtNumber1.Text, txtNumber2.Text)
```

As you type each line of code, notice the Intellisense prompt with the argument names.

5. Press F5 to test your application, as in Figure 4-8.

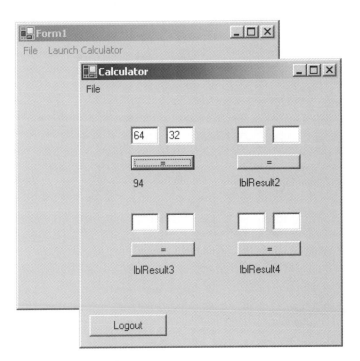

Figure 4-8. Testing our calculator program

Try entering a couple of small numbers in any of the TextBox controls and clicking on your button. Does it work as you anticipated? Are you sure you haven't made any typos in the code?

What happens if you put a breakpoint on your button click code by pressing F9 and then step through it line by line with F8? See how it all fits together? Also, what if you enter a word such as *twenty-one* in one of the TextBox controls and then click on your button? Hmm, how could you solve this? Would the IsNumeric or Val functions be useful here?

6.   Close your application when finished.

> **TOP TIP**   *Small aside, gang. We've not really talked about math in VB .NET, but it's pretty simple. You merely have different operators for different functions, used just as we've done here. So, we have + for addition, – for subtraction, / for division, and * for multiplication. Plus, the .NET framework already has a whole bundle of mathematical functions for you, hiding away in the* System.Math *namespace, such as Sqrt to determine the square root. Check it out in the code window, search the Help index, or press F2 to browse the namespace via the Object Browser.*

Hmm, a number-adding program. Call me Claire Voyant, but I can tell you're still not impressed. But it's more a concept thing; just be aware that functions are a cool way of working and can really help expand your application.

Let's say you were creating that F2K word processor we talked about earlier. How would you save files? Would you put all the code behind the Save menu item, then all over again behind that toolbar Save button, and then again behind the . . . nah, of course not.

Instead, you'd write it only once, perhaps as a method into which you pass the text you want to save. You can then add a load of file manipulation code, all accessible just by running a method such as SaveFile. Or you might package it up as a function that accepts your text and a filename as parameters and then returns a True or False, depending on whether the file save was successful.

Either way, expanding your applications with methods and functions makes your life easier. And, if you ever need to make any changes, you only have one place to look.

Cut bugs, code faster, be successful. This is the solution.

Wow, impressive talk, Karlos. Wonder if Anthony Robbins is looking for a sidekick . . .

Methods, Modules, Mayhem—Oh My!

How are you finding the learning process? Are you enjoying discovering how to expand your application—or simply debating over which hit man to hire? Either way, I'm really glad you've come this far.

In this fifth and final section of our chapter on expanding, we're going to look at modules. Now, you store your files in a folder, your wad in a wallet, *and your methods (and stuff) in modules*. Yes, it's another dodgy mnemonic, but it works. Sort of.

Modules are basically a holding place for your methods and functions, in addition to variables and objects. Let's take a peek at them now.

1. From the menu in your program, select Project ➤ Add Module.

2. Change the name of your new module to "modGeneral".

Your code window should look pretty bare, just holding the opening and closing lines of the module, like so:

```
Module modGeneral

End Module
```

Let's add a simple variable to this module.

3. Add the following declaration to your module:

```
Public Username As String
```

Hmm, looks a little different from the way we usually declare a variable, right? Well, they're not all *Dim*, you know, despite what the rumors say.

In VB .NET, you can add the Public or Private keywords to the front of pretty much anything: methods, functions, variables, objects. These keywords just determine what can see that item.

> **TOP TIP** *By default, the Dim statement is the equivalent of using the Private keyword.*

In modules, if you declare something as private, only the code within that module can see it. But, if you declare it as public, your entire application is able to access it. And that's just what we've done here: added a public variable that should be accessible from anywhere in our entire application.

> **TOP TIP** *Why bother messing about with all this Public and Private stuff? It helps you segment off code that will be used only inside a module and nowhere else. When developing larger applications, it's also possible that you'll find bugs creeping in where you've accidentally set an incorrect variable or some such. By restricting which parts of your application are allowed to see certain bits of code, you've limited the risk, hmm, about this much.*

4. Add a button anywhere to both forms in your application: your startup form and the calculator form.

5. Behind the button on your startup form, add the following code:

```
Username = "Strangely Brown"
```

6. Behind the button on your calculator form, add the following code:

```
MessageBox.Show(Username)
```

7. Press F5 to test your application. (See Figure 4-9.)

Figure 4-9. Strangely Brown (my pet Iguana, you know)

When you click on the first button on your startup form, it should set that "global" variable, and the second button on your calculator form should read it. Does it work? Where could this be useful?

8. When finished testing, close your application.

But this really isn't modules at their best. Creating a global variable is nothing; creating global methods and functions is everything. Obey your thirst.

However, I'm going to be cruel and leave this one to you. Before continuing, I want you to take our Add function from behind the calculator form and make it accessible to your entire application.

9. Move the Add function from your calculator form to your module, remembering to prefix it with the Public keyword.

10. Add code to your startup form to prove that you can access the Add method from anywhere in your application. For example, behind the form load event:

```
MessageBox.Show(Add(52, 23))
```

11. When finished, press F5 and test your application.

What happens? Can you access it from anywhere in your program? How about your existing code? Does the calculator still work?

Hmm, so what else could you use this for? How about putting all your really useful functions—entire blocks of code that manipulate files, dip into the registry, open files—into one generic, ready-to-run module? Wouldn't that cut down your development time drastically, and enable you to have instant access to reams of code? You bet your bottom dollar, kiddo.

Another thought: why not declare a form object behind your module, As New, like so:

```
Public MyCalc As New Calculator()
```

Now, whenever you need to show the calculator form in your application, you simply have to run MyCalc.Show(). This also ensures that you only ever have one instance of that form open at any one time.

So, you've had a glimpse of just what modules can do: they store stuff that can be seen by your entire application. And now it's up to you to put this knowledge to work. To get you started, try scouring Tutorial 8, "Tips and Techniques" and pulling together the most-useful snippets into your own ready-to-run code library.

Tsk, your own code library, eh? That's what you call expanding your application. Your mum would be proud.

CONCLUSION

Congratulations on completing the fourth chapter of Tutorial 1, "Beginning VB .NET"!

In this jam-packed session, we've looked at just how we can take our development techniques to the next level. We've found out how to use menus in our applications, experienced multiple forms, checked out the groovy world of methods and functions, and figured out how modules can help us build our programs.

Simple samples, maybe, but—now that you've grasped those oh-so-important concepts—you're on course to use these neat new skills in your next application.

Anyway, consider yourself officially *expanded*, a trait unsurprisingly familiar to most in the nerd world.

In the next, final chapter, we'll be concluding with a sneak geek peek at error handling, distribution, and that ever-so-friendly FAQ. So, y'all come back soon, ya hear?

But, until then, I'm your slightly nerdier host, Karl Moore, wishing you all a very enjoyable evening. Toodle-pip!

MENUS, METHODS, MODULES, AND MULTIPLE FORMS REVIEW SHEET

- You can graphically design menus in your application by adding the MainMenu control to your form.

- Every menu entry you create using the MainMenu control is actually an individual MenuItem control, each which its own click and select events.

- To add a new form to your project, select Project ➤ Add Windows Form from the menu.

- Forms are classes and should be treated in the same way as regular classes in the .NET framework. Every Windows form inherits a `.Show` method, which displays the form to the user. Here is sample code to display a form:

```
Dim objMyForm As New Form1()
objMyForm.Show()
```

- Every time the `As New` declaration is encountered in your code like this, a new instance of your form is displayed. One way to help ensure that only one instance of your form is ever created is to move your `As New` code to the Declarations section of your form, making it a form-level object. A better method is to make this a public `As New` declaration in a globally accessible module.

- Methods allow you to bundle together chunks of code that can be called simply by specifying their name in code. Here is a sample method, or *subroutine*:

```
Sub WriteToLog()
    ' code to write to log
End Sub
```

- Functions are different than methods in that they can "return" values. Examples of functions include MessageBox.Show and InputBox. Here is a sample function:

```
Function GetDateTime() As Date
    GetDateTime = Now
End Function
```

- Both methods and functions can also include parameters. Here is an example of a method that accepts parameters:

```
Sub LogAction(ByVal Action As String, ByVal CurrentDate As Date)
    MessageBox.Show(Action & " on " & CurrentDate & " logged!")
End Sub
```

- Calling a method with parameters is equally simple. Here is an example of a method to which we are providing arguments:

```
LogAction("Accessed Account #4293", Now)
```

- Modules are a holding point for variables, objects, methods, and functions. To add a new module to your project, select Project ➤ Add Module from the menu.

- Items in a module prefixed with "Public" are visible to the entire application, whereas "Private" items are visible to only that code within the module. Here's a sample of a public variable declaration:

```
Public MyPublicString As String
```

Errors, Setup, and Going from Here

"640K ought to be enough for anybody."—Bill Gates, 1981

THE END IS NIGH—BUT, FOR ONCE, in a good way. Yes, you're reading the fifth and final chapter of Tutorial 1, "Beginning VB .NET," where, over the next dozen pages, we'll be concluding our first look at the world of programming.

Now, now, put away those hankies.

We've already traveled a long way. Homer would be proud. Today, we'll be going just that little bit farther, with a look at how to handle errors in your application. We'll also find out how to pull together our own setup program in minutes.

As with all the last chapters of the tutorials in this book, we'll also finish with a FAQ—a selection of frequently asked questions—and spend some time figuring out where you can take your knowledge from here.

So, ready to jump straight back in? Then brace yourself, for the rather unglamorous world of error handling. Eww, yuck!

Handling the Errors

The Chinese call mistakes *opportunities*. I call them *annoying*.

But they're all around: that fender-bender on the way into work, the way in which I always manage to accidentally delete the wrong computer files, the new kid at number 54.

Oh, and, of course, code mistakes, errors, bugs.

Trust me, I'm a bit of an expert here. A typical Karl Moore application is buggier than than Bunny. No kidding. And this is just where error handling steps onto the scene: it's a method of dealing with problems in your code as they occur.

I'm not talking about typing errors here because the compiler usually catches those. I mean the errors that occur when your user runs that calculator program we built last week and enters *twenty-one* as one of the numbers. I mean the errors that occur when your program tries to manipulate a file that no longer exists. I mean runtime errors. I mean . . . *whoops!*

Thankfully, VB .NET has two main ways to handle runtime errors, and I'll be teaching you both over the next few pages.

Resume Next

The first method on the list is my absolute favorite for simplicity. It's called a Resume Next statement, and it essentially tells Visual Basic, "Hey, listen up mate. If you stumble across an error, just ignore it, sweep it under the carpet, and move on to the next line of code. Pretend nothing ever happened."

Okay, so perhaps Visual Basic doesn't use those *exact* words, but you get the idea. And how do you implement the Resume Next statement? Let's put our foot down and get moving.

1. Create a new Windows application in VB .NET.

2. Change its name to "LifezaWitch".

3. Add a button to Form1.

Next, we're going to add some code behind that button. This code will look fine at design time, but it'll generate an error when we run our application. Let's go.

4. Add the following code to respond to the click event of your button:

```
MessageBox.Show("Hello World! No error yet . . . ")
Process.Start("z:\amazing.doc")
MessageBox.Show("Everything is just fine, ma!")
```

Here, we're just displaying a message box, attempting to launch a presumably nonexistent file, and finally showing another message box.

5. From the menu, select Build ➢ Build (or press Ctrl+Shift+ B).

Next, let's figure out what happens when running our program in the real world.

6. Go to your project's Bin folder and run your executable, LifezaWitch.exe.

7. On Form1, click on your button.

If you don't receive an error message, it means you actually do have a Z: drive with a file on it called Amazing.doc, in which case you win the grand prize of a soggy Mars Bar. (Hilariously restrictive conditions apply; see `www.KarlMoore.com` for details.)

However, most of you should find yourselves staring at an error message (as shown in Figure 5-1), reading something like "The system cannot find the file specified."

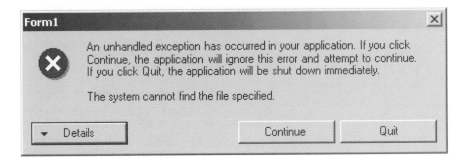

Figure 5-1. Oops, I did it again.

You have two options: continue or quit. Actually, you're lucky: in old versions of Visual Basic, you could only quit. But it still looks pretty unprofessional.

8. On the error message, click on Continue.

Notice what happens? That's right—nothing. The routine is exited, and your code stops running. You never get to see the next message box. So, how could we handle this in code? Well, Resume Next first!

9. Close your application when finished.

All it takes is a simple line of code to get VB .NET to ignore the error. And it goes a little something like this:

10. Add the following statement above the three lines of code you just entered:

```
On Error Resume Next
```

11. Repeat the preceding tests: building and running your program, then clicking on the button.

What happens here? The first line of code runs without problem. The second line kicks in, and, when an error occurs, VB .NET just ignores it and cunningly moves on. Finally, the third line of code—our message box—gets displayed.

> **TOP TIP** *The Resume Next action kicks into play as soon as the statement is encountered in your subroutine. You can turn it on at one point, and then turn it off later in the same subroutine by using the code* On Error Goto 0.

And that, my friends, is the Resume Next statement. It's a quick and easy fix: just add water and microwave for five minutes. But there's also another way, one that gives you a little more control. Enter stage right: the Try-Catch-Finally block.

Try-Catch-Finally

Think you already know everything you need to know about error handling? Not quite. This latest version of Visual Basic features structured error handling in the form of Try-Catch-Finally blocks. Huh?

It works like this. You put any code that may generate an error into a *Try block.* VB .NET tries to run this, and, if an error occurs, it's caught and the code inside your *Catch block* runs. Finally, whether an error occurred or not, VB .NET runs code in your optional *Finally block.*

Make sense? Okay, let's see it in action.

1. Change the code behind your button to:

    ```
    Try
        MessageBox.Show("Hello World! No error yet...")
        Process.Start("z:\amazing.doc")
        MessageBox.Show("No problemo, senor!")
    Catch ex As Exception
        MessageBox.Show("An error has occured: " & _
            ex.Message)
    Finally
        MessageBox.Show("Hey - I run regardless!")
    End Try
    ```

Notice how VB .NET automatically closes the Try block for you?

Here, we have three blocks of code: the Try block that tests the code, the Catch block that runs if an error occurs, and the optional Finally block that runs at the end of it all (which is useful for clearing up variables, objects, and such).

One slight point I haven't mentioned yet. As an extra here, we're catching the error as an Exception object called Ex, which provides us with further information about the error, such as the type of error and its description. In our code, we're simply displaying the Exception Message property.

> **TOP TIP** *You'll hear many programmers talk about exceptions whereas others talk about errors. Confused? In reality, they're exactly the same thing. However, as* exception *is the latest buzzword, it's worth dropping into the occasional conversation.*

What other properties are available to you with that Exception class? What do they do? To view a quick description, simply click on a property in the Intellisense list and read the tool tip message.

2. Run the same tests as before: build your program, run it, and click on your button, closing when finished. (If possible, turn on debugging and step through your code line by line.)

What happens? My screen can be seen in Figure 5-2.

```
Try
    MessageBox.Show("Hello World! No error yet...")
    Process.Start("z:\amazing.doc")
    MessageBox.Show("No problemo, seniore!")
Catch ex As Exception
    MessageBox.Show("An error has occured: " & _
        ex.Message)
Finally
    MessageBox.Show("Hey - I run regardless!")
End Try
```

Figure 5-2. An error is caught with Try-Catch-Finally blocks.

Do you ever get to see the No Problemo message box? When would that occur? How about the "I run regardless" message? Would that ever *not* display? And is it actually possible to completely remove that Finally block? Check it out.

Here's another experiment: try mixing the Resume Next and Try-Catch-Finally error-handling techniques in the same subroutine. Can you build the application now?

And so there, in a nutshell, we have error handling in VB .NET. The two main methods—Resume Next and Try-Catch-Finally blocks—both have their own advantages, and, although you might not be too keen on using them just now, you'll probably want to implement them as your application nears its release date.

That is, of course, unless you like homicidal users on your case. Been there, done that, got the scars. Trust me: it's not advisable. Just add the code.

Distributing Your Program

So, your application is looking sexy, your modules are full of methods, the bugs have gone, and your testers are showing their pearly whites. That can mean only one thing.

For me, I'm daydreaming. For you, it's time to distribute your application.

How? Well, it's pretty simple actually, and, back in those halcyon days of Chapter 1.1, I let the real trick out of the bag: you just copy and paste.

That's right. If the user already has the .NET framework installed, he or she needs only the EXE file (perhaps alongside any separate DLLs you've referenced), and everything is ready to roll. It's called XCOPY deployment, and it's just that easy to get your program out to the world.

Building a Setup Program

So, you can just copy and paste to deploy your application. But what are your other options? Well, you could always get out that wallet and shell out a bit of green on a third-party installation creator, such as Wise for Windows Installer.

But, if your wallet appears to be stuck tight—curious, that—then you may as well use VB .NET itself to create a setup program. And it's relatively easy: you simply add a setup project to your existing solution, tell VB .NET which files it should install and any shortcuts it needs to make, and then run a Build.

Let's check it out now.

1. Open a Windows application in VB .NET, or create a new one.

2. From the menu, choose File ➤ Add Project ➤ New Project.

Your one solution can contain multiple projects. Here, you have your core application, plus the following.

3. From the Add New Project screen, under the Setup and Deployment Projects folder, choose Setup Project.

4. Change its name to "MySetup" and click on OK.

You should be looking at a screen similar to the one shown in Figure 5-3. Exciting stuff, obviously.

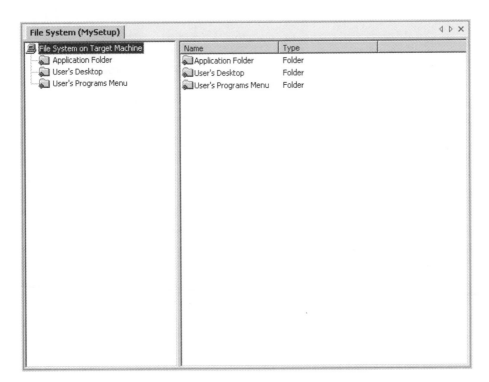

Figure 5-3. Your setup project

First off, let's give this setup application a little information about what it's installing.

5. If your Properties window isn't displaying properties for your MySetup project, click on MySetup in the Solution Explorer.

6. Next, for your application, specify values for the following properties as best you can:

- *AddRemoveProgramsIcon*: the icon that will appear in the Add/Remove Programs menu

- *Author*: your name

- *Description*: a brief summary of your program

- *Manufacturer*: your company name

- *ManufacturerUrl*: your company Web address

- *SupportPhone*: telephone number for support enquiries

- *SupportUrl*: Web address for support issues

- *Title*: the important one, the name of your application

That's a little basic information entered. Next, we need to tell this setup project what it actually needs to install:

7. Right-click on MySetup in the Solutions Explorer and select Add ➤ Project Output, as in Figure 5-4.

This is where we'll specify that we want this setup to install the EXE file from our main project.

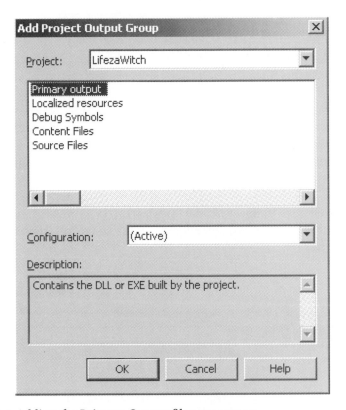

Figure 5-4. Adding the Primary Output file to our setup

8. From the dialog box that appears, select Primary Output for your project and click on OK.

You should notice a few onscreen changes. First off, you have a "Primary output" entry under MySetup, your final EXE. (Click on it for more details.) Plus, you should also have a detected dependency: dotnetfxredist_x86_enu.msm.

When VB .NET analyzed your project, it realized it was built to run on the .NET framework. Pretty clever, you see. And to ensure that your users can properly run your application, the whole .NET framework is bundled along as well, as a redistributable package called dotnetfxredist_x86_enu.msm.

What's next? We probably want to add a shortcut to the User's Programs menu. Let's check that out.

9. You should be looking at the File System view. If not, right-click on MySetup in the Solution Explorer, choosing View ➤ File System.

10. Click on the Application folder. You should see the primary output from your main project.

11. Right-click on "Primary Output from LifezaWitch (Active)" and select "Create Shortcut to Primary output . . . " (as shown in Figure 5-5).

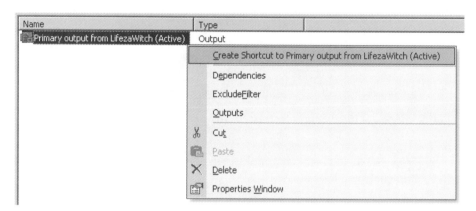

Figure 5-5. Creating a shortcut to the Primary Output file

This will create a shortcut to your core EXE file. But, right now, it's in the actual application folder and called something amazingly long and silly. Let's change that now.

12. Change the following properties of your shortcut:

   • *Name*: Change it to something more suitable, bearing in mind that spaces are allowed here.

- *Icon*: Don't go for the default; select a more personalized icon for your application.

- *Folder*: Change to the user's Program Menu.

> **TOP TIP** *This will create a shortcut directly on the Programs menu, without a subfolder. If you would prefer your own subfolder—which is particularly useful if you have extra files you want to create shortcuts for—then right-click on the User's Programs Menu folder and select Add ➤ Folder—then move your shortcut into the new folder. Remember, this is simply a representation of what will occur on the target machine. If you create a folder here, it will be created on the user's machine.*

Understand everything so far? Let's test it out in practice.

13. Build the entire solution, by selecting Build ➤ Build Solution from the menu.

Unfortunately, this process is about as fast as a minus 486, so you might want to go grab a coffee and bagel. After the chugging and churning stops (sometime in the twenty-third century), you'll receive a Build Complete message—and, quite simply, that's that.

14. Open your MySetup project development folder.

15. Open the Debug subfolder.

In here, you'll find your ready-to-release setup project. Even for a simple project, mine stands at about 15MB simply because of those redistributable .NET framework files.

It's also compiled into a Windows Installer MSI package, which brings with it many advantages, such as allowing Windows to handle the installation, restore your program setup should faults occur, and more.

But it also brings one particular disadvantage: if your user doesn't have the Windows Installer on their machines, it just won't work. At all. We'll look at that slight problem more in just a moment, but for now, let's test our setup program.

16. Install your own program now using the MySetup.msi Windows Installer package, as in Figure 5-6.

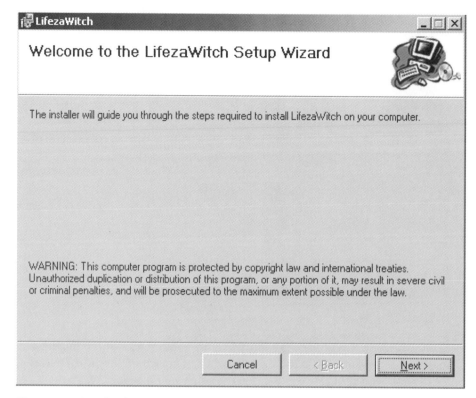

Figure 5-6. Our final setup application!

Impressed yet? Remember designing each of those user interface screens? When your installation is complete, do you get an icon on your Programs menu? Does the shortcut work? Also, what files do you find inside your actual application folder?

Next up, open the Add/Remove Programs applet from the control panel. Can you see your application? Notice how the icon appears next to your program? Try clicking on your application, then selecting "Support Information". Remember entering that information? If you're feeling all naughty, check out the uninstall functionality by click the Remove button. Go on, zap it from your machine!

Well hurrah and hujjah! Congratulations on building your own supercool setup program!

Going Further

Think that's as advanced as you can get with your setup project? Yeah, right. They're currently writing entire books on the subject, but thankfully we're not quite that boring. So, briefly, what other things can you do here?

Well, one top stop for you is the property page for your project. Try right-clicking on MySetup in the Solution Explorer and selecting Properties. Here, you can specify the output filename of your setup project; you can also select to optimize your setup package for size, ensuring smaller downloads for your clients.

Another important property here is the Bootstrapper. Remember we said that, if the user didn't have the Windows Installer on their machines, they wouldn't be able to run the MSI file? Well, changing the Bootstrapper option to Windows Installer Bootstrapper will create an actual EXE that will first set up the installer and then your MSI file, meaning it should run on literally any machine.

What else can you play with here? Once again, try right-clicking on MySetup in the Solution Explorer, but this time opening the View menu as shown in Figure 5-7. Here, you'll find a bunch of extra screens that are useful in customizing your setup.

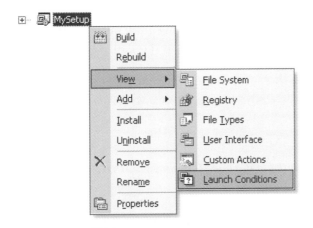

Figure 5-7. Choose a useful screen, any useful screen.

First off, you have the File System screen, which allows you to define where your application is installed, add any extras files, and incorporate shortcuts. Next is the Registry screen, which allows you to specify any registry keys you want to insert upon installation. File Types allows you to associate a particular file extension with your application, automatically.

The User Interface screen gives you more control over what the user sees, allowing you to change items such as the banner bitmap, welcome messages, and copyright text. Finally, we have the Custom Actions and Launch Conditions menus, which allow you to further personalize the experience by perhaps adding registry or file searches before allowing the installation to commence.

Powerful stuff, this install lark. And you can learn more about its intricacies by delving into "Setup projects, creating" in the Help index.

But, for now, it's a big cheer for you on getting this far! You've not only learned how to create an exceptionally groovy, bug-free application, but have also touched upon how to distribute it the professional way. Next, sit back, put those feet up, sip at that Starbucks coffee, and spend an enjoyable few minutes perusing the FAQ.

Which of these questions have you asked *yourself*?

FAQ

Books are a bit impersonal, don't you think?

In a classroom environment, I get instant feedback. If I don't explain a concept correctly, the rancid tomatoes sliding down my face give me a clue. In the publishing world, I have to wait for my next proposal to get turned down before I can take the hint.

So, as with the rest of the tutorials in this book, we're going to finish off with a bunch of frequently asked questions, taken straight from my own real-world classes.

Are you sitting comfortably? Then I'll begin.

I've created one of those If-Then statements, but VB .NET tells me I've got it wrong. What's the problem?

Writing your own If-Then statements can be a confusing practice, and it's incredibly common for programmers to miss out the End If statement or insert an End If when it's not required.

In brief, you can write two sorts of If-Then statements. First off, the one-liner that requires no `End If`, as so shown here.

```
If MyString = "Karl" Then MessageBox.Show("Welcome, Karl!")
```

Then we have the If-Then block, which runs code right up to the `End If` line, as so:

```
If MyString = "Exit" Then
    MessageBox.Show("Goodbye, User!")
    Application.Exit()
End If
```

It can be a real stumbling block at first, so make sure that you memorize this baby. It's quite easy really: just remember, the one-liners have no End. A bit like this book, really.

I'm trying to build my application and keep getting a message in the Task List saying: "'Sub Main' was not found in 'MyApp.Form1'". Eh?

I'll tell you what's happened. You've built your application and decided to be all good, renaming your forms to use standard naming conventions. The problem is, by default VB .NET remembers that it should display Form1, and, when you rename the form, it gets awfully confused and generates that error message.

To sort the situation, simply double-click on that message in your Task List and select your actual startup form. Then try building once again.

That icon that VB .NET puts on my forms is really annoying. Can I change it?

Absolutely! If you're feeling slightly dissatisfied with that strange block of colorful squares VB .NET automatically inserts as your form icon, you can select a new one by changing your Form Icon property.

If you can't find a suitable icon on your machine or the many Internet sites providing them for download (Developer Fusion at `www.developerfusion.com` has a very nice collection), then do it yourself, by checking out "Creating Your Own Icons" in Chapter 8.2, "Intermediate Tips and Techniques".

Is there like a master variable data type you can use? I tried out VB6 once and used the Variant a lot—however I can't find it in VB .NET. Has it disappeared?

Yes! With the shift to VB .NET, the old Variant of VB6 fame was thrown out the window. However, in VB .NET, we have the Object, from which practically everything in the .NET Framework inherits: forms, controls, variables, and infinitely more.

Therefore, if you create an Object, you'll be able to set it to absolutely anything, as in:

```
Dim MyObject As Object
MyObject = "Possible String"
MyObject = 23.231
MyObject = Now.Date
```

Of course, it's always best to declare and use the exact types you intend. This helps conserve memory and is deemed better programming practice. But if you're feeling lazy . . .

***I've been reading in a magazine about managed code and unmanaged code.
What's the difference?***

You may remember that back in the first chapter, we mentioned that something
called the Common Language Runtime (CLR) actually manages our code as it
runs. It also handles memory, enables different languages to talk together, sorts
a lot of the plumbing issues, and so on.

Basically, code that is interpreted and run by CLR is called *managed code*.
Pretty much any project you create in VB .NET will contain pure managed code.

If, however, you deal with COM objects (see "Using COM Objects" in
Chapter 8.3, "Advanced Tips and Techniques"), this is referred to as unmanaged
code. That doesn't mean it's a bad thing; it simply means that the CLR isn't
managing its memory and so on.

So, managed code is pure .NET code. Unmanaged code is everything else.

***You mentioned creating a setup program, but, with the sizes you were talking
about, well, I just don't have enough floppy disks! I'd prefer to have just
a "skeleton" setup program that downloads the Windows Installer and my
application files from the Net as and when required. Is that possible?***

You bet your bottom dollar. It's easy to create a small setup EXE file that checks
the target machine and downloads the required components on demand. In
fact, the Visual Studio .NET developers thought of that exact scenario and added
an option in there just for you.

So, how do you do it? First off, create your setup project as normal, then
open its project properties via the Solution Explorer. From here, change the
Bootstrapper option to Web Bootstrapper. You will be asked to provide a URL to
download both your Windows Installer MSI package (the Setup Folder URL box)
and a URL to download the Windows Installer itself (the optional Windows
Installer Upgrade box). (See Figure 5-8.)

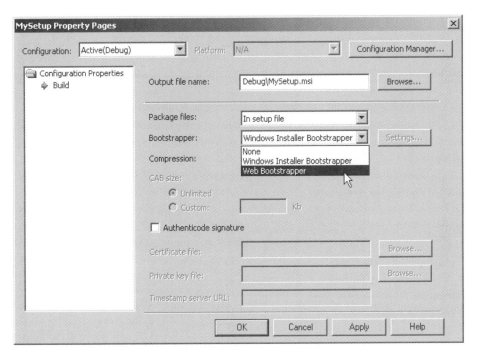

Figure 5-8. Changing the Setup Bootstrapper

Provide these details, and build your project. Your project will produce your final MSI package, alongside the InstMsiA.exe and InstMsiW.exe files (the two current Windows Installer installation packages). You'll need to make these files available in the URL you just provided to your setup.

The final distributable file here will be your setup.exe file. This should be very small, perhaps around 70KB. When run, it will attempt to download the necessary components from the locations you specified. Using this technique, you don't have to bundle the bulky Windows Installer bootstrapper and bog down your setup program; only the required components are downloaded as and when needed. It also ensures your users always get the latest version of your app. Supercool!

WHERE TO GO FROM HERE

This five-chapter "Beginning VB .NET" tutorial should have provided you with a solid grasp of your now-favorite programming language. But where do you go from here? How can you take your knowledge to the next level?

For a start, you need to keep playing with VB .NET. Read through the Review Sheets a couple more times. Fully digest all the vital points: where the .NET framework comes into play, what the main controls are used for, the difference between methods and functions, the life purpose of a module, how to handle errors, and so on.

And, if you don't quite understand something, keep working on it until you do. Don't give up! Stay curious! Plug away, browse the bundled examples, and ask questions on newsgroups because, when it does click, you'll feel like a genius. Or so I'm told.

So keep playing, keep pushing for that training course, keep making programs, and never give in.

What's your knowledge action plan from here? After celebrating your triumphant success in this tutorial, you'll probably want to move onto Tutorial 2, "Doing Databases", which teaches a whole bundle of groovy techniques for surviving in the real data-driven world.

Looking for a second opinion? Then here are my top third-party recommendations for moving forward.

- *Moving to VB .NET* (Apress, ISBN 1-893115-97-6): If you're moving to VB .NET from VB6, you're probably still trying to get your head around the changes. This great book helps you understand the true meaning of .NET.

- Other books: *Visual Basic .NET in Easy Steps* (Computer Step, ISBN 1-84078-131-9); *VB .NET Language in a Nutshell* (O'Reilly, ISBN 0-596-0092-9).

- `http://localhost/quickstart`: Got questions? This QuickStart tutorial from Microsoft is set up on your machine when you install Visual Studio; it provides answers to some of the most common developer questions.

- `www.vbforums.com`: This helpful community site prides itself on providing quick responses to questions on all areas of programming, whether you're a complete newbie or a VB antique.

- `www.dotnetjunkies.com`: "Putting the dot into .NET," this jam-packed site crams tutorials, tips, and sample code all into one impressive Web stop. It's a corny slogan, but the site is worth a bookmark.

- `www.dotnetwire.com`: Get the latest .NET news from the people who brought you VBWire.com. You'll find everything from developer article links to software update announcements that are posted every day.

- www.dotnet247.com: Describing itself as the first independent guide to .NET (I'm not saying a thing), you'll find this site a handy reference to the major namespaces.

- www.pinpub.com: The homepage of Pinnacle Publishing, which produces the popular *VBD* and *.NET Developer* magazines. The site includes free online content and opportunities to subscribe.

- msdn.microsoft.com/NET: The official MSDN .NET homepage from the software giant itself. It's full of technical resources, downloads, career maps, and more.

- microsoft.public.dotnet.languages.vb: The official Microsoft newsgroup for VB .NET language discussion. For speedier answers, try searching the archives first at www.googlegroups.com.

Don't forget that VB .NET is still brand spanking new, which means that some Web site material may disappear or books be replaced by newer titles. You can always check with Apress at www.apress.com for the latest.

CONCLUSION

Hurrah!! A huge congratulations and great big hug for completing Tutorial 1, "Beginning VB .NET"!

I'm your host Karl Moore, and over the past five chapters we've really traveled a long way. We started by looking at where VB .NET came from and how we could use its tools to "paint" ourselves a program. We then moved on to look at controls and how they each have their own special properties, methods, functions, and events.

Moving on, we uncovered the If statement, and learned how variables can make our applications more intelligent. We then spent a while exploring a few of the neat features hidden away in the .NET framework, plus uncovered a loop in action.

Next, we learned how to expand our application with menus and multiple forms, along with our own methods, functions, and modules. Finally, today, we looked at handling those nasty errors in our applications, and discovered how to create our own professional setup program.

Cool? You most definitely are. So a round of applause and well done once again! *<cheer>*

And so, until "Doing Databases", this is me signing off for the evening. Take care, goodnight, and God bless.

ERRORS, SETUP, AND GOING FROM HERE REVIEW SHEET

- Errors can occur in your application for a variety of reasons: perhaps the user has provided incorrect information or a requested file wasn't available. To avoid unsightly error messages, you deal with these situations using error-handling code.

- Error handling can be implemented in two main ways. The first is using a Resume Next statement, which simply ignores any errors and moves onto the next line of code. Here's an example.

```
On Error Resume Next
Process.Start("c:\badfile.txt")
MessageBox.Show("This runs, regardless!")
```

- The second method for handling errors—and a method that is new to this version of Visual Basic—is structured error handling, consisting of Try-Catch-Finally blocks. Here's an example.

```
Try
    Process.Start("c:\badfile.txt")
Catch
    MessageBox.Show("An error occurred!")
Finally
    MessageBox.Show("Finally is optional. " & _
        "It always runs after everything else - " & _
        "whether an error occurred or not.")
End Try
```

- You can retrieve more information about an error by reading the Exception object in a Catch block. You can find out more about handling specific errors by looking up "Try . . . Catch . . . Finally statement" in the Help index. Here is a generic Catch block example that reads the error message of your exception:

```
Catch ex As Exception
    MessageBox.Show("An error has occured: " & ex.Message)
```

- Your solution can contain multiple projects. The first step in creating a setup program for your application is to add a setup project to your solution. Many different types of setup projects are available; however, Setup Project is the best choice for most desktop applications.

- To add a new setup project to your solution, choose File ➤ Add Project ➤ New Project ➤ Setup Project. To add the output from your application to this setup project, select Project ➤ Add ➤ Project Output and select the Primary Output from your project, clicking on OK when finished. When finished, build your solution as normal.

- Beyond creating a standard installation, you can do much more with setup projects. To view the advanced editing screens, choose View ➤ Editor and select one of the menus. For more information on each, open it and press the F1 key.

Doing Databases

Introducing Databases

"I have traveled the length and breadth of this country and talked to the best people, and I can assure you that data processing is a fad that won't last out the year."—Editor-in-Charge of Business Books, Prentice-Hall, 1957

So, YOU WANT TO use databases, huh?

Looks like we're both in luck. You've just started reading Tutorial 2 "Doing Databases", and I've just started writing it. Over the next five chapters, I'll be revealing everything you ever wanted to know about databases but were too afraid to ask.

It'll be fun. It'll be easy. It'll be eye-opening. There'll be no confusing jargon, no excess nonsense, and certainly no sprouts. It'll be a smooth(-ish) journey, and I promise I won't bite.

So, what will I be babbling on about over the next dozen pages? Well, we'll start at the very beginning, which is a very good place to start (according to Julie Andrews). We'll open with questions such as . . . erm, what's a database? Why don't those tables have legs? What's Microsoft Access got to do with it? How do I build my own mini-database program in VB .NET? Why is grass green? What's the meaning of life?

(Well, let's get the philosophical stuff out of the way first. The meaning of life is 42 and grass is green because all of the other colors of the spectrum are absorbed and only the green is reflected, a process known as *subtractive color mixing*. Tsk, and they said this tutorial would be boring.)

After all the introductory stuff, we'll put our foot down and really start flying. We'll learn how to create our own database, figure out the power of SQL Server, understand how to integrate reporting into our applications, look at creating data-powered sites for the Internet, play in the wonderful world of transactions—and lots more.

Oh, yes. By the end of the next five chapters, you'll be creating transactional database-centric Web applications on your lunch hour. And I don't mean a Government-slacker-style lunch hour, either.

But, before we dive into that deep end, let's take a step back and ask ourselves one question: Exactly what are those things they call databases?

What Are Databases?

When I first started out in the programmatic world, I shivered at the *D* word. Eugh, who wanted to mess around with databases? Not me, I was here to program!

But it doesn't take long before you realize that, no matter what sort of program you're creating, databases can be awfully helpful and, in many cases, completely critical.

So, what exactly is a database? Well, it's essentially just a store of information. They often exist in the form of a simple file, just like a Microsoft Word file, say. You can shove information into this store or retrieve it from the store, typically with a few lines of code.

> **TOP TIP** *Looking to make friends and impress the opposite sex? At your next geeky cocktail party, try saying* DB *instead of* database. *It's sure to raise an eyebrow.*

Hmm, they don't sound terribly complex, do they? That's because they're not. However, most database wizards like to overcomplicate such what-nots in a bid to scare off any potential competition. And that's you.

Okay, let's think a little more about databases. Each database may include any number of tables, each of which you can imagine as an organized Excel worksheet. (See Figure 1-1.)

Each column in the worksheet will hold something different. For example, column A may hold a customer name, column B could store the postal code, and column C might keep track of the telephone number.

That's all a table is: a set of predefined slots or boxes into which you throw information.

	A	B	C
1	CustomerName	PostalCode	TelNumber
2	Mr K D Moore	CV10 9TS	07092 123 456
3	Mrs A J Lansbury	S13 0EJ	01142 654 321
4	Mr P Ustinov	PE13 9QU	0850 230 130

Figure 1-1. A table is a little like an organized Excel worksheet.

However, because we're supercool geeks, we're not allowed to call these boxes, erm, boxes. We need to call them *fields*, because it's the done thing and boosts your street cred.

Just like an Excel worksheet, you can add new entries to a table simply by filling in a new set of fields. (See Figure 1-2.) So, each time you need to add a customer, you simply fill out a new set of fields, putting the required information under the CustomerName, PostalCode, and TelNumber columns, and Bob's your uncle.

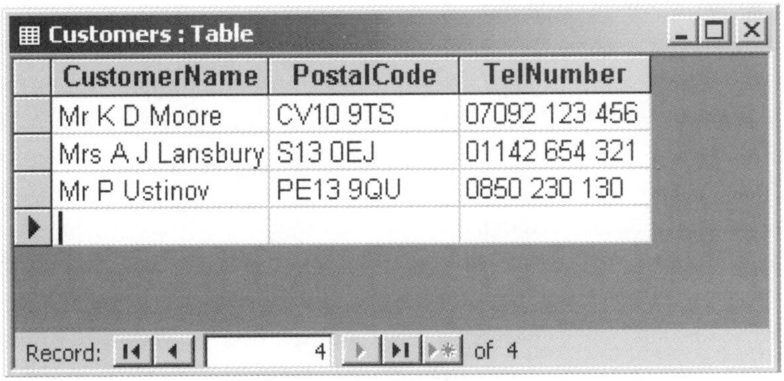

CustomerName	PostalCode	TelNumber
Mr K D Moore	CV10 9TS	07092 123 456
Mrs A J Lansbury	S13 0EJ	01142 654 321
Mr P Ustinov	PE13 9QU	0850 230 130

Customers : Table

Record: 14 ◄ 4 ► ►I ►✱ of 4

Figure 1-2. A real table in action

TOP TIP *You cannot eat your dinner off a database table. This is considered highly uncool in the database world. Also, it's unadvisable to graze sheep in a table field, no matter how free of foot-and-mouth it may be.*

Righto, let's run over all those wizzy DB terms one more time:

- *database*: a bunch of tables

- *tables*: store numerous rows of information

- *fields*: the boxes in a row, each holding particular bits of data

A database can also contain other widgets such as relationships and queries. You can even have a relationship with a query, but the Church doesn't commend it. Either way, that's in-depth geeky stuff, so we'll cover it later.

Now, for a moment, just imagine what you could do with such a store of information. You could record customer details and their related orders. Or maybe keep of log of which users are accessing your system and at what times. Or perhaps you just want to keep a track of lotto numbers so you can predict next week's lucky six.

That's the power of data. Just don't forget me if you snatch the jackpot.

Choices, Choices

So, you know what a database is. But how can you create one?

Well, first off, you need to decide which type you want to create. Yes, it's another technological stumbling block thrown in the works just to confuse us all. What are the options? Well, it all depends on what you want and how much cash you can get your greedy little mitts on.

You've got that expensive whopper of a database system called SQL Server for a start; it's used by corporations that need to store huge wads of information. (We'll be working with this from Chapter 2.4 onwards.) Then there's that thing they call Oracle, which is another database format used by people that generally don't like Microsoft.

However, one of the least expensive (but still exciting) types of database is an Access Jet database. You've probably seen them hanging around: they're MDB files and can be created with a few clicks using, unsurprisingly, Microsoft Access.

Now, if you don't have Access yet, you'd better add it to your Christmas list and be a good programmer. Oh, you might also want to keep your fingers crossed that it's currently the evening of December 24, because we'll be using the program in the very next section.

In fact, all this talk of databases has got me itching to get started. Hold on to the anorak and Coke-bottle glasses! It's time for us to explore a real-life database.

Exploring Northwind

I'm as bored as a pacifist's pistol with all this theory. Let's inject a little action into the party by getting down and dirty with an actual database.

1. Launch Microsoft Access.

2. Open the Nwind.mdb database.

The Nwind.mdb database is the infamous Northwind sample database that's distributed with Microsoft Access and some early versions of Visual Studio .NET. You'll have it somewhere on your machine, so have a search around. Mine is located in Program Files\Microsoft Office\Office\1033\ and is called Nwind.mdb; however, it's possible yours may be named FPNwind.mdb.

Let's explore.

3. In the Objects list, click on Tables. This will display all the tables in your database.

4. Double-click on the Customers table. (See Figure 1-3.)

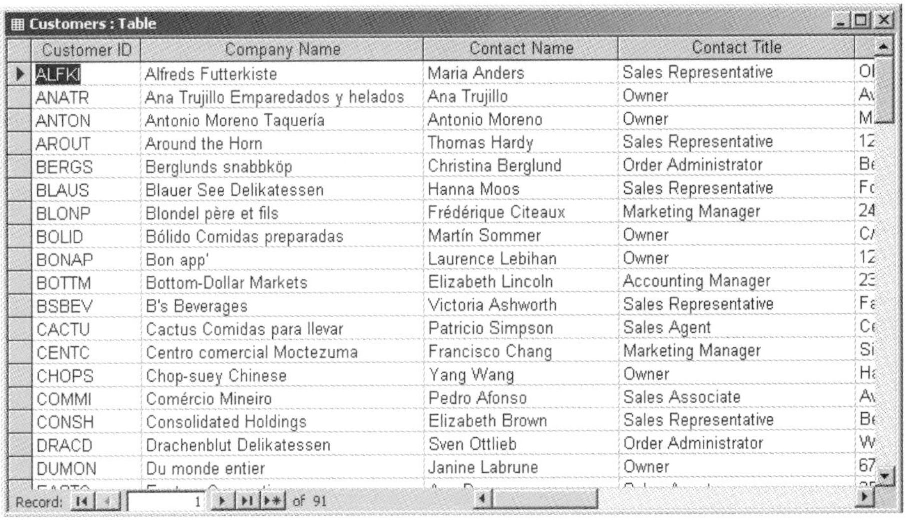

Customer ID	Company Name	Contact Name	Contact Title
ALFKI	Alfreds Futterkiste	Maria Anders	Sales Representative
ANATR	Ana Trujillo Emparedados y helados	Ana Trujillo	Owner
ANTON	Antonio Moreno Taquería	Antonio Moreno	Owner
AROUT	Around the Horn	Thomas Hardy	Sales Representative
BERGS	Berglunds snabbköp	Christina Berglund	Order Administrator
BLAUS	Blauer See Delikatessen	Hanna Moos	Sales Representative
BLONP	Blondel père et fils	Frédérique Citeaux	Marketing Manager
BOLID	Bólido Comidas preparadas	Martín Sommer	Owner
BONAP	Bon app'	Laurence Lebihan	Owner
BOTTM	Bottom-Dollar Markets	Elizabeth Lincoln	Accounting Manager
BSBEV	B's Beverages	Victoria Ashworth	Sales Representative
CACTU	Cactus Comidas para llevar	Patricio Simpson	Sales Agent
CENTC	Centro comercial Moctezuma	Francisco Chang	Marketing Manager
CHOPS	Chop-suey Chinese	Yang Wang	Owner
COMMI	Comércio Mineiro	Pedro Afonso	Sales Associate
CONSH	Consolidated Holdings	Elizabeth Brown	Sales Representative
DRACD	Drachenblut Delikatessen	Sven Ottlieb	Order Administrator
DUMON	Du monde entier	Janine Labrune	Owner

Figure 1-3. Our jam-packed Customers table

5. Scroll about the records.

So, here we have 91 records, each describing a customer. Each of these rows consists of multiple fields, each containing data according to which column it sits under.

Let's add our own customer now.

6. Scroll down to the bottom of the Customers table. (See Figure 1-4.)

7. On the empty row at the bottom, insert a little random data into each field. (Watch out: the Customer ID field will accept a maximum of only five characters.)

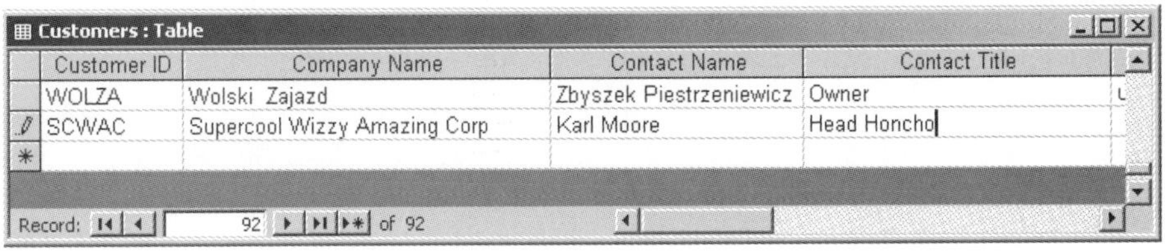

Customer ID	Company Name	Contact Name	Contact Title
WOLZA	Wolski Zajazd	Zbyszek Piestrzeniewicz	Owner
SCWAC	Supercool Wizzy Amazing Corp	Karl Moore	Head Honcho

Figure 1-4. Enter stage left: Supercool Wizzy Amazing Corp

8. Close the Customers table, and then reopen it.

9. Find and click on the record you just added in the Customers table. (It will now be sorted in alphabetical order.)

Interesting, eh? So, we've looked at the table and added our own customer. And, just as Access can create, so can Access taketh away. Yes, I'm talking about killing your record. Don't worry; they have no feelings. (At least they won't in a second or two.)

10. Select the record you just added by clicking on the arrow to the left of your Customer ID. (See Figure 1-5.)

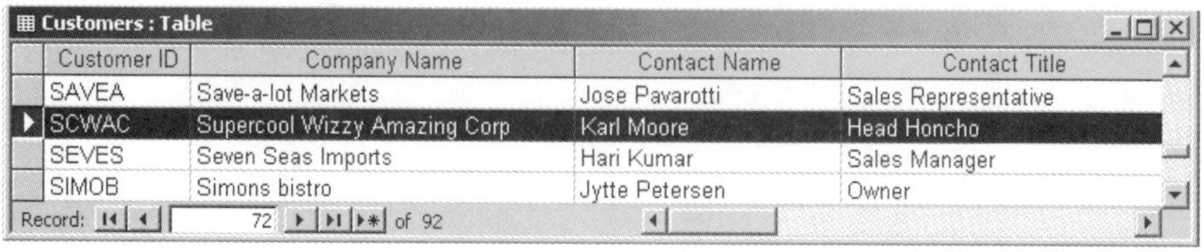

Figure 1-5. Selecting our row in Access

11. Press the Delete key.

12. When warned (as in Figure 1-6), click on Yes to confirm the delete.

Figure 1-6. You sure? You really sure?

Well, wasn't that fun? Now, let's conclude this exploration by taking a sneak geek peek at our Customers table in the nude. Ha, move over, *Playboy*!

13. Close the Customers table again.

14. Right-click on your Customers table and select Design View.

You'll be taken to a sheet as shown in Figure 1-7 that describes the database and shows field names and the types of data each holds.

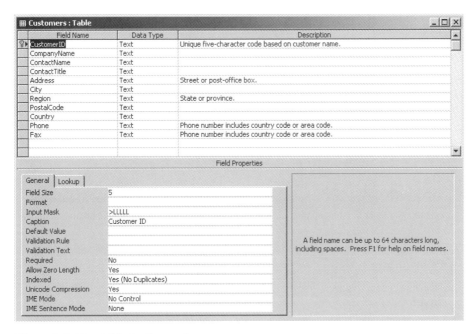

Figure 1-7. Our table in the nude

15. Have a look through the fields and the list of available data types.

Imagine that you were creating a table to hold orders. What data type would you use to store the quantity of each product? And what about the total cost of the order?

Also, note the little key next to our CustomerID field. It indicates that this is a primary key, a field that is unique to each customer. No two can be the same. This key is used in the Orders table to help link an order to a customer. We'll stumble across relationships like this accidentally-on-purpose in the next chapter.

16. Close the Customers table yet again.

Okay, so you're probably getting tired of databases by now. Yes, they look cool and allow you to add and delete records with relative ease. But how can you go and connect into them using your favorite programming language?

That's an awfully good question.

Doing the Data Bind

So, you want to connect into Access using VB .NET? Then don those bright green flares, stick an exaggerated afro wig on your head and "pass the Mojo, let's get groovy" as we prepare to do the Data Bind.

1. Create a new Windows application in VB .NET.

2. On the menu, select Tools ➤ Connect to Database.

Here, we're going to connect into our database, then display information from its Customer table in an editable grid. It's a simple data access application.

3. Click on the Provider tab and select the Microsoft Jet 4.0 OLE DB Provider.

Remember we were talking about the various types of database earlier? Well, here you select a different "provider" depending on what you're connecting to. Access databases use the Jet provider, whereas SQL Server uses the OLE DB Provider for SQL Server, Oracle uses the OLE DB Provider for Oracle, and yadda, yadda, yadda.

4. Click on the Next button.

5. In the first box, enter the database location or select it by clicking on the ellipsis (. . .).

6. Click on the Test Connection button, as in Figure 1-8.

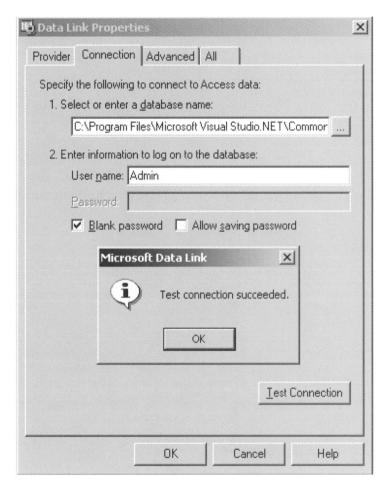

Figure 1-8. Testing our Access connection in Visual Studio .NET

You should receive a message congratulating you on being so amazingly good looking (or maybe just one saying "Test connection succeeded"). It really depends on your setup and vision.

7. Click on the OK button to the message, then OK again on the Data Link sheet.

The Server Explorer window should appear, probably to the left side of your screen. This lists details of all the database connections you've made through Visual Studio.

8. Expand your connection in the Server Explorer to view the list of Nwind.mdb tables. (See Figure 1-9.)

That's our connection made. But, right now, it's just sitting in Visual Studio .NET and has nothing to do with our actual program. Let's change that.

9. Drag the Customers table onto Form1. See Figure 1-10 for the result.

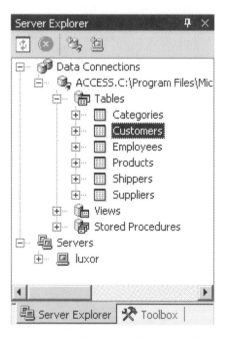

Figure 1-9. Viewing our Access tables using the Server Explorer

You'll notice that two widgets add themselves to the bottom of the screen. These work like regular controls, yet they have no visual interface and so aren't shown on the form. What do they do?

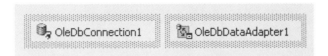

Figure 1-10. The result of dragging and dropping our Customers table

Well, let's imagine that talking to your Access database is a little like making a telephone call. The OleDbConnection widget is the telephone cable, the thing that handles the connection from your program to the actual database. And the OleDbDataAdapter thingy is what actually does the talking down that connection, asking the database for information or telling it to modify certain bits.

10. From the menu, choose View ➤ Toolbox.

11. In the toolbox, click on the Data tab.

12. Drag a DataSet control, seen in Figure 1-11, onto your form.

This is another invisible control, and it ties in with the OleDbDataAdapter object. You can imagine it as a virtual database, stored in memory. The OleDbDataAdapter talks to the database and can pass any information it gets

Figure 1-11. The DataSet control, which holds a set of data (surprisingly)

back to the DataSet control. You then edit information inside the DataSet control in any way you like. When you've finished, you pass the DataSet back to the OleDbDataAdapter, which in turn updates the database.

    13. In the Add DataSet dialog box that appears, click on "Untyped DataSet" and then on OK. (See Figure 1-12.)

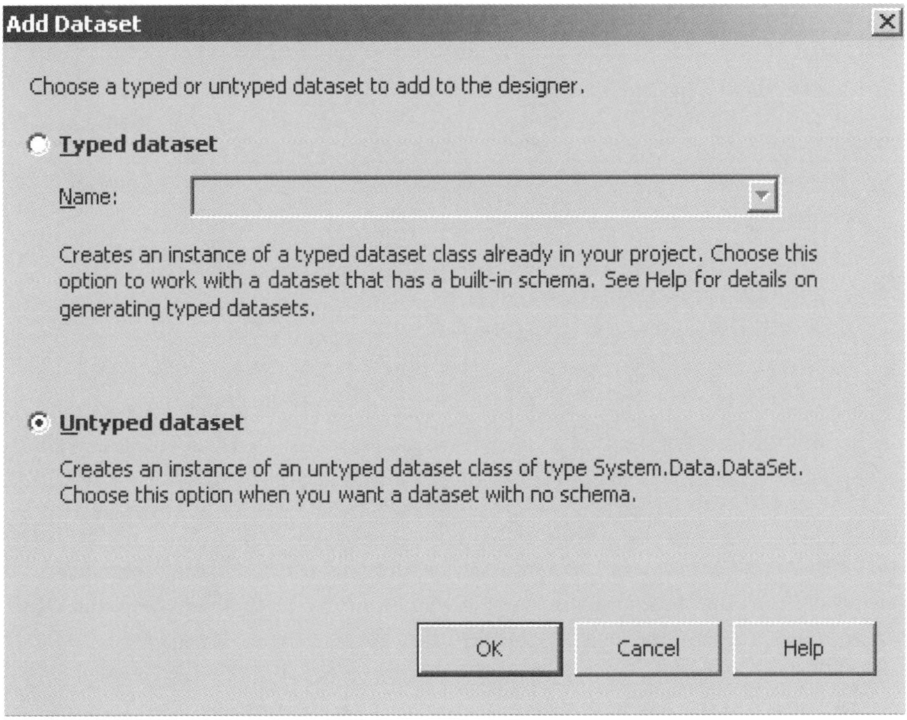

Figure 1-12. Untyped, please

By adding an untyped DataSet control, we're telling that rather nosy Visual Basic that we don't yet know what tables and fields this DataSet is going to hold. Okay, that's maybe a slight lie—it's the Customers table—but this step isn't essential, and I won't say anything if you don't. We'll discuss typed DataSets more in Chapter 2.2 anyway.

So, there we have the three main widgets added. With these, we should be able to connect in to our database. Yet we also need to actually display the data to our user in this application—but, uhm, with what?

14. In the toolbox, click on the Windows Forms tab.

15. Draw a DataGrid control out onto Form1.

Although this is a family show, I have to be a little explicit here. You see, the DataGrid control enjoys a bit of bondage, tying itself direct to a DataSet in the tightest manner possible.

Let's add code to help the DataGrid control experience this cheap thrill now. First, we'll fill the DataSet with information, then tightly bind it with our DataGrid control.

16. Add a button to Form1, changing its Text property to "Fill".

17. Behind its click event, add the following code.

```
' Fill the DataSet
OleDbDataAdapter1.Fill(DataSet1)

' Bind to DataGrid
DataGrid1.DataSource = DataSet1
```

The first line here tells the OleDbDataAdapter to start talking to our database, filling the DataSet with information from our Customers table. (If you remember, the OleDbDataAdapter was created when we dragged our *Customers* table onto Form1.) The second line tells the DataGrid to "bind" to the DataSet, displaying its information and changing the underlying data as our user edits the grid.

18. Add another button to Form1, changing its Text property to "Update".

19. Behind its click event, add the following code.

```
' Update the database
OleDbDataAdapter1.Update(DataSet1)
```

This line takes information from the DataSet, which may have been edited through the DataGrid, and ensures that the database is completely updated. This may involve deleting records, updating rows, inserting new data, *whatever*.

And that's it! Let's take five to test our new creation.

20. Press the F5 key to run your program.

21. Click on your Fill button. A little plus sign will appear on the DataGrid.

22. Click on the plus sign on the DataGrid to expand it.

23. Click on the Customers link.

You should be shown every record from the Customers table, as demonstrated in Figure 1-13.

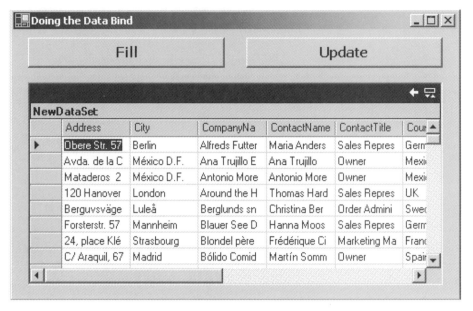

Figure 1-13. Browsing our final application

Have a good browse around. Neat, eh? (Please say yes. My Mom is reading.)

24. Try editing information inside the DataGrid: add a new record, delete that record, and update a record. When finished, click on the Update button.

25. After updating, restart your program, clicking on the Fill button again.

What do you see? Have your changes been fully applied to the database? What if you compiled this program and had two users running it, updating at the same time? How could you apply this binding technique to your work right now? Where could it be useful?

26. When finished, close your program and save the project.

Well, hurrah and hujjah! Talk about minimalist: you've just successfully completed your first powerful database application, all in under three lines of code! Sleek? I think so.

And I'm left feeling all proud now, which usually means it's time for a big pat on the back in traditional Conclusion-style.

CONCLUSION

Congratulations on finishing the first chapter of Tutorial 2 "Doing Databases"!

Over the past dozen pages, we've moved forward in leaps and bounds. We launched today's tutorial by figuring out exactly what databases are, and we spent a few nanoseconds understanding the different types that are available to us.

After checking our wallets and opting for the slightly cheaper Access route, we went on to explore tables behind the sample Northwind database, plus finally connected straight into the Customers list with our fully functional, updateable VB .NET database application! And all in just three lines of code.

Not bad for the first chapter, and completely painless too. You see? Trust me; I'm a psychotic maniac.

Next time, we'll be figuring out how to create our own database, and we'll look at the curious world of relationships. We'll also be checking out a more controllable version of form data binding, and we'll learn how you can get your live data straight onto the Internet.

But, until then, this is your host Karl Moore welcoming you to the world of databases. Well done once again, and goodnight!

CHAPTER 2.1

- Databases are just a storage place for information.

- A typical database includes multiple tables. A table has a predefined set of columns, with rows of fields containing data underneath. These rows are often referred to as *records*.

- There are many different types of database. SQL Server and Oracle are relatively expensive database systems that run live on a server, potentially handling trillions of records at a time.

- Microsoft Access also has the capability of creating a Jet MDB database. Although this is certainly cheaper than SQL Server or Oracle, it is also more limited in capability.

- You can connect straight into any database using Visual Studio .NET by opening the Server Explorer (View ➤ Server Explorer) and clicking on the Connect to Database icon.

- To connect into an Access database in your code (as we did in this chapter), you can use the OleDbConnection, OleDbDataAdapter, and DataSet objects. The OleDbConnection object sets up the connection, the OleDbDataAdapter talks to the database, and the generic DataSet object holds the disconnected data.

- The DataGrid control can bind itself directly to a DataSet, which means that any changes made to information in the DataGrid control are reflected in the bound DataSet.

- Presuming that you visually set up the OleDbConnection, OleDbDataAdapter, and DataSet objects on your form using the Server Explorer and toolbox, the following code demonstrates how to retrieve data into a DataSet, how to bind to a DataGrid, and how to update the underlying database following any changes.

```
' Fill the DataSet
OleDbDataAdapter1.Fill(DataSet1)
' Bind to DataGrid
DataGrid1.DataSource = DataSet1
' Update the database
OleDbDataAdapter1.Update(DataSet1)
```

Our Own
Database and VB .NET

"If you torture the data enough, it will confess."
—Ronald Coase, winner of the 1991 Nobel Prize in Economics

IN CASE YOU DIDN'T NOTICE the amazingly suggestive header just above these words, this is Chapter 2.2 of Tutorial 2, "Doing Databases". Today, we'll be boosting your developer knowledge once more, taking you even closer to database nirvana—and even further from that thing they call sanity.

Cuckoo.

But that's just a sacrifice every programmer makes.

Cuckoo.

So, what will we be covering today? We'll start by learning how to create our very own database using Microsoft Access, plus figure out how to get the best from our "relationships"—without having to resort to flowers and Godiva chocolates.

After that, it's all hands on deck to create a more powerful data binding form, and we'll even find out how to get our data live onto the Internet. All that in the next hour.

So buckle up and prepare for the ride; it's time to groove!

Cuckoo.

Creating Our Own Database

That Northwind sample we explored in the last chapter is great to demonstrate basic database principles, but let's be honest here: it's about as realistic as Munchkin Land. I mean, for a start, it purports to sell Uncle Bob's Organic Dried Pears to 21 different countries.

And, honestly, any company that deals with contacts such as "Hannah Moos" or "Zbyszek Piestrzeniewicz" needs a big-time reality check.

That's why we're going to ditch the dodgy samples now and get straight to creating our own Access database. Doing it yourself, hands-on, is always so much better than just watching.

Shall we begin?

1. Launch Microsoft Access.

We're going to create the backend database to a veterinary surgical office here. It'll hold details of the owners and their related pets. *Tsk*, and they said I couldn't do serious.

2. Create a new blank database, storing it on the root of your C: drive, if possible, as surgery.mdb.

That's our core database file created, but it doesn't do an awful lot yet. To be specific, I've seen more activity inside a slug. A dead slug. Sounds like your cue.

3. Under Tables, click on the New button.

4. In the pop-up dialog box, select Design View and click on OK.

You should be looking at your table in Design view right now. This is where we define the columns and types of data that the fields underneath should hold. How? Just enter a name in the Field Name box and select an appropriate data type from the next.

> **TOP TIP**   *Fancy a hint from a wise old man? Too many cooks spoil the broth. Fancy a tip from a long-term geek? Don't use spaces in your field names. It only results in awful, buggy code and broken families.*

5. Add the following fields to your table, as shown in Figure 2-1:

   • OwnerID, Text (plus change the Field Size to 5)

   • Name, Text

   • Address, Text

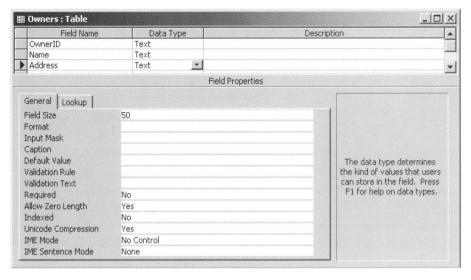

Figure 2-1. Designing our table

6. From the menu, select File ➤ Close.

7. Select Yes to save your table, naming it Owners. (If you receive a message prompting for a primary key, click on No.)

Primary keys are used in relationships for linking tables together. We don't need no stinkin' Access to do this automatically for us: we'll be adding relationships manually in the next section. Because we're all hard like that, you see.

For now, let's add ourselves a little sample data to this table.

8. In the Database window, double-click on the Owners table to open it.

9. Insert at least half a dozen creative entries. (See Figure 2-2.) In the OwnerID field of each row, use a unique five-character code. We'll expand on exactly why later.

Figure 2-2. Creative entries in the Owners table

Problem is, in its present state, our vet surgery database is ever so slightly limited. Why? Well, because a veterinary practice typically keeps records of its actual pets, not just the owners. (Strange, but true.)

What's to do? Well, I suppose we could try adding a field onto the Owners table, so you enter information as Figure 2-3 shows.

OwnerID	Name	Address	PetName1	PetType1
KARLM	Karl Moore	Moore Mansions, England	Bi-Curious George	Iguana

Figure 2-3. Storing pets next to owners

But that's no good for someone like me, with two pets: you've recorded Bi-Curious George, but what about Strangely Brown? So maybe you could change it to something like Figure 2-4.

OwnerID	Name	Address	PetName1	PetType1	PetName2	PetType2
KARLM	Karl Moore	Moore Mansions, England	Bi-Curious George	Iguana	Strangely Brown	Iguana

Figure 2-4. Storing multiple pets next to owners

But then you'll be forgetting my pet cow, Dizzy Daisy. And she's awfully sensitive to that kind of thing.

A better, more geektastic way of handling this would be to add another table to hold all the pet details and then link the two together using relationships.

Let's add that second table now.

10. Create a table called Pets (Figure 2-5) and add the following fields:

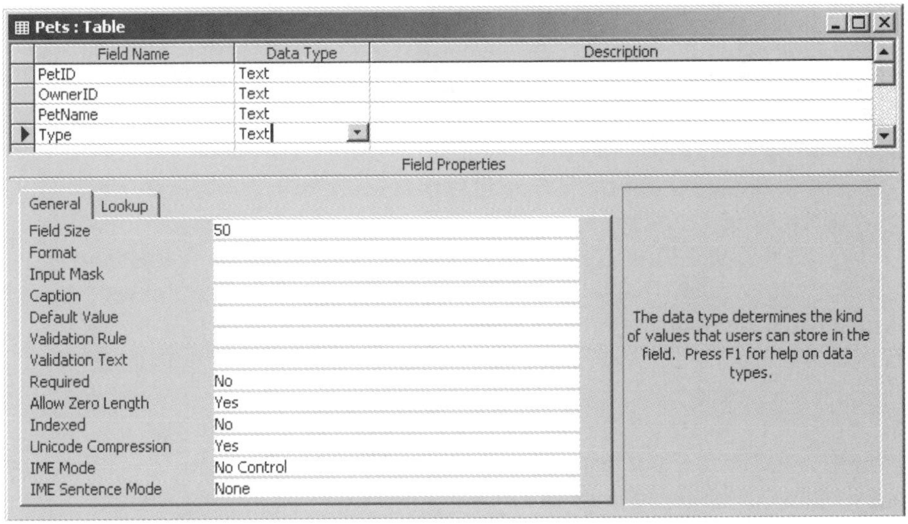

Figure 2-5. Creating our Pets table

- PetID, Text (plus change the Field Size to 5)

- OwnerID, Text (plus change the Field Size to 5)

- PetName, Text

- Type, Text

(Once again, if prompted to add a primary key when saving, click on No.)

This table will hold the pet name and type, plus the OwnerID so we can link each pet back to a relevant record in the Owners table. Our table also carries a PetID, which will be the individual ID of each pet.

That's our tables sorted. Now, what was I saying about relationships?

Adding Relationships

Think you know everything there is to know about relationships? I think not. You see, if men are from Mars, databases are from Uranus.

Yes, our databases have relationship issues, but thankfully we Dr. Ruth-types are here to sort them out. Now, in your database, you have two core tables: one holds the owners, and the other the pets. The problem is that Microsoft Access can't quite see the connection yet.

We know that our Owners table contains an OwnerID field and that each entry in the Pets table needs a valid OwnerID next to it, so we can tell which pets belong to which owner. However, you could go straight into the Pets table now and add a record containing a completely nonexistent OwnerID and, frankly, my dear, Microsoft Access wouldn't give a damn.

Why? It doesn't understand that all pets (barring strays) need to have owners. Why? Because it's thicker than the big-print edition of the complete works of William Shakespeare and needs your guidance. You need to add a *relationship*.

But, before doing that, you need to tell Access a little more about your fields. Firstly, you need to tell it that the Owners table will always contain unique OwnerID entries. Otherwise, you could end up with single pets linking back to multiple owners, right?

For this to work, we're going to change the OwnerID field into what is known as a *primary key*. A what? Well, as its name ever so slightly suggests, a primary key is the main field that *uniquely identifies* any one row. Setting OwnerID as the primary key ensures that we'll never get duplicates.

1. Open your Owners table in Design view, as shown in Figure 2-6.

2. Select your OwnerID field and click on the Primary Key button on the toolbar.

3. Close your Owners table and save the changes.

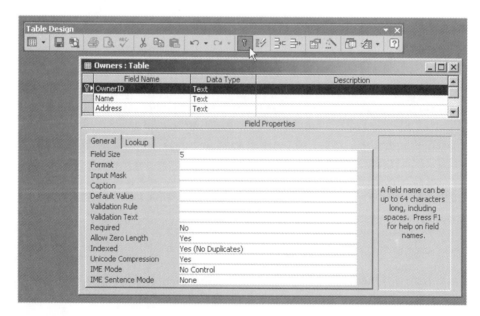

Figure 2-6. Specifying a primary key

However, that's not the only table that needs a key. As Access warned you earlier, for tables to be involved in a relationship, it's recommended that each contain a primary key, a unique identifier such as an automatically generated number.

In the Pets table, we've used another text field, a five-character PetID, for this. Let's add our second table key now.

4. Open your Pets table in Design view.

5. Select your PetID field and click on the Primary Key button on the toolbar.

6. Close your Pets table and save the changes.

Finished? As before, we did this to ensure that we don't get duplicate PetID entries in our table. Go try it out now. See what I mean?

So, we've created our primary keys, defining which fields in our tables uniquely identify the records within them. Next, we're going to actually define the relationship between our two tables.

7. From the Database window, select Tools ➤ Relationships.

8. Using the pop-up dialog box, add both of your tables to the Relationships window, and click on Close.

This is your plotting board. It's where you tell Access which bits of which tables link together. You've already told it that your Owners table OwnerID field will be unique, so it's put that in bold. It realizes this may be a "parent" field that could have "child" fields in another table.

Let's now create a relationship between the OwnerID field in the Owners table (the "parent" field, the primary key) and the OwnerID field in the Pets table (the "child" field, known as the *foreign key*).

9. Drag the OwnerID field in the Owners table across and onto the OwnerID field in the Pets table.

10. In the Edit Relationships dialog box that appears, check the Enforce Referential Integrity box, the Cascade Update Related Fields box and the Cascade Delete Related Fields box—and click on Create. (See Figure 2-7).

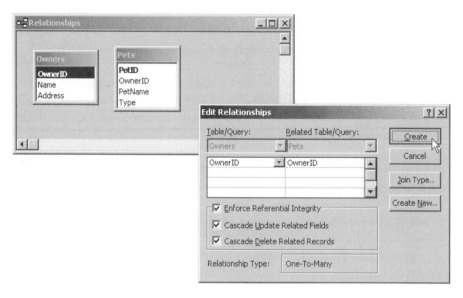

Figure 2-7. Creating our Owners-Pets relationship

Here, we've just told Access that there's a relationship between those two fields and that it should enforce referential integrity, meaning that it shouldn't allow pet entries without valid OwnerID values (thus ensuring the integrity of your data).

We've also told it to cascade updates and deletes, meaning that, if we change the OwnerID in the Owners table, it will automatically change the related OwnerID entries in the Pets table. Likewise, if we delete the record containing the OwnerID in the Owners table, all entries containing that OwnerID in the Pets table will be deleted. It just gives us a little more power.

> **TOP TIP** *Look at the Relationship Type box in the Edit Relationships dialog box. It says One-to-Many, meaning that there can only be one owner with a particular ID, although many pet records holding that ID. Spend two minutes memorizing that phrase—the* one-to-many relationship—*it's very relevant here and a real nerdy favorite.*

11. Close the Relationships window, saving your changes.

Go and try to enter a new pet now, using an invalid OwnerID value. What happens? Also, try deleting an owner who has pet entries. Do those pet entries get deleted too? Now think of your own business. Where do *you* have one-to-many relationships? Customers to orders? Offices to employees? Stomachs to meals? Suppliers to products? Would this information be useful in a database, and, if so, how could you create this in Access?

Also, there's a way that you could enhance our vet database even further, right now: by adding another table and inserting a second one-to-many relationship. Where would that be? What could the table hold? How could you do that? Have a quick think.

So, there we have our 30KB database, two tables, one relationship, and a partridge in a pear tree. *<wipes brow>*

If you thought that was easy to understand, then you'll love working with databases. Even the most complex-looking systems are exactly the same as the database we created today, although perhaps with a few more tables and an extra half-dozen relationships.

And, if you thought that was difficult—well, to be honest, I have to agree. When I teach this subject in real life, I typically start with "Let's create one table and put some data inside it." Two weeks later, we progress onto the second table, and, as the course draws to a conclusion, I quickly mention something about relationships, snatch my paycheck, and run.

You, however, got the works. What can I say? You guys are quick to mature. Either that, or I'm being exceptionally cruel.

Now, we'll work more on this second table and our relationship in a short while. For the moment, though, we've finished building our database, so let's move on to figure out how we can bind some of our owners data direct to both a Windows form and the Web.

Binding to a Windows Form

We're all looking for the quick-fix solution. The instant abdominal-toner. Lose-fat-while-watching-TV pills. Pheromone attract-anyone sprays. Data binding on Windows forms.

Did you spot the odd one out? If you haven't guessed yet, it's data binding—because it's one wonder that actually *works*. Trust me; I've been there, done the rest, and I'm still the same ol' Michelin man with the sexual prowess of a dead skunk and a body odor to match. Please, don't picture it.

Anyway, what is this data binding on Windows forms all about? Well, it enables you to set up your Windows form to hold fields from your database, then navigate through and edit records one by one. Users adore that sort of interface—and, rather usefully, these interfaces are incredibly quick to code as well.

How does it work? First off, you knock up your Connection, DataAdapter, and DataSet objects to get a hold of your data, as we did in Chapter 2.1. Then you tell Visual Basic that certain controls on your form will display certain fields. As you then move forward and backward within the DataSet, those controls are automatically updated. And, if you change any information in your controls, that's also reflected in the DataSet.

Fancy trying it?

1. Create a new VB .NET Windows application.

2. From the menu, select Tools ➣ Connect to Database.

3. As we did with the Northwind sample, link in to our surgery.mdb database. See Figure 2-8.

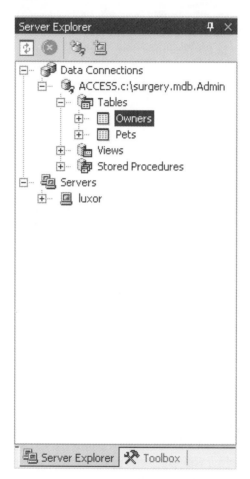

Figure 2-8. Accessing surgery.mdb via the Server Explorer

4. Drag the Owners table from surgery.mdb onto your form, as shown in Figure 2-9.

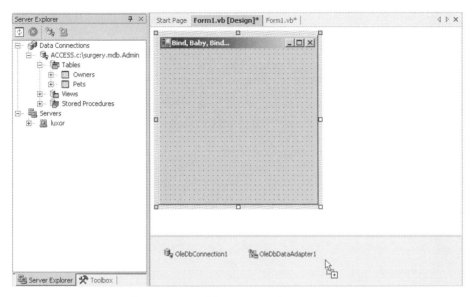

Figure 2-9. Dragging the Owners table onto our form

5. Using the Properties window, rename OleDbConnection1 to "connSurgery" and OleDbDataAdapter1 to "daOwners".

Next up, we need to add the DataSet. Now, in the first chapter of this tutorial, we added something called an *untyped DataSet*, which means that our program knows we're getting data but doesn't know anything about field names or what sort of data it is.

With a *typed DataSet*, however, we basically create our own DataSet object from a template that lists all our fields. This makes it easier to work with our DataSet and reduces the chance of programming errors. Plus, when working with your DataSet in code, it allows you to reference individual fields as actual properties. We'll look more at accessing DataSets in code both in the next chapter and in Tutorial 6, "Services Rendered".

Cool! Okay, let's continue now and create that template we've been talking about.

6. While on your form, select Data ➤ Generate DataSet from the menu.

7. Select the New option and, in the box, type "Owners".

8. Ensure that the Owners table from our OleDbDataAdapter control (daOwners) is checked.

9. Uncheck the "Add This DataSet To The Designer" box. (We'll add the DataSet manually.)

10. Click on the OK button when finished.

You'll notice that an Owners.xsd template schema has been added to the Solution Explorer. (See Figure 2-10.) Try opening that file. It's essentially a graphical representation of the fields of data to be held by your DataSet.

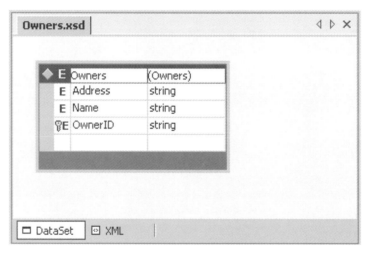

Figure 2-10. It's a graphical representation of your DataSet fields, you know.

TOP TIP   *When you generated this typed DataSet template, a lot of code was automatically added to your project to make it work. Some of this is behind Owners.xsd (try clicking on the XML button to view), although the majority is in Owners.vb (you'll need to click on Show All Files to see this). It makes interesting browsing, yes, but you don't have to worry about any of it. All this code is generated and handled automatically! It's also dead boring.*

Now, we're going to use this template to add a new owners DataSet to our project.

11. Open Form1.

12. From the data entries in your Toolbox, drag a DataSet onto your form.

You'll be given an option to make this an untyped DataSet (it doesn't know about the data it will be holding) or a typed DataSet (you tell it about your owners DataSet schema template). See Figure 2-11.

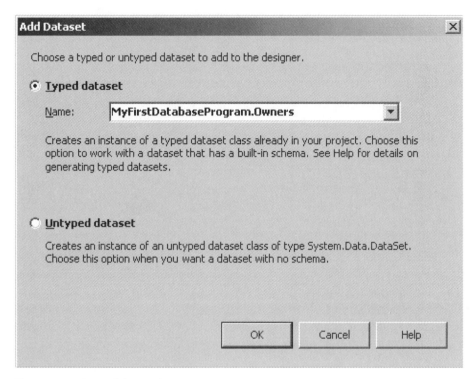

Figure 2-11. Type this, punk!

13. Choose the "Typed dataset" option and select your Owners schema.

14. Click on OK when finished.

You'll find that the Owners1 DataSet has been added to your form.

15. Change the Name property of your new DataSet to "dsOwners". (Make sure that you don't confuse this with the DataSetName property.)

Now that we have our DataSet that will hold the owners data, we need to design our form and tell it which boxes will display what information. Step aside, Michelangelo; it's time for us to slap on that beret and paint forms!

16. Design your form so it looks something like the one shown in Figure 2-12, making sure that you change the following Name properties:

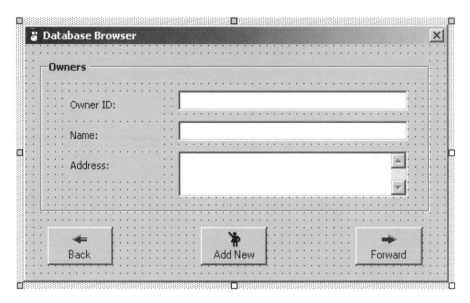

Figure 2-12. Our database browser

- *Owner ID TextBox*: txtOwnerID

- *Name TextBox*: txtName

- *Address TextBox*: txtAddress

- *Back Button*: btnBack

- *Forward Button*: btnForward

- *Add New Button*: btnAddNew

Next up, we need to bind our text boxes with the actual data:

17. For each text box, under the DataBindings section of the Properties window, change the Text listing so it points to the relevant field. (We wouldn't be able to view this list of fields if this was not a typed DataSet.) See Figure 2-13.

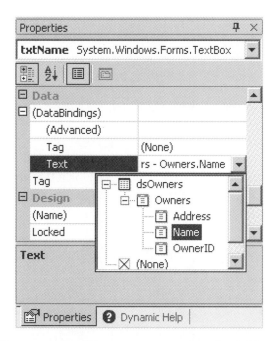

Figure 2-13. Binding our control Text property to a DataSet field

So, we've set up our database objects, designed our form, and bound the text boxes to fields in our DataSet. That means it's time to actually code, adding lines to both fill the DataSet and move around within it.

18. Double-click on a blank part of your form.

The code window should open, with a piece of code named Form1_Load. This will run whenever your form loads.

19. Change the Form1_Load method, so it reads as follows:

```
Private Sub Form1_Load(ByVal sender As System.Object, _
    ByVal e As System.EventArgs) Handles MyBase.Load
    daOwners.Fill(dsOwners)
End Sub
```

Here we're telling our DataAdapter to pour information from the database straight into our DataSet, which is then displayed in our bound text boxes. But, *newsflash*—how do we move around the rows in our DataSet, changing which one is currently displayed on our form?

20. Add the following code to respond to the click event of btnFoward:

```
BindingContext(dsOwners, "Owners").Position += 1
```

This code is talking direct to our form. It's telling it that all text boxes (and other controls) bound to the dsOwners "Owners" table should move forward one place, straight to the next record.

> **TOP TIP** *Here, we're using*
> `BindingContext(dsOwners, "Owners").Position += 1` *to add 1 to our current data position. This += operator is a great new way of increment-ing a value and saves excess code. Without it, you would have had to write* `BindingContext(dsOwners, "Owners").Position =`
> `BindingContext(dsOwners, "Owners").Position + 1.`

21. Add the following code to respond to the click event of btnBack:

```
BindingContext(dsOwners, "Owners").Position -= 1
```

22. Add the following code to respond to the click event of btnAddNew:

```
BindingContext(dsOwners, "Owners").AddNew()
```

Here, we're telling the data binding features of our form to add a new record to the Owners table of our dsOwners DataSet. This will then clear the text boxes, leaving them ready for you to add fresh data.

But our database application is currently about as useful as a waterproof teabag. Why? Because we haven't yet added any code to actually update the database. Let's do that now.

23. In the code window, select (Base Class Events) from the Class Name drop-down box.

This will fill the second drop-down with all the events supported by our form, such as click and load.

24. In the Method Name drop-down box, select the closing event.

25. Add the following code to respond to the closing event of Form1:

```
daOwners.Update(dsOwners)
```

Well, hurrah! It looks like that's about it. We've added the database objects, bound the controls, and typed a little code to tell the form what to do with its data binding. And now? Why, it's time to give this girl a whirl!

26. Press the F5 key to test drive your program.

There will be a slight delay as your form loads and the data is retrieved from surgery.mdb. Then, you'll be shown the OwnerID, Name, and Address fields in our text boxes, as in Figure 2-14. Try moving both forward and backward. What happens when you reach the end of your records and continue clicking on the Forward button?

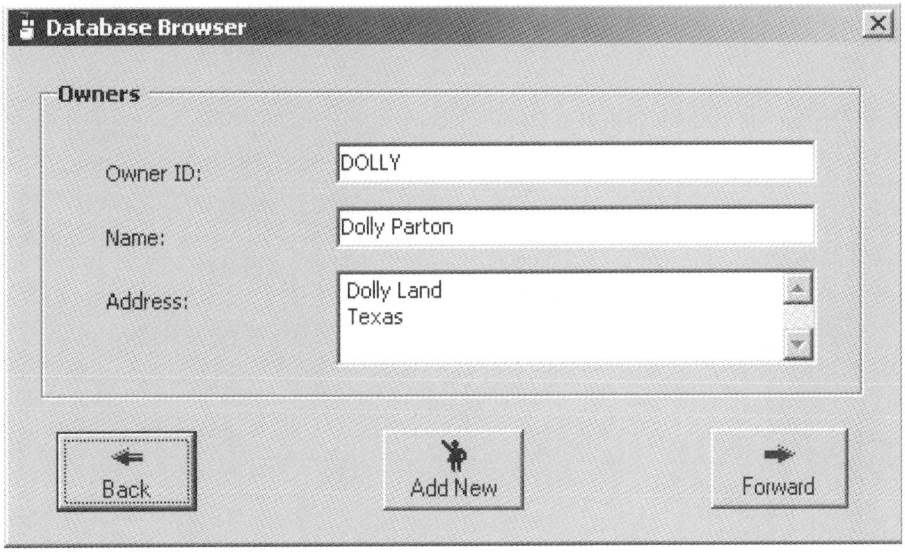

Figure 2-14. Our final database browser

Why not try adding a new record, too? Fill out the blanks, then navigate off and back onto your record. If you close your program and then reopen it, is that information still there? Has the database been updated?

Moving on, what if you were storing a True/False value in your database? What control could you bind that to?

But hold on a minute: we haven't added a feature to delete records from the database yet! Ohh, there's no time now; this dizzy chappie is scheduled to move on to another section. However, I'll leave you with this conveniently placed problem, alongside a couple of clues to help out:

- To delete a record from the DataSet, use

```
BindingContext(dsOwners, "Owners").RemoveAt(IndexNumber)
```

- To find out the IndexNumber of the current record, use

```
IndexNumber = BindingContext(dsOwners, "Owners").Position
```

Binding on the Web

Looking to slap your information on the Internet? In the golden olden days, it'd take more 1s and 0s than you'd find in Bill Gates' current bank account balance.

Thankfully, with VB .NET, it's all much easier. Admittedly, you don't have all the power you have with binding in Windows forms. You can't update or delete records using such a small amount of code, for example. But we'll leave all that fancy jazz for Chapter 2.4 when we'll build our own transactional Web application powered by a server database.

Come on, everyone go *whooo*!

Anyway, for now we're going to work on simply viewing our data over the Web. And that, my friends, is easier than Widow Twanky on a quiet night at the Hotpants Discothèque.

1. Create a new ASP.NET Web application, named "surgery".

This new application is basically your interactive Web site, and the WebForm1.aspx you see in Figure 2-15 is a page on that site.

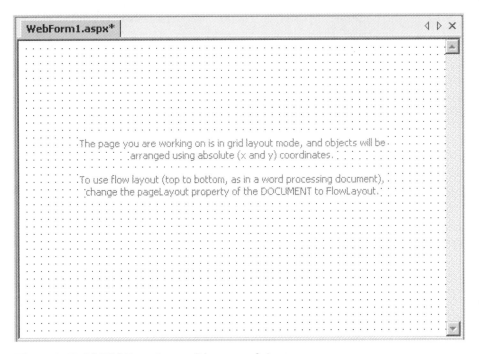

The page you are working on is in grid layout mode, and objects will be arranged using absolute (x and y) coordinates.

To use flow layout (top to bottom, as in a word processing document), change the pageLayout property of the DOCUMENT to FlowLayout.

Figure 2-15. It's WebForm1.aspx. It's pretty plain, too.

TOP TIP *If you've built ASP Web pages before, forget everything you know. This is ASP.NET and, with Visual Studio in hand, you can build fully functional sites in just the same way as you would a regular Visual Basic application: just paint and code! To find out more, check out Tutorial 3, "Working the Web".*

2. From the Server Explorer, access the Tables view of surgery.mdb.

3. As you did earlier, drag and drop your Owners table onto WebForm1.aspx.

4. Using the Properties window rename OleDbConnection1 to "connSurgery" and OleDbDataAdapter1 to "daOwners".

Next, we could generate a typed DataSet. In the last example, we did this so we knew which fields were available and so we could easily tell VB .NET which controls bound to what. We never actually needed to do this (in fact, we could have just skipped the step altogether), but making VB .NET aware of which fields it has available before it actually uses the data can make it easier to work with. I'm going to add a typed DataSet now.

5. While on your Web form, select Data ➢ Generate DataSet from the menu.

6. Select the New option and in the box type "Owners".

7. Ensure the Owners table from our OleDbDataAdapter control (daOwners) is checked.

8. Uncheck the "Add This DataSet To The Designer" box. (We'll do this manually.)

9. Click on the OK button when finished.

10. From the data entries in your toolbox, drag a DataSet onto your form.

11. Choose the "Typed dataset" option and select your Owners dataset.

12. Click on OK when finished.

13. Using the Properties window, change the name of your DataSet to "dsOwners".

That's our actual data-retrieval side of things sorted. Now we need something to display our data.

14. Draw a DataGrid control out onto your Web form.

15. Change its ID (Name) property to "grdOwners".

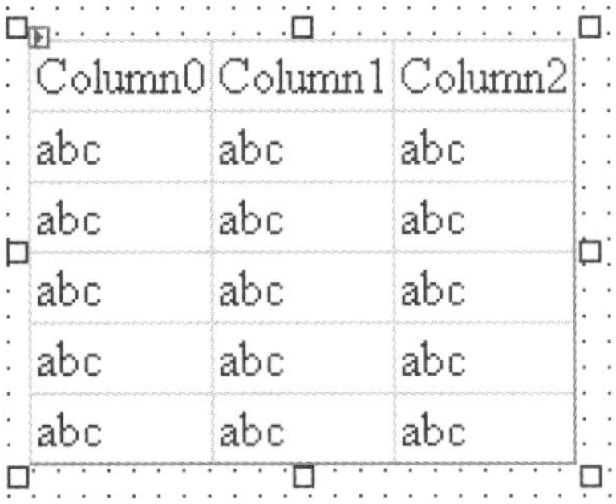

Figure 2-16. A rather dull DataGrid control

Figure 2-16 shows the beast that will hold your actual information. Looks a bit boring though, doesn't it? Let's pump up the volume, disco divas.

16. Just under the list of properties, click on the Auto Format link.

17. Select the Colorful 4 style from the list and click on OK. Plus, change the font name to Tahoma and the size to X-Small.

> **TOP TIP**   *In addition to changing the style of your DataGrid via the Auto Format link, you can also alter how it* behaves *by clicking on the Property Builder link. Check it out if you have a few spare minutes.*

Now it's time to add some actual code.

18. Draw a Button control at the top of your Web form.

19. Double-click on the button. You should be inside a subroutine that responds to the button click event.

20. Insert the following code:

```
daOwners.Fill(dsOwners)
grdOwners.DataSource = dsOwners
grdOwners.DataBind()
```

Here we start off by filling our actual DataSet and then binding it to the DataSource property of our DataGrid. So far, it looks just the same as our very first example project in Chapter 2.1. However, the last line of code is a little different. It's a DataBind method, and you need to run it before a Web form's DataGrid control will bind to its source. Standard procedure, ma'am.

21. Press the F5 key to test your application. Your Web browser should launch, opening your application, as shown in Figure 2-17.

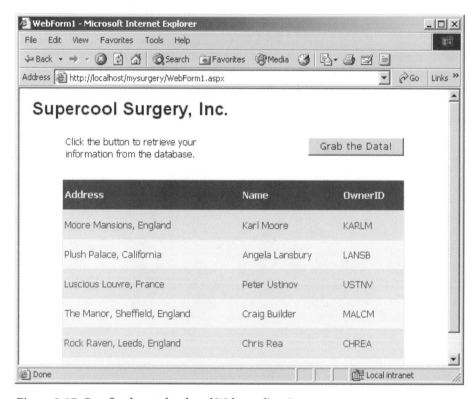

Figure 2-17. Our final pastel-colored Web application

What happens when you click on your button? Does the DataGrid fill (populate) itself with information from your Owners table? Can you edit any of this information?

Also, pay particular attention to the order of the fields. How has this order been decided? Can you change this? Try editing your actual DataSet XSD file, cutting and pasting the fields into a different order, then running again. Does this help?

22. When finished testing, close your Web browser.

Impressed yet? Amazed by the fact that you can write a few lines of code and generate a completely HTML-driven Web site? No? Oh, I see. You're not too keen because you're only accessing it on your local machine.

But this could be literally anywhere: your own machine, an intranet, the Internet, *anywhere*. All you need to do is copy your database and the Web application project (Project ➤ Copy Project) across to a relevant machine, and your site is live and ready to run. It's as simple as that.

Congratulations! Wahoo. Phew, what excitement! If my heart doesn't stop beating quite so fast, I fear I might just keel over right now! (What do you mean . . . it can be arranged?)

Using the Wizards

Among all the excitement, I've gone and accidentally forgotten to give you a relationships example. Sure, we set up the database and included relationships, but then we never used them in code.

Have no fear; we'll save all that for the next show. But, for now, I'd like to leave you with a little homework that should give you an idea as to how relationships could work in the programmatic world.

It's nothing too heavy; I just want you to run a couple of wizards. They'll re-create all the code we've typed today, not only better but in about ten seconds flat. And who said computers were useless?

1. Create a new VB .NET Windows application.

2. Select Project ➤ Add Windows Form.

3. Select Data Form Wizard and click on Open.

4. Try working your way through the screens, setting up a relationship between our two tables. See Figure 2-18.

5. When finished, add a button to your first form to open your new data form. Then use the F5 key to test your application.

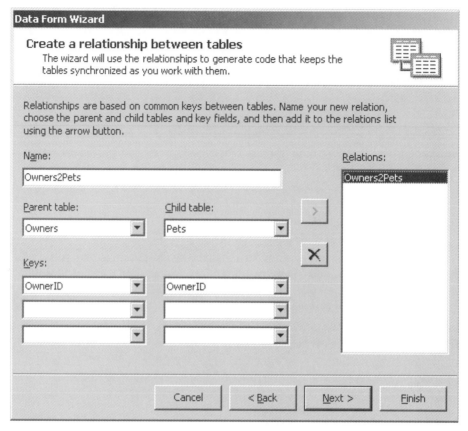

Figure 2-18. Creating a relationship with the Data Form wizard

Does it all work? What about the code behind this form? Does any of it look familiar? Let's do the same again now, this time on a Web site.

6. Create a new ASP.NET Web application.

7. Select Project ➤ Add Web Form.

8. Select Data Form Wizard and click on Open.

9. Try working your way through the screens once more, setting up a relationship between our two tables.

10. When finished, right-click on your DataWebForm1.aspx and select "Set as Start Page". Then press F5 and test your application.

How does this application work? Notice how this is a little more advanced than our own sample? Do you understand any of the code behind this Web form?

Keep tinkering around here and see just how you can customize each sample. Fingers crossed!

CONCLUSION

Congratulations on completing the second chapter in Tutorial 2, "Doing Databases"!

Today, we've really pushed out the knowledge boat. We started by creating our own database and soon delved into the puzzling world of relationships. After that, we figured out how to bind directly to controls on a Windows form, and looked at viewing data live on a Web site.

Finally, we checked out the cool wizards that are bundled with VB .NET, wizards that will automatically bind to Windows and Web forms for you. All automatically. What do you mean, *why'd I save that bit for last*?

For now, continue playing with databases. Try to create a few of your own, ones that represent real-life data storage needs in your company. Then attempt to link into them from Visual Basic. And, when you can do that, no problemo, go pushing it all even further.

Well, that's all for now. In the next chapter, we'll be talking to databases in their native language of SQL, figuring out how to access your data entirely in code, and creating our own mega-supercool program that actually understands the world of relationships.

Awww . . . how very sweet.

But, until then, I'm Karl Moore, wishing you a very good day.

Cuckoo.

CHAPTER 2.2

OUR OWN DATABASE AND VB .NET REVIEW SHEET

- The easiest way to create a Jet MDB database is by using Microsoft Access. To do this, launch Access, select Blank Database, and specify a location.

- The most important part of creating a database is setting up the tables. To do this in Access, click on Tables, click on the New button, choose Design View, and specify a name and data type for your fields.

- Relationships in a database allow you to link information from multiple tables using a key. For example, you might link entries in your Orders table to their parent entries in the Customers table, via a CustomerID key.

- Most relationships are of the one-to-many type, sometimes called *parent-to-child* relationships. This means that you have a main entry in one table and multiple related entries in another.

- For tables to be in a relationship, it is recommended that each table contain a primary key, a field that holds a unique value for each row. This could perhaps be an auto-incrementing number or a text ID value. To turn a field into a primary key in Access, highlight the field (or fields, if this is a "composite" primary key) in Design view, and click on the Primary Key button on the menu.

- To set up a relationship between tables within Access, select Tools ➤ Relationships from the menu. Add any appropriate tables to your Relationships view, then drag and drop the primary key field from your parent table onto the foreign key field on the child table. Make sure that the relationship type is correct, check the box if referential integrity is required, and then click on the Create button.

- Data binding is a feature of Windows forms that ties elements of a DataSet directly to certain control properties. For example, you might tie the CustomerName field of a table in your DataSet to the Text property of the txtCustomerName TextBox control.

- To use data binding in Windows forms, you first need to set up standard Access data connection objects (OleDbConnection and OleDbDataAdapter) by dragging and dropping your database table from the Server Explorer onto your form. You then need to create a typed DataSet from your DataAdapter object. Next, you need to bind elements of your typed DataSet to individual control properties, using the DataBindings property of each control. Finally, after filling your DataSet—`MyDataAdapter.Fill(MyDataSet)`—you can use code similar to the following to navigate and manipulate your records:

```
BindingContext(dsOrders, "Orders").Position += 1
BindingContext(dsOrders, "Orders").AddNew()
BindingContext(dsOrders, "Orders").RemoveAt(IndexNumber)
```

- Data binding in Web forms is not quite as powerful as that available in Windows forms. The most commonly used technique is to take information from your DataSet and display it in a customizable DataGrid control. These are read-only, and extra code is required to add and edit records. (See Chapter 2.4 for more information.)

- To bind data in Web forms using the DataGrid control, first set up the standard Access data connection objects and the typed DataSet (as before, with Windows forms). Finally, after filling your DataSet, execute code similar to the following:

```
MyDataGrid.DataSource = MyDataSet
MyDataGrid.DataBind()
```

- You can save time by running the wizards to generate your own, more complex data binding projects. To do this, create either a Windows application or ASP.NET Web application. Then, from the menu, select Project ➢ Add New Item ➢ Data Form Wizard.

Doing It Completely in Code

"Three things in life are certain; death, taxes and data corruption. Guess which just happened?"—Suggested Windows error message, source unknown

IT'S THE THIRD CHAPTER HERE IN "Doing Databases" and we're approaching the middle of the line, somewhere between the early days of defining a field and the more complicated world of transactions and report-demanding users.

As ever, I'm your host, Karl Moore, and you're a database genius. Today, once again, we'll be taking your knowledge straight to Another Level. And, who knows, maybe they'll make a song out of it.

"One Day-tabase in Your Life", "What a Field Believes", "Row over Troubled Waters". The possibilities are endless.

But cheap gags aside, what will we be covering today? We'll start by learning how to talk to databases in their own special language, SQL. We'll also figure out how to access databases completely in code. Oh, and it's about time we took a further look at relationships, too.

Hey, just call me Dr. Ruth.

All that coming up—so stay interested and let's party!

Talking the Talk

If you were traveling to Spain, you'd probably get out the ol' Spanish phrasebook, and, if you were tripping across to France, you'd learn a couple of French phrases. Likewise, if you were visiting Rome, you might memorize a couple of lines of, erm, Romanian.

Databases are not very different. In a perfect world, we'd be able to say to our database, "Listen, mate, I'm looking for the telephone numbers of all companies based in London. What can you come up with?" And it'd return a bundle of relevant records.

Welcome to an imperfect world, in which *we* need to speak *their* language. Thankfully, it's not awfully difficult, and, in this short section, we're going to get the lowdown on Structured Query Language (or *SQL*, if you're a hip and trendy author-type or personal friend of Bill Gates).

Let's launch Microsoft Access and take another peek at that Customers table.

1. Launch Microsoft Access.

2. Open the same Nwind.mdb database that we accessed in the first chapter of this tutorial.

3. Under Objects, click on the Tables box.

Here are all the tables in your database. Let's open our trusty favorite.

4. Double-click on the Customers table, and scroll about the records to refresh your memory. See Figure 3-1.

Customer ID	Company Name	Contact Name	Contact Title
ALFKI	Alfreds Futterkiste	Maria Anders	Sales Representative
ANATR	Ana Trujillo Emparedados y helados	Ana Trujillo	Owner
ANTON	Antonio Moreno Taquería	Antonio Moreno	Owner
AROUT	Around the Horn	Thomas Hardy	Sales Representative
BERGS	Berglunds snabbköp	Christina Berglund	Order Administrator
BLAUS	Blauer See Delikatessen	Hanna Moos	Sales Representative
BLONP	Blondel père et fils	Frédérique Citeaux	Marketing Manager
BOLID	Bólido Comidas preparadas	Martín Sommer	Owner
BONAP	Bon app'	Laurence Lebihan	Owner
BOTTM	Bottom-Dollar Markets	Elizabeth Lincoln	Accounting Manager
BSBEV	B's Beverages	Victoria Ashworth	Sales Representative
CACTU	Cactus Comidas para llevar	Patricio Simpson	Sales Agent
CENTC	Centro comercial Moctezuma	Francisco Chang	Marketing Manager
CHOPS	Chop-suey Chinese	Yang Wang	Owner
COMMI	Comércio Mineiro	Pedro Afonso	Sales Associate
CONSH	Consolidated Holdings	Elizabeth Brown	Sales Representative
DRACD	Drachenblut Delikatessen	Sven Ottlieb	Order Administrator
DUMON	Du monde entier	Janine Labrune	Owner
EASTC	Eastern Connection	Ann Devon	Sales Agent
ERNSH	Ernst Handel	Roland Mendel	Sales Manager
FAMIA	Familia Arquibaldo	Aria Cruz	Marketing Assistant

Record: 1 of 91

Figure 3-1. Hello, remember me?

Now, when writing programs in Visual Basic, you'll often want to ask your database certain questions and get information back. You might want a list of all of the customer IDs for example, or perhaps you need to know which organization has a contact named Liu Wong. You might even want a list of most expensive products, or details of all orders from a particular customer.

For now, let's figure out how we can ask such questions. We'll learn how to use them later.

5. Close the Customers table.

6. Back in the Database window, click on the Queries option.

7. Click on the New button.

8. Click on OK at the first pop-up box.

9. On the next Show Table form that appears, click on Close.

10. From the menu, select View ➤ SQL View.

You're currently in the question-asking screen. (See Figure 3-2.) It doesn't look like much, and that's because it isn't. But just watch the magic start when we begin asking questions. Sort of.

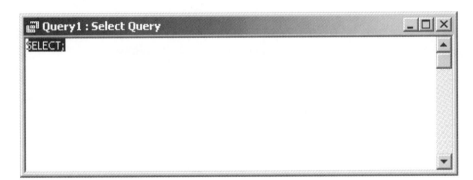

Figure 3-2. The SQL view, our question-asking screen

11. Into the Query1 window, type the following:

    ```
    Select CompanyName From Customers
    ```

12. Select View ➤ Datasheet View.

Here, you're asking the database to select the CompanyName fields from the Customers table. The Datasheet view shows you what your SQL statement returns, and it should look something like Figure 3-3.

Figure 3-3. The results of our SQL statement

TOP TIP *Most databases speak SQL. It's a language that consists of four main parts. You've got the Select bit, which we're dealing with now, plus you've got Insert to insert records, Update to update records, and Delete to zap 'em. We'll encounter these more later in this series, and you'll find examples on today's Review Sheet.*

13. Using the View menu, go back to SQL view.

Let's look at a few other questions you might want to ask your database. Try 'em out as we go through the list:

```
Select CompanyName, Address, PostalCode From Customers
```

Here, we're telling our database to return all the CompanyName, Address, and PostalCode fields from the Customers table.

```
Select * From Customers
```

In SQL geek speak, the asterisk (*) means "anything and everything." So here we're telling the database to give us all fields from the Customers table. Simple enough. Shall we move on?

```
Select CompanyName, Address, PostalCode From Customers Where City = 'London'
```

A bit more complicated, this one. We're asking the database to select the CompanyName, Address, and PostalCode fields for all Customers that have a City field of "London".

```
Select * From Customers Where Country = 'UK' Or Country = 'Canada'
```

Nerdier. Is that a word? Well, that's what we're getting with this sample. Here, we're selecting everything from the Customers table where the Country field is either the UK or Canada.

```
Select * From Customers Where Country = 'Mexico' And ContactTitle = 'Owner'
```

Slightly more unusual, this. We're getting full details on all customers based in Mexico that have an Owner as the key contact. Obviously small businesses, those.

```
Select PostalCode From Customers Where PostalCode Like 'WX*'
```

Finally, this sample is selecting everything from the Customers table for which the PostalCode begins with "WX". This works because that asterisk means "anything and everything," plus we've used the Like keyword. Interesting, eh?

Okay, question time: What statement would you use to display all the details of customers based in Mexico? How about companies that have phone numbers containing "555"? Tell me, how many companies have a contact whose name is Ann?

> **TOP TIP**   *If you need a list of field names to help you out, go back to the Database window by pressing F11. Then, select your table and click on the Design button.*

Hey, how much time do you have? If you've got a spare two minutes, try saving your "query" by selecting File ➢ Save from the menu. When we start accessing databases from our programs later today, you'll notice that we can use such queries in the same way as you do tables. In fact, you can treat them just like tables right now: try writing a query that gets its data from another query and not a table. What do you think? Observe your feelings and be sure to discuss them in the next group session.

Cheating at SQL

"If at first you don't succeed, try, try again."

The wise person who once uttered those words obviously hasn't read this book. If at first I don't succeed, I cheat. Simple dimple. Whether that means telling my boss I programmed Microsoft Word especially for him or nicking half my application code from the Internet, I really don't care.

Another nifty little cheat is getting Access to write your SQL what-nots for you. And it's incredibly simple. Here's how.

1. On the Query screen in the Access Database window, click on the New button.

2. Add the table(s) you want to query, clicking on Close when finished.

3. Double-click on the table fields to add to your query.

4. Type any criteria (the Where stuff) in the Criteria boxes under the desired fields, as shown in Figure 3-4.

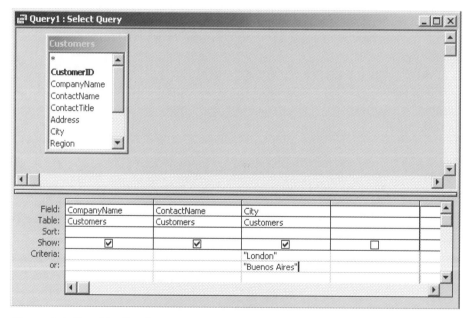

Figure 3-4. Graphically plotting our SQL statement

> **TOP TIP**   *For help on using the query window, press F1 at any time. That handy paperclip thing will be sure to lend a helping hand, and, for once, it actually presents a bunch of rather useful examples to work from. Try, for example, finding out how to order records alphabetically, count the number of rows in a table, or group by a particular field.*

5.   Using the menu, select View ➤ SQL View. (See Figure 3-5.)

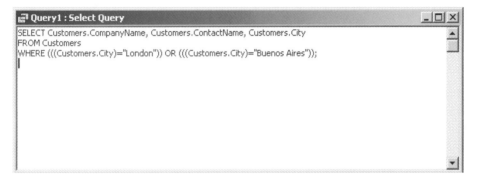

Figure 3-5. Our final SQL statement

And there you have your completed SQL statement, ready for saving as a query (sometimes called a *view* by boring types) or for use in your Visual Basic program when you need to ask such database questions.

Want to continue? No worries. Let's start to look at accessing databases in code, where we'll put some of the knowledge we've used so far into play. But keep this language fresh in your mind: in Chapter 2.4, you'll really give this SQL lark a good bashing. So stick with it, gang!

Accessing in Code

In the first two chapters, we learned how to connect into databases the fluffy way. It's quick, it's easy, and it's quick. It's easy, too. But true nerds prefer another way.

They don't like Visual Basic doing any of the work for them. They don't like VB .NET creating the OleDbConnection object. They don't like the designer automatically determining what should be selected from their tables.

So they do it all themselves, in code. And this holds certain advantages: you have more control, you can easily port your code anywhere, and sometimes it enables you to work with features that would be otherwise unavailable. Trust me, working completely in code can bring you a lot of benefits, plus it seriously boosts your street cred.

Uhm, so how do you do it? Well, there isn't just one simple method. No surprise there then. Instead, we have two core techniques: using Command objects in code, and using the DataSet to manipulate information coming from a DataAdapter.

Using Command objects in code allows you to execute SQL statements directly onto a database, perhaps updating a particular record or retrieving data into something called a *DataReader* (which is basically a read-only, one-table DataSet). Command objects require little coding and are relatively simple widgets, but, because I'm feeling all cruel, I'll save them for the next chapter.

You've already been introduced to the second main data access method (using the DataSet to manipulate information coming via a DataAdapter). Yes, you know exactly how this little beastie works. The only difference *here* is that you'll need to create all the individual objects in code.

> **TOP TIP** *Both of these techniques form the basis of ADO.NET, a buzzword covering all the data access objects in the .NET framework (under the* System.Data *namespace). It's a word you'll hear bandied about a lot in industry journals. Just remember, when you're accessing databases using any of the methods taught in this tutorial, you're using ADO.NET.*

So, think you can handle doing a DataSet in code? Hmm, pull down the blinds and turn on that computer. It's time to put you to the test with a completely-in-code program.

Our Completely-in-Code Program

Hmm, what completely-in-code program do you think we should create? Let's cast our minds back to the veterinary surgery database we built in the last chapter. How about an application that lists all the owners in our database and allows you to select, edit, and save the details of each one?

Sounds fair enough. We can expand this later to automatically display the pets for each owner too, using relationships. Okay, then, let's get busy.

1. Create a new Windows application in VB .NET called "CodeMode".

Let's start off by designing our actual application interface. I'll leave all the fancy features up to you; however, we really need only a half-dozen controls to get started. Here goes.

2. Add the following controls to your form, along with any appropriate descriptive blurb or decoration. (My screen is shown in Figure 3-6.)

- *ComboBox*—Name: "cboOwners"; Text: (blank); DropDownStyle: DropDownList

- *Label*—Name: "lblOwnerID"; Text: (blank)

- *TextBox*—Name: "txtName"; Text: (blank)

- *TextBox*—Name: "txtAddress"; Text: (blank); MultiLine: True

- *Button*—Name: "btnRetrieve"; Text: "Retrieve Owners"

- *Button*—Name: "btnSave"; Text: "Save Changes"

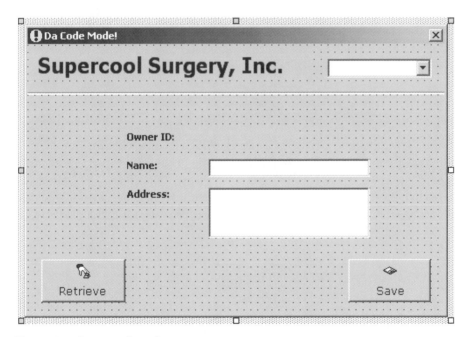

Figure 3-6. Our user interface

Declaring the Objects

That's our interface knocked together. Next, we need to think about code.

1. Open your code window.

2. In the Declarations area (top of your form, underneath `Public Class` and `Inherits`), add the following object declarations:

```
Dim objConnection As New OleDb.OleDbConnection( _
    "Provider=Microsoft.Jet.OLEDB.4.0;Data Source=C:\Surgery.mdb")
Dim objOwnerDA As New OleDb.OleDbDataAdapter("Select * from Owners", _
    objConnection)
Dim objOwnerCB As New OleDb.OleDbCommandBuilder(objOwnerDA)
Dim objDataSet As New DataSet()
```

Whoa, boy! What in the name of King Tutu the Tenth is *this*? Here, we're simply setting up the objects we need to use for accessing our data. Let's briefly look at each in turn.

```
Dim objConnection As New OleDb.OleDbConnection( _
    "Provider=Microsoft.Jet.OLEDB.4.0;Data Source=C:\Surgery.mdb")
```

Here, we're creating an OleDbConnection object. Remember that one? Earlier, we likened this object to a telephone cable. That thing we're passing to the object as an argument is something called a *connection string*. (You should've seen that in the Intellisense.) Now, if this is a telephone call, you can imagine that connection string as the telephone number. It provides details of the database you're connecting to.

> **TOP TIP**   *If you need to know the connection string for a particular database, you may as well let Visual Basic figure it out for you. Here's a great technique for doing just that: in Visual Studio .NET, select Tools ➤ Connect to Database. Fill out the blanks in the Data Link form, then click on OK. Select View ➤ Server Explorer and select your database. Then simply copy and paste the ConnectString from the Property window. For another, even simpler method, look up "Generating OLE DB Strings with Ease" in Chapter 8.3, "Advanced Tips and Techniques".*

Next, we'll set up our actual DataAdapter object, the wizzy what-not that actually talks down our telephone cable to the database.

```
Dim objOwnerDA As New OleDb.OleDbDataAdapter( _
    "Select * from Owners", objConnection)
```

As you can see, we're passing two arguments here. The first is our Select statement, the SQL question that our program will ask the database. (Does that make sense after our quick language course?). The second argument tells our DataAdapter which connection to use.

```
Dim objOwnerCB As New OleDb.OleDbCommandBuilder(objOwnerDA)
```

This looks weird, but it's actually pretty simple. The DataAdapter does a lot of talking with your database. When it grabs records, it does a Select. When it updates records, it needs to run an Update statement, plus you have Delete and Insert also.

Yuck, imagine writing all of those SQL statements in code! Well, just by adding this line here, the CommandBuilder fills out all the other statements for you based on your Select statement. Cool, eh?

```
Dim objDataSet As New DataSet()
```

And, finally, here we have our groovy little DataSet, just ready to be pumped silly with information. Ooh, matron!

So, there we have our core database objects setup: OleDbConnection to make the connection, our DataAdapter to talk to the database, the CommandBuilder to create the SQL Insert (and so on) DataAdapter commands automatically, and the DataSet to hold the information returned by the DataAdapter.

Adding the Code

Making sense so far? I hope that's affirmative, Doctor, because we're about to encounter even more code—code that will use the objects we've just created.

1. Add the following commented code to respond to the click event of btnRetrieve:

    ```
    ' Clears DataSet of any existing data
    objDataSet.Clear()

    ' Fill schema - adds table structure information to DataSet
    ```

```
' Not essential, but handles primary keys for us, etc.
objOwnerDA.FillSchema(objDataSet, SchemaType.Source, "Owners")

' Fills DataSet with info from our DataAdapter
objOwnerDA.Fill(objDataSet, "Owners")
```

Here, we start off by clearing our DataSet of any existing information. We then fill our DataSet with "schema" information from our table, such as the structure information, primary key details, and such. Finally, we fill the DataSet with the results of our Select query, giving it a virtual table name of "Owners".

So now we have our actual data and its structure in the DataSet. Next, we need to display some of that in our cboOwners ComboBox control, ready for the user to pick an owner.

2. Underneath that last chunk of code, behind the click event of btnRetrieve, add the following code:

```
' Empty combo box
cboOwners.Items.Clear()

' Loop through each row, adding the OwnerID to combo box
Dim i As Integer, strCurrentID As String

For i = 1 To objDataSet.Tables("Owners").Rows.Count
    strCurrentID = objDataSet.Tables("Owners").Rows(i -1).Item("OwnerID")
    cboOwners.Items.Add(strCurrentID)
Next

' Select first item in the list
cboOwners.SelectedIndex = 0
```

First off here, we clear any existing entries in the combo box. Then, we loop round all the rows in our Owners table and retrieve the value of the current row OwnerID field. This value then gets added to our ComboBox control. Finally, we actually select the first item in our ComboBox control.

> **TOP TIP** *Understand the loop? We're just looping around from 1 through to the number of rows in our Owners table, placing the loop number in the* i *variable. Still, you're probably wondering why we actually do* .Rows(i - 1) *when referencing a row? Well, all rows are zero-based, meaning that the first row is actually referred to as 0, the second as 1, and so on. Therefore, we subtract 1 from the loop number to get the actual row number we should retrieve. Clear as mud? Oh good.*

Hey, want to see how your program works so far? Let's give this baby a test run.

3. Press F5 to test your application. (See Figure 3-7.)

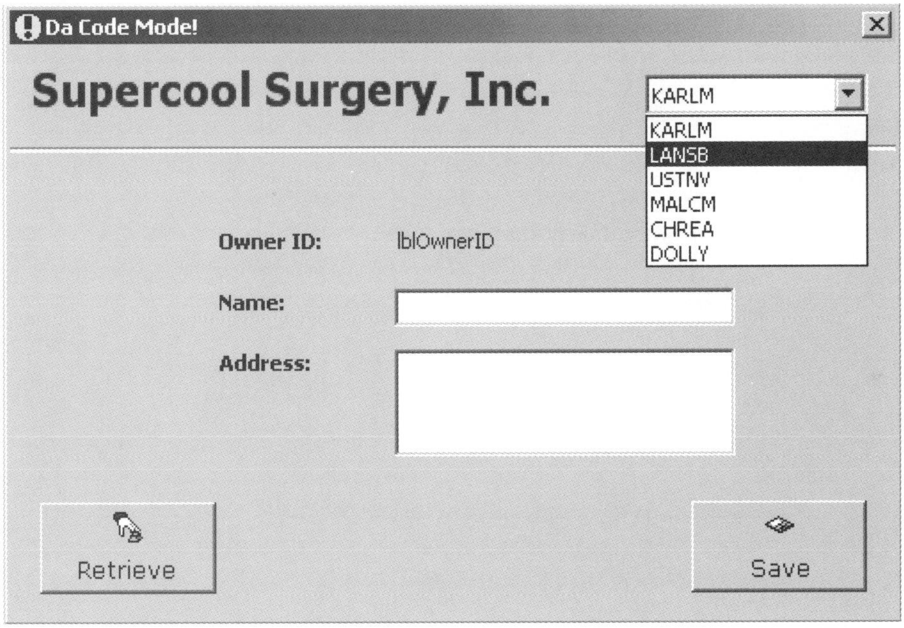

Figure 3-7. Our list of owners in action

Try clicking on your Retrieve button. What happens? How quick is your code? Does the ComboBox control get populated with a bundle of OwnerIDs? Notice how the first item in the list gets selected, thanks to your code? What happens right now if you select another entry in the list?

> **TOP TIP** *If you don't have many owners or pets in your database right now, this is a fantastic time to go add a few. Go on, make them weird and wacky;* Zachurius the Ninety-Seventh *and* Incredibly Suspicious Looking Sausage Dog *are a couple of suggestions to get you started.*

4. Close your application when finished.

Adding Even More Code

We've only written a *relatively* small amount of code and our application is already retrieving data. That's really good news. How are you finding it? Oh, that's not good news. In fact, that's an expletive.

But, still, we must move on, expanding our application so we can display information about each particular owner in the TextBox controls on our form.

For this, we're going to create our own method: FillOwnerDetails. It'll simply search for an OwnerID, then display that owner's details in our controls. Let's work on it now.

1. Add the following method to your form:

```
Public Sub FillOwnerDetails()

    Dim objRow As DataRow
    objRow = _
      objDataSet.Tables("Owners").Rows.Find(cboOwners.SelectedItem.ToString)

    lblOwnerID.Text = objRow.Item("OwnerID")
    txtName.Text = objRow.Item("Name")
    txtAddress.Text = objRow.Item("Address")

End Sub
```

Understand what's happening here? We're running the .Find function on our table rows. This takes a primary key as an argument (the SelectedItem.ToString on our ComboBox) and returns the row, a DataRow. Next, we take information from the fields in that DataRow and put it into our controls.

That method should help us take care of getting information out of our DataSet. But what about putting it back in? And no, you can't make this a read-only application. *Tsk, tsk.*

2. Add the following method to your form:

```
Public Sub StoreOwnerDetails()

    Dim objRow As DataRow
    If lblOwnerID.Text = "" Then Exit Sub

    objRow = objDataSet.Tables("Owners").Rows.Find(lblOwnerID.Text)

    objRow.Item("Name") = txtName.Text
    objRow.Item("Address") = txtAddress.Text

End Sub
```

Here, we start off by checking whether the current OwnerID label is blank. (In other words, check whether the user is currently looking at a record. If not, the program is probably just loading, so exit the method.) Next, we just find the record with our OwnerID again, then amend the field values.

But these chunks of code aren't clever enough to just run when they should. Instead, we need to tell our VB .NET program when they should step in.

3. After the existing code behind your btnRetrieve click event code, add this line:

```
FillOwnerDetails()
```

Next, when the user selects a new owner from our ComboBox control, we need to save any changes from the existing data, and then refill the screen with the new owner details. Let's add that now.

4. Add the following code to respond to the SelectedIndexChanged event of your ComboBox:

```
StoreOwnerDetails()
FillOwnerDetails()
```

Excellent! Just one more thing. Our whole application works a treat, but we haven't yet added any code to actually update the backend database, only the local DataSet. Well, no problem; this last bit is easy.

5. Add the following code to respond to the click event of btnSave:

```
objOwnerDA.Update(objDataSet, "Owners")
```

Alrighty, genius coders, that's our entire application finished! And you're still smiling. That's good. Okay, let's give this little number a trial run.

6. Press F5 to test your application. (My final application is shown in Figure 3-8.)

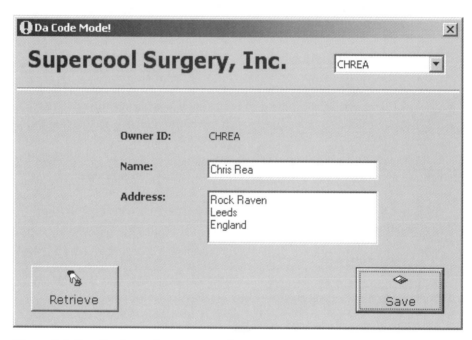

Figure 3-8. Our final veterinary surgery browser

What happens when you click on your Retrieve button? Do your Label and TextBox controls instantly populate with the information of the selected owners? What if you update an owner's details, move to another owner, and then move back? Also, try modifying some of the information, clicking on Save, and then restarting your application. Did the changes save? And what happens if you don't click on Save at all?

7. When finished, close your application.

Congratulations on completing your first database application—completely in code!

Going Even Further

Hey, hold on just one little minute! I may be about as dense as a brick's molecular structure, but most database applications actually allow you to add records, too. Oh, and delete them.

Well, we'll not be doing that here. Why? Well, let me be more specific. *I* won't be doing that here. *You* will.

Before moving on to the next section, check out the following code snippets, then update your application so the user can also add and delete owners. Don't forget that you don't always have to use a TextBox control to accept user data, the InputBox function will suffice. You'll see what I mean later. Okay, here goes and best of luck!

- To add a row to a DataSet:

```
Dim objRow As DataRow
' Create a new DataRow object for this table
objRow = objDataSet.Tables("TableName").NewRow
' Edit each field value
objRow.Item("FieldName") = "Value"
' Officially add the DataRow to our table
objDataSet.Tables("Owners").Rows.Add(objRow)
```

- To delete a row from the DataSet:

```
objRow.Delete()
```

If you're up for the challenge, here's a further puzzler. What if you add two rows with the same primary key value? Does VB .NET pick up on this? How does it know, without sending the information back to the database first? How could you implement error handling to catch something like this?

I'm out of here before she blows. See you in the next section!

Expanding with Relationships

Tsk, relationships, eh? Not quite my thing. I tried it once, after seeing a hippie video promoting "Make Love, Not War!" So I married—and ended up doing both.

So, you might ask what this not-quite-Dr-Ruth is doing teaching you about relationships. Well, when talking about those programmatic wonders that can help make your DataSets cooler than Austin Powers on the pull, I'm actually not too bad. *Those* relationships are simple. It's the Venus thing I can't understand.

Right then—relationships. Imagine that the users of the program you've just finished have decided that they didn't want to browse just owners, they also wanted to view pets. What a pain!

How do we handle that? Well, in this instance, we might grab data from both our tables, putting it all into our single DataSet. Then, we could set up an OwnerID relationship between the two tables (in code), and move onward from there.

To start this, we need to declare a couple of DataAdapter-related objects to actually talk to the database and grab our data.

1.   Add the following declarations to your form:

```
Dim objPetDA As New OleDb.OleDbDataAdapter("Select * from Pets"_ ,
    objConnection)
Dim objPetCB As New OleDb.OleDbCommandBuilder(objPetDA)
```

Here, we're just creating a DataAdapter to run a Select command from our Pets table, plus a CommandBuilder to fill out all those extra Insert, Update, and Delete commands—just as we did with our Owners table. Next, we need to actually get information from our DataAdapter into the DataSet.

2.   You already have code behind your btnRetrieve click event. Underneath where you fill the DataSet with owner data, and just before you clear the ComboBox control, add the following code:

```
' Fill our DataSet with info from the Pets table
objPetDA.FillSchema(objDataSet, SchemaType.Source, "Pets")
objPetDA.Fill(objDataSet, "Pets")

' Setup our relationship
objDataSet.Relations.Clear()
objDataSet.Relations.Add("Owners2Pets", _
            objDataSet.Tables("Owners").Columns("OwnerID"), _
            objDataSet.Tables("Pets").Columns("OwnerID"))
```

You can probably understand the first couple of lines here: we're just retrieving data in the exact same way as earlier. But what about that last line of code?

Here, we're adding a relationship to our DataSet called "Owners2Pets". We're telling the DataSet that the parent column is OwnerID in the Owners table. The child column in this relationship is OwnerID in the Pets table. Make sense?

That will actually set up our relationship, but it doesn't really do anything until we use that relationship, in code. To demonstrate the principle here, we're going to simply add a list box to our form, then create a method that fills it with

details of pets belonging to the currently selected Owner. Understand?
Hokily-dokily!

3. Draw out a ListBox control on the bottom of your form, changing its
    name property to lstPets. See Figure 3-9.

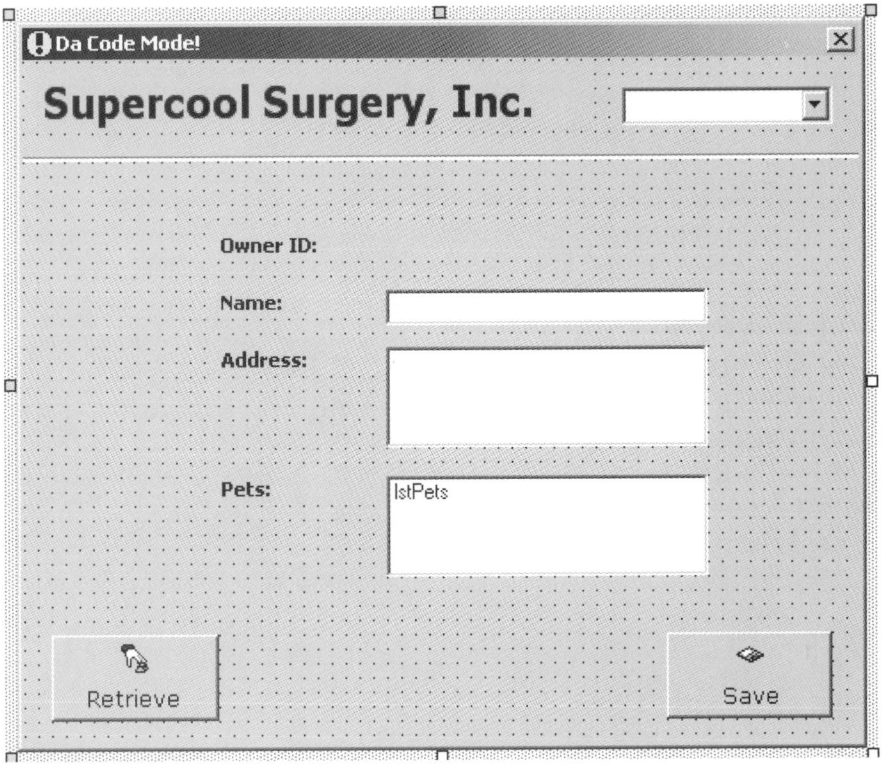

Figure 3-9. Adding our list box to hold pet details

Next, let's add ourselves a little code to actually use our relationship.

4. Add the following method to your form:

```
Public Sub FillPetDetails()

    Dim objOwner As DataRow, objPet As DataRow
    Dim strPetEntry As String

    ' Clear any existing pets
    lstPets.Items.Clear()
```

```
            ' Find the current Owner record
            objOwner = objDataSet.Tables("Owners").Rows.Find( _
                cboOwners.SelectedItem.ToString)


            ' Loop through each child record for this row, as per
            ' the Owners2Pets relationship. Then, add details of
            ' each child row to lstPets.
            For Each objPet In objOwner.GetChildRows("Owners2Pets")
                strPetEntry = objPet.Item("PetID") & ", " & _
                    objPet.Item("PetName") & ", " & objPet.Item("Type")
                lstPets.Items.Add(strPetEntry)
            Next


        End Sub
```

Here, we begin by clearing any pets currently in our list box. We then locate the record for the currently selected owner. Next up, we cycle through each child row of this parent record, using a For Each loop. With each cycle, details of the current child row are stored in objPet, which we then collect details from and add to our list box. And that's that!

But, of course, we still need to tell our program when it should run this code. Tsk, we programmers simply have to do everything, don't we?

5. Add the following to the very end of your btnRetrieve click code (underneath your FillOwnerDetails() call):

```
FillPetDetails()
```

6. Add the following at the bottom of your existing code, to respond to the SelectedIndexChanged event of cboOwners:

```
FillPetDetails()
```

Now, when the form first fills, it should display all pets for the current owner, and, with each change of our ComboBox, all the new details should appear. Want to try it out?

7. Press F5 to test your application. (Figure 3-10 shows my application.)

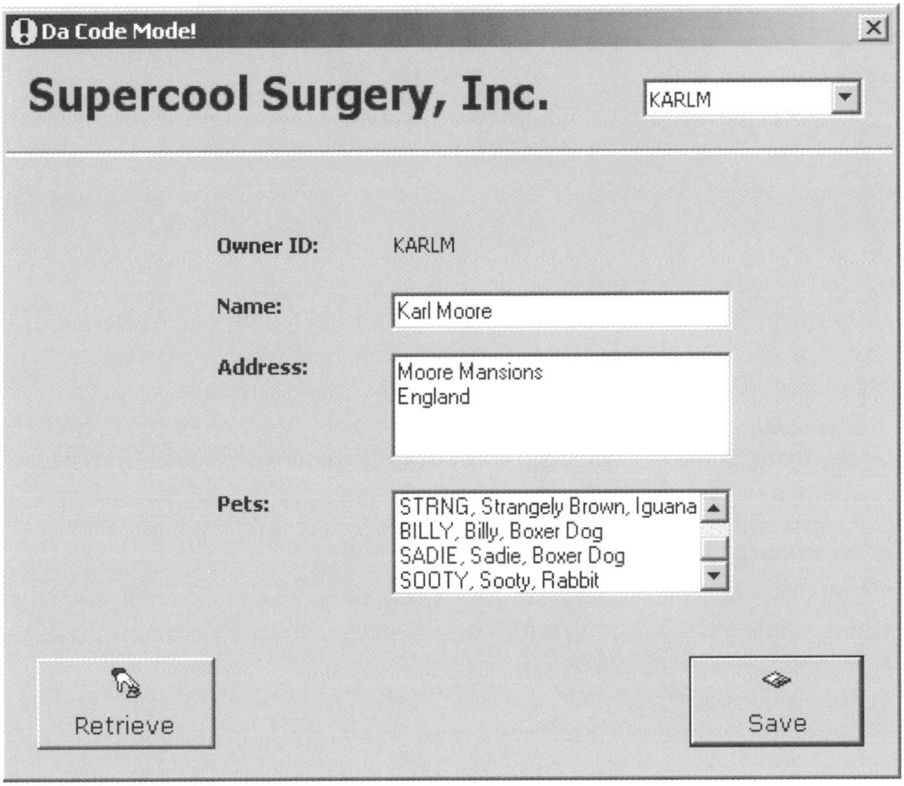

Figure 3-10. The result of our relationship code

Try clicking on your Retrieve button and browsing the owners. Does it all work as expected? What if you add an owner (as per the earlier exercise)? Presumably they have no existing pets? Try adding new pets to that owner using Microsoft Access. Do they immediately display in your application, or do you have to click on your Retrieve button once again?

8.   When finished testing, close your application.

Hurrah and hujjah! Once again, you've really excelled. You've implemented a supercool, amazingly fantastic relationship in code and lived to tell the tale. Well done!

Can you think where you could implement this sort of programmatic relationship in your own applications? What do you think would happen if you tried to add a pet containing an invalid OwnerID to your DataSet now? Also, do you have any ideas as to how you could push this sort of example even further? How do you think you could improve the user interface? Go on; take a few seconds out to think of the glitzy possibilities.

Oh, and you'll note that once again I've left a whopping great big functionality gap in our sample application. That's right: you can't add, remove, or edit any pet records here.

Why not try adding that now? Go on. Oh, go on. Go on, go on, go on, go on, *go on.*

CONCLUSION

Wahoo! Congratulations and mega-amazing respect, my friend!

In today's jam-packed session, we've really covered some turf. We started by learning to talk SQL, the preferred language of database wizards, plus figured out an Access cheat that allows us to easily generate SQL statements in seconds.

Moving on, we soon discovered how to access our database completely in code—a feat that will gain you high-ranking kudos in the nerd world, as well as giving you more power in the code window. Do you think you could make your data access code even simpler by putting it in methods and functions, behind modules in your application?

After our core data access code, we took our project even further by discovering how to add relationships to our DataSets. Suddenly, all that relationship jazz we learned in the last chapter seemed to make sense.

Erm, it did, right?

Next time, we'll be looking at moving on from Access into the grand world of SQL Server, and we'll really get down and dirty with that SQL language. There's still a lot, lot more to come. But trust me, it'll be an exciting ride.

In fact, I bet you haven't felt this excited since the last time you sneezed.

And, on that rather pleasant thought, this is your smiling host, Karl Moore, wishing each of you a very enjoyable evening—wherever you are in the world. Nighty night!

CHAPTER 2.3

- Most databases speak in Structured Query Language (SQL). You can write SQL statements to select records, insert records, update records, and delete records.

- Here are examples of Select, Insert, Update, and Delete statements:

```
SELECT * FROM customers

INSERT INTO customers (id, name, address)
    VALUES('123', 'Peter Ustinov', '21st St, France')

UPDATE customers
    SET name = 'Angela'
    WHERE id = '123'

DELETE FROM customers
    WHERE id = '123'
```

- When working with an Access database, the following is a generic code template for manipulating your data:

```
' General object declarations
Dim objConnection As New OleDb.OleDbConnection( _
    "Provider=Microsoft.Jet.OLEDB.4.0;Data Source=c:\mydb.mdb")
Dim objDataAdapter As New OleDb.OleDbDataAdapter( _
    "Select * from MyTable", objConnection)
Dim objCommandBuilder As New OleDb.OleDbCommandBuilder(objDataAdapter)
Dim objDataSet As New DataSet(), objRow As DataRow

' Fill your DataSet with schema information
objDataAdapter.FillSchema(objDataSet, SchemaType.Source, "MyTable")

' Fill your DataSet with the result of your SQL statement
objDataAdapter.Fill(objDataSet, "MyTable")

' Add a record
objRow = objDataSet.Tables("MyTable").NewRow
objRow.Item("ColumnName") = "Value"
objDataSet.Tables("MyTable").Rows.Add(objRow)
```

```
' Find and edit a row
objRow = objDataSet.Tables("MyTable").Rows.Find("PrimaryKeyValue")
objRow.Item("ColumnName") = "Value"

' Delete a row
objRow.Delete()

' Update the backend database
objDataAdapter.Update(objDataSet)
```

- You can create relationships in your databases. These can be replicated inside your DataSet with a few lines of code, making your program more reliable and intelligent. Here is a generic code template for creating a DataSet relationship:

```
objDataSet.Relations.Add("RelationshipName", _

objDataSet.Tables("ParentTableName").Columns("PrimaryKeyName"), _
          objDataSet.Tables("ChildTableName").Columns("ForeignKeyName")
```

- Once you have set up your relationship in code, you can use it to easily navigate through parent and child records. Here is an example code template for utilizing a relationship:

```
' Get access to current row
objParentRow = objDataSet.Tables("ParentTableName").Rows(0)

' Loop through each child record for this parent row
For Each objChildRow In objParentRow.GetChildRows("RelationshipName")
    MessageBox.Show(objChildRow.Item("AnyColumnName"))
Next
```

SQL Server, Web Applications, Transactions...Oh My!

"Data expands to fill the space available for storage."
—*Parkinson's Law of Data*

FANCY JOINING THE BIG BOYS? I sure hope so, because in this chapter we'll be learning how to do just that.

We'll be moving away from Microsoft Access, opting rather for the world of SQL Server. We'll learn how to create our own server database, and we'll figure out how we can manipulate data via commands in our code.

We'll also spend time looking at transactions, which is something that most programmers tend to run away from. Please, promise me you won't.

Today's session will be fun, fast, and full of funky code. Raring to go? Boot up, log on, and let's get started!

Joining the Big Boys

Whenever the great inventor Thomas Edison guided visitors around the displays of novel gadgets that filled his home, someone would always ask, "With everything here so modern and innovative, why do your visitors still have to push their way in through that old-fashioned turnstile?"

And Edison would chuckle with delight and say, "Because, my friend, every single soul who forces his way through that old turnstile pumps three gallons of water up from my well and into my water tank!"

True innovation. Edison was no longer playing with his LEGO kit; he'd moved on, he'd joined the big names in his industry, he'd made the big time. And that's exactly what I'll be showing you today.

No, not how to build a well-pumping turnstile; rather, I'll be demonstrating how we can move from playing with trusty Access on to the eternally reliable world of SQL Server, the database of choice for professional Microsoft developer wizards with good looks.

So, just what is SQL Server? Well, it's a database system. We've already seen one such database system: the Jet MDB files that Access creates. Other types are available, too, such as Oracle and FoxPro databases. Even an Excel file can be manipulated as a database.

However, SQL Server is one of the most powerful, and the .NET Framework includes built-in data objects that are optimized specifically for this system. We'll be looking at some of those today.

How is this SQL Server different from Access? For a start, it isn't just a file. SQL Server is a database product that actually runs "live" on a computer, perhaps somewhere on your network or over the Internet, just waiting to accept new data or serve requests. It's also faster and more efficient than Access, plus maintains a log of all changes so you can even "rollback" to a particular date and time should you need to do so.

In fact, SQL Server is typically seen as the crème de la crème of database systems. It's one of those skills you can demand big bucks for. And we'll be figuring out how to use it today.

Now, before we can get started, you actually need to get SQL Server 2000 up and running. Either slap in the installation CD or get your network administrator to give you the address of a development server. Go on, tell him to hurry up. Slap him if required. Don't worry; just blame me.

However, it's just possible that a few of you readers may be getting slightly concerned at this point because I'm talking about installing SQL Server, and, unless you've got a wallet the size of Wichita, you might not actually have this package available.

Not to worry. Microsoft thought about that, and, to help the terminally short-of-cash, it bundled something called *MSDE* with the .NET Framework. What's MSDE? Well, it stands for the *Microsoft Desktop Engine*, and it's essentially a cut-down version of SQL Server that limits the number of simultaneous requests. It also ships without any of the extra graphical tools, such as the Enterprise Manager.

Thankfully, we'll be doing all of our database work from within Visual Studio .NET anyway, so you won't lose out in the slightest. Just ensure that, before continuing, you install one of the following:

- SQL Server 2000: Insert the installation CD or use an existing development server.

- MSDE: Run the InstMSDE.exe file from your Program Files\Microsoft Visual Studio .NET\FrameworkSDK\Samples\Setup\MSDE folder.

> **TOP TIP** *Our favorite software giant is unfortunately experiencing major difficulties in making up its mind as to exactly what* MSDE *stands for. Sometimes it's referred to as the* Microsoft Desktop Engine, *whereas other references talk about it as the* Microsoft Data Engine. *The former seems most prominent in .NET documentation, but I think it really depends on the weather. Just to be safe, stick with* MSDE. *Sounds cooler, too.*

Creating a Server Database

So, you've installed SQL Server and want to get right to creating your own database? The time has come, the Walrus said.

1. Launch Visual Studio .NET; however, don't create a new project.

2. Select View ➤ Server Explorer.

We can use the Server Explorer to create our own databases, live on our SQL Server machine.

3. If you cannot see the machine containing SQL Server listed under Servers in the Server Explorer, click on the Connect to Server button and specify the machine details.

4. Expand your database server, and open the SQL Servers entry.

5. You'll be looking at all the instances of SQL Server on this machine. (See Figure 4-1.) Double-click to expand the instance you want to use (probably the one bearing the server name).

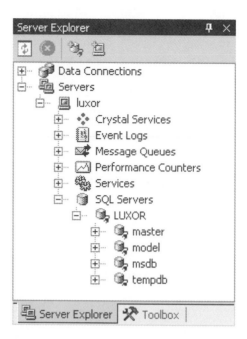

Figure 4-1. Exploring SQL Server via the Server Explorer

You should be looking at a list of the existing databases on this instance of SQL Server. You'll probably see Master, which holds details about your database itself, plus maybe Pubs and Northwind (remember that?), both of which you can explore. Erm, later—for now:

6. Right-click on your SQL Server instance (in my case, LUXOR under the SQL Servers entry).

7. Select New Database from the pop-up menu.

8. Enter a new database name of KeepFit, then click on OK. (See Figure 4-2.)

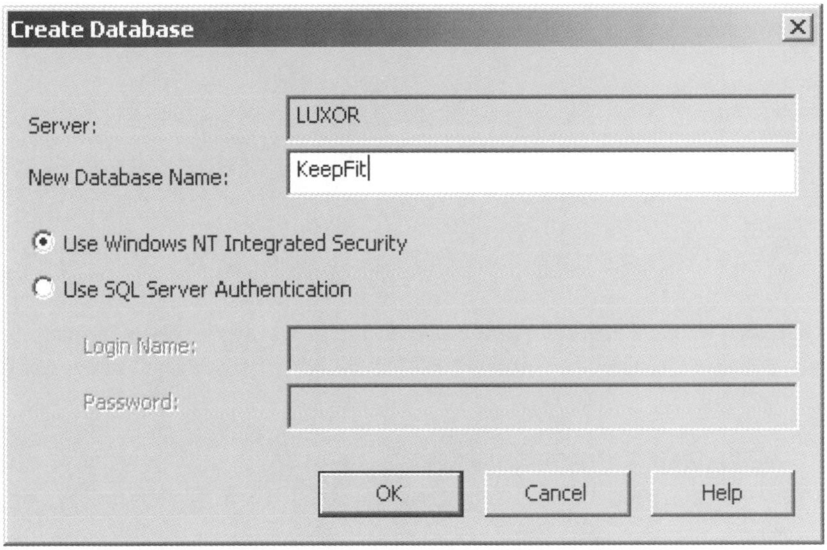

Figure 4-2. Creating a new SQL Server database

You know, I've never quite understood all this health stuff. On my last trip to the gym, the attendant showed me around the club store: half of the store was products for weight loss, and the other half was products for weight gain. Go figure.

But, regardless, it's for a gym just like my own that you'll be creating this groovy little database. So pack that Lucozade and prepare those dumbbells as we think about our new system.

Now, what sort of tables should we have? Hmm, I think just two for now: one to hold details about our members, the other to store information about each of their transactions (perhaps a log of their purchases at the club store, their gym visits, or which premium classes they attended). We'll call that one Sales. It's probably a good idea to add a relationship in there, too—for good taste, you know.

Don't forget that, although some databases may get a little more complex than our example here, they're never any more difficult. Personally, I've worked on the National DNA Database over here in the United Kingdom, and, trust me, that beast has more tables and relationships than *Ikea* and *Sex in the City* combined. But it's not actually more difficult; there's just more of it.

Designing the Tables

Okay, let's sort out those tables.

1. Expand the Server Explorer so you can see the Tables entry, underneath your KeepFit database.

2. Right-click the Tables entry and select New Table.

This is where we enter details about our table, just as we would in Access. (See Figure 4-3.) Sure, we have a couple of extra options, but nothing to worry about.

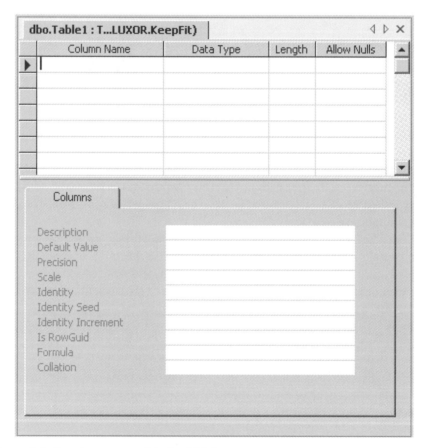

Figure 4-3. Creating a new table for SQL Server

Let's create that Members table first.

3. In the first Column Name box, enter "MemberID".

This field—or column—will store the actual Member ID. We're going to make this an automatically incrementing number.

4. In the Data Type drop-down box, change the data type to "int".

Whoa! We have a few more data types here than with our Access friend. They're not too scary though: the most important are int (holds an integer) and varchar (holds a string of text), alongside datetime, decimal, smallmoney, timestamp, and uniqueidentifier. You can find a full list of the various types and what they can hold in Appendix F.

5. Uncheck the Allow Nulls box.

In database terms, a null indicates that the value hasn't been specified. Because we don't want "nothing" to be put in as the MemberID, we don't allow it by unchecking this option.

6. In the options at the bottom of your screen, change the Identity property to Yes.

The Identity property is what makes this an automatically incrementing field. Take a peek at the Identity Seed and Identity Increment properties that have now become available. The next time you add a row to this table, SQL Server will automatically place a value into this field, starting with Identity Seed and going up by whatever the value of Identity Increment is.

In other words, we've just created an automatically incrementing membership number!

7. Right-click on your MemberID column and select Set Primary Key.

Remember doing that in Access? Here, we're just telling SQL Server that this is the one field that uniquely identifies each record: no two will be the same. We'll be using this field when creating a relationship with our other table later.

8. Add the following columns to your table, also. (See Figure 4-4.)

    •   Name: varchar; Allow Nulls: False

    •   Address: varchar; Length: 100; Allow Nulls: False

    •   TelNo: varchar; Length: 15; Allow Nulls: False; Default Value:
        Not Available

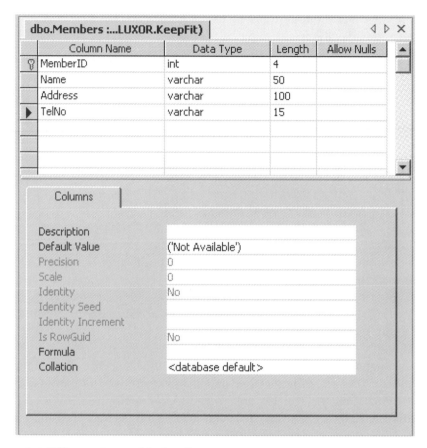

Figure 4-4. Filling out our table details

Understand this? We're using a couple of unexplained features here, but I'm sure you can determine their use yourself. If not, you'll see them in action later.

9. From the menu, select File ➤ Close.

10. Save the changes, calling the table "Members".

Next let's create our Sales table. This will keep a log of what members have paid for.

11. Create a new Sales table, with the following columns (see Figure 4-5):

- SaleID: int; Allow Nulls: False; Identity: Yes; Primary Key

- MemberID: int; Allow Nulls: False (this is our foreign key)

- Description: varchar; Allow Nulls: False

- Charge: smallmoney; Allow Nulls: False

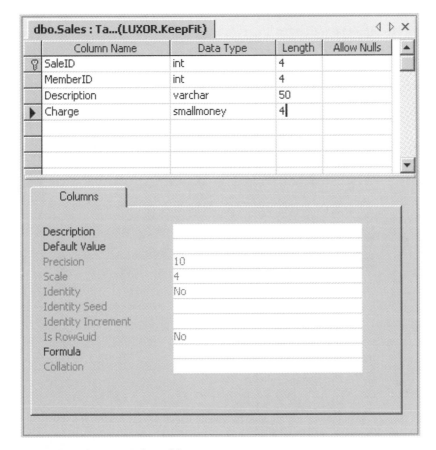

Figure 4-5. Creating our Sales table

Adding Relationships

Everything understandable so far? Next, let's set up our relationships. In Access, you'd use the Relationships window to do this. With SQL Server, you use a database diagram. The only real difference is the name and about a thousand dollars.

1. In the Server Explorer, right-click on the Database Diagrams entry under your KeepFit database and select New Diagram.

2. Using the pop-up window, add both of your tables to the diagram and click on Close.

Next, we're going to actually create the link between our two tables.

3. Drag the MemberID primary key from our Members table and drop it on the MemberID foreign key in our Sales table.

4. In the Create Relationship dialog box, click the checkboxes so they look similar to Figure 4-6. Click on OK when satisfied with the relationship.

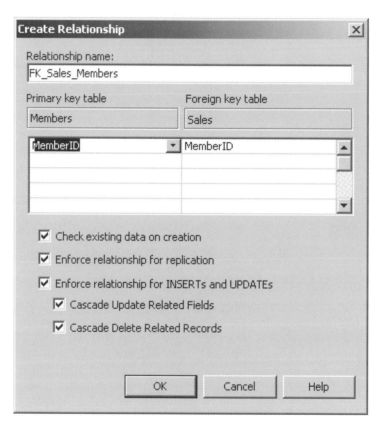

Figure 4-6. Defining the relationship between our Members and Sales tables

TOP TIP *Confused by your diagram? Does your relationship not exactly touch both MemberID fields? Don't worry. You view the relationships down to only the table level, and not actual field-to-field links. If you want it to look all smart, however, try rearranging manually with a little nifty mouse work, then print it off and impress the boss with your new "took-five-hours-to-design-this" data schema. Time for another golfing lunch, I feel.*

5. When finished, select File ➢ Close from the menu.

6. Save your database diagram as "KeepFitDiagram". (See Figure 4-7.)

7. Click on Yes to any warnings about saving tables.

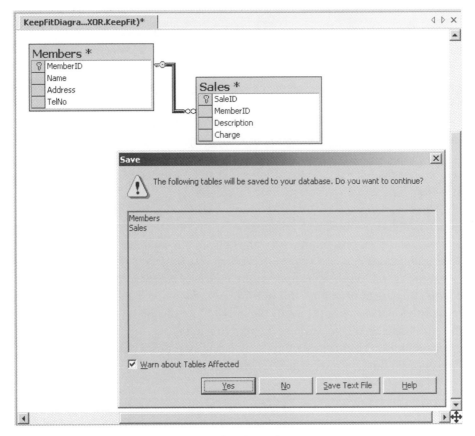

Figure 4-7. Designing and saving our database diagram

And that's it! You've just created your very own SQL Server database, capable of holding zillions of records, logging thousands of transactions, running live over your network or the Internet, and providing your own business with a stable, secure database system. All in under ten minutes. Tsk, is that value for money or what?

No, no, don't say *what*. Publisher will kill me.

Next up, try opening your Members table by double-clicking on it in the Server Explorer. Go on, add a few members. Notice what happens to the MemberID field? Also, what if you don't enter a telephone number? And can you add a row if you don't specify an address? Why is that?

Also, try entering a few sales entries too (perhaps products purchased from the store or pricey indoor tennis sessions). You have to enter a valid MemberID here. What happens if you don't?

Have a good play around. Enter at least a half-dozen new records. (We'll need them later.) And, when you're ready, let's move on.

Creating a Transactional Database-Powered Web Application

I have to admit, somewhere inside me is a real geek just begging to be set free.

How do I know? Well, I just love technical-sounding words. You know, like *OOP-based integrated technical solution*, or *distributed wireless automation servers*, or *transactional database-powered Web application*.

Each sounds jolly complicated, but, in reality, they're all about as difficult as scratching your left ear. Admittedly, this isn't an easy task for some—Van Gogh, say—but, for the main, it's pretty much a breeze.

However, I digress. The point I wanted to make was that creating a transactional database-powered Web application isn't really all that difficult. However, let's start at the very beginning: what the hell *is* a transactional database-powered Web application?

Well, it's basically a Web application that uses a database. Oh, and the application also uses transactions, one of those professional database features that most developers leave to the nerdy big knobs. But, oh, not us—we'll be joining the elitist high brow by covering even this area today.

Fancy kicking off? Let's start creating our transactional database-powered Web application! Now, everyone say, "Whooooooo!"

Okay, maybe later.

Designing Our Web Page

Let's kick this practical off by designing the front page of our Web application.

1. Create a new ASP.NET Web application in VB .NET, changing its location to `http://localhost/keepfit`.

2. Using the Solution Explorer, rename WebForm1.aspx to "default.aspx".

3. Change the Title property of default.aspx to "Welcome to Keep Fit Online!"

> **TOP TIP**   *Default.aspx is one of the first default files that your Web server looks to display when someone accesses your location, your virtual directory. This means that, instead of typing in something like* `http://localhost/keepfit/WebForm1.aspx`, *your user will now only have to type* `http://localhost/keepfit` *and default.aspx will be displayed automatically.*

4. Decorate your Web form in a manner similar to Figure 4-8, making sure that you add the following controls:

   • *Hyperlink*—ID: lnkNewMember; Text: "Add New Member"; NavigateURL: newmember.aspx

   • *Hyperlink*—ID: lnkNewSale; Text: "Add New Sale"; NavigateURL: newsale.aspx

   • *TextBox*—ID: txtFind; Text: "(All)"

   • *Button*—ID: btnFind; Text: "Display Member:"

   • *DataGrid*—ID: grdMembers; AutoFormat: Colorful 1

   • *Label*—ID: lblInfo; Text: "Further Info Will Appear Here"

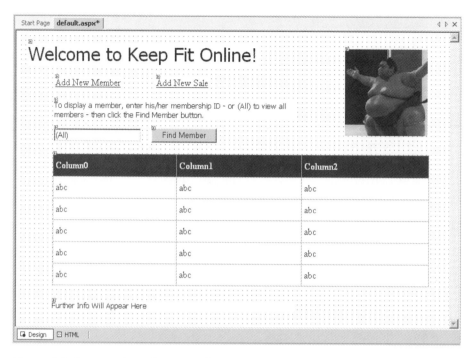

Figure 4-8. Our user interface, sorted

Writing the Code

So, what exactly will this page do? Well, it'll basically just provide details about our members. The user will be able to click our Display Member button, and, if they've entered a member number into txtFind, that particular member should be displayed. However, if they've left the default (All) in the text box, we want all members to be shown in our DataGrid.

Fancy coding that now?

1. Add the following code behind the click event of btnFind:

```
' Setup our core objects, mainly for use with our database
Dim objConnection As New SqlClient.SqlConnection _
    ("server=.;database=KeepFit;trusted_connection=true")
Dim objCommand As New SqlClient.SqlCommand _
    ("Select * from Members", objConnection)
Dim objReader As SqlClient.SqlDataReader
```

```
' Check whether the user wants to search for a particular member -
' if so, change the .CommandText SQL string
If txtFind.Text <> "(All)" Then
    objCommand.CommandText = "Select * from Members where MemberID='" & _
        txtFind.Text & "'"
End If


' Open our database connection
objConnection.Open()


' Get the results back into our DataReader object
objReader = objCommand.ExecuteReader


' Bind our DataGrid to our DataReader object
grdMembers.DataSource = objReader
grdMembers.DataBind()


' Tell the user how many records our DataGrid is displaying
lblInfo.Text = "Displaying " & grdMembers.Items.Count & " record(s)"


' Close objects
objReader.Close()
objConnection.Close()
```

Okay, so you're scratching your head. That's understandable. Lice probably. No, seriously, this is weird code. Let's explain it line by line.

```
Dim objConnection As New SqlClient.SqlConnection _
    ("server=.;database=KeepFit;trusted_connection=true")
```

Here, we're setting up the object to gain us a connection to our SQL Server database. Remember in the last chapter we used the OleDb.OleDbConnection object for this? The OleDb objects handles most databases; however, the .NET Framework also bundles with an almost identical set of objects under the SqlClient namespace that are designed to work specifically with SQL Server. These objects offer a whole bunch of performance features, such as connection pooling, which help save system resources.

So here we're just setting up our connection object, passing in a connection string as an argument.

> **TOP TIP** *You might be wondering why we use a period for the server location in our connection string. Well, this simply tells the object to look for the instance of SQL Server on your local machine. You can change this to your own machine name or any network or Internet address. For more help on connection strings, highlight the SqlConnection class name and press the F1 key. You'll also get details on how to specify a username and password to access your database, if required. Alternatively, check out the third question in the FAQ to Chapter 2.5.*

In the next bit of code, we're setting up a couple of extra objects.

```
Dim objCommand As New SqlClient.SqlCommand _
    ("Select * from Members", objConnection)
Dim objReader As SqlClient.SqlDataReader
```

First is SqlCommand, which is just that: an SQL command. We're passing it our command text, a Select statement, and our connection object as parameters.

Next, we're declaring a DataReader object, which is like a cut-down version of the DataSet.

> **TOP TIP** *All of the objects we're working with here are also available under the OleDb namespace, although with slightly altered names. Also, it's worth remembering that you can work with the DataSet using objects in both the OleDb and SqlClient namespaces. The only real difference between your OleDb and SqlClient code should be the slightly altered connection string and a prefix change from OleDb.OleDb to SqlClient.Sql.*

Over the next few lines of code, we're checking whether our TextBox control contains the text "(All)".

```
If txtFind.Text <> "(All)" Then
    objCommand.CommandText = "Select * from Members where MemberID='" & _
        txtFind.Text & "'"
End If
```

If it doesn't, the user has presumably entered a MemberID to search for, in which case we change the CommandText property of our Command object.

```
objConnection.Open()
objReader = objCommand.ExecuteReader
```

Here, we're opening our database connection, then running the ExecuteReader function of our Command object. This returns data from our Select command straight into our DataReader object.

```
grdMembers.DataSource = objReader
grdMembers.DataBind()
lblInfo.Text = "Displaying " & grdMembers.Items.Count & " record(s)"
```

You've seen code like this before. We're just binding to our DataGrid and displaying a count in our Label control.

```
objReader.Close()
objConnection.Close()
```

Finally, we close our DataReader object and the database connection. Does everything make sense so far? Do you understand what this part of your application is supposed to do?

2. Press F5 to test your application. (See Figure 4-9.)

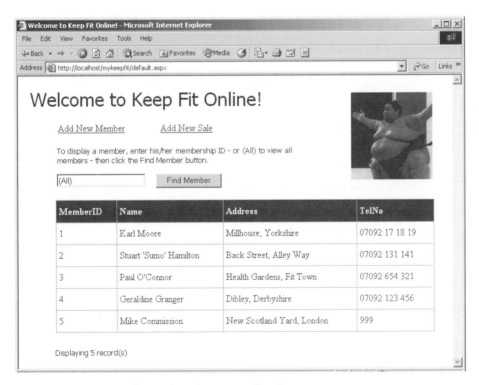

Figure 4-9. Viewing all members in our application

Try clicking on the Find Member button without specifying a specific MemberID. Do you get all the members displayed in your colorful DataGrid? Notice your Information label? Also, what if you specify a valid MemberID then click on the Find Member button again? And how about entering an invalid MemberID?

Close your browser when you're finished testing. Are you satisfied? Did it all work as you expected? Congratulations! As a reward, you may take a short holiday.

Enjoy it? Let's move on.

But Why the Two Systems?

Wondering why we need the Command and DataReader objects, when we could just use the DataAdapter and a DataSet?

Never fear, there's a perfectly rational explanation. Unfortunately, the DataAdapter and DataSet objects are relatively expensive. No, not in the champagne-caviar way; rather, they carry a fairly large memory overhead due to all the advanced features they support (such as multiple tables, internal relationships, XML integration, search functions, and so on).

The Command object, however, is as close as you can get to your actual database, and is exceptionally lightweight, which is particularly good for use in high-demand Web applications.

That's why we have the two: one is more feature rich but with a larger memory impact, whereas the other is simple and lightweight (great for straightforward commands). It's always a little confusing at first though, particularly for me. But, then again, I'm about as bright as a total solar eclipse.

Now, so far we've only done a simple Select using the no-messing Command object, alongside a little binding with the DataReader. However, you can also execute Update, Delete, or Insert statements with the command in almost the same way.

And we'll see just how to do this in the next section.

And Now, Adding Data!

Hmm, the thing is, your application can only display data at the moment. And, although it's nice and funky-looking and could probably earn you a couple of '70s revival awards, it's not awfully functional.

What you need is the ability to add data. That's why we added those two links to your default.aspx page: Add New Member and Add New Sale. Hey, you knew there would be a reason, right?

First off, we're going to deal with adding a new sale. This will take a MemberID and add a new record to the Sales table. Simple dimple. After that, we'll work on adding a new member. This is the transactional bit, wherein we add a record to both our Members and Sales tables at the same time.

But I'm jumping ahead of myself. First things first: let's add a new sale.

1. Add a new Web Form to your application (Project Add Web Form), called "newsale.aspx".

If you remember, our New Sale link navigates to this page. Okay, let's slap together the user interface.

2. Decorate your Web form in a manner similar to that shown in Figure 4-10, ensuring you add the following controls:

    *   *TextBox*—Name: "txtMemberID"

    *   *TextBox*—Name: "txtDescription"

    *   *TextBox*—Name: "txtCharge"

    *   *Button*—Name: "btnSaveSale"; Text: "Record this Sale"

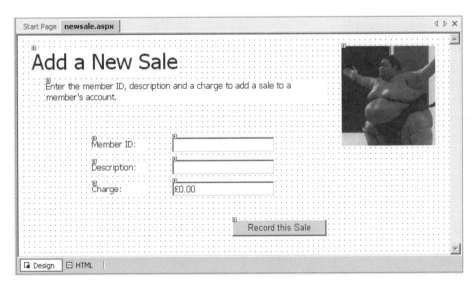

Figure 4-10. Designing our Web page (healthy man snapshot optional)

And now, it's time to add the code.

3. Add the following code to respond to the click event of btnSaveSale:

```
' Setup the connection
Dim objConnection As New SqlClient.SqlConnection _
    ("server=.;database=KeepFit;trusted_connection=true")
' Create the final SQL string to execute -
' remembering that only text strings are
' enclosed in 'apostrophes'
Dim strSQL As String
strSQL = "INSERT INTO sales(memberid, description, charge) " & _
    "VALUES('" & txtMemberID.Text & "', '" & _
    txtDescription.Text & "', " & txtCharge.Text & ")"
' Create our Command object
Dim objCommand As New SqlClient.SqlCommand(strSQL, objConnection)
' Open the Connection, execute the command, close the connection
objConnection.Open()
objCommand.ExecuteNonQuery()
objConnection.Close()
' Take user back to first page
Response.Redirect("default.aspx")
```

Yes, it looks scary at first glance, but it's actually much simpler than the last chunk we stumbled across.

We start off by declaring our regular Connection object. Then we generate an Insert SQL statement, based around information entered by our user. (You can look up examples of Insert statements in either the SQL Server Books Online help, or buried inside the VB .NET index.) Next, we simply create our Command object and execute the command against our database.

This should add a sales record to our database. But does it?

4. Press F5 to test your application.

You should be taken straight to your default.aspx page. Click on the link to add a new sale.

Enter a valid MemberID in the first text box, a description in the second, and a charge in the third, then click on your Record this Sale button. (Your screen should look something like Figure 4-11.) Are you taken back to your main page? Notice how fast that occurred? What if you close your browser and open your Sales database via the Server Explorer? Can you see your new entry?

Figure 4-11. Logging a new sale in our application

5.   When finished testing, close your browser.

In a couple of minutes, we're going to get even more complicated and add multiple records to our database, all under a "transaction." But, before that, let's think about how we could improve our application right now.

The first thing that strikes me here is that our system requires staff with more memory than Tony Buzan and Big Blue combined. They'd either have to remember every single MemberID for each time they wanted to add a sale, or they'd be constantly viewing all the members, finding the ID they wanted to add a sale for, then opening the Add Sales page and going from there. How incredibly boring.

How about adding a drop-down box here that displays a list of MemberID values alongside their names? In code, you'd simply need to grab that MemberID from the drop-down list and you're rocking. To get started, all you'd need to do is execute a simple Select statement into a DataReader, then write a mini loop to add the values. (See this chapter's Review Sheet for how you might do this). You might even want to take advantage of the Text and Value properties of individual ListItem objects to help you make this even more user friendly.

Also, what would happen if you entered a *word* in the Charge box? And how about if you specified an invalid MemberID or entered an apostrophe in any of our fields, thereby messing up our SQL statement? What then?

Well, we can add checks for all these potential problems—using the IsNumeric() function to see whether something is a number, for example. However, just in case you miss anything, I'd suggest you implement a little error-handling code to deal with any "issues" that may crop up. (A Try-Catch-Finally routine is probably your best bet.)

> **TOP TIP** *Extra apostrophes in your SQL statements can cause real problems. One solution is to use the* Replace() *function to swap all single apostrophes for double apostrophes. These are allowed and interpreted by the database as singles. An alternative is to use parameters, which also help simplify your code. For more information on both of these techniques, check out the FAQ in Chapter 2.5.*

Go and have a stab at these desired additions right now. And don't worry if you stumble across problems along the way. Remember, they're not problems, they're opportunities. Let's just hope none of them are insurmountable opportunities.

Seriously though, you gain three times as much knowledge from your mistakes than you do from a trouble-free ride. So, when that error message fills your screen, smile and be merry.

When you're ready, let's move on. But at least spend ten minutes addressing these little problems first. And if you don't, well—uhm, well, I might just come round there and—erm, oh boy. *Pretty please?*

And for My Next Trick...Transactions!

Start talking about transactions in the nerd world and half the crowd will try to change the subject, worried that you'll start questioning their knowledge. The other half suddenly needs to use the restroom.

Only the few real BO-branding database wizards will stop and talk joyously on the subject. Why? It's one of those crème-de-la-crème features that most employers would love you to know about, but the majority of developers simply steer clear in fear.

But the fear isn't warranted: using transactions in the database world is about as difficult as blowing your nose. That's why I've decided we should add them to our application, right here, right now.

So, just what is a transaction? Well, you've probably heard that term bandied about in the banking world. A typical financial transaction might involve taking some dough out of one account and putting it into another.

Now imagine that you're running the database system for that bank. I walk into one of your branches and ask to transfer all the laundered money in my account across to my associate up in bonny Scotland.

Your computer system then goes and removes all the money from *my* account, ready to transfer over to my boss, Mr. McDodgy. Then—can you believe it—the machines crash. The network has fallen over due to too many simultaneous Doom sessions.

Therefore, I wait around impatiently for the reboot. And, when the machines come back on, I'm told that *my* account now stands at £0.00 and not a penny was transferred to Mr. McDodgy.

Tsk. All that stealing—and for nothing. That's technology for you.

But in a real *transaction*, you wouldn't be able to do this. Both actions would have to be completed—money deducted from my account and added to the McDodgy account—for the transaction to be a success. If this didn't occur, the transaction would cancel itself. It would "rollback."

So, a transaction is a set of instructions that must be completed as a whole, or not at all.

> **TOP TIP** *As you can see, a transaction is a pretty simple concept to understand. Still, if you want to join the nerdy types mentioned at the beginning of this tutorial, search about the Internet for the ACID transaction theory. This provides you with the official lowdown on what all transactions should have: atomicity, consistency, isolation, and durability. Oh, the joy.*

Let's demonstrate transactions in our own application now.

1. Add a new Web form to your application and name it "newmember.aspx".

2. Decorate your Web form in a manner similar to Figure 4-12, adding the following controls:

   - *TextBox*—Name: "txtName"

   - *TextBox*—Name: "txtAddress"; Rows: 4

   - *TextBox*—Name: "txtTelNo"

   - *Button*—Name: "btnAddMember"; Text: "Add Member"

Figure 4-12. Designing our New Member page

Here, we're going to allow the user to add a new member. As we add this person to the Members table, we also want to log a £25 joining fee against the Sales table. This is our transaction. If we can't add the member or can't add the joining fee, we don't add anything. These are our instructions that must be completed as a whole or not at all.

Now, to start a transaction, you simply run the `.BeginTransaction` function of our Connection object. This returns an SqlTransaction object. You then run your individual commands, telling the Command object it's in a transaction. At the end, you can `.Commit` the transaction, permanently saving any database changes you've made. Alternatively, you can `.Rollback`, say, if an error occurred, undoing any changes since the start of the transaction.

Let's add our code to do all this now.

3. Add the following code to respond to the click event of btnAddMember:

```
' Setup the database objects
Dim objConnection As New SqlClient.SqlConnection _
    ("server=.;database=KeepFit;trusted_connection=true")
```

```vb
Dim objCommand As New SqlClient.SqlCommand("", objConnection)
Dim objTransaction As SqlClient.SqlTransaction, strSQL As String

Try

    ' Open connection and begin transaction
    objConnection.Open()
    objTransaction = objConnection.BeginTransaction

    ' Make the Command object aware it's in this transaction
    objCommand.Transaction = objTransaction

    ' Generate SQL statement and execute to
    ' add a new Member to our Members table
    strSQL = "INSERT INTO members(name, address, telno) " & _
        "VALUES('" & txtName.Text & "', '" & txtAddress.Text & _
        "', '" & txtTelNo.Text & "')"
    objCommand.CommandText = strSQL
    objCommand.ExecuteNonQuery()

    ' Retrieve the Member ID for our new member, the automatically
    ' generated identity value (See Top Tip for explanation of this)
    Dim intAutoNumber As Integer
    strSQL = "SELECT @@Identity"
    objCommand.CommandText = strSQL
    intAutoNumber = objCommand.ExecuteScalar

    ' Add an initial joining fee to the Sales table
    strSQL = "INSERT INTO sales(memberid, description, charge) " & _
        "VALUES(" & intAutoNumber & ", 'Joining Fee', 25.00)"
    objCommand.CommandText = strSQL
    objCommand.ExecuteNonQuery()

    ' Commit successful transaction, close connection
    objTransaction.Commit()
    objConnection.Close()

    ' Move back to main page
    Response.Redirect("default.aspx")
```

```
        Catch
            btnAddMember.Text = "Cannot Add Member!"
            objTransaction.Rollback()
            objConnection.Close()

        End Try
```

> **TOP TIP** *In our code here, we're retrieving the automatically generated primary key value for our member by running the special SQL Server statement "Select @@Identity". This returns one single field containing the last identity value added under this connection: in other words, our new member ID. We then retrieve this using the* `.ExecuteScalar` *function, which very simply returns the first field of the first row returned by the statement.*

Wow! Big code momma! You've seen pretty much all of this already. But let's briefly explain away some of the important transactional bits.

```
Dim objTransaction As SqlClient.SqlTransaction
```

This is where we declare our transaction object. As soon as we begin our transaction, we can use this object to commit or rollback our changes.

```
objTransaction = objConnection.BeginTransaction
```

Here, we're initializing our transaction object using the `.BeginTransaction` function, telling the connection that the transaction is beginning.

```
objCommand.Transaction = objTransaction
```

The Command object needs to know exactly which transaction it's taking part in. So here, we're setting its Transaction property to our actual Transaction object.

```
objTransaction.Commit()
```

This line actually runs after everything else. If the code reaches this stage, no errors have occurred, so we can happily commit the transaction, saving all our changes.

```
objTransaction.Rollback()
```

However if problems do crop up, our error-handling code steps in and performs a rollback, automagically undoing all the data alterations we made.

Understand everything so far? Let's give our code a quick whirl.

4. Press the F5 key to test your application.

On the default.aspx screen, click on your Add New Member button. Type in a name, address, and telephone number, and then click on the Add Member button. What happens? Do you get sent back to the main page? If so, check whether a record has been added to both your Members and Sales tables. Has it worked?

Also, what if an error occurs between adding the Members record and adding the Sales record? Try adding the following chunk of code to generate an exception (error) somewhere in the middle of your routine:

```
Throw New Exception("Error! Beep! Buzz!")
```

This will raise an exception, meaning your error-handling code will kick in and perform a rollback. Try running your code with this modification and seeing what happens. Does just *one* record ever add itself to your database, without the other?

5. When finished testing, close your browser and open the champagne.

CONCLUSION

Yeah, yeah, wave your hands in the air like you just don't care.

A big *well done* on battling through to the end of Chapter 2.4! It's been a long day, and I think you deserve a rest. Before that, however, let's quickly review what we've covered over the past couple of hours.

We started our session with a look at SQL Server and how it differs from Access. After that, we moved on to create our own database in this system. Next up, we figured out how to create a light-impact Web application that can read from and write to our database using Command objects. And, to add a little spice, we even made it transactional. What fun!

If you're looking for a little homework, try improving our KeepFit Web application and database system. I hear the users now want to be able to view member account totals live on the system. How could you do that? Maybe add up the totals in code, or generate a "Sum query" SQL statement using the Access designer? And what about updating member details, too?

Go have a play around! And on that note, I'll leave you to it.

My eyes are feeling heavy, and that means its time to part. So from me, Karl Moore, the warmest wishes for a very pleasant evening. Ta ta!

CHAPTER 2.4

SQL SERVER, WEB APPLICATIONS, TRANSACTIONS, ...OH MY REVIEW SHEET

- SQL Server is a robust, scalable database system. It is more powerful than Microsoft Access and runs live on a Windows machine, awaiting client commands. MSDE (Microsoft Desktop Engine) is a cut-down version of SQL Server.

- You can create your own SQL Server database, design tables, and input data using the Server Explorer in Visual Studio .NET. Simply expand your server (use the Connect to Server toolbar button if not visible), and then open the SQL Servers entry to get started.

- Of all the data types available when creating tables in SQL Server, the most common are int (integer), varchar (string of text), smallmoney, uniqueidentifier (to store a globally unique identifier (GUID)), datetime, decimal, and timestamp.

- You can plot out your relationships in SQL Server by dragging and dropping key fields in a database diagram. This is the equivalent of the Relationships window in Microsoft Access.

- The .NET Framework includes objects in its System.Data.OleDb namespace for accessing general databases. It also bundles with a bunch of almost identical objects, fine-tuned for accessing SQL Server. These can be found in the System.Data.SqlClient namespace.

- The Command object enables you to get as close to your database as you can, executing SQL statements straight against the connection. Here is an example of executing an Insert statement using a Command object, using the SQL Server classes.

```
Dim MyConnection As New SqlClient.SqlConnection _
    ("server=.;database=KeepFit;trusted_connection=true")

Dim MyCommand As New SqlClient.SqlCommand( _
    "INSERT INTO mytable(val1, val2) VALUES('Mr', 'James')", MyConnection)

MyConnection.Open()
MyCommand.ExecuteNonQuery()
MyConnection.Close()
```

- The DataReader object acts as a mini DataSet, allowing you to view the results of Select statements returned from the Command object. Here is an example of this, using the SQL Server classes.

```
Dim MyCommand As New SqlClient.SqlCommand("SELECT * FROM MyTable", _
    MyConnection)
Dim MyReader As SqlClient.SqlDataReader

MyReader.Open()
MyReader = MyCommand.ExecuteReader

Do While MyReader.Read = True
    MessageBox.Show(MyReader.Item("MyColumnName"))
Loop

MyReader.Close()
MyConnection.Close()
```

- You can discover the last identity value you inserted under SQL Server by running the Select @@Identity statement. This returns one single field containing the identity value last inserted during the connection.

- The .ExecuteScalar function of a Command object returns the value of the first field in the first row returned by your statement. When you need to retrieve only this single value, this function replaces the complexity of the DataReader.

- A *transaction* refers to a bunch of statements that must be completed as a whole or not at all. These are used in the database world to ensure the integrity of data. Here is a generic template for using transactions, using the SQL Server classes.

```
Dim MyTransaction As SqlClient.SqlTransaction
MyTransaction = MyConnection.BeginTransaction

Try
    ' Perform Command processing here, remembering
    ' to set the Transaction property of any Command
    ' object equal to the MyTransaction object
    MyTransaction.Commit()
Catch
    ' Errors occured, so rollback any changes made
    MyTransaction.Rollback()
End Try
```

Designing Reports and Going from Here

"I have no data yet. It is a capital mistake to theorize before one has data. Insensibly one begins to twist facts to suit theories instead of theories to suit facts"—Sherlock Holmes, the detective creation of Sir Arthur Conan Doyle

TWEED JACKET? CHECK. Coke-bottle glasses? Check. Roll-on BO? Check. Stick-on beard with added soup? Check.

Looks like we've got everything prepared for when you graduate from Doing Databases later today. And, if you don't have any of the above, you can always borrow mine. In fact, I think my beard hosts a couple of mice too, though I've not seen Tom and Andrea since 1973.

Anyway, nonsense and mice aside, what will we be learning in this fifth and final chapter? Well, we'll start by discovering how to deliver reports to the masses using a nifty little application bundled with Visual Studio. NET. And, as with every last chapter of a tutorial, we'll also review those frequently asked questions, plus figure out how you can take your database knowledge even further.

But time is running out, and that's not a good thing. So, fellow dudes, what are we waiting for? Are you raring to get started? Can you feel the excitement? Everyone say "Yeeaah!"

Now I'm going to just have to *presume* you did that.

Reporting with Crystal

Users can be damnably picky sometimes.

They want programs; you create programs. They want pretty paperclip animation characters to keep them amused; you create pretty paperclip animation characters to keep them amused. They want programs that don't crash; you remove paperclip animation characters that once kept them amused.

After all that, they realize that they actually want reports, too. They say they're putting information into this database system and now they want something back out of it. What?

Well, you could always just photocopy the "How to Write SQL" chapter and hand it out with a quick memo telling them to see this document if they have any database questions. But, if you actually want to keep your job, I'd better inform you that you can incorporate reports into your programs in six main ways.

1. Set up a bunch of reports in Access and link them to your data source.

2. Grab your data, and then manipulate it in Excel—completely in code, using COM Automation. (See "Using COM Objects" in Chapter 8.3, "Advanced Tips and Techniques", for more information.)

3. Display your data in on a Web Form and tell your user to click on Print.

4. Just *don't* (my personal favorite).

5. Retrieve your report data in code, then pass it straight to the printer. (This is neither easy nor pretty; see "Printing from Your Program" in Chapter 8.3, "Advanced Tips and Techniques", for information.)

6. Use the really groovy Crystal Reports designer (*hint, hint*).

The most popular of all these options is Crystal Reports, a neat reporting tool that's bundled with Visual Studio .NET. It allows you to create and incorporate cool-looking reports into your programs within minutes.

Creating Our Own Reports

How? Let's figure it out by knocking together our own report based on the Xtreme database, a neat sample distributed with Crystal Reports that supposedly belongs to a mountain bike manufacturer. Ahh, if only all databases were that exciting. Let's take a quick peek.

1. Launch Access and have a browse round the Xtreme.mdb database, which is most likely located in Program Files\Microsoft Visual Studio .NET\Crystal Reports\Samples\Database\.

The two tables we'll be looking at in this short session are Customer and Orders. Spend a couple of minutes getting acquainted with the sort of data these two beasts hold.

2. Create a new Windows application in VB .NET.

First off, we're going to design the actual form that will display our report.

3.   Design your solution so it contains a form that includes at least one Button control and the CrystalReportViewer control (right at the bottom of the toolbox).

Mine looks something like Figure 5-1, although yours can be completely different (and will probably look one heck of a lot smarter, too).

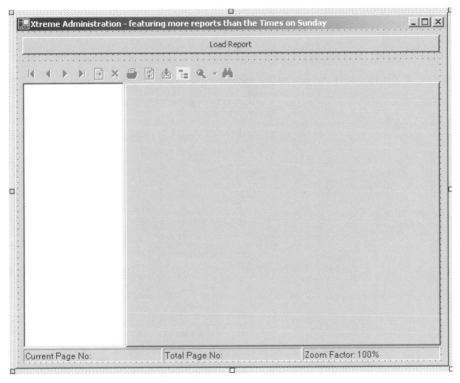

Figure 5-1. Our form, brandishing the CrystalReportViewer control

Hey, look at that CrystalReportViewer control! Your form instantly looks amazingly professional, and you've already got an excuse for the week's worth of golfing you unofficially bunked off for last week: "Yes, boss, I was programming this incredible interface!" Trust me, it works.

Anyway, there we have the actual report viewer. The problem is that some things work best in pairs. Morecambe and Wise. Michael Douglas and Kathleen Turner. Bonnie and Clyde. Oh, and report viewers and *reports*.

And, because we don't yet have a report for our viewer, let's knock one together now.

4. From the menu, select Project ➤ Add New Item.

5. Select Crystal Report from the long list of templates and click on Open.

> **TOP TIP** *If you get hassled to register your Crystal Decisions application, either follow the prompts or choose to register later. Watch out, though: you can use the program only thirty times before it forces you to give Crystal the lowdown.*

You'll be asked what sort of report you want to create, as shown in Figure 5-2.

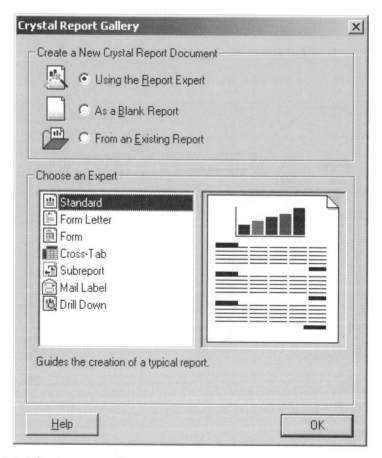

Figure 5-2. Selecting a type of report to create

The easy answer here is simply to select "Use the Report Expert" and select the type of report you're looking to generate. Then let Crystal Reports do the rest for you.

But, because I'm feeling all self-torturing today, let's start from scratch.

6.   Choose the "As a Blank Report" option and click on OK.

You should be staring at a pretty featureless screen at the moment—nothing but a bunch of gray lines and white squares. (See Figure 5-3.) Well, surprisingly enough, this is the very basis of your amazingly supercool report.

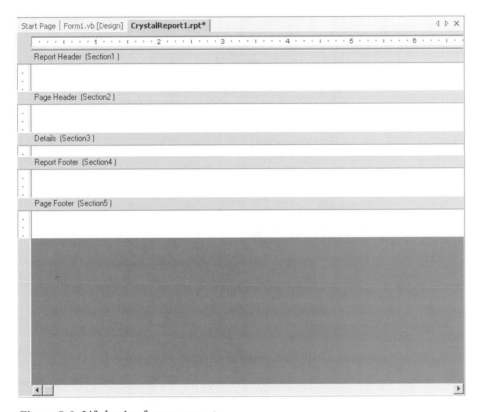

Figure 5-3. Life begins for our report.

Now, if you've ever created reports in Microsoft Access, you'll probably feel quite at home with this screen. However, if you haven't, you'll probably want to pay attention.

Here, you have a bunch of sections. Right now, you have the Report Header, which appears just once right at the top of your report. This is great for a company logo or report title. Next up is the Page Header, which will appear under the Report Header on the first page and then again at the top of each subsequent page. This is where you'd usually put the descriptions of fields used in your reports.

Next, we have the Details section, which actually displays your data. So, imagine you were displaying all customers; you would put the customer fields in this section and they'd be repeated on your report for each customer.

Onward and we've got the Report Footer, which might make for an interesting summary or copyright notice, as it's only displayed after the very last Details item.

Finally, we have the Page Footer, which is displayed at the very bottom of each page. You'd typically put the page number or some fantabulous-looking, page-separating line here.

Now that you've completely memorized that short list, let's move on to add an actual reference to our Xtreme database, then throw our report together.

7. Using the Field Explorer to the left of your screen, right-click on the Database Fields entry at the top and select Add/Remove Database from the pop-up menu.

Next, we need to select our database.

8. In the pop-up Database Expert box, double-click on the Database Files folder.

9. When the Open dialog box appears, select our xtreme.mdb database. (See Figure 5-4.)

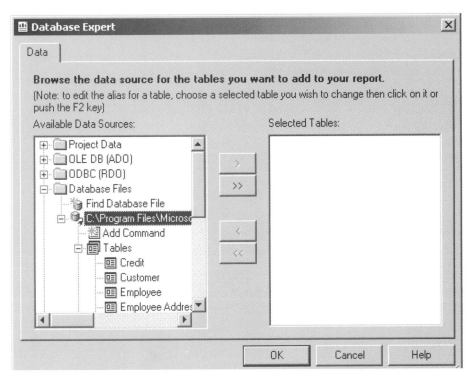

Figure 5-4. Selecting a data source for our report

TOP TIP   *If you wanted to use a DataSet in your application as the source of your data, you could simply select Project Data, ADO.NET DataSets, in the Available Data Sources box. And, if you wanted to connect into an SQL Server database, you'd use the OLE DB (ADO) option.*

10. Expand the Tables view and move the Customer and Orders tables across to the Selected Tables list box.

11. When finished, click on OK.

You'll be taken to another screen to help you plot relationships between the two tables. (See Figure 5-5.)

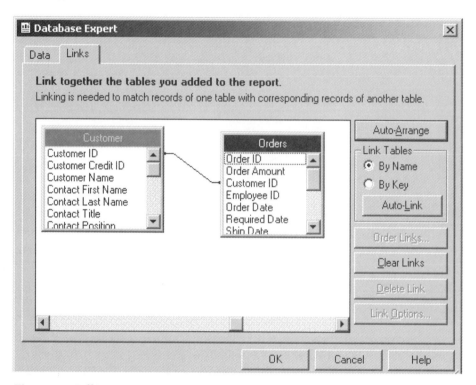

Figure 5-5. Telling our report about the Customer-Orders relationship

This is where you can tell your report which fields link with each other. However, in our sample, this has been automatically detected. If it hadn't, it's easy to create a relationship: simply drag one field onto the other.

12. Review the relationships created and click on OK to close the Database Expert dialog box.

Designing Our Report

You're now ready to start adding actual data to your report. In this report, we're looking for a basic list of customers along with their core contact details.

1. In the Field Explorer, expand the Database Fields link and then the Customer table.

2. From the list of fields, drag and drop (then resize!) six or so items that you deem important into the Details section of this report. (See Figure 5-6.)

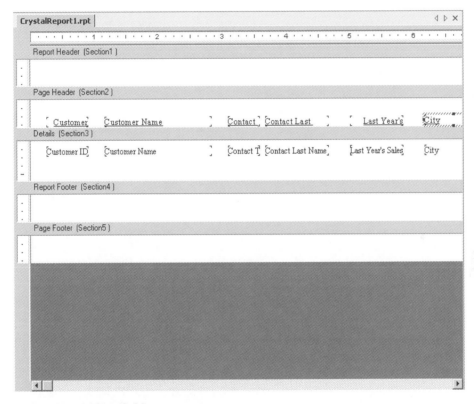

Figure 5-6. Adding fields to our report

> **TOP TIP** *Notice how the Field Explorer ticks off each individual field as you add it to your report? This helps you keep track of what data you've included so far.*

And that's about all we need to get our core information out of the database. Now let's make it look all pretty, smoothing out a few edges.

3. Drag a couple of the design widgets from the Crystal Reports section in the toolbox onto your report, such as the Text object and the Box object. (Right-click and select Format to visually change the properties of both.)

4. Expand the Special Fields section of the Field Explorer and add the page number to your Page Footer section.

Righto, Figure 5-7 shows our finished core report.

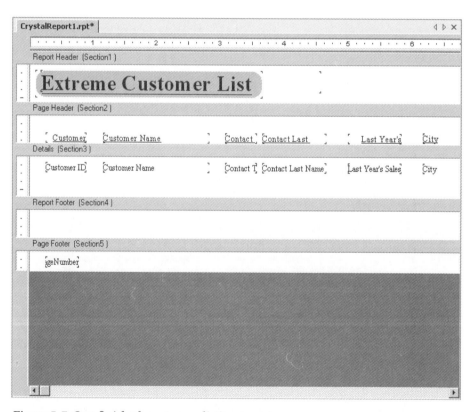

Figure 5-7. Our finished, customer-listing report

Next, we need to run this report and get it displayed on our form.

5. Go back to your form and, behind the click event of your Button control, insert the following code:

```
CrystalReportViewer1.ReportSource = New CrystalReport1()
```

Okay, so we'll probably get spanked by the Naming Convention Police for this line, but you get the gist here. We're setting the ReportSource of our CrystalReportViewer control equal to a new instance of CrystalReport1, our newly designed report.

6. Press F5 to run your application.

Try clicking on your button to test the report, as in Figure 5-8. What happens? Does it all work as expected? Can you print the report? How about zooming? Do you need to add more code to do this or does the viewer control handle it all for you?

Also, should your data be in this order? Try going back to your report design, clicking the "A-Z" Sort Order button on the menu and sorting by the customer name, then testing your application again. Has it made a difference?

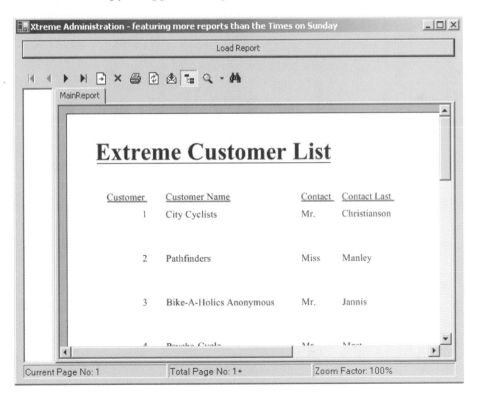

Figure 5-8. Displaying the report in our application

And There's More . . .

Think that's about it with Crystal Reports? Don't bet on it. We've only seen the simplest of reports—however, you can get a *lot* groovier.

Grouping is one of the most powerful features. Imagine, for example, that you need a report listing all your customers and their related orders. How can you do that?

First, you need a reference to both Customer and Orders tables in your report and to set up a relationship between them (which we've already done). Next, you'd need to tell the report to group by the customer name and list the orders in your Details sections. Let's do that now.

1. Delete everything on your report right now.

2. Right-click on any blank area, selecting Insert ➤ Group from the pop-up menu.

3. Select the CustomerName field from your Customer table, then click on OK.

4. Using the Field Explorer, drag and drop key fields from the Orders table into the Details section.

5. When finished, press F5 to test your application.

What happens? My offering is shown in Figure 5-9. Notice how Crystal Reports automatically lists the company names next to your report for easy navigation? It's friendly like that, see.

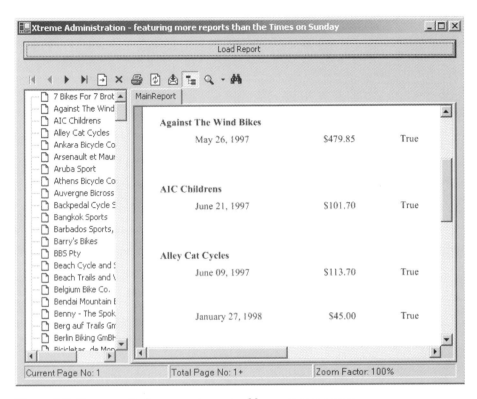

Figure 5-9. Our new Orders report, grouped by customer name

TOP TIP *To change the way in which Crystal Reports displays your data, right-click on a field and select Format. This is particularly useful with date and money fields. I've done exactly that with the Order Date field shown in Figure 5-9.*

Anyway, what else might you want to play around with here? Well, try clicking on the Insert Chart button on the toolbar. Can you get Crystal Reports to display a 3-D pie chart, summarizing Xtreme sales by year? If you have a spare few minutes, try checking out the Parameter Fields entry in the Fields Explorer, too. Right-click and look at the options. How could this help you customize each user's reporting experience?

You can also expand even further. For example, instead of storing the reports directly in your application—as we just did here—you can allow the user to pick one, set the ReportSource of your CrystalReportViewer control to the filename, and the final report will be displayed.

Imagine how easily expandable and maintainable that could be. I'm dribbling already.

Want to find out more? Then it's time for you to explore a few of the Crystal Report samples that ship with VS .NET. Try opening your Program Files\Microsoft Visual Studio .NET\Crystal Reports\Samples folder and browsing around. You'll find VB .NET code samples, the Xtreme.mdb database, and a bundle of ready-to-run reports.

With a little exploring and an eager mind, you'll soon learn how to add all these wizzy features to your own reports—and have them looking more professional than the president of Professionals Incorporated just after making his National Professional Speech to the Association of Conglomerated Professionals.

And that's pretty professional.

FAQ

Still have a few niggling questions? Not entirely clear about a particular concept? Run through our list of frequently asked questions and see if you can find a solution.

Back in the first chapter, you started talking about database terminology. Since then, I've noticed a lot of people use certain phrases interchangeably. For example, they talk about fields and columns as though they're the same thing. Is this right? Is a database the same as a data warehouse? Are there any other terms that are used side by side?

It's easy to become overwhelmed with the mass of weird-sounding words you'll find in the database world. Let's try to clear up a little of the confusion now.

First off, databases. You'll often hear these referred to by their type, such as SQL Server or Access, or perhaps shortened to just *data* or *data source*. But this isn't the same as a data warehouse, which is a system that allows your users to create reports and gain business knowledge from company data.

Next up, tables are always called *tables*. Not too difficult, that one. And each table can hold multiple rows, which are often referred to as *records*. A table also contains columns, with fields underneath each column.

However, the distinction between *columns* and *fields* is often blurred. After all, without fields you would have no columns, and without columns you would have no fields. Therefore, be aware that even Microsoft uses these two terms interchangeably.

You can also have queries in your database, which are just stored SQL Select statements. These are sometimes called *views*. Stored procedures are also available in certain database systems, although we didn't cover them in this tutorial. (See the last question for more information.)

What's the difference between an Access database and a Jet database?

There's really no difference. When you create a database in Access, you're creating something called a Jet database. It's just an MDB database standard created by Microsoft.

When accessing SQL Server, I need to specify a username and password. How can I do this?

If the instance of SQL Server you're connecting into requires a username and password, you need to specify this in your connection string. As an example, the following connection string connects into a server called MySQLServer, for the database MyDatabase, using a username and password of MyUserName and MyPassword. Original, eh?

```
Server=MySQLServer;Database=MyDatabase;UserID=MyUserName;Password=MyPassword
```

Look up the ConnectionString property of the SqlConnection class for more information.

I've been using the DataReader and get an awful message back saying that I need to close it first or something. What's happening?

When you use the DataReader to read data through the Command object, this holds a live conversation with the database. Information is literally streaming down the line directly into the DataReader to be used in your code.

Therefore, before you can read data into the DataReader a second time, you need to close the first "conversation" from your DataReader object by running its `.Close` method. That should sort your problem.

I'm running my code and getting an error: "Object reference not set to an instance of an object." I don't understand what's happening. Is it me?

This crazy little error occurs when you try to use an object that hasn't yet been set to anything. For example, if the error occurs on a line where you're using your DataSet object, it's probable that you haven't declared that object properly. Make sure all such objects are always set to a new instance of its class, for example: `Dim MyDataSet As New DataSet()`.

My company is apparently using XML files to send data to other organizations. Can you explain what this is? Is it possible to create XML files from my data?

XML stands for *eXtensible Markup Language* and is really just structured text. It looks a little like HTML and can be easily manipulated in code. Here is an example XML document.

```xml
<?xml version="1.0" ?>
<books>
  <book>
    <author>Moore</author>
    <title>Surviving in the Wild</title>
    <price format="sterling">19.99</price>
    <pubdate>20/05/2002</pubdate>
  </book>
  <book>
    <author>Briggs</author>
    <title>Making Your Money Work</title>
    <price format="dollar">31.95</price>
    <pubdate>17/02/2003</pubdate>
  </book>
</books>
```

Can you create XML files from your data? Absolutely! When using DataSets, it's incredibly simple to either read or write your information straight into an XML document. Simply call the WriteXml and ReadXml functions. For example:

```vb
' Write data to XML document
MyDataSet.WriteXml("c:\mydoc.xml")
' Read data from XML document
MyDataSet.ReadXml("c:\mydoc.xml")
```

For more information, look up "Reading an XML File" and "Using DataSets and XML" in Chapter 8.2, "Intermediate Tips and Techniques".

You talked about how apostrophes can ruin your SQL statements. How come?

Imagine you were writing an application that took a member name from a TextBox control to incorporate into an SQL statement. If the user entered a name with an apostrophe in the box, the resulting SQL statement may end up something like:

```
SELECT * FROM members WHERE name='Sinead O'Connor'
```

The extra apostrophe here renders this an invalid SQL statement, and it will result in an error. To get around this, you can simply replace all single apostrophes from the name with double apostrophes. These are automatically understood as singles by your database.

You can use the `Replace()` function to do this. Look up "Replacing Text the Easy Way" in Chapter 8.2, "Intermediate Tips and Techniques", for more information.

Another method of handling this if you're working with a Command object is to use parameters. Parameters automatically handle apostrophes, and they can greatly simplify those often complex SQL statements.

How do they work? You begin by building your Command object as usual, changing your SQL statement so it includes little "placeholders" where your actual field values should be. Then you add those actual values to the parameters collection of your Command object and execute the query as normal. Parameters work with all SQL statements: Select, Insert, Delete, and Update. The following sample code demonstrates this technique in action with an Insert statement:

```
' Create our template SQL statement with placeholders
Dim strSQL As String
strSQL = "INSERT INTO Stock(productid, description, quantity) " & _
    "VALUES(@ProductID, @Description, @Quantity)"

' Declare our Command
Dim objCommand As New SqlClient.SqlCommand(strSQL, objConnection)

' Add the parameter values
objCommand.Parameters.Add("@ProductID", 4515)
objCommand.Parameters.Add("@Description", "Magoo's Amazing Rubber Chicken")
objCommand.Parameters.Add("@Quantity", 439)

' Execute as normal
objConnection.Open()
objCommand.ExecuteNonQuery()
objConnection.Close()
```

What exactly are stored procedures?

Stored procedures are basically *mini scripts* that are stored with your database. They typically consist of simple logic and SQL statements, and they can accept and return parameters. They simplify development because they allow you to move the SQL from your application to the database, allowing for added security and better maintenance; plus, they are "compiled" and therefore quicker to run than SQL coming straight from your program. To execute a stored procedure, you'd typically call it using a DataCommand, passing any parameters as we just did. Although SQL Server supports stored procedures, these are not possible in Microsoft Access. For more information, look up "stored procedures, executing in ADO. NET" in the Help index.

WHERE TO GO FROM HERE

There's always something new to learn in the database world—and no tutorial could ever hope to cover it all. Still, over the past five chapters you've gained an excellent footing, but how can you take that knowledge even further?

Here are my recommendations for taking your database power straight to the next level.

- *Database Programming with Visual Basic .NET* (Apress, ISBN: 1-893115-29-1): Handy in-depth look at accessing data from within your VB .NET applications. Covers everything from data-bound controls to message queues, and everything in between.

- Other books: *Professional ADO.NET* (Wrox, ISBN: 1-861005-27-X); *ADO.NET Core Reference* (Microsoft Press, ISBN: 0-735614-23-7).

- www.gotdotnet.com: Yes, it's Microsoft's own site dedicated to priming its developers with all the latest information. Includes a host of interesting data links.

- www.swynk.com/sql/: If you're looking to learn more about SQL Server, this hot Web stop boasts a mass of tips and tutorials, all free. You'll find similar resources for all the other Microsoft .NET Server products here, too.

- www.aspalliance.com/wisemonk/: Alongside its random book recommendations, this site hosts an interesting selection of database and ASP.NET articles. Worth a surf.

- www.nakedvariables.com: Whether you're wanting the latest on hardcore multitier ADO.NET data access techniques or the underground scoop on how to create top-notch objects in .NET, this handy developer link station brings you the best of the rest—all on one page.

- www.dotnetextreme.com: Great site, packing a bundle of small how-to guides. Includes features on data access with ADO.NET.

- microsoft.public.dotnet.framework.adonet: The official Microsoft newsgroup for discussion about the ADO.NET classes. For speedier answers, try searching the archives first at www.googlegroups.com.

Remember, the world of .NET is still relatively new and constantly changing. These resources were chosen due to their quality and apparent stability; however, if you experience any problems, you can always stop by Apress for the latest at www.apress.com.

CONCLUSION

Doesn't time fly when you're having fun? Please, no swearing.

Yes, it's that time again: the end of a chapter and, today, the end of another epic book tutorial. It's been an arduous journey, but we've reached the end of our roller coaster database ride—and lived to tell the tale.

Congratulations! I'm really pleased you've worked so hard. It's been difficult, but we've gotten there. So, just what have we learned over these past five chapters?

Well, we launched the first chapter of this tutorial with a look at just what databases are and how you can easily bind your data to a Windows form. We then moved on to look at how we can create our own Access database, with relationships—plus, explored how we could connect that information straight to the Web.

We then soon uncovered some of the more advanced topics, such as learning how to talk the database language of SQL and understanding how to access our data entirely in code. Next up, we started to look at the more powerful SQL Server database system, plus used it to create the Keep Fit database, then went on to write our own transactional Web application that manipulated its records.

Today, we've touched on the world of reporting and how you can use the Crystal Reports tool to help quiet demanding users, plus answered a few frequently asked questions. Finally, we found out how you can take your database knowledge straight to the next level.

And that leads us here, right now, to this very sentence.

Guess that's my cue to say goodnight. So, until the next tutorial of this book, this is your host, Karl Moore, thanking you for your very enjoyable company. I hope you've learned a lot. Toodle-pip!

DESIGNING REPORTS AND GOING FROM HERE REVIEW SHEET

- Crystal Reports allows you to generate reports and display them in your applications. The package is bundled with Visual Studio .NET.

- To add a new Crystal Report to your application, select Project ➢ Add New Item ➢ Crystal Report. To add a Crystal Report viewer to either a Windows or Web form, draw out a CrystalReportViewer control onto the screen.

- A regular report typically consists of five sections: the Report Header, which appears once at the top of each report; the Page Header, which appears at the top of each report page; the Details section, which displays once per each data item you are displaying; the Report Footer, which appears once after the very last Details item; and the Page Footer, which appears at the bottom of each page.

- You can create reports and store them as RPT files, then load them as requested in your application by setting the .ReportSource property of your CrystalReportViewer control to the RPT file path. Alternatively, you can create the reports as part of your application and simply set the .ReportSource property equal to a new instance of your report, like this:

```
MyCrystalReportViewer.ReportSource = New MyCrystalReport()
```

Working the Web

The ASP.NET Revolution

"I took the initiative in creating the Internet."—Al Gore

LOOKING TO KNOCK TOGETHER YOUR own interactive Web sites? In the past, it was pretty darn difficult.

Back in the early days, most Web sites were nothing more than a bundle of static HTML pages—and about as exciting as Bill Gates' cardigan collection. Languages such as Perl and JavaScript became available for programmers to add interactivity, but, unless you were smarter than Einstein at his daughter's wedding, actually putting these tools to good use wasn't all that easy.

The hours ticked by and Microsoft eventually unveiled their own Web offering—something called *Active Server Pages* (*ASP*). This was a system that enabled you to create dynamic, interactive Web pages using Visual Basic-like code. However, this relied on you mixing your own code among a mass of HTML, all inside an ASP page—making development stickier than an explosion at an Israeli toffee factory.

And, at the end of the day, none of these techniques came even close to the *richness* of Windows applications that many people were using each and every day. In short, a Web developer's life was tough.

But, when Gates and his merry gang of programmers disappeared into a phone booth recently and emerged brandishing a clingy superhero outfit and the .NET Framework, he brought with him the solution.

How come? The .NET Framework includes ASP.NET, the next version of ASP. And this new and wizzy release allows you to build fully interactive, highly impressive Web sites in minutes, sites that you can roll out with a simple copy-and-paste. It's true.

"How?" I hope I hear you crying. "What's the secret?"

I'm your shockingly nerdy host Karl Moore, and welcome to Tutorial 3, "Working the Web." Over the next three installments, I'll be getting down and dirty with Web applications, showing you all the top insider tricks in the shortest possible time. No messing.

So, what are you waiting for? Oh, me. Right. Okay, then!

How It All Works

In the past, building interactive Web sites was about as easy to understand as the groupies behind `www.PylonOfTheMonth.co.uk`, and just about as exciting. However with ASP.NET, that's all changed. So, how does this new way of working . . . work?

Well, you start the whole process by creating a Web application project, which essentially represents your interactive site. Your Web application typically consists of one of more Web forms, which are ASPX pages on your site.

Next, you "paint" these Web forms in much the same way as you would design a Windows form. You add controls to make the page look pretty. You put Visual Basic code behind control events to glue it all together. You put links on each page to take you to the others.

And when you've finished? You simply build your Web application. This creates a bundle of ASPX files—plus a DLL file containing your actual code—and puts them all on your Web server, awaiting the next visitor.

Now, imagine that one of those friendly users decides to access your site. They tap the address of one of your ASPX Web forms into their browser. As soon as the request comes through to your machine, the .NET Framework starts whizzing and whirring. It runs any required code in your DLL, does any processing it needs to, then passes back the final ASPX page as a simple HTML document.

That's right. No confusing downloads, no ActiveX controls (as with earlier versions of Visual Basic that "allowed" you to create interactive Web sites)—just HTML as plain as a Boeing 747. And that means your site will work with any operating system, from Windows to the Macintosh.

Interested yet? Me too. Let's launch this part of the book with a simple site to demonstrate some of these key concepts—then we'll get a little geekier.

> **TOP TIP** *Before getting started with any ASP.NET application, you need Internet Information Server 5.0 or above installed on your machine. If you don't have it, you can't play the game.*

Creating Your First Site

Are you sitting comfortably? Then I'll begin the practical.

1. Launch VS .NET and create a new ASP.NET Web application, changing its location to `http://localhost/hello`. (See Figure 1-1.)

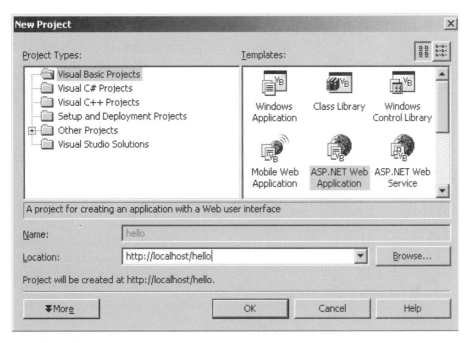

Figure 1-1. Creating a new ASP.NET Web application

Yes, this is going to be one of those amazingly original Hello World applications. We'll expand out and create our own online reservation system later, but, for now, let's get used to working with ASP.NET.

> **TOP TIP** *If you get a warning about Internet Explorer being offline or some such, launch Internet Explorer, cancel any attempts to dial up, then click on File and uncheck Work Offline. Tsk, computers, eh?*

You should now be looking at a pretty boring, dotted screen, christened WebForm1.aspx. This is the ASPX Web page that your end users will see.

Move your eyes over to the left of your screen. See the toolbox? These are controls you can use on your Web forms, similar to the way you have controls you can use with regular Windows forms. Let's try a couple out now.

2. Drag and drop a Button and TextBox control anywhere on your Web form.

Next, cast your beautiful eyes over to the bottom right of your screen. Notice the Properties window? Again, just as you'd have with Windows forms, it's here you can change the properties and behavior of objects you're working with.

3. Change the Text property of your button to "Say It To Me".
    (See Figure 1-2.)

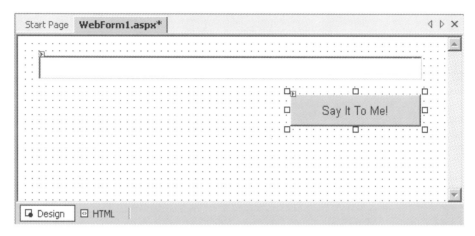

Figure 1-2. Painting our Web page

To complete our eye exercise regime, raise your blinkers ever so slightly so that the Solution Explorer comes into view. These are all the files that are included by default in your Web application project. Erm, so what do *they* do?

What Are Those Project Files?

Damn, I was afraid you were going to ask that. Well, we cover all of this in Appendix B, but I guess there's no harm in being repetitive.

First off is the AssemblyInfo.vb file. Open it up and take a look. When you build a Web application, all your code gets compiled into a DLL file called an *assembly*. This AssemblyInfo.vb file stores data about that file, such as version and copyright information. Oh, the excitement.

Moving on, the Global.asax file is like a global class. You could put code here to run whenever requests are sent to your Web application, or when errors occur. Next up, the Styles.css cascading stylesheet can be used to set default HTML styles. (We'll look at these later.) And then the VSDISCO file includes informational links about any Web services that you implement here (not used in this project, see Tutorial 6, "Services Rendered").

Next, we have Web.config, which stores settings for your Web application, such as whether debug messages should appear when an error occurs, how long before a session times out, and so on. And, finally, we have your actual ASPX pages.

> **TOP TIP**   *If you really want to see what makes up the WebForm1.aspx page, go into design mode and click on the HTML button at the bottom of your page. The top line here lists your actual code file, plus which part of our compiled DLL this page will "inherit" its code from at runtime. Also, pay attention to all those <asp:> tags. As the .NET Framework is serving pages up, these are translated from actual Web Form controls into regular HTML controls. These special <asp:> tags simply allow the .NET Framework to identify that this is a control you may want to manipulate in your code.*

This is all worth knowing, but still about as interesting as the System.BillCrosby namespace. Thankfully, we'll only be covering the most important and exciting Web site creation techniques in this tutorial, so if you really want to find out more about a particular file here, consult the Help index.

Adding Code

Let's put our foot down now for the event you've all been waiting for. We're getting juicy: we're adding code.

1.   Double-click on your button.

You should be taken to the code window. This is actually WebForm1.aspx.vb, the code behind your WebForm1.aspx page. Although the code content here might be different from Windows forms, you'll notice that the structure is still pretty much the same.

Here, we have a public class called WebForm1. You can see that it inherits some of its functionality from `System.Web.UI.Page` and that your Button1 and TextBox1 controls have been declared.

Before the `End Class` here, we also have the load event listed, ready for you to insert code into—plus, of course, our button click event. Let's add code to that now.

2.   Add the following code to respond to your button click event:

```
TextBox1.Text += " Hi Worldies!"
```

So, let's recap. Now, when somebody visits our site and clicks on the button, we want to take the Text property of our TextBox control and add " Hi Worldies!" to the end of it. How will that work in real life? There's only one way to find out.

3. Press the F5 button to test your application.

4. Click on your "Say It To Me" button a few times. (See Figure 1-3.)

Figure 1-3. Our final Web application, in full IE6 glory

What happens? Try removing the text and clicking again. What if you type something in yourself and click? Does it remember what you entered?

Also notice how, each time you click, the Web form is being "posted back" to the server, the code runs and fresh HTML results are returned? Where is that code running? Do you understand the concept here? Does everything make sense?

So many questions, so few answers. Ho-humm.

Getting Bigger and Better

What's that? You don't think a Web site that constantly appends "Hi Worldies!" to a TextBox is going to attract investors? Really?

Well, that's *their* loss. Still, just to be on the safe side, let's go ahead and build ourselves a slightly more complex system, one that organizes doctor appointments. Patients—hopefully the non-dying, well-enough-to-surf-the-Internet sort—can come along and book appointments with their favorite doctor online. Save all that time-wasting telephone rubbish.

The requested appointment time can then be instantly checked against the doctor's workload, and, if the slot is available, booked there and then. Erm, okay, so perhaps we're not going to implement *all* those fancy features right now, but it will look a bit like an appointment booking system. Sort of. Ish.

Creating Our Project

Let's launch this slightly more in-depth example by creating a new project. Great starting point, that.

1. Launch VS .NET and create a new ASP.NET Web application called "appointment" by changing its location to `http://localhost/appointment`.

You should be looking at WebForm1.aspx. The first thing we're going to do here is turn off the grid layout mode. When this is on, your controls always stay in the exact same place no matter how the user resizes his or her Web browser. I don't like this, so let's go with the more traditional flow layout.

2. Click on WebForm1.aspx, so it appears in the Properties window.

3. Change the PageLayout property of WebForm1.aspx to FlowLayout.

Adding Text to a Web Form

The first thing we want to do on our site is welcome visitors. Because we're all friendly like that. Here goes.

1. Click inside WebForm1.aspx and type "Welcome to the Surgery!"

Unfortunately, this title has about as much sex appeal as a vitamin pill. Let's alter this by changing the font we just used.

2. Highlight your "Welcome to the Surgery!" text.

3. Select the Verdana font from the Font Name drop-down box on the toolbar.

4. Change the font size to 5.

5. Make the selected text bold.

In a slightly less obvious font now, type a description of the doctor's practice and describe how users can make an appointment by filling out the form and clicking on our up-and-coming "Click Here to Book this Appointment" button. (See Figure 1-4.)

6. Enter any blurb text underneath the title in a smaller font.

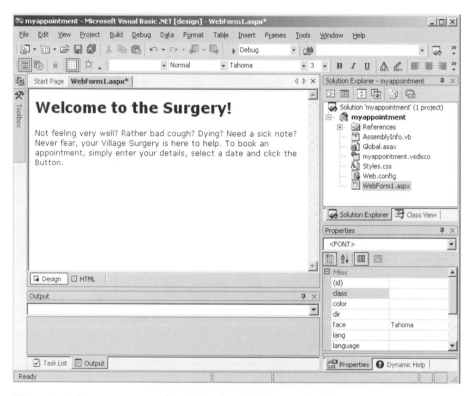

Figure 1-4. Our program so far: titles, descriptions, and all

Using the ID Property

The time has come, the Walrus said, to talk of many things. Like adding boxes for the user to enter his or her name and telephone number.

1. Type "Name: " on a new line in your Web form.

2. Drag and drop a TextBox control to the end of this line.

3. Change the ID property of this TextBox to "txtName".

The ID property is just the same as the Name property in Windows forms. It's our way of referring to the control in code.

4. Do the exact same for a "Telephone Number: " field.

5. Change the ID property of your Telephone Number field to "txtTelephoneNum".

So, we have somewhere for the user to tell us about themselves. Okay, so there's no complicated database matching or client searching going on here, but I'm feeling awfully lazy.

And it's for people like myself—lazy boys—they invented some really great Web controls to slap straight onto our forms, such as the Calendar.

6. Type "Select Date:" on a new line in your Web form and press the Enter key.

7. Drag and drop a Calendar control on the current line.

8. Change the ID property of your Calendar control to "calDate".

Wow! See that? As in Figure 1-5, you'll be shown a fully working, HTML-based calendar without all the work. Without any work, in fact.

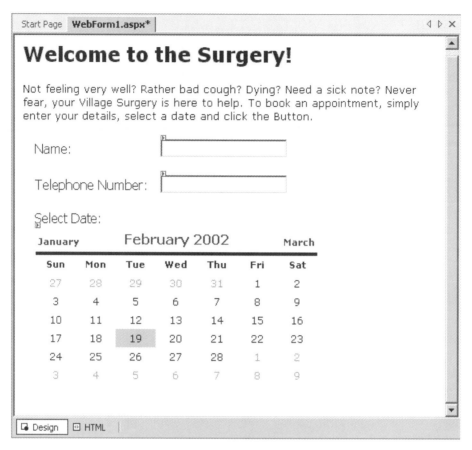

Figure 1-5. Our Web form, sporting the Calendar control

Something like this would've taken an absolute age to code or an absolute fortune to purchase back in the golden olden days of ASP.

But we supercool, hip-hop, new-age programmer types have it sorted in two flicks of a cat's whisker. Or something like that. It's cool, and that's all we need to know.

Testing Our Application

So, how does this calendar thing work? What does it feel like? Let's test our little application so far.

Press F5 to launch your Web form. Have a play around with your calendar. Try selecting one of the dates. What happens? Do you notice how the whole page is resubmitted back to the Web server (probably your local computer)? And did you see how the background color of the date you select changes?

Also, if you've got a few spare minutes, try viewing the source of your page. In Internet Explorer, you do this by selecting View ➤ Source. (See Figure 1-6.)

```
WebForm1[3] - Notepad                                        _ |□| x|
File  Edit  Format  Help
<!DOCTYPE HTML PUBLIC "-//W3C//DTD HTML 4.0 Transitional//EN">
<HTML>
        <HEAD>
                <title>WebForm1</title>
                <meta name="GENERATOR" content="Microsoft Visual Studio.NET 7.0">
                <meta name="CODE_LANGUAGE" content="Visual Basic 7.0">
                <meta name="vs_defaultClientScript" content="JavaScript">
                <meta name="vs_targetSchema"
content="http://schemas.microsoft.com/intellisense/ie5">
        </HEAD>
        <body>
                <form name="Form1" method="post" action="WebForm1.aspx" id="Form1">
<input type="hidden" name="__EVENTTARGET" value="" />
<input type="hidden" name="__EVENTARGUMENT" value="" />
<input type="hidden" name="__VIEWSTATE" value="dDwOMjg1NTYwMTI7Oz4=" />
```

Figure 1-6. The source of our ASPX page

See all that HTML? Remember writing that? Even the Calendar control design has been translated into pure HTML, even though you'll soon be treating it in code as a regular object. That's the .NET Framework being clever. And that's good, because most of my code is thicker than iced tapioca.

You might also want to observe the "__VIEWSTATE" bit in the HTML source. This is a hidden field that contains encrypted information. Think about how you just clicked a date on the Calendar control and the whole form was resubmitted. Did you notice how any text entered in the TextBox controls remains there, no matter how many times you select new dates?

That's the job of the __VIEWSTATE field: to maintain the "state" of your Web form. It stores and encrypts the state of your controls and ensures that their properties remain the same so you don't have to mess around putting the old values back into TextBox controls and such every time the user selects a new date. It's there to save you time, and, if you've ever used the old ASP tools, you'll find it a complete heaven-send.

Yes, you've died, and I am the Holy One. Now send me your checks.

> **TOP TIP**   *We'll be stumbling across the* __VIEWSTATE *field again in the next chapter. However, if you want to stop a control from having its state stored like this, set the EnableViewState of the specific control to False. Try it out on a TextBox to see the difference.*

Finishing the Design

Hmm, we've not yet finished our application however. Let's get it sorted. *Then* send me your checks.

1. Close your browser when finished to return to your Web form in design mode.

2. Try changing the BackColor, BorderColor, and ForeColor properties of your Calendar control to improve its appearance. Alternatively, click on the Auto Format link and choose a style.

    What other Calendar properties can you change? Have a quick browse down the list.

3. Underneath the Calendar control, type "Time: ".

4. Drag and drop a TextBox control to the end of this line.

5. Change the ID property of this TextBox control to "txtTime".

    Hokily dokily, that's the data input controls finished with. Next we need to add a button for the user to click and submit the information, plus some sort of label onto which we confirm to the users that their appointment has been booked.

6. Drag and drop a Button control to the bottom of the page.

7. Change the Text property of your button to "Click Here to Book this Appointment".

8. Change the ID property of your Button control to "btnBook".

9. Finally, underneath everything else, drag and drop a Label control.

10. Change the Font property of your label to something noticeable—a large bold Arial, for example, with a red ForeColor.

11. Remove any existing text in the Text property of your Label control.

12. Change the ID property of your Label control to "lblInformation". (See Figure 1-7 for the final user interface.)

Figure 1-7. Our final user interface

Adding the Code

We're ready to add a little code to make all this work together. First off, we're going to write code to confirm the appointment.

1. Double-click on your button. You should be taken to the code window.

2. Add the following code behind your button click event:

```
lblInformation.Text = "Thank you, " & txtName.Text & ". " & _
    "Your appointment has been booked for " & _
    calDate.SelectedDate & " at " & txtTime.Text & ". " & _
    "Be there . . . or be ill!"
```

Here, we're simply setting the Text property of our label equal to a mixture of our own text and properties of the various Web controls we've used.

Next, because we haven't told the user how to enter a time—as 9 PM or 21:00 or whatever—we're going to suggest a time. In the real world, we'd perhaps use a database to determine the next available slot. Here, we're going all manual.

3. Add the following code to respond to your page load event:

```
txtTime.Text = "09:00"
```

Hmm, when do you think this code will run? We'll find out when we finally see our masterpiece in action. And now seems like a pretty good time for that, don't you think? I mean, I'm not doing anything important. Got a spare couple of minutes yourself?

4. Press F5 to test your application. (See Figure 1-8.)

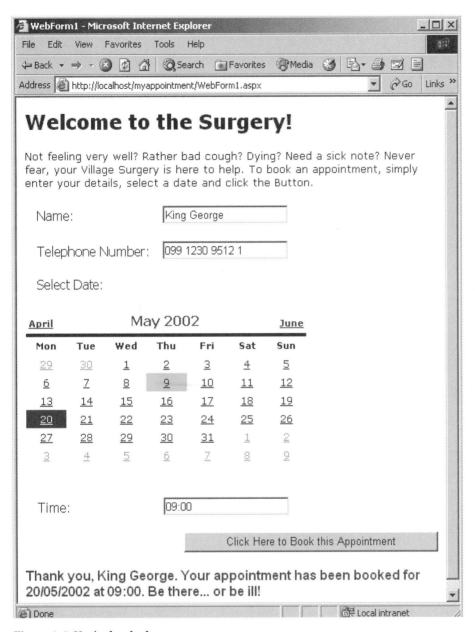

Figure 1-8. You're booked, son.

Try filling out all the blanks, selecting a date, and clicking on your button. What happens? Does it all work as you expected?

Run your application again and try entering everything except the date. What happens? How can you prevent this? Also, what if the user enters a time, such as 03:00, when your offices are closed? How can you stop that from happening?

Let's boot up the brain for a couple of extra questions, too. What if the user enters no data at all? What happens then? How do you think you could prevent that? An If statement? Try checking out some of the extra Web Form controls, too. Do you think any of these could help you validate a field?

Have a play around: the controls here are the real secret to building yourself a great Web application. And we'll be looking at some especially exciting ones next.

The Greatest Controls Ever Sold

Sometimes you need to know a little about your tools before you can really begin to use them.

It wouldn't, for example, be fair of me to pass you a Geiger counter and ask you to check Becquerel levels. Neither would it be fair of me to ask my dad to program the video recorder. And neither would it be fair to ask you to design a Web site without me telling you about all the controls that you have available.

Thankfully, there's a solution to each of these: (a) take a course in radiology, (b) read the VCR manual, and, most importantly for this section, (c) read on.

Now, if you peruse the toolbox displayed when creating Web applications, you'll notice it's pretty packed. We've seen some of these before—the Label, TextBox, and Button controls, for example.

But there are other newbies that we haven't yet stumbled across, such as the AdRotator and RequiredFieldValidator. These are the sort of widgets we'll be looking at now.

And to help keep up the interest, I've split them all into six separate sections: the Linkers, the List Types, the Validation Bods, the Data Trio, the Option Controls, and the Visual Bunch.

At the end of the first five sections, you'll see a little "Try it now!" note. (There isn't one for the Data Trio, because we won't be covering the data controls in any great detail.) Wherever you see these three powerful words, go and experiment. Play with the control; try implementing it in a sample ASP.NET Web application. If you don't, you won't remember what you need to do when working in the real world. (I'm relying on your honesty here.)

Ready? Then affix that thinking cap and study each of the following controls carefully, making sure that you complete the related mini tasks. Some of these controls are big and important; others are small and trivial. Play with them as you see fit, but watch out! In the next chapter, I'll be setting a little test to check your knowledge on a few of these beasts, so make sure you at least partially superglue down that thinking cap. Let's move on.

The Linkers

You can use two main link controls in your Web applications, and, although they look exactly the same, they actually do two completely separate jobs. Let me show you what I mean.

First off, we have the Hyperlink control, as shown in Figure 1-9.

Figure 1-9. The Hyperlink control

If you've ever surfed the Web, you'll have stumbled across hyperlinks. Well, this is the same—except in control version, meaning that you can manipulate it in code. Try playing with the Text, NavigateURL, Target, ImageUrl, and ToolTip properties.

Next up, you have the LinkButton control (Figure 1-10), and, although this little beast looks like a hyperlink, it is in fact a cunning disguise. Instead, the LinkButton control works just like a regular button and even has a click event you can write code underneath. Try playing with the Text, ToolTip, and AccessKey properties.

Figure 1-10. The LinkButton control

Both the linkers are simple, yes, but nonetheless critically important.

Try it now!

Create a new ASP.NET Web application and test both of these controls. Try writing code to respond to the click event of your LinkButton. Also, what does the ToolTip property do?

The List Types

Okay, so you haven't seen any flashing lights or amazing knock-your-socks-off Web controls yet. And we're not going to cover any revolutionary ground in this section either. Rather, this part covers more of those bare necessities—for the times you want to select something from a list. I'm talking about the DropDownList and ListBox controls, as shown in Figure 1-11.

Figure 1-11. The DropDownList and ListBox controls

You've seen them before, but how do you use them? Let me give you a quick lowdown. First, you need to add items to the list by editing the Items property, either via the Properties window or in code. For example, you might want to add an item to either the DropDownList or ListBox control in code, like this:

```
ListBoxOrDropDown.Items.Add("No problem, Houston")
```

Or we might want to clear the list:

```
ListBoxOrDropDown.Items.Clear()
```

What else can you do? Well, perhaps you want to kick start the user into selecting an item. You can select one for them, using the SelectedIndex property (starting at 0 to select the first item):

```
ListBoxOrDropDown.SelectedIndex = 0
```

Other things you can do with your lists include adding items that contain text and a related value. For example:

```
Dim MyItem As New ListItem()
MyItem.Text = "Joan Briggs"
MyItem.Value = "M98W23D"
ListBoxOrDropDown.Items.Add(MyItem)
```

Here, we're adding an item that appears as "Joan Briggs" but that has an underlying value of M98W23D. This is useful for storing ID values, such as database keys and such.

Finally, you can find out what the user has selected by checking the SelectedItem property, like so:

```
MyVariable = ListBoxOrDropDown.SelectedItem.Text
MyVariable = ListBoxOrDropDown.SelectedItem.Value
```

Both of these controls also support the SelectedIndexChanged event, which fires off whenever your user selects a new item in the list.

Yes, the list types are about as plain as the color white, with added white, but they do their job—and well, too.

Try it now!

Create a new ASP.NET Web application and add a list box to your Web form, filling with sample items using the Properties window. Then test the SelectedIndexChanged event by adding code to put the currently selected item text in a Label control. Does it work? What if you changed the list box for a drop-down list? Does it break your code?

The Validation Bods

In the old world of ASP, validation was a sticky subject. It made developers stop, shiver, and instantly consider a career in farming. To most, it brings back memories of buggy If statements and more code crosschecks than you can wave a huge Web server at.

But, in ASP.NET, validation is a real breeze. It allows you to easily validate data the user has entered via a bundle of neat new controls. How does it work? You start by adding one of the validation controls to your form, such as RequiredFieldValidator or CompareValidator. Then you provide it with more information as to what it needs to check, using the Properties window.

When your Web form is next submitted—because, perhaps, the user has clicked one of your buttons—the validation takes place. If an error has occurred, the Validation control becomes visible, displaying its error message to the user. (See Figure 1-12.)

Let's check a sample.

Figure 1-12. The Validation controls

1. Create a new ASP.NET Web application.

2. Drag TextBox, Button, and RequiredFieldValidator controls onto WebForm1.aspx.

The RequiredFieldValidator control checks whether another control is empty. If it is, that's invalid and an error is raised. We want to ensure that the user enters something in our TextBox1 here, such as a username, say, so let's change the relevant properties of our RequiredFieldValidator control now.

3. Change the following properties of the RequiredFieldValidator control:

- *ErrorMessage*: "You must enter a username!"

- *ControlToValidate*: TextBox1

4. Press F5 to test your application.

Don't bother entering anything into your TextBox control. Just click your button. What happens? Yes, before even posting back to the server, an error is generated. And, as soon as you enter a value and move off the text box, see how it disappears? Clever stuff.

So, we've learned a little about the RequiredFieldValidator control: it checks for a value in another control. What other validation widgets are available? Let's get nosy.

There's the RangeValidator control, which checks that a control value is between a particular range. To use this, check out the ControlToValidate, MinimumValue, MaximumValue, and Type properties.

Next, we have the CompareValidator control, which has two general uses: it can compare a control value with a predefined value or it can compare two text boxes. To demonstrate the first, if you wanted to check that TextBox1 contained a number greater than 5, you would change the ControlToValidate property to TextBox1, the Operator to GreaterThan, the ValueToCompare to 5, and the Type to Integer.

However, if you wanted to check whether TextBox1 and TextBox2 held the same information (perhaps as password verification fields or some such), you would change the ControlToValidate property to one TextBox, ControlToCompare to the other TextBox, and the Operator to Equal.

On top of all this, we have the RegularExpressionValidator control, which allows you to check the format of a control value. So, you might want to check for the @ symbol in an email address, for example, or that the user has entered a five-digit ZIP code. To use this, change the ControlToValidate property and select a ValidationExpression from the available options, or specify your own.

Finally, we have the CustomValidator control that allows you to specify your own validation JavaScript code, there for when the regular validation controls just aren't good enough. Check out the Help index for more information on how to do this.

We should note a couple of quick points about these validation controls, however. As you will have noticed, each comes with its own ControlToValidate property. They also have a Display property, which determines whether the control always stays in the same place (*static*) or is created in that spot when an error occurs (*dynamic*). My suggestion is to set this to dynamic.

Other common properties include EnableClientScript. Remember earlier when the validation checks were performed without even needing to post back to the server? That was done using regular JavaScript. If you don't want to use that, set this property to False.

Think we're finished yet? You should be so lucky—just a few more points to go.

The ValidationSummary control can also be found in your toolbox. This control can either automatically display a summary of all validation errors found either in a message box or on the Web page. Your call. Check out the ShowSummary and ShowMessageBox properties.

Anything else? You bet. You might be wondering how to check for validation errors in your code. After all, let's say that your user clicks a button and validation errors occur. That button may just be about to add all that invalid data to a database somewhere! How can you check? Simply use the IsValid property of your Page object. For example, you might use code like this before the rest of your database-adding button code:

```
If Page.IsValid = False Then Exit Sub
```

One last point: a bunch of button-like controls, such as the Button (naturally) and LinkButton, contain a CauseValidation property. Set this to False if you're creating a Cancel button. In this way, the client-side validation checks won't occur when clicked.

Phew! Can I have a nap now?

Try it now!

Create a new ASP.NET Web application and test some of the more advanced controls we've covered here. Can you get them to work? Try pushing validation to its limits!

The Data Trio

Need to display chunks of information on the Web? Never fear! ASP.NET comes bundled with a trio of groovy controls that are specially designed to work with whole blocks of data.

First off (and most importantly), we have the eternally groovy DataGrid control. If you've already taken Tutorial 2 "Doing Databases", you'll know exactly how to use this little beast.

Let's recap what we did back then. First off, we created our DataSet, filled with information from our database. Then we slapped a DataGrid control onto our form, set its DataSource property to our DataSet, then ran the .DataBind method—a little like this:

```
Dim MyDataSet As New DataSet()
' ... populate DataSet from database ...
MyDataGrid.DataSource = MyDataSet
MyDataGrid.DataBind()
```

> **TOP TIP** *Although you may* usually *set the DataSource property of your DataGrid to a DataSet, you don't have to. You have plenty of other options: you could bind it to a DataView, a DataTable, a DataReader, a HashTable, an ArrayList, and more. You've seen some of these objects in previous chapters. Check out the Help index to find out more information.*

You also get the DataList and Repeater controls with ASP.NET, and these allow you to bind to data sources in a similar manner. The DataList control creates a customized HTML table with a new row for each item in the data source. The Repeater control essentially follows your own instructions for how it should display data, then repeats it for each item in the data source. (See Figure 1-13 for examples.)

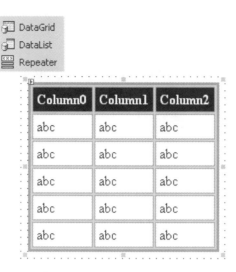

Figure 1-13. The DataGrid, DataList, and Repeat controls

You can get pretty advanced with this data trio. For example, you can "page" the information you display in a DataGrid or DataList control, meaning that you ask ASP.NET to automatically split its information over multiple pages. You can also really personalize your rows with the DataList and Repeater controls, perhaps using added hyperlinks or extra images and buttons.

So, you know it's possible. However, we won't be covering the Data Trio in any real further detail, so, if you're looking to really push out the boat with these widgets, you'll need to get researching.

Try checking out "DataGrid control, overview", "DataList control, overview", and "Repeater control, overview" in the Help index for more information. Each of those headers also packs a bundle of samples that are sure to more than answer your questions. Alternatively, hang around until Chapter 3.3 where I'll be listing a whole bunch of resources that'll enable you to take your ASP.NET knowledge even further.

The Option Controls

Want the user to select an option? Yes or No? Male or Female? Pickle, anchovy, or a big dollop of mayo? Then you're probably looking for one of the check or radio controls. Let's review your options.

First up, you have the CheckBox control. This gives you one singular checkbox that you can check. Or not. It's pretty simple to use too: you just look at the Checked property for its True or False value.

Next, we have the CheckBoxList control. This allows you to have multiple checkbox items all inside one control. It actually inherits from the same base as the DropDownList and ListBox controls we saw earlier, and, as before, you use the Items property to add items to the list. (See Figure 1-14 for examples of the CheckBox and CheckBoxList controls.)

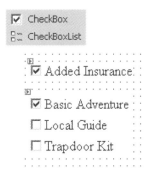

Figure 1-14. The CheckBox and CheckBoxList controls

But how do you know which items have been selected with the CheckBoxList? With the DropDownList and ListBox controls, the user typically selects only one item—so you can use the SelectedItem property. But this returns only the first item. To find out which others have been selected, you have to cycle through each in code, checking the Selected property. Here's a quick demonstration:

```
Dim i As Integer

For i = 0 To MyCheckBoxList.Items.Count - 1
    If MyCheckBoxList.Items(i).Selected = True Then
        MyCheckBoxList.Items(i).Text = "You Selected Me!"
    End If
Next
```

Moving on, the RadioButtonList control once again inherits from that same base as the DropDownList and ListBox. You just use the Items property to add individual RadioButton items to your control, then find out which has been selected via the SelectedItem property.

The next control on the Toolbox is the singular version of the RadioButtonList, our friend the RadioButton. Each radio button is a control on its own, and you can group a bundle of them together so that only one is selected at a time, by setting the GroupName property. Cool stuff. (See Figure 1-15 for examples of the RadioButtonList and RadioButton controls.)

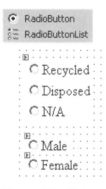

Figure 1-15. The RadioButtonList and RadioButton controls

My personal recommendation is that, when you need to use checkboxes, go for individual CheckBox controls—and, when you need to use radio buttons, choose the RadioButtonList. You'll find both of these most appropriate for regular applications.

Try it now!

Create a new ASP.NET Web application and try adding three items in
a RadioButtonList control, then try reading which option was selected.
What could such a control be used for? Could you use three CheckBox controls
for this instead?

The Visual Bunch

ASP.NET ships with a whole bundle of other controls that provide a heap of rich
functionality and do their own jobs very well but that don't neatly fit into an easy-
to-describe category. Still, they look pretty, so their home is in this section.

Who lives here? Well, we have the AdRotator, Image, ImageButton, Calendar,
and XML controls. Let's briefly cover each of these now.

Want to rotate a bunch of advertisements on your site? Heck, who doesn't?
It's the backbone income-generator for most Web stops, and the AdRotator control (Figure 1-16) helps you accomplish the task with a minimal amount of fuss.

Figure 1-16. The AdRotator control

How does it work? First off, you create an XML advertisement file, which lists
each banner ad you want to display, alongside a related link URL, the impression
distribution, a caption, and keyword. (Look up "AdRotator control, overview" in
the Help index for how to create such a file.) Next, you slap the AdRotator control
onto your Web form and point its AdvertisementFile property to your XML document and let ASP.NET do the rest!

One thing you might want to play around with here is setting the
KeywordFilter property at runtime, perhaps depending on which area of the Web
site your user is visiting. This will pull up the ads using that keyword, helping you
to serve up advertisements that are more targeted.

Want to display an image on your Web form? The Image control can help out.
(See Figure 1-17.) Not much else to say here really, except that if I were you I'd be
checking out the ImageUrl property.

Figure 1-17. Image control

TOP TIP *Instead of adding an Image control, you might want to click on the HTML tab on the toolbox and insert a regular Image element directly—or, add an <IMG> element by going into the HTML view of your Web form. If you can do it this way, why bother including a Web control to do the same sort of job for you? Simply because it allows you more power. You can change the Image control's properties at runtime with a line or two of code. However, you can't edit an <IMG> element quite so easily! The same goes for a hyperlink.*

Okay, so maybe the ImageButton control (Figure 1-18) doesn't look like the Button or LinkButton controls, but it's still a button. Sort of. Basically, you just set the ImageUrl property, then go on to write code behind its click event. No probs!

Figure 1-18. The ImageButton control

Next up is a control that you've already grown to love and cherish. Yes, it's the Calendar control, and it's a calendar. (See Figure 1-19.) Surprising, I know. But this is a really great control and you'll find a few interesting properties to play around with here: NextMonthText, NextPrevFormat, ShowGridlines, TitleFormat, and more! Oh, and there's a neat SelectedChanged event, too. How very useful.

Calendar

<		May 2002				>
S	M	T	W	T	F	S
28	29	30	1	2	3	4
5	6	7	8	9	10	11
12	13	14	15	16	17	18
19	20	21	22	23	24	25
26	27	28	29	30	31	1
2	3	4	5	6	7	8

Figure 1-19. The Calendar control

Finally is the XML control, as shown in Figure 1-20. As you may have guessed, this little number displays an XML document, formatting it per the instructions in an XSL (Extensible Stylesheet Language) file. To use it, specify an XSL file as the TransformSource property, then set the Document property to an XmlDocument object, the DocumentContent property to an XML string, or the DocumentSource property to a filename—and let this baby do the rest. It'll be pretty darn helpful as the XML standard becomes more commonplace in the development world. The Help index will bore anyone interested with full, gory details. Oh joy.

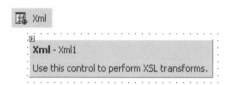

Figure 1-20. The XML control

Try it now!

Before moving on, create a new ASP.NET Web application and test each of these controls. See if you can write code to respond to the ImageButton click event. Also, try throwing together your own advertisement file. How do you get on? Could this be useful in the real world? And could it be used for anything apart from just advertisements?

We've finished exploring all of the most interesting ASP.NET Web controls. Some are big, some are small, some are about as useful as the Pope's wedding tackle. But you've been introduced to more of the key players now, which should help you make better interface decisions when designing your next Web application.

And we'll save *that* event for Chapter 3.2. For now, it's time to wrap up!

CONCLUSION

Well done on completing the first chapter here in Tutorial 3, "Working the Web"!

In this short introduction, we've taken a lightning tour of building ASP.NET Web applications. We started off by understanding how the .NET Framework serves up intelligent Web forms, then moved on to create a couple of groovy samples. Along the way, we explored concepts such as how the __VIEWSTATE field maintains control state, and we figured out just what files make up a standard Web application.

After that, we moved on to look at some of the Web controls, taking time out to play with everything from the AdRotator to the Validation controls, completing a bundle of mini exercises along the way. Erm, you did complete the exercises, right?

But we're still only scratching the rather clichéd tip of that iceberg. Next week, you'll be figuring out how to really expand your site, with a look at the top ten code snippets you just won't be able to live without. All that, and much more, coming up.

However, until then, this is me, Karl Moore, wishing you a very pleasant evening. Keep investigating all those controls, my friend—and *ciao* for now!

CHAPTER 3.1

THE ASP.NET REVOLUTION REVIEW SHEET

- ASP.NET is part of the .NET Framework. Its predecessor was ASP (Active Server Pages).

- Using Visual Studio .NET, you can create ASP.NET Web applications. Each Web application typically consists of one or more Web forms, which each represent interactive ASPX pages on your site.

- To create a Web application using VB .NET, paint your Toolbox controls onto a Web form, set properties as appropriate, and add Visual Basic code to glue it all together.

- Every ASPX page request made to your server is intercepted by the .NET Framework. The framework takes the information given, processes it, and runs any relevant code, then returns results to the client. Typically, all code is run on the server side.

- The .NET Framework *thinks* before sending results back to the client. For example, if the client browser supports only HTML 3.2, it will attempt to send only pure HTML 3.2 back. If, however, the target client supports some of the more advanced Web control and document features you may have used in your pages, these are sent down the line.

- In Web forms, the "state" of your controls is handled automatically, using the hidden __VIEWSTATE field. For example, the __VIEWSTATE may store the Text property of your Label control, ensuring that that property remains the same, no matter how many times the user resubmits their form, and so on.

- You can stop the .NET Framework recording __VIEWSTATE information for a particular control by setting its EnableViewState property to False.

- ASP.NET is bundled with a set of Validation controls to allow you to easily implement simple input data checks. These are RequiredFieldValidator, CompareValidator, RangeValidator, RegularExpressionValidator, and CustomValidator. You can check whether a page is "valid" using the IsValid method of the Page object.

- Three main data controls are bundled with ASP.NET: DataGrid, DataList, and Repeater. The DataGrid control is specifically designed for data binding, whereas the others allow for powerful customization.

- The AdRotator control allows you to manage advertisements on your site through an XML-based AdvertisementFile. You can also specify keywords through the KeywordFilter property to allow you to target users better.

Ten Top Code Snippets You Can't Live Without

"The Internet is a great way to get on the Net."—Bob Dole

IT'S TIME TO GET SERIOUS. That's right: put away the *Beano* comics and get out *Programmer's Weekly*.

In the last chapter, we picked up the essentials, figuring out how to create a basic site, how to work with controls in code, and basically how the whole ASPX dream fits together.

But that was then and this is now. Erm, obviously.

Today, we'll be spending our entire session looking at ten top code snippets, techniques from my own groovy development workshops that you'll find yourself using in virtually every application you develop.

And, because I'm feeling all cruel, we'll conclude with a little ASP.NET test to check your current knowledge level. Prizes and all, you know.

So close that door, sit down with your cup of java, and boot up that cranky 286. It's time to party!

Erm, program. I meant *program*.

The Top Ten List

A monk signs up at a local monastery and takes a vow of silence that allows him to say but two words every two years—and only in the presence of the head monks. Well, two years pass, and he is called up to the head monks.

"What are your two words, brother?" asked the head monk. "Cold floors" came the reply. The head monk raised an eyebrow, but nodded and the monk went on his way. Another two years pass and once again the monk is called upon for his two words.

"What are your two words, brother?" asked the head monk. "Bad food" came the reply. Again, there was a nod and he left the assembly. More time passed and, now in his sixth year, the monk was called into the room once again for his biannual two words.

"What are your two words, brother?" asked the head monk. "I quit!" said the brother.

"Good!" came the sharp reply. "You've done nothing but complain since you got here!"

Oh boy, please, stop laughing. But you can't blame me for trying to keep the air light and breezy: you see, after this, it's all incredibly serious. You're going to learn the top ten coding techniques you'll use all the time in your Web applications.

At the end of each technique, you'll see the "Try it now!" note, where you should go and experiment, playing with the technique and implementing it in a sample ASP.NET Web application.

And, of course, we have that test coming up. So study carefully, or it'll be detention and fifty lines.

Are you ready? Strap yourself in tightly; this might be a turbulent ride. Height restrictions apply. Okay, let the tips rip!

1. Redirecting the User

Need to send the user to another page? If you just need a link, the Hyperlink control is probably what you're looking for. But, if you need to redirect in your code, you're best with the Redirect method of the Response object. Let's see that in use:

```
Response.Redirect("MyWebForm.aspx")
Response.Redirect("http://www.karlmoore.com/")
```

> **TOP TIP** *If you've worked with ASP before, you'll already be acquainted with the Response object—along with Application, Request, Server, Session, and User. All of these objects are still available in ASP.NET—all officially under the Page object and almost identical to the classic ASP objects. There's no amazingly difficult learning curve here. We'll be covering some of the best features of these objects today, but, if you're interested in finding out more, check the Help index.*

> **ANOTHER TOP TIP** *The Page object refers to your current page. You don't need to type* Page *before being able to access objects such as Response or Session, because it's intrinsically implied. However, if you ever get lost and don't know where to find your solution, try typing* Page. *and browsing through the available objects. You'll find it a useful starting point.*

So, that's how to redirect a user in code. It's a simple sample to start us off—not very interesting, though an essential code snippet for your developer's tip bag.

Try it now!

2. Setting Cookies

You've probably heard of cookies before, and, no, I'm not talking about those things you nibble at supper with a cold glass of milk. Rather, cookies on the Web are little information files that are stored on the user's computer—and your site can use them to store and retrieve details.

For example, you might save the username in a cookie. Then, when the user next accesses your site, you might read the username from that cookie and make it the default logon. Or perhaps you'll store the users' geographical location, so you can display appropriate weather forecasts each time they visit.

So, how do you create a cookie?

```
Dim MyCookie As New HttpCookie("preferences")
MyCookie.Values.Add("username", "Karl")
MyCookie.Values.Add("country", "UK")
MyCookie.Values.Add("lastvisit", Now.Date)
MyCookie.Expires = DateTime.MaxValue
Response.AppendCookie(MyCookie)
```

Here, we're creating a "preferences" cookie that stores values for "username", "country", and "lastvisit". It's also good practice to set expiry dates on cookies. Here, we're setting it to the maximum value of the DateTime object, which basically means it never expires. Finally, we append the cookie using our Response object.

So that's how to create—and even update—a cookie. But what about reading them?

```
Dim MyCookie As HttpCookie
MyCookie = Request.Cookies("preferences")

If Not MyCookie Is Nothing Then
    Dim Username As String
    Username = MyCookie.Values("username")
End If
```

Here, we're creating a HttpCookie placeholder, then setting it to our preferences cookie via the Request object. If the cookie exists (in other words, if MyCookie is Not Nothing), we then use it to retrieve the "username" value.

Try it now!

3. Remembering the User Session

Every time a user visits your site, your Web server gives you access to a Session object. This is basically a server store of information that is particular to that user and their one session at your site.

You typically put into that store only data that you want to save for the period of their session. As an example, last week I created a data input site that contained multiple wizard-style input pages. So I temporarily stored the data from each page in the session, and collated it all at the end.

So, how do you add information to the Session object for a user? It's pretty simple:

```
Session.Add("LastViewed", "NP4922")
```

And you can read information from the Session object just by accessing that Session object once more:

```
Dim MySessionObject As String
MySessionObject = Session.Item("LastViewed")

If Not MySessionObject Is Nothing Then
    txtLastViewed.Text = MySessionObject
End If
```

In both the samples here, we've set and retrieved the value of a string. But the Session object can hold just about anything—from an Integer to a Hyperlink control to an instance of a class. Anything.

It's worth noting that the Session object will typically become invalid when the user closes the browser window, or if they remain inactive at the site for twenty minutes or longer. You can change that default time value by editing the <sessionState> element in the Web.config file.

Also, you can remove objects from the session, or ditch it altogether, using code such as:

```
Session.Remove("LastViewed")
Session.Abandon()
```

Try it now!

4. Looking at the Browser

Sometimes it's good to know what browser your user is using. You might want to log it in your statistics, so you know whether most visitors will be able to view some of your more advanced features. Or you might want to find out which are using AOL, so you can warn them about potential compatibility problems. Or you might just want to find out which are still using Internet Explorer 2.0, so you can have a good laugh.

Either way, you do all of this using the Browser property of the Request object. Let's look at a few code snippets showing it in action:

```
Dim MyText As String

' Returns the browser type (ex: IE6)
MyText = Request.Browser.Type

' Returns the browser name (ex: IE)
MyText = Request.Browser.Browser

' Returns the browser major version number (ex: 6)
MyText = Request.Browser.MajorVersion

' Returns the platform (ie, WinNT)
Label1.Text = Request.Browser.Platform

' Returns a True if using AOL
If Request.Browser.AOL = True Then
    MyText = "You've Got Mail!"
End If

' Returns a True if supports VBScript
If Request.Browser.VBScript = True Then
    MyText = "You browser can run VBScript!"
End If

' Returns a True if supports background sounds
If Request.Browser.BackgroundSounds = True Then
    MyText = "I can annoy you with music!"
End If

' Returns a True if supports cookies
If Request.Browser.Cookies = False Then
```

```
MyText = "Your browser (a) has cookies turned off, or (b) is real old"
End If
```

Try it now!

5. Finding the Referrer and URL

Want to find out where your user came from? Whether they clicked through from a completely different site or from one of your own pages, the UrlReferrer property of the Request object will help you find out. It's kind like that, you see.

Let's look at a sample of its usage:

```
Dim MyReferrer As String
MyReferrer = Request.UrlReferrer.AbsoluteUri
```

You can also find out what page you are currently "on" by checking out the Url property of the Request object. Why would you want this? Well, many sites display the current Web address (also known as the *URL*, or *Uniform Resource Locator*) somewhere on their page as standard practice. Here's a sample:

```
MyURL = Request.Url.AbsoluteUri
```

Also, here's a smarter use: imagine you have an account with a Web host and two addresses pointing to that same account. Let's say, `www.karlmoore.com` and `www.whitecliff.net`. However, when someone visits the Karl Moore site, you want to show your personal site—and, when someone visits White Cliff, you want to show the business site. However, you only have one hosting account and both of these Web addresses are pointed at it, right?

The solution is to simply create an opening page in ASP.NET. On that page, check the Url property: depending on which site the user requested, redirect them to the appropriate page or subdirectory. Oh, and because you'll require only the one host, you'll save yourself a huge wad of cash in the process. Supercool!

Try it now!

6. Is This a Postback?

As you start developing Web applications, you'll probably find yourself putting a lot of initialization code behind the page load event.

Let's imagine a scenario. You're creating a doctor's reservation system, like we did last week. In the page load event, you're setting a TextBox control to a suggested appointment time. The user fills in the details to book an appointment and then clicks on a button to confirm the appointment.

The problem is that, when the form posts itself back and then returns with the confirmation, the page load event runs again—meaning that your TextBox control gets set to that suggested time once more.

Whoops! Therefore, if you're going to put initialization code in your page load event, check the IsPostBack property of your Page object. This returns a False if this is the first time the page has loaded. Let's look at that in action.

```
If IsPostBack = False Then
    ' code here only runs once,
    ' when page first loads
End If
```

You might not think it now, but this code snippet is jolly useful in the real world. Trust me. I'm a programmer.

Try it now!

7. Get the User IP Address

Need to grab the user's IP address? Plenty of sites log such information for security reasons. And you can access this data via the UserHostAddress property of the Request object, like so:

```
Dim MyAddress As String
MyAddress = Request.UserHostAddress
```

You can also get the DNS name of the remote client by using the UserHostName property. With regular dial-up Internet users, this will typically return a service provider machine address.

Try it now!

8. Uploading a File

In the golden olden days, uploading a file was Mission Impossible. Most developers ended up digging deep to purchase a third-party add-on to help them achieve the desired result. But not in the wonderful world of ASP.NET.

So, how do you do it? Well, first you need to add an instance of the File Field element to your form. (You can find this under the HTML tab in the toolbox.) The File Field element allows users to select a file on their local machines, with the goal of uploading it. You've probably seen such a widget when sending attachments via mail sites such as Hotmail and Yahoo! (See Figure 2-1.)

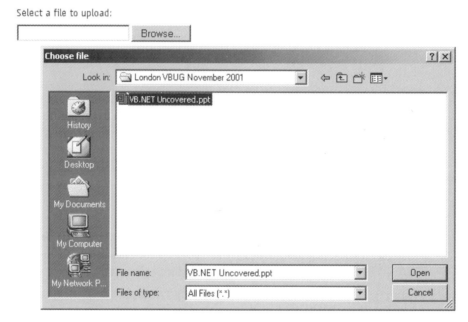

Figure 2-1. The File Field element in action

However, the problem is that this is an actual HTML element, not a control. And, if you remember, we said earlier that you can't work with HTML elements in code—that is, unless you make a couple of slight alterations.

You'll need to select your element first to view its details in the Properties window. From here, you need to give it a name by changing the ID property, then make it available to ASP.NET by right-clicking on the control and clicking on "Run As Server Control". This changes the "runat" property to "server". ASP.NET should now be able to see and work with the control.

That's the first real change—pretty simple stuff so far. Let's move on.

Now, most forms on the Internet just pass about regular chunks of data, and most browsers handle typical forms with absolute ease. But here, we need to tell the browser that it won't be passing back regular form text this time. Instead, it may need to post back actual file information—and, for the browser to do that, we need to tell it to use a different "encoding type." It'd be nice just to set an "encodingtype=file" option, but that doesn't sound technical enough.

Rather, in the HTML view of your Web form, you need to add this parameter to the <FORM> tag: encType="multipart/form-data". After the change, your whole <FORM> tag may look something like this:

```
<form id="Form1" method="post" encType="multipart/form-data" runat="server">
```

That's the second change. For our final alteration, you need to add code to actually take the selected file, then save it somewhere on your server machine. How? Simply add one line of code, like this:

```
NameOfFieldFieldElement.PostedFile.SaveAs("c:\temp\testfile.txt")
```

And that's it. With just a couple of small edits and a line of code, you've implemented a full upload routine.

> **TOP TIP**   *If you're looking to grab the original filename, just check out the MyFile.PostedFile.FileName property.*

> **ANOTHER TOP TIP**   *If you're dealing with multiple users, you want to be careful that you don't accidentally overwrite other user files using code like this. It may be worthwhile writing your own code routine to generate unique file names for each upload.*

Try it now!

9. Using a Query String

If you've ever run a search at any of the top engines, you'll probably have seen a query string in action. For example, run a "Karl Moore" search at MetaCrawler.com, and the resulting search screen will have a URL looking something like this:

```
http://search.metacrawler.com/crawler?general=Karl+Moore
```

Everything from the question mark onward is the query string. The concept is pretty simple; extra bits of information are stored in the actual URL, which can be easily retrieved. It's a way of passing information to other pages.

So, for example, you may have a main index page that allows the user to select products from an online catalog. Each of these items has a unique ID number, with full descriptions stored in your online database. What happens when the user clicks on each individual product? Will you be creating a separate page to hold the details of every product you stock?

Sounds a bit time consuming, doesn't it? A much better way would be to create a general page that can display details of any one of your products. Then, from your catalog, send your user to that page to display more information, along with an extra parameter as part of the query string, like so:

```
http://www.yoursite.com/displayproduct.aspx?id=490
```

But how does your displayproduct.aspx page know which product to load from the database? It just checks the QueryString property of the Request object, like so:

```
Dim MyID As String
MyID = Request.QueryString("id")
```

What other real-life instances could you use this for? A site search? A page to view news stories? Have a quick think.

Also, there a few extra considerations to make when using query strings. Firstly, when adding a parameter to the query string, you should first encode it. Why? Well, imagine that you weren't dealing with an ID number but a search term. If someone types in "Karl Moore", you need to insert a + sign between the words Karl and Moore. Spaces, "angle brackets" and certain other symbols aren't allowed in query strings and need to be encoded first.

To automatically encode your whole parameter value, use the UrlEncode function of the Server object, like this:

```
Dim MyURL As String
MyURL = "http://site/mypage.aspx?search=" & _
    Server.UrlEncode(">Karl + Mark's Forum!<")
```

There's also a UrlDecode function of the Server object, which will help you reverse this process when requesting the QueryString property.

One more note: you can easily create your own forms for users to enter a query value parameter and have them submit it directly to your own page. An example of this could be:

```
<form method="GET" action="http://search.metacrawler.com/crawler">
<input type="text" name="general"><input type="submit" value="Search Now">
</form>
```

Here, we're using the GET form method rather than POST. This takes our INPUT controls' name and value, adding them to the query string. So, if I entered "Karl Moore" in the above HTML form and submitted it, the resulting URL would be:

```
http://search.metacrawler.com/crawler?general=Karl+Moore
```

It's just another useful way of building up a query string. Of course, users could always bookmark this address directly, meaning that they'd have no need to submit forms with each and every visit.

Anyway, that's it. No more notes, over and out.

Try it now!

10. Adding to the ViewState

You've heard about the ViewState before. When working with Web forms, ASP.NET uses a hidden HTML field that contains encrypted details of your Form control properties. (See Figure 2-2.)

This is how it manages to maintain the state of your controls between each form post. When you post your form back to the server, it first decrypts that data and re-creates the form as it was when sent to you. It then applies any changes, such as new values you've entered in text boxes, and, finally, it runs your actual code.

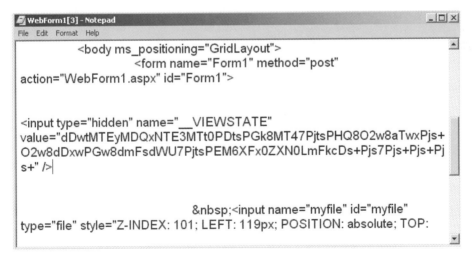

Figure 2-2. The encrypted __VIEWSTATE *field*

All that clever state management, previously unseen in the Web programming world, thanks to the hidden __VIEWSTATE field.

You can also use the power of ViewState by *adding* to it. If you have values you want to temporarily add to the encrypted __VIEWSTATE, simply use the ViewState object. Let's see it in use:

```
' Add items to the ViewState
ViewState.Add("User", "Karl")
ViewState.Add("Display", 100)

' Referencing an item in the ViewState
Dim MyUser As String
MyUser = ViewState.Item("User")

' Removing from the ViewState
ViewState.Remove("Display")
```

Don't forget however that your __VIEWSTATE information remains only while the user is submitting on that one Web form. If they move away, you will no longer be able to access the information. If you need to store information longer, you'll probably want to use the Session object or cookies.

Also, by default, most controls on your form have their state monitored and recorded in __VIEWSTATE. If you don't want a control to have any changed properties stored in the ViewState, set its EnableViewState property to False.

Try it now!

Quiz Time

I hate examinations. I took a computer design examination a few months ago, and my results were so low, I hear they were last spotted by Alice in Wonderland half an hour after she pondered, "Hmm, I wonder what's down that hole."

Still, my psychologist says I need to face up to this fear; I need to confront it head-on. Therefore, let's dive into a little quiz: ten simple questions based on everything you've learned so far. Oh, and there are no answers either, so you either need to know your stuff, or be exceptionally good at scouring pages.

Ready? Make sure that you answer each one fully before continuing.

1. You are creating a Web application to run a hotel. The accommodations include three main types of bedrooms: Complete Dive, Relatively Decent, and the Ultra-Glam Suite. Which control would be best for allowing the user to select this option?

2. You're creating a page for your surfers to subscribe to your newsletter, *Weighty Watchers Weekly*. You've decided to get the user to enter their email address twice to ensure that it's typed correctly, displaying an error message if it isn't. Which control would you use for checking this, and what properties would you set?

3. Finally, you've finished creating that "Email Us!" form. The user enters some details and clicks on the button, but, instead of just a simple "Submit", you want to display an animated email button. When the user clicks on it, you want your code to run and send their message. Which control would be most appropriate here?

4. While designing your application, you've figured out that you need to remember different pieces of information for different lengths of time. For example, you might want to remember a username for the entire session, whereas other pieces may need to be best stored for the longer term. What state-management technique could you use to store information temporarily, for just one page? For one entire Web site session? Permanently? List the three main techniques and how you could use them.

5. What property would you use to find out if the user was running a version 6 browser?

6. Imagine that you've created a product lookup page that utilizes a query string. How can you read the value of an item in the query string?

7. You're running a site that allows users to upload their own MIDI files for possible inclusion on the site. You have to make three core changes to your Web form to implement an upload routine. What are they?

8. You're getting a lot of hits to your specialty wood site from BillsHardwareHouse.com, and you want to reward each with a special offer on your homepage. How can you figure out whether a visitor came from Bill and display an offer as appropriate?

9. The catalog search function you've been working on is almost complete. However, if a user searches for an invalid character—such as a space or equal sign—an error occurs. Before you send the user to that page, you've forgotten to encode your parameter values. How do you do that? And how do you later decode them?

10. What is a postback? And how can you tell in code if your form has already been "posted back'?

CONCLUSION

Corr blimey, missus! Yes, it's another complete chapter overrun, but boy has this one been action packed.

We've spent today learning the top ten Web development techniques you'll find yourself using in almost every site you create. We've learned how to personalize each visitor's session, which objects to use when you want to find out more about your users, the three changes you need to make to accept a file for upload—and much, much more.

And, with each of the ten tips, you went off and tested your new knowledge in your very own Web application. I know you did, really.

Finally, we concluded with a knowledge quiz to test some of the key concepts we've stumbled across so far. And you scored an amazing 10 out of 10. Amazing. Amazing. Truly amazing.

So a big well-done to you, my friend—and thanks for sticking with me through all the rough stuff!

What's next? Well, there's just one more chapter to go in this tutorial, where we'll explore authentication in our applications, look at a bundle of supercool quick tips to take your site to the next level, and find out how we can get our final application out to the big, big world. And, naturally, we'll have our usual FAQ list and "Where to Go from Here" section.

All that, next time. And so, until then, this is your host, Karl Moore, signing off for tonight. Goodnight!

CHAPTER 3.2

- To redirect the user to another page in code, use:

```
Response.Redirect("mypageorsite.aspx")
```

- To check where the user last came from, use:

```
Request.UrlReferrer.AbsoluteUri
```

- You can tell whether a page has been "posted back" to the server by checking the IsPostBack function of the Page object.

- You can read data from a query string by checking the QueryString property of the Request object, like this:

```
MyVar = Request.QueryString("queryparametername")
```

- The three main ways of managing state in your applications are: adding to the ViewState, utilizing the Session object, and implementing cookies.

- You can use the ViewState object to add and retrieve automatically encrypted data from the hidden __VIEWSTATE field. The __VIEWSTATE exists with only the current page and does not persist when the page changes. Here is an example of adding to the ViewState:

```
ViewState.Add("ViewsPerPage", 100)
```

- Every visitor to your site holds a unique session with your server, and you can utilize the Session object to add and retrieve data from the current user's session. All items stored in the session are held on the server and have a default timeout period of twenty minutes. (To change this, edit the Web.config file.) Use this object to store data to be used during the period of that one site visit. Here is an example of adding to the session:

```
Session.Add("Username", "Karl")
```

- Cookies enable you to store small chunks of data more permanently on the user's machine. To create a cookie, you declare a new HttpCookie object, add individual value sets to the cookie, then add it using the AppendCookie method of the Response object. Here is an example of setting and reading a cookie:

```
Dim MyCookie As New HttpCookie("style")

' Set the Cookie
MyCookie.Values.Add("backcolor", "blue")
MyCookie.Expires = DateTime.MaxValue
Response.AppendCookie(MyCookie)

' Read the Cookie
MyCookie = Request.Cookies("style")
If Not MyCookie Is Nothing Then
    Dim MyBackcolor As String
    MyBackcolor = MyCookie.Values("backcolor")
End If
```

3.3

Authentication, Tips, Distribution, and More

"When will the highways on the Internet become more few?"
—*George W. Bush*

WELCOME TO THE THIRD CHAPTER in . . . wow, did you hear that? We're on the third chapter! Well, slap me silly and call me Sally, that means this is the last part in Tutorial 3, "Working the Web"!

Just one more block of hard work and you're officially a supercool Web guru. And that means big cars, expensive holidays, and gold medallions that would make even Mr. T envious.

So, what's on the agenda today? To start off, we'll explore the world of authentication, allowing users to sign in and out of your site. After that, we'll spend two minutes figuring out a couple of neat tricks that can really improve your sites, then we'll discuss how you can actually get your ASP.NET applications out to the world.

And it doesn't stop there. Before concluding, as ever, we'll talk about where you can take your Web programming knowledge from here, then answer all those frequently asked questions.

So, are you ready? Onward, knights. . . .

Securing Your Sites

You know, I used to be a trusting soul. Right up until about five years of age.

I'd won a fortune on a Blackpool slot machine. (Well, it was about fifty pence in tuppence pieces, which roughly equated to five sweet mixes, but, back in those days, if you had five sweet mixes, you had a fortune.)

As the pennies dropped, I rushed to tell my mum of the win. She instantly turned toward me and asked, "Where's the money now?"

"Just at the machine," I said, still smiling innocently, completely oblivious to any potential problem. Mum grabbed my young arm and rushed over to the Two Pence Master Blaster.

Gone.

It was at that point that my instinctive distrust of fellow human beings started to set in. I don't lend anyone my house key. I have a triple steel lock on my bedroom door. And my Web sites are more secure than Fort Knox on code red.

Hmm, security. Yes, it's another smooth Karl Moore link, but distrust isn't always a bad thing—*especially* if you consider it when you build your Web sites. And that's just what we'll be discussing in this section.

The Types of Authentication

Let me ask you a question: Who can access your Web applications *right now*? Well, all your sites run through Internet Information Services (IIS), which determines who can and can't view your content. And, by default, any Web application created via Visual Studio .NET isn't secured at all.

In other words, right now, any surfer can view any page in your Web application.

Although that's not always a bad thing, there are times when you might want to prompt your surfer for a username and password to figure out exactly who they are. They need *authenticating*.

How can you do that? As ever, yet another plethora of weird and wonderful options are open to you. And, for your viewing pleasure, here they are: all the types of authentication available under ASP.NET.

- *Windows*: This is where you get the user to provide you with a username and password that directly maps to a Windows account. Any work the user does on the site after that is done under this account name. It's most useful for corporate intranets and the like.

- *Passport*: Sites such as Hotmail.com now all link back to a single Passport account. You can implement such a feature on your own site, too (for a slight fee, *naturally*). For more information, visit `www.passport.com/business/`.

- *Forms*: This is the most popular type of authentication. It allows you to restrict access to all your application pages until the user enters valid credentials.

In this section, we'll be dealing with absolutely the most common method: using forms authentication in your application. For samples using the other techniques, check out the Help index.

So, how does forms authentication work? Once turned on, every time a surfer accesses a page in your Web application, a check is made to see whether the user is logged on. If not, they're sent to our login form (by default, login.aspx).

At this stage, if valid credentials are entered, you officially authenticate the user, sending a cookie containing an identity key to their machine. They're then redirected back to the page they originally requested. And if the credentials they enter aren't valid? Well, you whip them silly.

Sounds fair enough to me.

Setting Up Forms Authentication

Intrigued by forms authentication? Want to have a go at setting it up right now? Please, say yes.

1. Create a new Web application, changing its location to
   `http://localhost/letmein`.

By default, your Web application is about as secure as Cynthia Payne's chastity belt, so we need to change that. How? We edit the Web.config file, telling it to use forms authentication and providing a list of valid usernames and passwords.

2. Open the Web.config file (see Figure 3-1) and change the
   <authentication> element, so it reads as follows:

```
<authentication mode="Forms">
    <forms>
        <credentials passwordFormat="Clear">
            <user name="karl" password="moore" />
            <user name="strangely" password="brown" />
        </credentials>
    </forms>
</authentication>
```

```
Web.config                                                            ◁ ▷ ✕
    <!--    AUTHENTICATION
            This section sets the authentication policies of the appl:
            "Forms", "Passport" and "None"
    -->

    <authentication mode="Forms">
        <forms>
            <credentials passwordFormat="Clear">
                <user name="karl" password="moore" />
                <user name="strangely" password="brown" />
            </credentials>
        </forms>
    </authentication>

  ☐ XML    ☐ Data
```

Figure 3-1. Editing the Web.config file

This might look a little confusing, but Web.config is just an XML document, a file that contains structured information within "elements" (akin to HTML tags). We're just editing some of that information here, specifying new settings.

TOP TIP   *Other options for the authentication mode element are Windows, Passport, and None (the default). Also, watch out for the potential pitfall here: everything in the Web.config file is case sensitive!*

ANOTHER TOP TIP   *Here, we're setting the passwordFormat attribute to Clear. This tells ASP.NET that we're storing our passwords in plain text. Although our surfers can't access this document, it still isn't all that secure, because as internal colleagues with access to your server could view the list. Therefore, you should always encrypt the passwords to SHA1 or MD5 standards. For more information on how to do this, look up "passwordFormat attribute" in the Help index (using the Visual Basic and Related filter).*

So, that's the forms authentication added, along with our list of usernames and passwords. Next, we need to tell Web.config to deny access to anyone that isn't forms authenticated.

3. Still in the Web.config file, within the <authorization> element, remove the `<allow users="*" />` line. This line grants access to anyone.

4. Still within the <authorization> element, add the following line to deny access to all anonymous users (that is, those not authenticated):

    ```
    <deny users="?" />
    ```

Whenever a page in your application is accessed now—and your user is not authenticated—they will be forcibly redirected to login.aspx. Oh, *feel* the power! And, no, you don't need your hands for that.

> **TOP TIP** *You can change the default page of login.aspx by editing the Forms element of your Web.config file to include the loginUrl parameter, as so:* `<forms loginUrl="myloginpage.aspx" />`.

Next, let's work on our actual site. Admittedly, it's going to be a small site. Actually, a tiny site. To be specific, it'll have only two pages: a logon screen and a regular page. Let's get on with the logon page first.

5. Using the Solution Explorer, rename WebForm1.aspx to "login.aspx".

6. Decorate the form as you deem appropriate (see Figure 3-2), ensuring you add the following essential controls:

    *   *TextBox*—Name: txtUsername

    *   *TextBox*—Name: txtPassword; TextMode: Password

    *   *CheckBox*—Name: chkPersist; Text: "Remember Me"

    *   *Button*—Name: btnLogin; Text: "Logon"

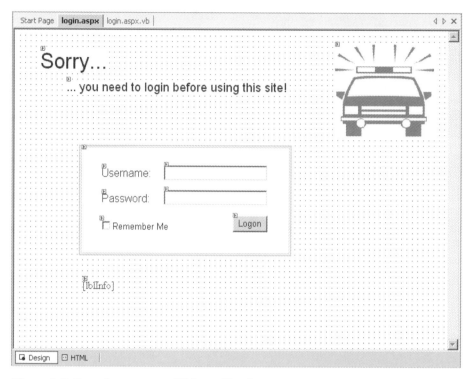

Figure 3-2. Our almost-secure Web application

- *Label*—Name: lblInfo; Text: (blank); ForeColor: Red

Our lovely user will skip along to this page, enter their credentials into the TextBox controls, and click on our button. Behind the button, we'll check that they're a valid user. If they are, we'll authenticate. If not, we'll exterminate. Simple, really.

Classes, Code, Controls—Oh My!

To do the authentication, we need to work with the FormsAuthentication class, which is part of the System.Web.Security namespace. Now, we can either type in System.Web.Security.FormsAuthentication every time you need to access the class, or "import" that namespace so you can use its functionality direct. Uhm, let's go for the latter:

1. In the code behind login.aspx, add the following above the class definition (the bit starting with Public Class):

```
Imports System.Web.Security
```

Next, let's add code to actually authenticate the user.

2.   Add the following code to respond to the click event of btnLogin:

```
If FormsAuthentication.Authenticate(txtUsername.Text, txtPassword.Text) = True Then
    FormsAuthentication.RedirectFromLoginPage(txtUsername.Text, chkPersist.Checked)
Else
    lblInfo.Text = "Invalid credentials - please try again, you hacker type, you!"
End If
```

What's our code doing here? It starts by actually checking the user credentials against our stored list, using the Authenticate method of FormsAuthentication. If this returns False, there's no match, so we tell the user to go take a hike.

However, if the Authenticate method returns True, we move on into our If statement. The next line uses the FormsAuthentication class again, running the RedirectFromLoginPage method, passing in the username and a True/False value depending on whether chkPersist is checked.

This RedirectFromLoginPage method does all the dog work. It sends back the encrypted cookie, then takes the user back to the page they initially tried to access. In other words, if they were trying to access members.aspx and ASP.NET realized they weren't authenticated, it would take them to our login form here. After successfully entering their credentials, an encrypted cookie would be set, and they'd be taken back to that original members.aspx form. How nice.

You might be wondering just what those parameters to RedirectFromLoginPage are. The first simply specifies the username logged on, and the second True/False value determines whether the encrypted cookie should "persist" (in other words, whether it should expire as soon as the user closes their browser or remember their details for the next time, "persisting" the user logon between sessions).

If you want an application to be particularly secure, don't give the user this persist option—always set the parameter to False. This ensures that nobody can ever impersonate your surfer just because they're using his/her computer. However, if you need authentication only to personalize a site or allow access to nonpersonal information, you might want to go for this.

Righto, that's our login form sorted. Next, let's create our main form. This will just contain one label that will welcome the user and offer a logout button. Oh, what functionality!

No, that was a question. What functionality?

3. From the menu, select Project ➤ Add Web Form.

4. Christen your new form default.aspx and click on Open.

> **TOP TIP**   *Remember that default.aspx will be the first file to be loaded when your Web application virtual directory is accessed, that is,* `http://localhost/letmein/`.

5. Decorate your form as you deem appropriate (see Figure 3-3), making sure that you add the following essential controls:

   - *Label*—Name: lblWelcome; Text: (blank)

   - *Button*—Name: btnSignout; Text: "Sign Out"

Figure 3-3. Our default.aspx page (I know you're impressed.)

Yes, it's about as exciting as Anne Robinson's hen night, but it'll suffice for this sample. Let's add a little code to spruce up the scene.

6. Add the following code to respond to the page load event of default.aspx:

    ```
    lblWelcome.Text = "Welcome, " & User.Identity.Name & "!"
    ```

Here, we're just setting our label to a quick welcome message. We're referencing the `User.Identity.Name` property, which will contain the authenticated username we gave when using the RedirectFromLoginPage method earlier.

We're almost there now. We just need to add code to sign the user out, then take them back to our login page.

7. Add the following code to respond to the click event of btnSignOut:

    ```
    System.Web.Security.FormsAuthentication.SignOut()
    Response.Redirect("login.aspx")
    ```

Testing Our Finished Application

Well, hurrah and hujjah with big fancy knobs and curly frills, we've finished! Let's compile our Web application.

1. From the menu, select Build ➢ Build Solution (or use the `Ctrl+Shift+B` shortcut).

Next, let's give our final Web application a whirl!

2. Launch Internet Explorer and try to access `http://localhost/letmein/`.

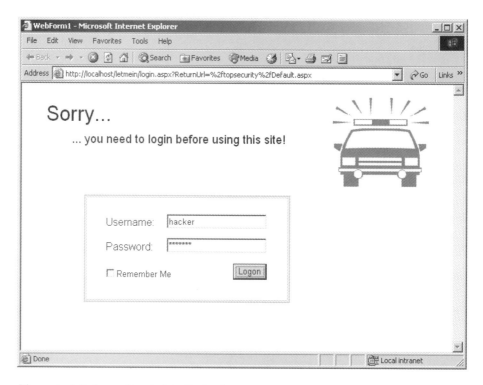

Figure 3-4. Being redirected to the login.aspx page

Even though you would typically load the default.aspx page, your security settings should have kicked in and you should be automatically directed to login.aspx, with the "ReturnURL" in the query string. (See Figure 3-4.)

Try submitting an invalid username and password. What happens? Now try slapping in a set of credentials that work—"karl" and "moore", for example. (For now, do not check Remember Me.) If valid, the page should automatically send back the encrypted cookie, plus redirect you to your first requested page, default.aspx.

As that page loads, it should greet you with your username, plus offer a Sign Out button. Has that worked? Where else would it be useful to reference that username? Perhaps when adding a record to a database?

Now try clicking on the Sign Out button. This removes the authentication cookie and takes you back to the login.aspx page. To prove you're signed out, try clicking back to the default.aspx once again. Now click on Refresh. What happens? Can you reload that page?

Next, try logging in again, this time using the Persist option. Then, instead of signing out, close your browser and try accessing the site again. What happens?

All these questions leave me feeling like Hercule Poirot, so at this point I'd like to say congratulations! You've just finished your very first Web application utilizing the latest in ASP.NET authentication. Supercool!

Expanding the Authentication

Don't tell me. I can guess your next question. You're thinking that you don't really want to store all those credentials in the Web.config file, aren't you? You'd rather look up the username and password, and then do your own comparison, right?

Hmm, fair point. And the solution is about as simple as an exceptionally simple thing, made even easier and with added simplicity.

In the last example, we used the Authenticate function to verify whether the user was valid. Well, just replace this with your own verification code, perhaps a little database script to grab the valid password then compare with the user input. After that, continue as normal, using the RedirectFromLoginPage method as we did earlier.

In other words, to use forms authentication with your own data source, simply write the code and don't bother with that Authenticate function. It only checks user details against the Web.config file and returns a True or False, which isn't very useful.

> **TOP TIP** *If you want to store passwords in your database, you might be interested in reading "Using Simple Encryption" in Chapter 8.3, "Advanced Tips and Techniques".*

Incidentally, if you go down this authenticate-it-yourself route, it means you can remove all your users from that Web.config file. In fact, you can now replace the entire <authentication> element and all its lovely little children with just:

```
<authentication mode="Forms" />
```

How very quaint. And that, my friends, is authentication.

Improving Your Site

So, you've created your mega-cool site and the visitors are flocking. You're making full use of the greatest Web controls this side of Saturn and are churning out more cookies than Miss Mary in July. How can you improve what you've done so far?

Well, I hear it's difficult to develop on perfection. But, just in case, here are a few top tips to help keep your site above the crowd.

Using FrontPage to Design

You probably already have Microsoft FrontPage on your machine. It's now distributed with Office and allows you to easily knock together exceptionally
cool-looking Web pages within minutes. My tip?

1. Before really getting into your programming, get the design right first.
    Knock together at least a few base pages using FrontPage (see Figure 3-5).
    Then, go into FrontPage HTML view and copy all the code.

2. Next, flick over to VB .NET. Open one of your Web forms in Design view,
    then switch to HTML mode. Remove all the existing HTML, excluding
    only the yellow line at the top. This is what tells ASP.NET where all your
    actual code for this page lies and is pretty darn important. Paste
    all your HTML code after this line.

3. Finally, you need to add one extra HTML tag. As its name suggests, a Web
    form is all about actual forms, <form> tags that are processed on our
    server. But our page right now doesn't have any of these tags right now;
    we've just overwritten the one that existed. Add it back by inserting
    something like:

    ```
    <form id="MyForm" method="post" runat="server">
    ```

    just underneath the opening <body> tag, and </form> just above the
    closing </body> tag. Now continue your Web application development
    as normal.

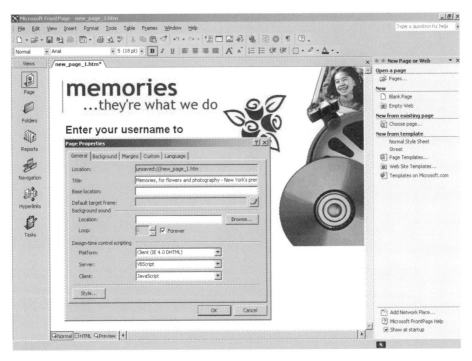

Figure 3-5. Using FrontPage to design great user interfaces

And that's how you can exploit both the design power of FrontPage and the programmatic power of ASP.NET at the same time.

Adding Advertisements

Advertisements can provide a source of revenue for your site. Perhaps you use a banner exchange scheme or have signed up with an actual advertising agency, such as BurstMedia.com. Either way, the AdRotator control can help you.

1. To use the AdRotator to add advertising to your site, your first stop is to create an advertisement file. This is essentially an XML document that stores core details about each of your advertisements (image file links, URLs, and alternative text), all alongside impressions and keywords.

2. Next, simply add the AdRotator control to any relevant pages (see Figure 3-6), changing its AdvertisementFile property to reference the document you just created. You can also specify a keyword as the KeywordFilter property, should you wish to target your ads.

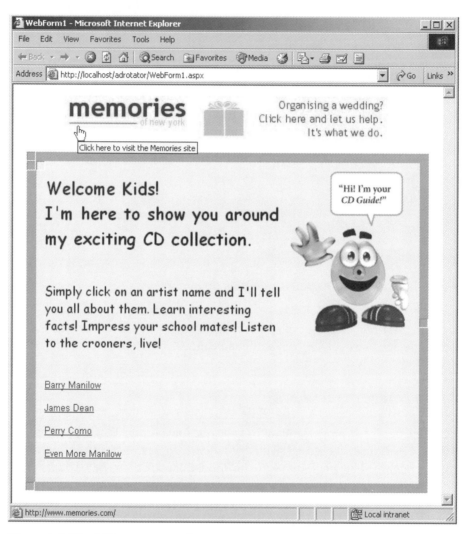

Figure 3-6. The AdRotator control in action

A full walkthrough of this entire process is given in the Help index. Simply look up "AdRotator control, overview" and select the result, "Introduction to the AdRotator Web Server Control".

Getting into Styles

Ever used styles in Word? They allow you to define how certain parts of your document look, just by editing a central style tag. They give you the power to change the appearance of a whole document in just a couple of clicks.

Imagine if you could set something like that up for your entire Web site. Imagine if you could simply change one setting in one file and suddenly every heading on your site changes from Verdana to Tahoma.

Let's take that one stage further. Imagine if you could use that power to instantly add light backdrop images to every table on your site. Or make all your links green, turning pink as you hover your mouse over them. Oh, now *that's* style.

All that just by editing one file? Yup, it's all possible right now, using cascading stylesheets (CSS files). This isn't a feature that's new with ASP.NET; it's been around a good few years. It basically allows you to remove all formatting information from your Web page files: no more colors, no more font names. You simply create a bunch of styles ("classes") and assign each item or paragraph on your form to one of those styles.

If you ever need to change the appearance of any of these elements, simply change the one stylesheet.

How can you define and use your own styles with Visual Studio .NET?

1. In your Web application, open Styles.css, the file that stores your styles. Don't be frightened by the existing styles defined here; they're not as confusing as they look. If instead you want to start afresh and add a new CSS file to your project, select Project ➢ Add New Item ➢ Style Sheet.

2. You are now in the integrated CSS editor. To create a style, select Styles ➢ Add Style Rule from the menu. This is where you tell the editor what you want to create: either you want to change the way that elements look (such as the default color of a hyperlink or table layout) or you want to create your own style (where you design your own style, then use it where necessary on your pages). To change an element, click on Element and select one from the drop-down list. To create a new style, click on Class Name and enter a new name for your style.

3. Move the new style rule across to the list box by clicking on the > button and then on OK. A very simple definition of your style will appear in the Styles.css window, probably looking something like:

```
.myStyle
{
}
```

4. To add formatting information to your style, click on its name, then select Style ➢ Build Style from the menu. You can use this powerful formatting window to describe how your element or style should appear, choosing anything from colors to cursors, capitalization to custom bullet points. When finished, click on OK to build the style.

5. Next, open a Web form (or other HTML-based document in your Web application) that you want to use with this stylesheet. Somewhere within the <head> tag, add the following, replacing Styles.css with the name of your own stylesheet:

```
<link rel="stylesheet" type="text/css" href="Styles.css">
```

6. This will automatically apply any defined element styles to this page. If you created your own style and want to apply it to an individual Web control, try changing its CssClass property to the name of your style (such as "myStyle", for example). (See Figure 3-7.)

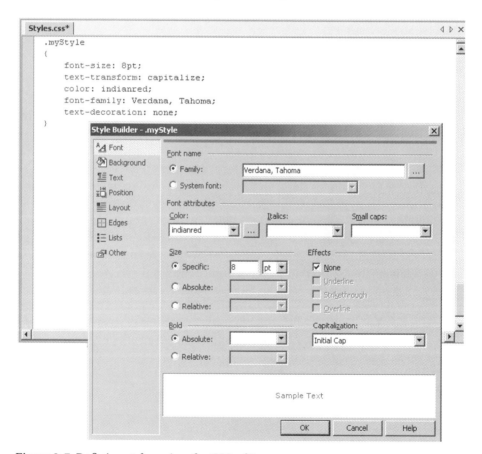

Figure 3-7. Defining styles using the CSS editor

And that's how you can define your own generic styles and apply them to your forms, instantly.

For a more in-depth explanation of CSS files and how you can use them in your Web pages, look up "CSS Editor" in the Help index, then click on the "Introduction to Cascading Style Sheets" link. You might also want to check out the top CSS tutorial from Joe Burns at `www.htmlgoodies.com`.

Using smartNavigation

Want to know how you can annoy your users? Force them to scroll right down to the bottom of your Web page to enter a value into a TextBox, then make them click on a button. The screen will go blank as the form is submitted and the page reloads. After a few seconds, the top of the new page will appear—and the user will have to scroll all the way back down to get back to where they were.

What a waste of time.

Thankfully, every ASPX page includes a little-known smartNavigation property. Despite its rather confusing name, this is really a "focus enforcer." It takes the user back to the control they were working with when the form was submitted, and it also doesn't display the next page until it has fully loaded (meaning you don't get that "flicker" effect).

How do you use it? Simply set the smartNavigation property of your Web Form to True. And why not? This neat feature may only work with Internet Explorer 5 or above, but, if your browser doesn't support it, ASP.NET will detect this and just serve up a regular page, minus the smartNavigation frills. Super!

Deployment

Hmm, deployment. Introducing this subject, I feel a little like Zsa Zsa Gabor's fifth husband: I know how to do it, but how do I make it seem interesting?

I can't. You see, deployment is always one of those topics that gets shoved to the back of any book. It's the ultimate cure for insomnia and about as interesting as a hermit's diary. Well, you've been duly warned, so let's ask ourselves how we can deploy our Web application, without dropping off into Slumber Land.

We're going to start with the easiest method of deploying your site. Let's say you've created a Web application on your own machine and just want to make it available to others on your network. How can they access your new intranet site?

Easily. In fact, you don't need to do any more work at all. Your users simply need to launch a Web browser, tap in `http://yourmachinename/ yourapplicationname/`, and that's it!

Too good to be true? I think not.

But what if you want to deploy your Web application to another Web server on your network? Then you need to use the Copy Project feature, which will copy all the ASPX files and your compiled DLL code file across, plus configure IIS to run your application.

How do you use that feature? It's amazingly simple: just open your Web application and, from the menu, select Project ➤ Copy Project. Then, select your destination project folder (such as http://anothermachine/ yourapplicationname/), select the "Copy only files needed to run this application" option button and click on OK. That's it!

But don't tell me: this doesn't apply to you, right? You've just bought yourself an account with one of the new ASP.NET hosts and need to zap your files across the Net. How do you do it then? Easy! Just copy them!

This copy-and-it-just-works method of deployment is something people from the old programming world find it difficult to get their heads around. There's no registering, no messing about: just "XCOPY" and the job is done.

So, log on to your account via FTP. You'll have direct access to your virtual directory, as configured in IIS. From here, you can upload your files. But what do you upload?

Simply open your actual project folder, probably in INetPub\wwwroot\AppName\, and upload all your ASPX files, alongside Web.config, possibly Styles.css (if used), Global.asax, and your VSDISCO file (if you have created a Web service in this project). In brief, upload any file that isn't used by Visual Studio .NET to store your code or details about your project. That means upload anything that doesn't have .vbproj, .webinfo, .vb, or .resx extensions.

Next, still via FTP, create and open a subfolder called "Bin". Then open your own local project Bin folder and transfer the DLL assembly containing your compiled application code across. And that's all you need to do.

Application deployed, end of tedium: over and out, Roger Wilco.

> **TOP TIP** *If you wish, you can even create a setup program for your Web application. Although this serves limited use to us in this context, it could be useful in certain situations. Find out more by looking up "deploying Web applications" in the Help index.*

> **ANOTHER TOP TIP** *If you don't yet have a .NET hosting account, the Web Hosting link on the Visual Studio .NET start page recommends a number of top hosts, such as MaximumASP.com and iNTERHOST. You can upload projects direct to these providers simply by clicking the "Upload directly to your <provider> account" link. Check it out!*

FAQ

Still got questions? I can sympathize; the world of Web applications is large, and there's always something new to learn. So, before we conclude this tutorial, let's review a few of the most frequently asked questions and see if we can answer a few common puzzlers.

I'm concerned about my Web.config file. If I use authentication and put a bunch of usernames and passwords in it, then upload to my site, isn't that incredibly insecure?

You'd think so, but the virtual directory your files are hosted in will have already been set up (either by Visual Studio .NET or your ASP.NET host) to stop this from occurring. Try downloading the file yourself by typing its address directly into your Web browser. You can't access it, right?

When an application error occurs that I haven't handled, my user sees a chunk of code and a mass of ugly messages. How do I stop this from happening?

As you develop your Web applications, debugging is switched on by default. This enables you to get all those wondrously detailed error messages that ASP developers would've died for. When you've finished working on the project, however, it's best to turn debugging off because it'll make your site faster and stop VS .NET from generating the PDB (program debug) file in your Bin directory. This essentially contains a copy of your code and is what ASP.NET reads from when it gives you those error messages.

To stop it from being created, we need to first tell our project that this application is ready for release. To do this, change the Solution Configurations drop-down box on the menu from "Debug" to "Release". Next, turn off debugging in the <compilation> element of Web.config, by changing it to `<compilation debug="false" />`.

This will stop your code from being displayed; however, it won't stop those awful generic error message pages. However, you can always replace those with your own custom message page simply by altering the <customErrors> element in Web.config to something like `<customErrors mode="On" defaultRedirect="genericerror.aspx" />`.

I've added code to the SelectedIndexChanged event of my DropDownList control. But, when I run my application and change the selected item, nothing happens! What went wrong?

Although you've written code to respond to that event, by default any changes to the DropDownList—or indeed most controls—don't automatically cause a post-back to the server.

To enforce a postback, try setting the AutoPostBack property of the control to True, and watch as your code runs as expected. Sorted!

I want to check what the user has selected from my ListBox control in code. However, if they haven't selected any item, my code causes an error. How can I check whether the user has actually selected something?

You need to check whether the SelectedItem property of your ListBox is "not nothing". Here's a chunk of code to demonstrate this concept:

```
If Not ListBox1.SelectedItem Is Nothing Then
    ' something selected, code goes here
End If
```

How can I open a link in a new window, using the Hyperlink control?

Simply set the Target property of your Hyperlink control to _new. You can also set this to _search to display the link in the Internet Explorer search bar. For more uses, check out "Target property" in the Help index.

I heard that, if I wanted to use Secure Sockets Layer (SSL) for my ASP.NET Web site, it works in just the same was as with ASP. Is this correct? Where can I find more information on the topic?

It certainly is. There's no difference at all, and it's a great way of encrypting data during HTTPS browser posts, giving the user confidence that any data they trans-fer is secure. To find out more about using SSL, and Web application security in general, look up "SSL, Web application security" in the Help index.

The controls that I use on my Web forms are great. Will Microsoft release any new ones?

Absolutely. In fact, the software giant has already made its Internet Explorer WebControls expansion pack available for free download on its MSDN site, plus the market has now opened up for third-parties to develop their own—all of which means quicker, easier, and more-sophisticated Web projects. Find out more about Microsoft's new Web controls by visiting msdn.microsoft.com.

One of my pages loads a lot of data from my main database. It's working with no problem right now, but, when the users really start hitting my site, I'm a bit worried it might get overloaded. Is there anything I can do here?

ASP.NET incorporates a neat little feature known as *caching*. This allows you to store pages between requests, so your server machine isn't continuously bogged down processing code.

For example, you might mark your news page to be cached, expiring after five minutes. When the first user accesses that page, your code runs, the page is generated (perhaps from data in your database), and then it's all cached. Anyone accessing your page within the next five minutes will simply have that cached version served to them. Best of all, it's often as simple as adding a single line to your ASPX page.

You can learn more about how to incorporate caching in your applications by looking up "ASP.NET, overview" in the Help index, selecting the "Introduction to ASP.NET Web applications in Visual Basic" listing, and following the "ASP.NET Caching Features" link at the bottom of the page.

I'm building a stock market Web site, but right now it's very inefficient. When my user makes a request, I need to copy a complete table of data from the stock exchange into my database. Then I need to load this into a DataSet, get the required value, and show it on a page. Not very tech-savvy, right? It would be best just to have one DataSet for all my pages, perhaps updating it every five minutes. Is there any way to have items exposed to my entire application like this, and not just a page or user session?

Although we've not covered it in-depth in this tutorial, your ASP.NET Web application has access to the Application object. This is the object that raises many of the events in Global.asax, allowing you to run code whenever your application starts and finishes. It's an object that is global to your entire application, not just one particular user session.

You can also store data or objects in the Application object, just as you would with the Session object. So, for example, you might want to store that DataSet in the Application object, like so:

```
Dim MyDataSet As New DataSet()
Application.Add("StockValues", MyDataSet)
```

In your code, you may check when this DataSet was last updated and perhaps refresh it at set intervals. Also, be sure to code carefully to ensure multiple clients don't attempt to update the DataSet at the same time. It might also be worthwhile looking up the SyncLock keyword, which may be able to help out in such situations.

For more information specifically on Web data access strategies, look up "cache, datasets" in the Help index.

WHERE TO GO FROM HERE

Looking to learn more about building your own Web applications? You're in luck. This is one of the areas of .NET that is overwhelmed with resources. And here are my pick of the crop, a bundle of recommendations that'll help take your knowledge right to the next level.

- *Moving to ASP.NET* (Apress, ISBN 1-59059-009-0): From Web forms to Web services to mobile applications, this book covers everything ASP.NET, with sections on related goblins such as databases, too.

- *Professional ASP.NET* (Wrox, ISBN 1-861004-88-5): A little large perhaps, but this book has it all and infinitely more. If you're looking for the ultimate reference, this is it. It's not necessarily bedtime reading, but very complete.

- `http://localhost/quickstart/aspplus/`: Got questions about using ASP.NET? This QuickStart tutorial from Microsoft is installed on your machine when you install Visual Studio and provides you with all the ASP.NET essentials.

- `www.411asp.net`: This is the Yahoo! of ASP.NET sites. This jam-packed, categorized site offers help for all, including a special beginners section. How nice!

- `www.asptoday.com`: This Wrox site is a great little stop, showcasing a mass of articles and site mailing lists.

- `www.aspfree.com/aspnet/`: It may look a little tacky, but this site is a heaven-send. It features a mass of external links, sample chapters from some of the leading ASP.NET publications, and a bundle of incredibly useful, exclusive tutorials.

- `www.asp.net`: Only Microsoft could own such an exclusive address. The site lists all the latest books, community sites, and code samples.

- `www.4guysfromrolla.com`: When you think ASP.NET, think 4 Guys from Rolla. At least, that's what the site begs. Not too sure myself, but it *does* pack a big collection of FAQs and more tips than you can wave a Web farm at. Worth a surf.

- `www.ibuyspy.com`: An entire site from Microsoft, built wholly in ASP.NET. With downloadable code.

- `microsoft.public.dotnet.framework.aspnet`: The official Microsoft newsgroup for ASP.NET discussion. For speedier answers, try searching the archives first at `www.googlegroups.com`.

But the world of .NET is still a new one, so remember that books become outdated and Web sites drop every day. To get the very latest, try heading down to Apress at `www.apress.com`.

CONCLUSION

Yeah, baby, yeah! We made it right through to the end of "Working the Web". And we're still relatively sane. Blub, snigger, hehe, schner, schner, look, Peter Pan!

Hey, I said *relatively*.

In today's session, we started off with a look at authentication and how we can use it to secure our Web applications. We then moved on to discuss how we can improve our site using FrontPage, advertisements, stylesheets, and smartNavigation.

After that, we talked about deployment and looked at how you can take your Web knowledge even further. We then reviewed a bundle of frequently asked questions, answering some of those niggling puzzlers you've probably asked yourself already.

And so here we are, at the end of yet another part in this book. We've briefly explored the large, exciting and (with ASP.NET) incredibly *quick* world of the Web. You've learned everything you need to know to start building your own mega-cool Web applications, plus infinitely more.

So get to it—and keep playing. The Web is an exciting place, and there's nothing like the challenge of creating your own masterpiece. Today and tomorrow, ASP.NET is the best tool for doing that. Channel the power!

Dear friends, it's time for me to say goodbye once again and wish you all the very best in developing for the wired world. Take care, God bless, and, until the next time, night night!

CHAPTER 3.3

- By default, authentication in your ASP.NET applications is handled by Internet Information Services (IIS). You can override this setting by editing the <authentication> element in Web.config. The three options are *Windows* to use integrated Windows authentication, *Passport* to use Passport authentication (www.passport.com/business/), or *Forms* (the most popular) to implement your own username and password setup.

- With forms authentication, you redirect all unauthenticated users to a login page (login.aspx, by default). From this page, you can verify credentials, then send an encrypted cookie bearing the user identity down to the client machine.

- Before forms authentication will fully work, you need to deny all anonymous users access to your site. You do this by removing the <allow users="*" /> line from your Web.config file, replacing it with <deny users="?" />.

- To authenticate a visitor, use the RedirectFromLoginPage method. The following sample sends an encrypted cookie down to the client machine, telling it MyUsername is logged in, along with the MyPersistBoolean value, which states whether the cookie should persist after the user finishes his or her browsing session. The user is then taken to their originally requested page after logging on, or default.aspx if none was specified:

```
System.Web.Security.FormsAuthentication.RedirectFromLoginPage(MyUsername, _
    MyPersistBoolean)
```

- To log out from forms authentication, removing your encrypted cookie from the client machine, use code like this:

```
System.Web.Security.FormsAuthentication.SignOut()
```

- To find out which user is currently logged in, check the User object, like this:

```
MyUsername = User.Identity.Name
```

- The smartNavigation feature allows you to maintain the control focus between form submissions; it also allows you to remove the "flicker" when posting data back to Web sites. This feature works automatically with Internet Explorer 5 and above. To turn it on, just set the smartNavigation property of your Web form to True.

- To deploy your ASP.NET Web application to another network server using Visual Studio .NET, select Project ➤ Copy Project from the menu and specify the destination server and project folder. You will need to ensure that the "Copy only files needed to run this application" option button is selected and that you have appropriate permissions (or relevant credentials) to deploy this application.

- If you need to FTP your ASP.NET files to an IIS virtual directory, copy across all your ASPX, CSS, CONFIG, ASAX, and VSDISCO files from your project directory. You will also need to create a Bin folder, copying across the compiled DLL assembly from your own.

Going Mobile

Introducing the Mobile Internet Toolkit

"Reading computer manuals without the hardware is as frustrating as reading sex manuals without the software."—Arthur C. Clarke

IT'S LIGHTWEIGHT, STABLE, TECH-SAVVY, brimming with code—and to be frank, pretty darn stunning. But enough about me, let's introduce you to this thing they call the *Mobile Internet Toolkit*.

Once upon a time, someone decided that the Internet would be the next big company craze. So, technology officers throughout the globe made strategic decisions to ditch desktop applications in favor of browser-based solutions.

Finally, after quite a learning curve, developers sighed a breath of relief as their sites were rolled out. Then that mysterious trendsetter decided that regular browsing simply wasn't good enough—and that anyone needed to be able to access any data at any time using any device.

And "any device" meant mobile phones, pagers, handheld computers and, of course, toasters.

Now, from a programmer's perspective, that got a little difficult. First, you had to decide which devices you wanted to target. Not everyone talked the same language, and some offered desirable I'd-love-to-use-that features over the lesser models. Some of these devices had large displays too, whereas others could barely display a few lines, so you had to figure out "pagination" also. Then you actually needed to build the site and incorporate interactivity. Oh, what fun.

But, finally, after burning more midnight oil than a cross-country lorry driver, a few of the more elite developers managed to create such mobile sites. Then the market unveiled new mobile machines and the nightmare continued.

Not a pretty picture, is it? To be exact, I've seen prettier pictures in the Freddy Krueger image archive. And, if you're a traditional Visual Basic developer, the skills gap may have put all thoughts of such groovy Web what-nots right out of your mind anyway.

Well, it's time to rethink.

Alongside the release of Visual Studio .NET, Microsoft unveiled the Mobile Internet Toolkit (MIT), essentially an extension to the .NET Framework that it promises will make building such mobile sites an absolute doddle. And, for once, it's actually telling the truth.

Welcome to "Going Mobile"—I'm your host, Karl Moore, and over the next two chapters we'll be finding out exactly what the MIT is all about and how you can use it to build fantastic device sites to impress your boss and drive customers to your business. From creating a simple Hello World application right through to crafty tricks of the trade, we've got it all covered.

So tuck in tight as we start the journey. Onward!

How Does It Work?

So, how does it all work? Well, after you have Visual Studio .NET and the MIT installed, you simply create a mobile Web application in much the same way as you'd create a regular Web application.

That means you drag and drop controls onto an ASPX page, then make it all interactive by adding regular VB code to respond to events.

> **TOP TIP** *If you haven't built Web forms in ASP.NET yet, you'll find it an enjoyable jump from traditional ASP. You simply add controls to a page, and then interact with them using the regular form-style VB code you're already acquainted with. Mobile applications are just the same—and, best of all, you're still coding in your favorite language. For more information, check out Tutorial 3, "Working the Web."*

Three lines of code, two stiff vodkas, and a simple build later, you'll have your compiled application, which is typically a bunch of ASPX files and a supporting DLL assembly.

Finally, all you need to do is access the pages using your mobile device. Just tap out the address and that's it!

But what about writing code to target individual devices? What if I'm using something in my application that's not supported by that particular phone? Well, unsurprisingly enough, the .NET Framework handles all that for you.

When your page is accessed, just as with ASP.NET Web forms, the .NET Framework does a lot of thinking and translates your content into something that the recipient can actually understand. And, if that means converting an HTML combo box into a Wireless Markup Language (WML) option list because that's all a particular device supports, it'll handle it for you. (WML is the Wireless Application Protocol (WAP) equivalent of HTML. You can find the full list of markup languages supported by the MIT in today's Review Sheet.)

In other words, you simply write all the code for your mobile pages once, then let the .NET Framework worry about the plumbing. Well, hurrah and hujjah for that!

Creating Our First Mobile Application

Righto. You now know some of the sticky problems of the past, and how this new and wizzy way of working should save you hours of development. That's our cue to actually see it all in action!

Before you get started however, it's a pretty good idea to get the actual Mobile Internet Toolkit installed on your machine. Don't worry, penny pinchers; it's a completely free download that weighs in at around 4MB. Grab your own copy online from http://msdn.microsoft.com/vstudio/nextgen/technology/ mitdefault.asp.

You'll also want to get one of the mobile emulators onto your machine. These ensure you can view your application as it might look on a real-life device, not just in the all-frills Internet Explorer. In this tutorial, we'll be using the Microsoft Mobile Explorer emulator, which is also available as a free download from the preceding address.

Creating Our Mobile Web Forms

As soon as you've installed all the essentials, you're ready to rock 'n' roll. But let's walk through our first mobile application instead.

1. Launch Visual Studio. NET.

2. Click on the New Project button.

3. Under the Visual Basic Projects folder, highlight Mobile Web Application.

4. Change the location to http://locahost/mobileapp and click on OK. (See Figure 1-1.)

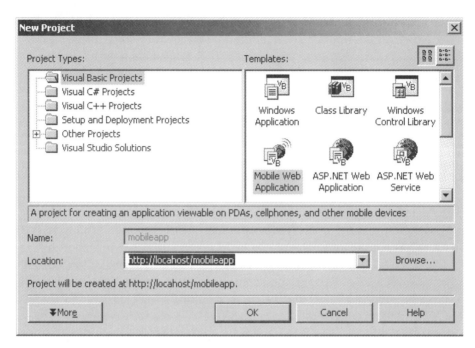

Figure 1-1. Creating our new Mobile Web Application

Your project will be created at the location and you'll be shown the file MobileWebForm1.aspx. On the page, you'll see a Form control called Form1. A Form control is the equivalent of one "screen" or "page" on a device.

5. Change the ID property of Form1 to "Logon".

> **TOP TIP** *You can add multiple screens to your ASPX page by simply dragging and dropping another Form control. You can then link between the pages using the Link control or by setting the ActiveForm property of the page.*

Let's get editing our page. We're going to create a logon form that allows users to enter their credentials.

6. Drag and drop a Label control inside our logon form, changing its ID property to "lblTitle".

7. Alter the Text property of lblTitle to "Welcome!" (See Figure 1-2.)

8. Change the StyleReference property of lblTitle to "title".

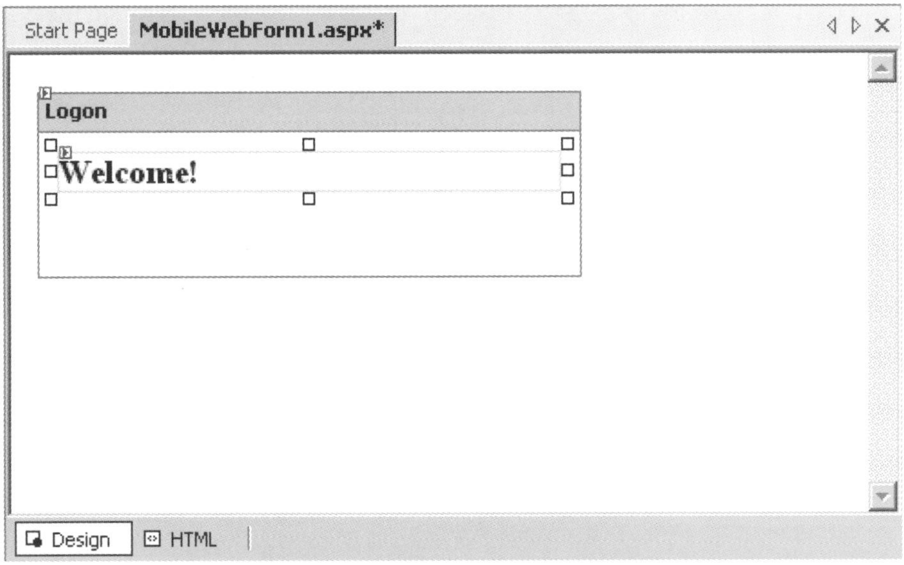

Figure 1-2. Designing our form

The StyleReference property tells the .NET Framework generally what sort of information you are displaying in the label. Here, we're selecting the *title* option, meaning that the .NET Framework will attempt to make the text in this label more prominent, if the target device supports it.

9. Drag another label onto the logon form, changing its Text property to "Please enter your username and select Logon."

10. Add a TextBox control underneath your existing controls, changing its ID property to "txtUsername".

> **TOP TIP** *If you're adding a TextBox that should accept only numbers, try changing the Numeric property to True. Although this has little effect on regular browsers, it will change the input mode on many mobile devices and could seriously increase usability.*

11. Add a Command control (cmdLogon) underneath your existing controls, changing its Text property to "Logon".

The Command control is the equivalent of an ASP.NET button and looks like a simple hyperlink on many mobile devices.

So, there's our simple data entry screen sorted. But, browsing through that list of available controls in our toolbox, I've noticed something from my days creating Web applications. It's the RequiredFieldValidator, and it can help me ensure that the user has entered a value into the Username box.

12. Add a RequiredFieldValidator control (rfvUsername) underneath your existing controls, changing its ErrorMessage property to "Please enter a username!"

See how the StyleReference property has already been set to *error*? What do you think this does?

13. Change the ControlToValidate property of rfvUsername to "txtUsername".

Supercool! Next up, we're going to create our second form. This will simply welcome the specified user to our system with a simple message.

14. Drag and drop another Form control underneath your existing logon screen, changing its ID property to "Welcome". (See Figure 1-3.)

15. Add a Label control (lblWelcome) to your welcome form, removing its default Text property value.

16. Alter the StyleReference property of lblWelcome to "title".

Figure 1-3. Our completed mobile form

Adding the Code

Next, we're going to add code to make it all work. Nothing too complex just yet, but it'll demonstrate exactly how easy it is to create your own mobile application.

1. Add the following code to respond to the click event of cmdLogon:

```
If Page.IsValid = True Then
    lblWelcome.Text = "Welcome, " & txtUsername.Text & "!"
    ActiveForm = Welcome
End If
```

First off here, we check whether the page is valid. If you sat through Tutorial 3, "Working the Web", you'll have already seen this. It returns a True if all validation on the form has passed. If the page isn't valid, we don't run any code and our Validation control error message should automatically display.

However, presuming the validation passes with no problem, our code goes on to set the Text property of our label, welcoming the user. Next, we set the ActiveForm equal to Welcome, which changes the currently visible form.

Finished? Then it's time to compile your application.

2. From the menu, select Build ➤ Build mobileapp (or press CTRL+SHIFT+B).

Testing Our Application

Ready to see our program in action? Let's try it out in Internet Explorer first off.

1. Press F5 to test your application in Internet Explorer.

See it all in action? Admittedly, this is about as exciting as visiting the restroom. But mobile applications weren't built for Internet Explorer, they were built for mobiles. Oh, and emulators. So let's see how our application might look on your device.

2. Launch the Microsoft Mobile Explorer emulator. (In Visual Studio, select View ➤ Mobile Explorer Browser ➤ Show Browser. Otherwise, select Start ➤ Programs ➤ Microsoft Mobile Explorer.)

3. In the URL box, type `http://localhost/mobileapp/MobileWebForm1.aspx` and press the Enter key.

You should be viewing your logon form, as shown in Figure 1-4. Notice how different it looks to the page in Internet Explorer? Pay special attention to what that StyleReference property did. Also, look at your TextBox and Command controls. Haven't *they* changed!

Figure 1-4. Our application in the Mobile Explorer Emulator

4. Using the Up/Down buttons, highlight the Username box.

5. Click on the button just underneath Edit to change the contents of the box.

6. Next, type in a username and click on the OK button when finished.

7. Now use the Up/Down buttons to highlight the Logon button and click on OK.

What do you get back? Is this what you expected? Now try visiting the Web site again, this time without entering a username. Does the validation kick in? Hurrah and a big pat on the back for you, my friend!

Exploring the Controls

They say a good workman never blames his tools. But, even if you did, I wouldn't hold it against you. After all, you guys haven't even been introduced yet.

Beloved reader, please meet the Mobile Web Form controls. Mobile Web Form controls, meet beloved reader.

Let's explore every one of the widgets in your toolbox right now, running over their individual specialties and finding out how each can help you build super-cool device applications.

Don't forget to play around with an instance of each control as we explore its possibilities. And, if you need more information on any particular control, either press F1 while it's selected or try checking out the Mobile QuickStart tutorial installed on your machine at `http://localhost/MobileQuickStart/`.

Let's get started.

Form

You've seen this widget before. It's a Form control, as shown in Figure 1-5. You can slap one or more of these onto a MobilePage. Each represents an actual page on the target device. By default, the form at the top of your page is shown first.

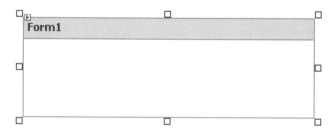

Figure 1-5. The Form control

Panel

If you've used the panel in Windows forms, this is its Web equivalent. (See Figure 1-6.) It's basically a holder, a container of other controls. What benefits does it bring? As an example, hiding the panel will hide all controls underneath it, and setting the stylesheet properties of the panel ensures that all of its child controls inherit those settings, and so on. Thrilling stuff.

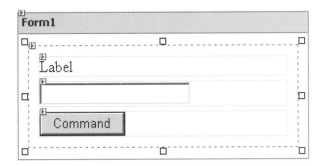

Figure 1-6. The Panel control

Label

It's trusty, faithful, and does its job extraordinarily well. Yes, it simply displays text—but it's awfully good at it. The StyleReference property here is particularly useful, allowing you to set its default display style. See Figure 1-7.

Figure 1-7. The Label control

TextBox

You know it, I know it, but it never hurts to reintroduce an old favorite. It's the TextBox control, and it accepts user input. (See Figure 1-8.) On various devices it renders differently, from a regular box through to a completely separate input screen. The most interesting properties to check out here are Numeric, Password, and MaxLength—so long as the target device supports them.

Figure 1-8. The TextBox control

TextView

Imagine that your user has requested the local weather predictions for the coming month. Unless he or she lives in the it's-too-darn-hot Sahara, you really can't display that on a line or two using the Label control. That's where the TextView control comes into play: it supports whole chunks of text and automatically handles the "pagination" (the splitting up into multiple device pages) for you. See Figure 1-9.

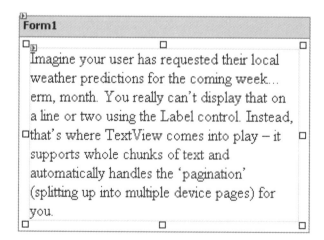

Figure 1-9. The TextView control

Command

Similar to the Button control used to build Web applications, the Command control comes with its own click event for you to react to. Why not just call it a button? To avoid confusion, because, depending on what a device supports, a Command control can look like anything from a regular button to a simple hyperlink. (See Figure 1-10.)

Figure 1-10. The Command control

Link

It's essentially the Hyperlink control, rendered as a plain, selectable link on most devices. (See Figure 1-11.) Simply use the NavigateUrl property to tell the Link control where it should take the user—whether it's another form on the page, another page on the site, or a completely separate resource.

Figure 1-11. The Link control

PhoneCall

Okay, so perhaps Internet Explorer won't be able to use this control, but many devices can make outbound calls and require the number data tagged in a certain way. Using this control does it all for you. Just set the PhoneNumber and Text property. For those devices that don't support phones, try filling out the AlternateUrl and AlternateFormat properties instead. (See Figure 1-12.)

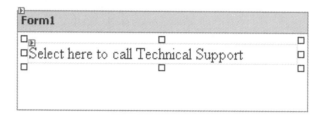

Figure 1-12. The PhoneCall control

> **TOP TIP**   *The AlternateFormat property of the PhoneCall control will automatically replace {0} with the Text property and {1} with the telephone number on devices that do not support phone calls.*

Image

Images are a sticky subject in the world of mobile devices. Some don't support them, some support only certain formats, and some support only certain, rather uncommon formats. We'll be spending time in the next chapter dealing specifically with this topic. The key properties to play with here are AlternateText, ImageUrl, and NavigateUrl. The Image control is shown in Figure 1-13.

Figure 1-13. The Image control

List

The List control (Figure 1-14) works in two modes: boring and exciting. In the boring mode, it simply displays a list of items, which you manipulate via the Items collection (either using the Properties window or in code as you would a ComboBox control). However, just by adding code to respond to the ItemCommand event, each item in the list is automatically hyperlinked. When you click on each item, simply reading the e.ListItem argument passed into the event enables you to find out what was clicked and make your move. That's the exciting mode, great for creating your own device menus. Hey, it's your call.

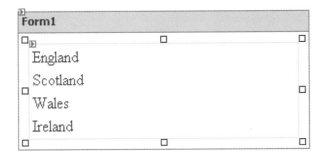

Figure 1-14. The List control

SelectionList

Is it a drop-down list? Is it a checkbox? Is it a radio button? No, it's the SelectionList control, which incorporates all these visual elements and more. (See Figure 1-15.) When you want the user to select from a list, this is the control for you. First off, you set the type of control to use with the SelectType property (which may in fact render differently depending on the target device), then you use the Items collection to manipulate the list. The control also has a Selection property that provides a reference to the first selected item.

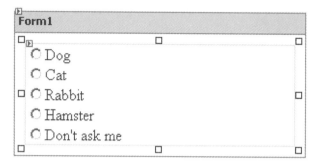

Figure 1-15. The SelectionList control

ObjectList

If you want to display a list of objects and their related properties, allowing the user to perform actions on those objects, the ObjectList control can come in handy. (See Figure 1-16.) You can see this little number demonstrated on the Mobile QuickStart tutorial at `http://localhost/MobileQuickstart/util/RunSample.aspx?src=ListControls%2fObjectList.src`.

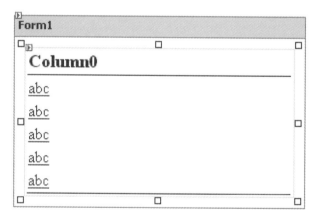

Figure 1-16. The ObjectList control

DeviceSpecific

Device-specific content can be sent down the wire in many ways, and using the DeviceSpecific control is one of them. (See Figure 1-17.) We'll be learning more about this way of working in the next chapter.

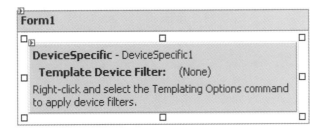

Figure 1-17. The DeviceSpecific control

StyleSheet

You've already seen the StyleReference property in action; it presents you with an intrinsic list of potential styles. However, with the StyleSheet control (Figure 1-18), you can add your own (right-click, select Edit Styles) or attach a stylesheet ASCX file via the ReferencePath property.

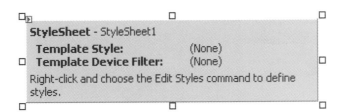

Figure 1-18. The StyleSheet control

Calendar

On capable devices, the Calendar control (Figure 1-19) renders as a complete calendar. On lesser models, it produces a submenu that allows the user to either type a date or select one from a list. Exceptionally clever and an extremely useful asset in our mobile Web forms toolbox. Interesting properties here include CalendarEntryText, SelectionMode, SelectedDate, and VisibleDate.

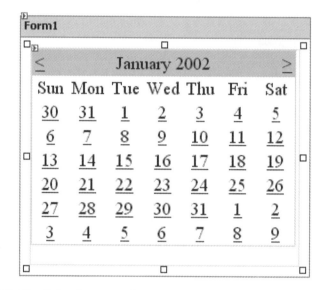

Figure 1-19. The Calendar control

AdRotator

Similar to the Web forms AdRotator, this control (Figure 1-20) allows you to specify advertisement images (or alternative text on image-unfriendly devices), all according to the XML-based advertisement file. Top properties include AdvertisementFile, KeywordFilter, ImageKey, and NavigateUrlKey.

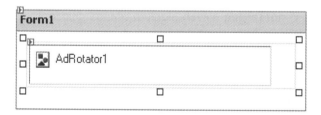

Figure 1-20. The AdRotator control

Validation Controls

Incorporating the RequiredFieldValidator, CompareValidator, RangeValidator, RegularExpressionValidator, CustomValidator, and ValidationSummary, the Validation controls (Figure 1-21) provide all the functionality you find with regular Web forms. They help ensure the integrity of your form data and work in much the same way as the regular ASP.NET validation controls you use with Web forms.

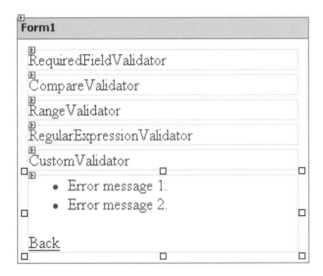

Figure 1-21. The Validation controls

I'm Playing Around

What's that? You want to go home? You're about as bored as the Visual Basic Orgy Club president? You've not felt this tired since the last time you watched the rerun of *Who Will Take Leadership? Nine Hours of Election Results*?

Okay, okay, I can take a hint: I'm talking and you're not doing. That's why, in this section, it's time for you to get all hands-on. I'm going to set you a couple of tasks, and, before you move on, I'd like you to complete each of them. Promise?

- Your name is Madame Cza Cza, princess of the night skies. You've diversified into the world of WAP and are looking to create your own mobile site delivering astrology readings. Try creating an application that allows the user to select their sign on the first form using the SelectionList control, after which they are shown their reading on a second form, using Label and TextView controls.

- Your name is Mr. Bean, lord of the geeks. You've finally released that amazingly cool software program and are creating ways of allowing your users to help themselves. You've decided to create a page somewhere on your support site that allows device users to call you. Try creating an application that includes a support page, using the PhoneCall control, linking directly to your offices if call functionality is available.

- Your name is Roger Victor, captain of one of those great big flying machines. However, the technology division of your airline is running seriously short of staff, so *you* have been asked to create a device site for customers. Nothing fancy right now, just a simple menu screen allowing the user to navigate to different screens—to book a flight, check flight status, or upgrade a flight. Try creating an application that includes a List control menu, with each item linking to a different form.

Should I trust you to create each of these apps? Hmm, those eyebrows are a bit close together. And I see a slight squint there. But, hey—reality check—this is a book, so I can't force you. But, if I smile sweetly and flutter these eyelids, maybe you'll do it. Uhm, please?

And to think they told me authoring was glam.

CONCLUSION

Congratulations on reaching the end of today's session!

You're reading "Going Mobile", and, over the past hour, we've really covered some ground. We started with a look at what mobile applications are and how they fit into the big picture. Next up, we looked at how they work in the real world, and went on to build and test our own sample mobile application, with thanks to the Mobile Explorer.

After that, we took a closer look at the individual mobile Web Form controls available to us. We—sorry, *you*—then securely affixed that practical head and built three supercool test applications to help you really get familiar with some of the essentials.

In the next chapter, we'll be doing it all again. No, not literally; that'd be rather boring. Instead, we'll be firing up Visual Studio .NET once more to take our mobile applications even further: from figuring out how to use images in our programs through to dealing with different device capabilities through to remembering the user, plus everything in between.

So long as "everything" is a FAQ.

But, until then, this is me, Karl Moore, signing off for tonight. See you next time!

CHAPTER 4.1

- The Mobile Internet Toolkit (MIT) is a Visual Studio .NET–integrated extension to the .NET Framework. It includes the runtime files needed to create your own mobile sites, ready to serve up to anything from mobile phones to microwaves.

- The MIT is a free 4MB download available from Microsoft, at msdn.microsoft.com/vstudio/nextgen/technology/mitdefault.asp.

- The device sites that you create using the MIT inherently support three markup languages: HTML 3.2, cHTML, and WML.

- HTML is the standard markup language used in browsers such as Internet Explorer and Netscape. cHTML (Compact HTML) is essentially a subset of regular HTML elements, alongside a few mobile-specific elements used on a number of cell phones.

- WML (Wireless Markup Language) is an XML-based standard used for displaying content on narrowband devices, such as cell phones and pagers. Imagine that WML is the WAP version of HTML (WAP stands for *Wireless Application Protocol*, which is almost the mobile equivalent of HTTP).

- Typically, each mobile Web application you create consists of one or more ASPX pages. Each mobile page needs to hold one or more Form controls, which are essentially "screens" on the target device. In a regular application, each form will hold numerous controls.

- The first form on a page is the first "page" to be displayed to the user. The easiest way to change the current form is to set the ActiveForm property in code.

- To add a new mobile Web form to your application, select Project ➢ Add New Item, and select a new mobile Web form. To move between mobile Web forms in code, use a Link control or your MobilePage RedirectToMobilePage function, like this:

```
RedirectToMobilePage("mypage.aspx")
```

- A wide range of mobile Web Form controls are available to help you build productive mobile applications. These include the PhoneCall control which allows call-supporting devices to dial out, the List control which allows you to display a standard list or create a menu, the Calendar control which allows your user to select a date, and the Validation controls which allow you to ensure the integrity of your form data.

- One of the ways in which the .NET Framework mobile extensions differ from regular ASP.NET applications is that the content sent down the wire is customized for each individual device. As an example, if you used a Command control (the equivalent of an ASP.NET Button) in your application, on some devices it would be sent down as a regular HTML Submit button, whereas on others it would be rendered as a clickable hyperlink.

- To assist future expansion, ASP.NET allows for manufacturers to create their own device adapters. These plug into the .NET Framework, allowing you to target new devices with differing capabilities, such as larger screen sizes or an improved range of input controls.

Your Device, Filters, Images, Memory, and More

"Documentation is like sex: when it is good, it is very, very good; and when it is bad, it's still better than nothing."—Dick Brandon

IS IT A BIRD? IS IT A PLANE? Is it a suspicious looking sausage dog? Nope, it's the second chapter in Tutorial 4, "Going Mobile", and this is your friendly author back to help take your mobile knowledge to even greater heights.

And I don't just mean know-how-to-create-a-basic-site heights. I'm talking the whole Kilimanjaro here. Oh yes.

So far, we've explored some of the basic concepts behind creating a mobile Web application, and looked at the range of controls available to us. And today? We'll start out by finding out exactly what the device looking at your ASPX page is capable of, plus how we can use that knowledge alongside filters to help us display images.

After that, we'll ask—do you remember? And if not, we'll tell you how, using the Session object. Confused? You will be.

All that and more coming up today. So pull up a pew and prepare for another hands-on session.

Finding Out about Your Device

They say all men are created equal, though some more than others.

It's a principle that applies straight to the world of mobile devices. Some are amazingly fantastic and can do just about anything. Others are about as technologically advanced as a bent paperclip. Therefore, it sometimes helps to find out just what your device is capable of . . . in code.

Let me show you what I mean.

1. Create a new mobile Web application in VS .NET, located at `http://localhost/thespymachine/`.

Now, you can tell exactly what the device your page is being delivered to supports by using the Device object, which is basically an instance of the `System.Web.Mobile.MobileCapabilities` class. It gets automatically created when your page is requested and tells you everything you could ever want to know about your target device. And then some.

Let's give it a whirl.

2. Add a Label and a Command control to your form. (Don't worry about naming conventions for now.)

3. Add the following code to respond to the click event of Command1:

```
If Device.CanInitiateVoiceCall = True Then
    Label1.Text = "You can make calls from this device!"
Else
    Label1.Text = "Just TRY making a telephone call from this! LOL!"
End If
```

Here, we're checking whether our device can initiate voice calls. If it can, we're setting the Text property of our label. And, if it can't, we're doing the same. Only differently. Or something.

Quick note: notice the long list of properties that appeared after you typed "`Device.`"? These all provide more information about your device, and we'll be looking closer at some of these in just a few minutes.

4. Press F5 to test your application in Internet Explorer. (See Figure 2-1.)

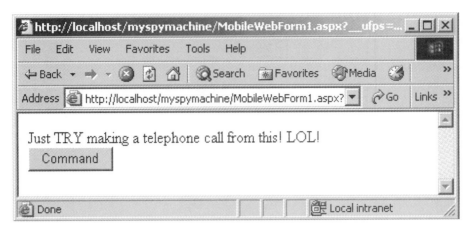

Figure 2-1. Our final application, through Internet Explorer

Testing our application now, what happens when you click on the Command button? You should be told that you can't make a telephone call. And that's right. Next, let's try it out on a real phone (read: *emulator*).

5. Launch the Microsoft Mobile Explorer (In Visual Studio, select View ➤ Mobile Explorer Browser ➤ Show Browser).

6. In the URL box, type
    `http://localhost/thespymachine/MobileWebForm1.aspx`
    and press the Enter key.

7. Click on the OK button to press the Command button.

What happens? My offering is shown in Figure 2-2. It should tell you that your mobile *can* make calls. Wonderful! And very true!

Figure 2-2. Our final application, this time in the Mobile Explorer

But without wanting to infringe on any Carpenters' copyrights, we've only just begun. You can use plenty of other Device properties to help you find out more about the devices visiting your site and exactly what their capabilities are. And imagine how you could use that data: to suggest features, load more-advanced pages, and log exactly what sort of machines are accessing your application.

Top Twelve Device Properties

Problem is, the Device object contains more properties than France contains French people. Therefore, you need a cut-down list of all the really juicy stuff. And I think that's my cue to introduce the top dozen properties.

- *Browser*: Whether it's IE, Pocket IE, Microsoft Mobile Explorer, MyPalm, or some other beast, the Browser property gives you the name of your client browser.

- *CanInitiateVoiceCall*: Returns a True if the device can call someone.

- *CanSendMail*: Returns a True if the device supports the "mailto:" method of sending email, such as a Link control that has the NavigateUrl property set to "mailto:karl@karlmoore.com".

- *Cookies*: Returns a True if the device supports cookies.

- *HasBackButton*: Can your users move back? This property returns a True if they can. This is great for deciding on whether to hide or implement your own Back button mechanism.

- *IsColor*: Returns a True if the device uses a color monitor.

- *IsMobileDevice*: Now, is that really a mobile, or are they just faking it with Internet Explorer? This property returns a True if they're using a recognized mobile device.

- *ScreenCharactersHeight*: Returns the approximate number of lines you can get onto a screen.

- *ScreenCharactersWidth*: Returns the approximate width of the display in characters.

- *ScreenPixelsHeight/ ScreenPixelsWidth*: Returns the approximate height and width of the display in pixels.

- *SupportsBodyColor*: Returns a True if the device can display the backcolor of a form.

- *SupportsBold/ SupportsItalic/ SupportsFontName/ SupportsFontColor/ SupportsFontSize*: Allows you to check whether certain text properties are available on the device.

- *Plus all the regulars*: When using the Device object, you get all the usual things you find when working with the `Request.Browser` property, such as the ability to retrieve the browser version, check the platform, and so on.

Which do you think are the most interesting? And how could you use these?

8. Try enhancing "thespymachine" project so it fills a TextView control with everything you know about the user and their device.

Now that you can find out so much about the device using your application, you should be able to think of a few interesting uses for this information. Perhaps use CanInitiateVoiceCall to set the appropriate properties of your PhoneCall control? Or maybe use the ScreenCharactersHeight and ScreenCharactersWidth properties to estimate how much information your user's screen can display? How about the CanSendMail property?

Have a think about how you can combine these new properties with your existing controls to improve your applications. Then build a completely new mobile Web application that uses *at least two* functional Device properties to make it better.

Make sure you keep the design clean and simple, while still very functional. And, if you even think about moving on before you've done it, I'll give you a big slap at the very next Tech Ed. Get to it now.

Finished? Hurrah! Well done and congratulations on successfully figuring out how to identify the capabilities of devices using your application and changing what you send down the wire accordingly.

Next up, I'm going to show you another way to do it. It's a way of simplifying the Device object. It's a way of setting device-specific properties at design time, without the need for any additional code. It's a common way of working, and it all revolves around filters.

Filters? What *am* I talking about?

A Word about Filters

Sometimes using that Device object isn't the best way of working. Why? For a start, you don't always want to write actual code just to target a device, plus the Device object itself isn't always the easiest to use.

For example, how can you tell whether your particular device prefers its content rendered in HTML? By checking whether the PreferredRenderingType property returns "html32". Not too obvious, that one.

And what if you want to check whether your target device prefers its images as GIFs? You probably want to use the PreferredImageMIME property to see whether it returns "image/gif".

Oh yes, that sort of code sounds stickier than Sticky the Stick Insect immediately after his visit to Sticky Land, Stickyville, up on Planet Sticky. And that's pretty sticky.

That's why you can set up filters in your mobile applications. It's something you'll stumble across often, and it's definitely worth a mention.

Try opening the Web.config file in any mobile project right now. This is the file that stores all your application configuration settings. Down near the bottom of this XML document, you'll find the deviceFilters element, with multiple filter items contained within it.

Let's look at one of those now.

```
<filter name="isHTML32" compare="PreferredRenderingType" argument="html32" />
```

Here we have a filter called "isHTML32". This property compares the PreferredRenderingType property of our Device object and checks whether it returns "html32". If it does, this filter is deemed True; otherwise, it's False.

Don't worry about how you actually use this filter in real life, just get your head around the concept first. Let's look at another.

```
<filter name="supportsVoiceCalls" compare="CanInitiateVoiceCall" argument="true" />
```

Our filter here, supportsVoiceCalls, checks that the CanInitiateVoiceCall property is equal to True. If it is, the filter is set to True; otherwise, it's False.

Using Filters

So, filters allow you to simplify using the Device object. They're like customized device properties. But how can you use them? I feel a sample coming on. (Either that, or the Chinese I had for dinner is playing up).

1. Create a new mobile Web application, at the location
    `http://localhost/filterfun`.

2. Drag a Label control onto Form1.

3. Change its Text property to "Don't Talk, Baby!"

This is going to be a simple experiment. You might remember setting the Text property of a label depending on whether the device is capable of placing a phone call earlier. Let's do that now using *no* extra code.

4. Under the Device Specific properties of TextBox1, click on the ellipsis
    (. . .) next to the AppliedDeviceFilters property.

Welcome to the Applied Device Filters dialog box, as shown in Figure 2-3. This is where you select the filters you want to use with this object.

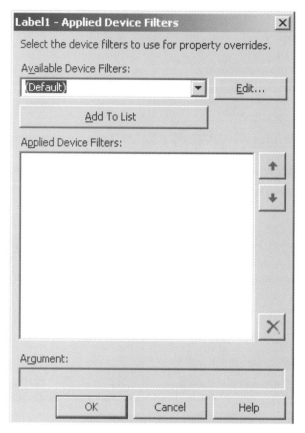

Figure 2-3. The infamous Applied Device Filters dialog box

5. Select the supportsVoiceCalls filter from the Available Device Filters list.

6. Click on the Add To List button, then on OK.

So, what properties of this control should we set if supportsVoiceCalls is equal to True for our device?

7. Click on the ellipsis (. . .) next to the PropertyOverrides property of TextBox1.

The Property Overrides dialog box (Figure 2-4) is where you can select a particular filter, then tell your application what properties of your control to set if this filter is True.

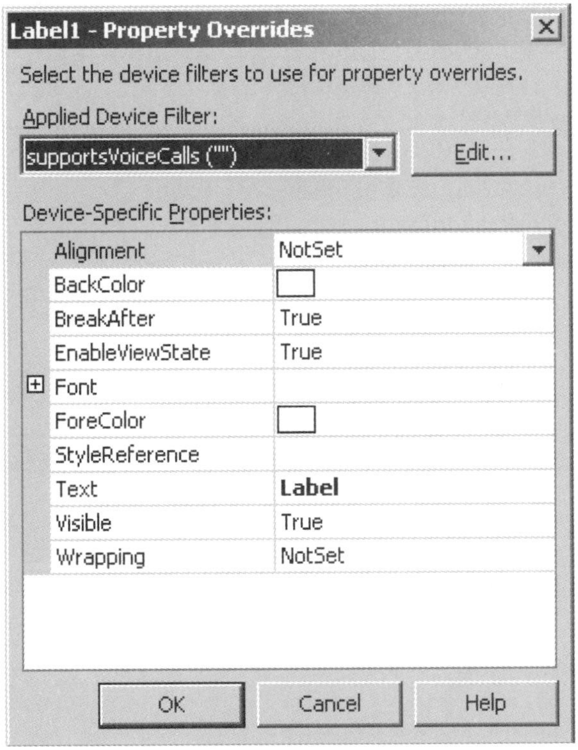

Figure 2-4. The also-infamous Property Overrides dialog box

Your current supportVoiceCalls filter should be selected.

8. In the Property Overrides dialog box, change the Text property to "Talk, baby, Talk!"

9. Click on OK when finished.

Now imagine that a user visits our mobile Web application. When this control loads, it will evaluate whether the supportsVoiceCalls filter is True. If it is, the Text property is overridden and set to "Talk, baby, Talk!"

If you flick over to your mobile Web form HTML view, you'll see your work with the Properties window has automatically generated the following ASP.NET DeviceSpecific code inside your label declaration:

```
<DeviceSpecific>
<Choice Filter="supportsVoiceCalls" Argument="" Text="Talk baby talk!"></Choice>
</DeviceSpecific>
```

Let's test our code now.

10. Build your mobile Web application.

11. Test your new site in both Internet Explorer and the Microsoft Mobile Explorer (MME).

What happens? My application is shown in Figure 2-5.

Figure 2-5. Our application, using filters to override the Text property here

Do you see how filters can be used like this to override certain properties, depending on the device and *without* coding the Device object? Let's crank up my rather rusty brain machine and spend a quick minute thinking about what this means.

Pause for Thought

Right then. We know what filters are and how you can apply them via the Property Overrides dialog box. We know they enable us to override certain properties depending on the device, without coding the Device object. But when would we use them?

In a word or eleven, simply *whenever you need to target a particular device or its capabilities.* For example, you might want to welcome a user especially if they're using a Nokia or Ericsson phone (by using the isNokia7110 and isEricssonR380 filters, for example). Or perhaps you want to check whether the user supports color (supportsColor) before setting that ForeColor property. Another idea could be to display a longer site introduction on more-capable devices, while keeping it short and snappy on mobiles with limited displays. Or maybe you even want to revisit that old favorite, supportsVoiceCalls, before altering certain properties of your PhoneCall control.

If you're feeling particularly randy, you could even set up your own filters, just by adding another <filter> element to your Web.config file. For example, the following filter checks whether the device is capable of sending email.

```
<filter name="supportsMail" compare="CanSendMail" argument="true" />
```

You might use this with a Link control. By default, you could set the control to link to your Web site, either by setting it manually using the Properties window or by adding it to the (default) device filter through the Property Overrides dialog box. However, if the supportsMail device filter equates to True, you might override the NavigateUrl property with a "mailto:" string, for example.

This is all nice and sweet, but, when using filters, you need to remember a few key rules, too. First of all, the filters are processed in the order you list them in the Applied Device Filters dialog box. In other words, if supportsColor equates to True and is listed before isHTML32, the override properties for supportsColor will be set.

Another little point: the Argument property in the Applied Device Filters dialog box allows you to compare the property behind that filter to another value. For example, selecting the supportsVoiceCalls filter and specifying an argument of False will result in that filter "running" when the CanInitiateVoiceCall property equals False.

Understand? Supremo! But surely that's it for filters? First off, don't call me Shirley. And secondly . . .

Displaying Images, Using Filters

In the introduction, I promised to teach you how to display images in your mobile Web applications.

And now this section has arrived, you're probably wiping that brow, thanking the Almighty that we've finished dealing with Device code and Web.config filters and all that confusing, pointless rubbish. Phew!

The thing is, erm, we haven't. At all. In fact, if filters were the name of a groovy high-tech shop, images would be its biggest customer.

Allow me to explain. Not all wireless devices were created equal. We know that. Some support HTML, some support WML, and some support cHTML. Some have huge color monitors; others have teeny green screens.

And now you want to display images on a device. First consideration? *Size matters*—and, in a curious twist, in this world *smaller is better*. Too big and your picture might not fit on the screen. Still, you can always check the capabilities of the device using the properties you've already uncovered.

But there's an even more important issue you'll stumble across (and then grow to hate) when it comes to dealing with images. Which format do you use? HTML devices typically support GIF files, whereas most WML devices traditionally support WBMP files, whereas still others can display regular bitmaps (BMPs).

So how do you do it? Well, you'll need to start off by creating files of each type. Then you'll set up a couple of the intrinsic image-related filters to find out what image format the target device prefers, and then change the ImageUrl property of your Image control as appropriate.

Let's see what I mean.

1. Create a new mobile Web application, at the location
    `http://localhost/images/`.

First off, we need to get our images ready. We'll be using GIF, WBMP, and BMP files.

TOP TIP *Wondering what a WBMP file is? Me too. It's apparently a wireless bitmap, an image format created specifically for wireless devices. If you want to create your own WBMP images, check out PhotoShop Pro, or one of the many shareware image-editing programs available on the Internet. (Try* www.download.com *for starters). Alternatively, surf down to* www.wappictus.com *for a free image library and online WBMP drawing applet.*

2. Select Project➤ Add Existing Item.

3. Change the Files of Type filter to "All Files".

We're going to use three sample images that are distributed with the Mobile Internet Toolkit in this sample. By default, they can all be found in the Program Files\Microsoft Mobile Internet Toolkit\QuickStart\samples\SpecialFeatures\ folder.

4. From the SpecialFeatures folder, select html-image.gif.

5. Repeat the operation to add wml-image.wbmp and wml-image.bmp to your application.

This simply copies those images across to your application folder, plus lists them in the Solution Explorer. Next, we're going to add an Image control to our form.

6. On MobileWebForm1.aspx, add an Image control to Form1.

7. Using the AppliedDeviceFilters property dialog box, add the prefersGIF, prefersWBMP, and (Default) filters; then click on OK. (See Figure 2-6.)

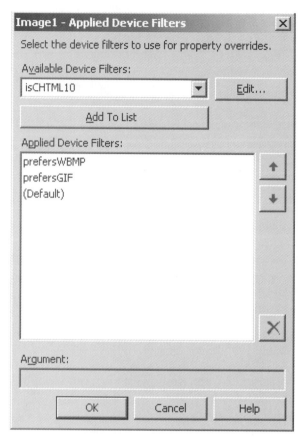

Figure 2-6. Apply the device filters.

Do you know where these filters come from? Which properties of the Device object do they look at? Where can you find this information? Next, let's set up our control to display the different files depending on the device preferences.

8.   Open the Property Overrides dialog box via the PropertyOverrides property of your Image control.

9.   Under the prefersWBMP device filter, change the ImageUrl so it references wml-images.wbmp.

10. Under the prefersGIF device filter, change the ImageUrl so it references html-image.gif.

11. Under the last (Default) device filter, change the ImageUrl so it references wml-image.bmp.

12. Click on OK when finished.

If you flick back to the HTML view behind your mobile Web form, you'll see the following DeviceSpecific code has been generated for you. Notice how the (Default) option doesn't include a filter name?

```
<DeviceSpecific>
<Choice Filter="prefersWBMP" ImageUrl="wml-image.wbmp"></Choice>
<Choice Filter="prefersGIF" ImageUrl="html-image.gif"></Choice>
<Choice ImageUrl="wml-image.bmp"></Choice>
</DeviceSpecific>
```

Understand what's happening here? Hold on, yes, yes, my psychic feelers can detect a definite nodding. Okay then, let's go build and access our site.

13. Press the F5 key to view your mobile Web application in Internet Explorer.

Because this is an HTML device, the prefersGIF filter should equate to True, and html-image.gif should be displayed. Does it? And for our next trick:

14. Place your mobile Web application on a machine that's accessible from the Internet.

15. Using a WML-only device (such as a standard mobile phone), try accessing your site through WAP. (If this isn't possible, use a pure WAP simulator, such as the Nokia download listed in today's FAQ.)

Does the WBMP image display itself? (See Figure 2-7.) What does it look like? What else could you do with the Image control? Try checking out the Alignment and AlternateText properties.

Figure 2-7. The wireless bitmap (WBMP) image, displayed in the Nokia simulator

Anyway, congratulations, you've just learned how to display images on virtually any device in the solar system! Erm, except perhaps a Macintosh. They're just not cool, OK?

Do You Remember?

Men who served in the Royal Navy under Admiral Sir James Lawry Gregory used to call him "Pope Gregory" because he was never wrong. Throughout World War II, while maintaining rigorous discipline and doing everything by the book, he was the hero of the North Sea convoys and led brilliant naval exploits in the Mediterranean.

It seemed the man had no weakness at all, except for one curious little idiosyncrasy. Every morning after breakfast he would retire to his stateroom, open his strong box, and study a piece of paper for five whole minutes.

For years, every man who served under him speculated about what was on that page.

Then one day the great admiral was urgently called to the bridge, leaving his quarters without locking the safe. While he was busily occupied, two of his junior officers dared to slip into his cabin and look at that note that he studied so carefully each morning.

It read: "Starboard on the right, Port on the left".

True story. Sounds like his memory was about as good as mine. Thankfully, however, your mobile Web applications don't have to share the same fallibility.

What do I mean? Often in your applications it's important that you *remember*—anything from a simple username through to data-holding objects. You saw how to do this for ASP.NET Web applications back in Tutorial 3, "Working the Web", by using cookies or the ViewState, for example.

However, the mobile world is a little different. Allow me to explain.

First off, cookies are a bit of a no-go. The majority of mobile devices don't support cookies, so, unless you know all your clients will be using particularly plush phones, steer clear.

That's not the only change. With mobile applications, the ViewState (which helps maintain our control properties) is not stored with the page but on the server, due to most phones not being able to handle such an amount of data. That means the ViewState expires along with the session, typically after twenty minutes of inactivity.

Interesting differences. But what does it mean for your applications? Two things.

First off, your best option for storing temporary data for a user is via the Session object. We learned how to use this in Tutorial 3, "Working the Web".

```
Dim MyVariable As String

' Add an item to the session
Session.Add("Username", "karl@karlmoore.com")
' Retrieve an item from the session
MyVariable = Session.Item("Username")
' Remove an item from the session
Session.Remove("Username")
```

The second lesson is that storing more-permanent information is best done using the query string. Remember that? You could add information to the query string and get the user to bookmark that page. When they revisit, you simply read from the query string and go from there.

For example, you might run the following code on your signup page:

```
Dim strQueryString As String

' Create query string
strQueryString = "user=" & Server.HtmlEncode(txtUser.Text)

' Redirect user to the page
Me.RedirectToMobilePage("members.aspx?" & strQueryString)
```

They will then be redirected to the members page, with a URL such as http://www.karlmoore.com/private/members.aspx?__redir=1&user=karl@karlmoore.com.

> **TOP TIP** *That's right: the* Response.Redirect *method of moving between pages isn't recommended in your mobile Web applications. Apparently, it can produce "unexpected results." Nothing to do with me, I assure you. Anyway, in its place you have this lovely* RedirectToMobilePage *function. Marvelous.*

Now, behind that members.aspx page, you might want to run code similar to the following:

```
Dim strUser As String

' Get and decode user data
strUser = Request.QueryString("user")
strUser = Server.HtmlDecode(strUser)

' Use the data in code
lblWelcome.Text = "Welcome, " & strUser & "!"
```

If the user bookmarks this page, the next time they access it directly the query string will be used to retrieve their details.

Okay, so it's about as secure as my rich Uncle Albert's staircase *<evil laugh goes here>*, but it's great for storing usernames or generic personalization settings across sessions. Pahh, who needs cookies?

Anyway, that's how we remember stuff when it comes to the mobile world. You've seen all the techniques before, but there are a few key differences when working with wireless devices.

And now you know about 'em. Alrighty!

FAQ

Still scratching your head over mobile Web applications? Maybe this neat roundup of frequently asked questions will hold the answer.

You say that the Mobile Internet Toolkit will target any device, no matter which "language" it speaks. My boss doesn't accept that this beast works by magic. He asks exactly which languages it supports.

The Mobile Internet Toolkit can send back content to your mobile device in any one of three formats: HTML, cHTML, or WML. But just what are these?

First off, you have regular HTML (Hypertext Markup Language), the standard markup language understood by browsers such as Internet Explorer and Netscape Navigator. After that, you have cHTML (Compact HTML), which is a markup language that's used on certain cell phones. It's essentially a mini version of HTML, with a few extra phone-specific tags thrown in for good taste. After that, you've got WML (Wireless Markup Language), an XML-based standard designed specifically for describing a user interface on wireless phones.

Incidentally, WML is part of WAP (the Wireless Application Protocol). This is a group of communication standards for wireless devices as proposed by the WAP Forum, for use on everything from phones to pagers to PDAs.

I know that .NET is the best thing since automatically-sliced bread. But this is now, and, in five years' time, surely all the mobile functionality they've bundled will be out of date? Won't everyone be on the Wireless Watch Web by then?

Good question and absolutely one of my very first puzzlers. Imagine a revolutionary new device is released: how do you support the fresh features? And what if the device uses different markup elements not currently found in HTML or WML?

Thankfully, Microsoft says it's already thought of this (*phew*). The answer is for manufacturers to create their own device adapters, which are runtime classes ready to plug into the .NET Framework.

These adapters will allow you to program for the new devices and take advantage of any new features. It also means that your application will work with the latest and greatest, all with a simple upgrade.

Write once, run anywhere. Not a bad little principle.

Earlier, you told me that the view state of a mobile Web form is now stored on the server. What if the user moves back a page and then resubmits the last form? Won't the server ViewState be out of synch with the page?

Erm, yes. Well spotted. As you know, by default, the ViewState of a mobile Web form is now stored on the server. If the user moves back on their device, then resubmits, the ViewState used on the server would be out-of-date.

To sort this problem, your server maintains a small history of ViewState information (by default, six individual sets). When sending content to your device, an identifier is added to the query string sent, which is later used to check which chunk of ViewState information to use.

You can change the default history of six history sets to ten, for example, by adding the following line to Web.config, inside the <system.web> element:

```
<mobileControls sessionStateHistorySize="10" />
```

Incidentally, it's worth noting that, wherever possible, you don't want to store information in the ViewState. It's an extra strain on resources, and, on busy wireless sites, could end up really slowing down your server. Therefore, where possible, set the EnableViewState property of individual controls (or your entire page, DOCUMENT in the Properties window) to False.

I'm happy testing my application with the Microsoft Mobile Explorer. However, are any other emulators available? I would really like to see how my program works on a Nokia 6210, for example, without having to rack up a whopping great big phone bill!

I know that feeling. I'm a bit of a scrooge myself, and, thankfully, there's a rather cheap solution: the Internet and a handful of third-party emulators.

First on our hit list, you have the ever-popular Nokia Mobile Internet Toolkit, a free download that includes its own emulator. Weighing in at 17MB and available from www.forum.nokia.com, sounds like this one is right up your alley. Another popular simulator is the OpenWave Mobile Browser, which is also a free download and available from developer.openwave.com/download/.

That should get you off to a start, but, if you're hungry for more, check out Microsoft's official lowdown on which emulators they've tested with the MIT at msdn.microsoft.com/vstudio/device/mitdevices.asp.

I'm now using multiple forms on one ASPX page, but fellow developers are finding it difficult to keep track of my forms and what they do. Is there a way to add notes to each form?

Officially, no. However, one little trick you might want to check out is to simply type text directly onto your page, above each form. Like controls such as the StyleSheet that get added directly to the page, this text will never be displayed to the user and provides you with just the sort of annotation required.

WHERE TO GO FROM HERE

Although we've covered everything you need to know to get your first mobile sites out to the world, there's always something new to learn. So let's review the books, sites, and newsgroups that can help in your explorations of the Mobile Internet Toolkit.

- *Mobile .NET* (Apress, ISBN 1-893115-71-2) If you want to dig down deep behind the mobile .NET scene, this book is definitely worth a browse. Covering everything from the MIT to the Mobile Information Server to SQL Server CE: if it's big time in the small world, it's in.

- *Building .NET Applications for Mobile Devices* (Microsoft Press, ISBN 0-7356-1532-2) The official mobile how-to from our favorite software giant. Thorough, but expensive.

- http://localhost/MobileQuickStart/: Got questions about using the Mobile Internet Toolkit? This QuickStart tutorial from Microsoft is installed on your machine when you install Visual Studio and provides you with all the MIT essentials.

- support.microsoft.com/highlights/mitk.asp: The official Microsoft support page for the Mobile Internet Toolkit.

- www.dotnetextreme.com: Great site, packing a bundle of small how-to guides. Includes features on mobile technology.

- www.ibuyspy.com/portal/: Part of the Microsoft sample ASP.NET site, the IBuySpy.com portal allows you to browse the site using a portable device such as a mobile phone or the MME. After you've finished browsing, visit www.ibuyspy.com to view the mobile code.

- www.gotdotnet.com: Microsoft's own .NET training portal, this site holds a mass of articles, source code, and third-party links. Includes its own Mobile section.

- microsoft.public.dotnet.framework.aspnet: The official Microsoft newsgroup for ASP.NET discussion. For speedier answers, try searching the archives first at www.googlegroups.com.

Keep in mind that sites disappear from the Net and books get replaced by even bigger books. To be sure of the latest, try heading down to Apress at www.apress.com.

CONCLUSION

Congratulations on finishing the "Going Mobile" tutorial!

Today, we've learned how to give our wireless sites that real edge. We started off by looking at the Device object and how we can use it to check out the capabilities of our target. After that, we uncovered filters and discovered how they can help us send images down to practically any device.

Next up, we talked about remembering data on mobile devices, and, because this is the last chapter in this tutorial, we concluded with a list of frequently asked questions and found out where to go from here.

Oh yes, and we learned that starboard is on the left, and port on the right. Or is it . . . oh, whatever.

Anyway, the Microsoft Internet Toolkit is an important addition to your developer's toolkit and can help you build powerful device sites in minutes. Even if you don't think that your organization currently demands such groovy technology, after exploring the possibilities, I'll bet you find a use within the next six months.

And, if you don't, make sure you do. Yes, that makes sense. Trust me, it's cutting edge, it's cool, and it'll help you provide a whole new service with just a little extra work.

Also, if you've built your existing Web or Windows applications using objects, you'll find it a complete doddle to reuse your existing code. What are objects, you ask? Oh, good question, and, if you don't know yet, all will be revealed in the next tutorial.

But, until that time, this is your host, Karl Moore, thanking you for your company and wishing you a very enjoyable evening. *Ciao* for now!

CHAPTER 4.2

YOUR DEVICE, FILTERS, IMAGES, MEMORY, AND MORE REVIEW SHEET

- The Device object is an instance of the
  `System.Web.Mobile.MobileCapabilities` class and enables you to discover
  the capabilities of your current device, via properties such as
  CanInitiateVoiceCall and IsColor.

- Filters are essentially custom properties listed in the Web.config file. They
  allow you to compare the properties of your Device object and return
  a True or False. Here is an example filter as defined in the deviceFilters element of Web.config:

  ```
  <filter name="supportsMail" compare="CanSendMail" argument="true" />
  ```

- Filters can be accessed via the PropertyOverrides property of your controls.
  This enables you to select individual filters and alter properties accordingly, allowing you to target content for specific devices/capabilities.

- One popular use of filters is in displaying images on the target device.
  Some devices support GIF, others prefer WBMP (wireless bitmap), and the
  rest typically opt for BMP. You can determine which image to send back by
  overriding the ImageUrl property of the Image control, depending on the
  bundled prefersGIF and prefersWBMP filters.

- There are two key state management changes between ASP.NET Web applications and mobile Web applications. Firstly, most mobile devices do not
  typically support cookies. Secondly, the user ViewState is stored on the
  server in the session.

- To store data for the one user session, simply add to the current user
  session, like so:

  ```
  Dim MyVariable As String
  ' Add an item to the session
  Session.Add("location", "Warwickshire, UK")
  ' Retrieve an item from the session
  MyVariable = Session.Item("location")
  ' Remove an item from the session
  Session.Remove("location")
  ```

- Although many wireless devices cannot support cookies, one technique for storing more-permanent information is to send the users to a page containing their username or personalization information in the query string. It can then be suggested that the user bookmark this page. On their next visit, you can read information from that query string and rebuild their own customized page.

Using Objects

Why Objects Are Important

There comes a time in every programmer's life when hair starts to grow in unexpected places and the vocal chords suddenly take a Barry White–style plunge. It's the stage at which *Superman Weekly* is ditched in favor of *Visual Basic Developer*. It's also when many coders begin to realize that a solution consisting of mere forms and modules just ain't enough. I call this the *change*.

Sure, you know the framework classes, and, yes, you understand databases, but, in the enterprise world, employers want that *something extra*. And that something extra is OOP (object-oriented programming). It's a skill that shows you've moved on from the tinkering stage, a résumé add-on that puts you right up there with the big boys.

Maybe you've heard that OOP acronym before. Uhm, but what does it mean? It means you know how to build "objects" and use them in your code. And that means you can write procedures that can be used over and over again. It means you know that objects can help you develop bug-free, easily maintainable applications.

Basically, using objects—being an OOP programmer—is a completely wizzy way of working. It starts off by making your life a little harder, then makes it one hell of a lot easier.

Today, we're going to learn more about objects and how they're important. We'll also figure out "classes" and what they've got to do with objects, plus we'll even build our own and understand how to put them to work in the real world.

In the next chapter, we'll be taking all of this even further, finding out how you can use your new skills to put objects inside "assemblies" and possibly earn yourself a few bucks in the process.

Just don't forget my 15%.

But, before we sign the contracts, let's start by asking ourselves—uhm, so just what is an object? Or, to put it another way—what the *hell* am I rambling on about?

What Are Objects?

Want to know something that might just make your day? Cue the drum roll—*you're already an object programmer*. Yup, that's right. I may have never met you, but I'll bet my brother's bottom dollar you are.

You see, every time you access a database, you're using objects, such as an SqlConnection object. Every time you write to a file, you're using objects, such as a FileStream object. Every time you need to display one of your project forms, you create a *new instance of your form class.* You create an *object.*

So, what exactly is an object? Warning! Geeky description straight ahead: *An object is an instance of a class.*

We've already seen classes, remember? Behind the scenes, every form you create is really a class. When you need to display a form, you create a new instance of that class; you create a new, completely independent *object.*

In other words, a class contains the code, and an object is that code in action. It's like the TextBox class and an instance of the text box. Or a cookie cutter and all those yummy cookies.

But, food analogies to one side, just what's so special about objects? Let's review the top three big benefits.

1. Objects allow for simplicity.

Imagine a television remote control. You press the "1" button and the television tunes itself into BBC 1. Or CNN. Or whatever. You press the power button and the television turns itself off. You press the brightness button and suddenly your screen looks like a close-up of that famous "White Cat Drinking Milk on a Snowy Day" masterpiece.

Now, unless you're a television repair geezer (which I'm kind of hoping you're not), you don't need to know how all this works. You just press the button, and it jumps into action.

This applies to objects too. After all, you don't really know what is happening when you use an instance of the SqlConnection class to access your data. It probably makes two-dozen further calls to some pretty obscure routines, then talks low-level geek speak with the database. But what do you care? You just use the object and it works.

Geeks like to call this *encapsulation.* They like to say it's a way of using an interface without needing to be aware of the internal implementation. And I'm pleased for them. I really am.

But in English? Objects allow you to use functionality without having to be aware of what's going on under the hood. What else?

2. Objects allow for reuse.

Let's say that you've developed a supercool spell checker. Your boss is over the moon and thinks it works really well in your new email program. In fact, it's so good, he thinks you should use the same functionality in that new Writer word processor you've created.

What do you do? There are two key options, and the first includes a lot of copying and pasting. Oh no.

However, if you created your spell checker as a class (compiled into a separate DLL), both your applications could create new objects from that class and use that same base of functionality—just by referencing it—regardless of what .NET language they're developed in.

> **TOP TIP** *Officially, for a programming language to be fully object oriented, it needs to allow objects to support certain qualities (encapsulation and inheritance, for example). You can find the full lowdown on these terms and just what they mean in the FAQ (in Chapter 5.2). It has some fancy, sure-to-impress words waiting there for you.*

3. Objects allow for maintainability.

You've finished that groovy application for the marketing department. When they click on the magic button, it dips into a dozen databases and produces relevant promotional sales figures.

But they're complaining that the sales-per-year figure doesn't tally with the last twelve sales-per-month totals. Whoops. Time to spend nine hours debugging all that calculation code to figure out just what went wrong.

Damn that department. After all, it was only last month when they called complaining they couldn't access your system. Why? The sales team had moved its database to another server, breaking your code. So you spent another nine hours going through that muddled mass of spaghetti code to change all the server references.

What a pain. But, if you'd used objects—well, you would've known exactly which property retrieved the sales-per-month figures and could've instantly located the error. And, due to the centralized nature of objects, you would've known exactly what part grabbed data, allowing you to easily implement any database server changes in a matter of seconds.

Updating any programs that used your objects would also be as simple as dishing out a new DLL.

So, objects allow for simplicity, code reuse, and maintainability. They're also darn cool. And, for the rest of today, we're going to spend our time looking at how we can create our own object, based on a Dog class.

Surreal? I think so. Boring? Never!

It'll all make sense later. Trust me; I'm a programmer.

Starting Small

In this section, we're going to begin by creating our own basic Dog class and then use it as an object. After that, we'll expand it to include a whole bundle of extra features.

Let's dive straight into the deep end.

1. Create a new Windows application in VS .NET, called "MyKennels."

Now, remember that objects are "live" instances of a class. And classes are just chunks of code, a lot like the code in a module except used in a different way. Let's add a class to our project now.

2. From the menu, select Project ➢ Add Class.

3. Change the name to "CDog" and click on Open. (See Figure 1-1.)

> **TOP TIP** *Just as there are naming conventions for text boxes (txt) and forms (frm), there are also two suggested prefixes for classes used inside your project. The first is an uppercase "C," and the second is a lowercase "cls." I personally prefer the former.*

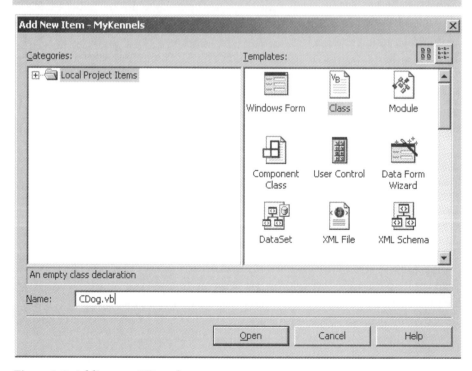

Figure 1-1. Adding our CDog class

You should be staring at a pretty empty screen. Here, we have our file, CDog.vb, that holds just two lines. The first indicates the start of the class, and the second indicates the end of the class. And in between? We have nothing.

This big blank blotch of white is where you slap your class code. And it'll be your home for the next few minutes, as we get typing.

4. Declare the following variable in your CDog class:

```
Public Name As String
```

Okay, so perhaps that didn't take a few minutes—but I'm male, I exaggerate. However, we've already done everything necessary to start using our CDog class as an object. No, really.

So, *vot haff ve crrreated?* Good question. Let's find out.

5. Open Form1.vb in the Designer.

6. Draw a button out onto your form.

7. Add the following code to respond to the click event of Button1:

```
Dim MyDog As New CDog()

MyDog.Name = "Billy Moore"
MessageBox.Show(MyDog.Name)

MyDog = Nothing
```

Let me explain what's happening here. We start off by creating a new instance of our CDog class. MyDog is now our object, the thing we work with. Next, we set the Name variable inside our object, and then read it in a message box.

Finally, we set our MyDog object equal to Nothing. This basically tells VB .NET that we've finished working with it and to release any memory used by the object.

> **TOP TIP** *Actually, that's a lie. Instead, this last line simply marks the object as not being used anymore. When the .NET Framework next runs the "garbage collection" process (`System.GC.Collect`), it will automatically clear memory used by the object. Although you're not strictly required to set any object to Nothing, it's a good practice to get into because it makes your code neat and controlled.*

8. Press F5 to test your application.

What happens when you click on the button? Does it all work as you expected? Top stuff! But, at the moment, you probably can't see any real difference between code in our class or, say, a module. Well, you can create multiple instances of a class in code: completely separate, individual widgets running in memory. We'll see that in action next.

9. Change the code behind the click event of your button to:

```
Dim MyDog As New CDog()
Dim MyDog2 As New CDog()

MyDog.Name = "Billy Moore"
MessageBox.Show(MyDog.Name)
MyDog2.Name = "Sadie Moore"

MessageBox.Show(MyDog2.Name)

MyDog = Nothing
MyDog2 = Nothing
```

This is almost exactly the same as our last chunk of code, except here we're using two different widgets, MyDog and MyDog2. Both of these objects are based on our CDog class, yet they are completely independent of one another.

Think back to our cookie cutter analogy. Our CDog class is the defining cookie cutter, and our MyDog and MyDog2 objects are the cookies. And I'm dribbling already.

10. Press F5 and test your application.

See what happens? When you click on your button, you should get two message boxes—one saying Billy Moore, the other Sadie Moore—both of which are exceptionally cute boxers, I might add. What if you read the value of MyDog.Name after you set MyDog2.Name? What would you get back? Check it out. Yes, they're completely independent of each other.

Now, programmers often build classes around real-life objects—such as a Customer or an Order class. So, in this sample, each dog already has a name. What other properties could we add?

11. Declare the following variable inside your CDog class:

```
Public Age As Short
```

12. Back on Form1, change the code behind your button click event to:

```
Dim MyDog As New CDog()
Dim MyDog2 As New CDog()

MyDog.Name = "Billy Moore"
MyDog.Age = 5

MyDog2.Name = "Sadie Moore"
MyDog2.Age = 8

MessageBox.Show(MyDog.Name & " is " & MyDog.Age & " years old")
MessageBox.Show(MyDog2.Name & " is " & MyDog2.Age & " years old")

MyDog = Nothing
MyDog2 = Nothing
```

Yes, it's incredibly similar to the last chunk, but here we're using the new Age variable.

13. Press F5 and test your application. (See Figure 1-2.)

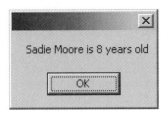

Figure 1-2. Our class-powered application

You should receive a message box displaying the name and age of each lovable pooch. Aww, bless. Now try setting the age of one of the dogs to 1,000. Or perhaps 30,000.

See what happens? That's right. Bugger all. That's because a Short variable can store any value right up to 32,767. But it doesn't make sense for a dog to be over 30,000 years old—unless it's *exceptionally* well kept.

So, how can you handle situations like this?

Adding Properties

Variables are great for storing simple data inside an object, but you can also add properties to a class, which give you much more control.

You might, for example, have a property that stores the salary of a particular employee. Or the name of a database to read from. Or (and this is your stop) the age of your pooch.

Now, a typical property consists of two parts: a Get and a Set. Your Get chunk of code runs when you try to read a property, and the Set chunk runs when you try to set a property. For example, look at this sample property:

```
Private shtAge As Short

Public Property Age() As Short
    Get
        Return shtAge
    End Get
    Set(ByVal Value As Short)
        shtAge = Value
    End Set
End Property
```

If we added this to our class, it'd work much like the Age variable. When someone runs `MyDog.Age = 5`, the Set block of code runs, passing in the new value as the Value parameter. If, however, someone reads the age, like `MessageBox.Show(MyDog.Age)`, the Get block of code runs, returning the value of `shtAge`.

Get the gist? Hmm, maybe. But, right now, this is only working exactly like a standard variable, except with a lot more code. However, properties also allow you to have a lot more control over what sort of data is and isn't acceptable. Let's demonstrate that now.

1. Remove the Age variable from your CDog class.

2. Declare the following "internal" variable behind the class:

   ```
   Private shtAge As Short
   ```

TOP TIP *When you declare anything inside a class as Private, it means that only code within the class can see it. If you declare something as Public, it means that any code using this class can see that item. Exactly the same as modules, really.*

3. Type the following code in your class, then press the Enter key:

```
Public Property Age As Short
```

VB .NET will automatically finish the property for you, with Get and Set routines.

4. Edit your property so that it reads:

```
Public Property Age() As Short
    Get
        Return shtAge
    End Get
    Set(ByVal Value As Short)
        If Value < 50 Then shtAge = Value
    End Set
    End Property
```

The only real change here from our original example is we're doing a little checking in code before setting our variable. We ensure the age value being set is under 50 (allowing for world-record-setting pups with wrinkles and white beards).

That means MyDog.Age = 30 would work. However, if you ran MyDog.Age = 75, it would fail to set the property. Of course, you could always display an exclamatory message box at this point or throw an error back at the calling code (using the Throw statement); however, I'm feeling all kind today.

5. Switch back to the code window behind Form1.

6. Click on the first line of code where we set the Age property and press F9 to set a breakpoint: MyDog.Age = 4.

7. Next, click on the first line of code where we read the Age property and press F9 again:

```
MessageBox.Show(MyDog.Name & " is " & MyDog.Age & " years old").
```

Now let's test run our application.

8. Press the F5 key to run your program.

9. Click on your button.

The code should pause on the lines of code where you added breakpoints.

10. When the code pauses, slowly observe what happens by stepping through each line with the F8 key. (See Figure 1-3.) To run your code as normal again, press F5.

```
Public Property Age() As Short
    Get
        Return shtAge
    End Get
    Set(ByVal Value As Short)
        If Value < 50 Then shtAge = Value
    End Set
End Property
```

Figure 1-3. Stepping through our class code

Do you see what happens? Notice how the Age property goes through the Get block when you read a value? And how the Set block runs when you try to set a property?

So there we have it—properties in a nutshell. They're like properties you work with all the time in VB .NET, and they're better than regular variables because they allow you more control.

Top stuff.

Bettering Properties

We've figured out that properties can be really useful in helping you have more control over the data that your object stores. Sometimes, however, certain properties could be better dealt with.

I mean, say you have four types of customers: Enterprise, Medium, Small, and New. Or three different types of scouring methods in your Search class: FloppyDisks, HardDisks, and Network. Wouldn't it be nice to pick one of these options from a predefined list, rather than setting the object property to some obscure number or a string of text?

Oh yes. And you can, with crazy lil' things called *enumerations*.

1. Insert the following code into your CDog class:

```
Public Enum CoatType As Short
    BigAndShaggy = 1
    ShortCrewCut = 2
    PoodleStyleAfro = 3
    Unknown = 4
End Enum
```

This Enum is an enumeration. In other words, it's a list of possible options.

You might wonder why we need the As Short and all those numbers next to each option. Well, behind the scenes, VB .NET remembers each option as a number, storing your selection as a numeric data type. By using As Short and assigning numbers ourselves, we're just controlling the process.

But try removing them, so you just have a plain Enum with options inside. It still works, right? Right.

> **TOP TIP** *Actually, the numbers next to an enumeration can be really useful if you want to put this information into a database. As BigAndShaggy really translates to the number 1, you could insert it directly into an efficient database number field. This means that you have the power of using English descriptions in code, yet can still maintain a sleek database design.*

So, we've created our list of possible options. Next, we're going to add a property that allows our programmer to select one of the options. To start with, we need to declare the internal variable to hold the data.

2. Declare the following variable behind our CDog class:

```
Private shtCoat As CoatType
```

Here, we've declared a private variable to hold one of our CoatType options. Next, we need to add our actual property.

3. Add the following property to your CDog class:

```
Public Property Coat() As CoatType
    Get
        Return shtCoatType
    End Get
    Set(ByVal Value As CoatType)
        shtCoatType = Value
    End Set
End Property
```

Do you understand what's happening here? Supercool! We're almost there now. Next, we're actually going to test out how this property works in the code window.

4. Flick back to Form1.

5. Remove all the code behind your button and replace it with:

```
Dim MyDog As New CDog()
MyDog.Name = "Billy"
```

6. On the next line, type "MyDog.Coat =".

See what happens? As you hit that equals key, a list of possible options crop up, your own groovy option list! And you can now select any of these.

Except the Afro one. Billy certain doesn't have an Afro coat. Nor a Big and Shaggy one come to think of it. In fact, just select the Short Crew Cut option.

7. Finish typing the code:

```
MyDog.Coat = CDog.CoatType.ShortCrewCut
```

Where have you seen an enumeration used like this before? Hmm, have you ever tried to set the Align property of a text box in code?

Righto, next up we're going to read our property in code. Now, if you read it direct in code (that is, MyDog.Coat), you'll get back the actual number you assigned that particular option. However, if you read the .ToString property of Coat (that is, MyDog.Coat.ToString), you'll get back the actual option name.

Let's add some code to read that now.

8. Append the following to your existing code:

```
MessageBox.Show("The coat of your dog is: " & MyDog.Coat.ToString)
MessageBox.Show("The number for that option is: " & MyDog.Coat)
```

Understand what this is supposed to do? Actually, there are many different ways of reading which option we chose. Another would be to use a Select Case statement, like this:

```
Select Case MyDog.Coat
    Case CDog.CoatType.BigAndShaggy
        MessageBox.Show("You have a big, bouncy, bushy pup!")
    Case CDog.CoatType.PoodleStyleAfro
        MessageBox.Show("Your pooch is pretty, petit and, erm, pooch-like!")
    Case CDog.CoatType.ShortCrewCut
        MessageBox.Show("Your dog contains more bounce than a rubber ball factory!")
    Case CDog.CoatType.Unknown
        MessageBox.Show("I have no idea about your dog. Don't think you do, either!")
End Select
```

Try it out if you want, typing each line in yourself for the full effect. Okay, so you don't have to do this; it's simply another way of reading your property. But, hey, I get paid per line of code.

Great stuff. Now, just one more rather familiar statement before we test. We need to mark MyDog as no longer being used. What do we do?

9. At the end of all your existing code, help free up memory by adding the following line:

```
MyDog = Nothing
```

10. Press F5 to run your application, and then click on your button.

See what happens? Impressed? Did you expect all this? Welcome to the wonderful world of enumerations!

Methods, Functions, Parameters—Oh My!

So, we've already figured out how to add variables, properties, and enumerations to our classes. What else can you do?

Well, for a start, you've got methods. Yes, bog standard methods. You first met them back in "Beginning VB .NET" and have been using them regularly in all your projects since (haven't you?). They're typically chunks of code that perform an action, and, in this world of classes, they're back with a vengeance.

Let's demonstrate.

1. Insert the following code into your CDog class:

```
Public Sub Bark()
    MessageBox.Show("Woof! Woof!")
End Sub
```

And that's it! Here we have a regular method inside our class you can call simply by running a command like `MyDog.Bark()`.

2. Replace the code behind your button on Form1 with:

```
Dim MyDog As New CDog()
MyDog.Name = "Billy"
MyDog.Bark()
MyDog = Nothing
```

Notice how, when you hit the period key following `MyDog`, `Bark` appears as a purple diamond, whereas `Name` and `Age` appear as a little blue hand pointing to some sort of list. (Okay, *you* tell me what it is.) Those icons are to help you distinguish the types of items inside your class. What is the icon for your enumeration?

3. Press F5 and test your application.

Everything work as expected? Great! But that's not all: you can also add functions to your class in pretty much the same way. Just add them and run. Let's add a rather zany sample function right now.

4. Add the following function to your CDog class:

```
Public Function Feed(ByVal FoodName As String) As String

    If FoodName = "PASTA" Then
        Return "Yuck! Take it back."
    ElseIf FoodName = "BOUNCERS" Then
        Return "Hmm, my favorite. Please sir, more . . . "
    Else
        Return "Woof! Thanks for the " & FoodName
    End If

End Function
```

5. Add code to the click event of your button on Form1 to call this function.

6. Press F5 to test your application.

What happens? Does your function work? What icon does this procedure have?

Now, let's imagine that I requested my class have a Sleep method. I'd call this each time I wanted my pooch to take a cat—or rather a dog—nap. But how would I know when my little bundle of joy has awoken?

Good question. And the answer is to use *events*.

You know when someone types into your text box thanks to its TextChanged event. And you know when someone clicks on your button with that eternal click event.

How do you know when your pup wakes up? Enter stage left: the Awake event.

Events

Events are a great way of informing the person using your class when something happens. Whether it's to tell them the database has been fully updated, or an error occurred reading one of your files during the BatchUpload method, or your pup has woken up. The possibilities are endless.

How does it work? Firstly, you define an event, which means that you tell VB .NET what the event will be called, alongside any extra parameters. You typically define this event at the top of your class for simplicity, a little like this:

```
Public Event OnAdd(ByVal CustomerID As Integer, ByVal CustomerName As String)
```

Then, when you need to "raise" an event in your code, you simply tap into the RaiseEvent method. So here, we might have one big routine that takes a customer log file and adds each person to our database, calling the OnAdd event each time one has been successfully added, passing the CustomerID and CustomerName, like this:

```
RaiseEvent OnAdd(42921, "Ben Sherman")
```

Understand how this could work? Let's add an event to our own class now.

1. Declare the following event behind your CDog class:

```
Public Event Awake()
```

Still, you can't wake up unless you've slept, so let's implement a Sleep method. In such a method, I could be doing literally anything: adding customer information to a database, creating a mound of individual management reports, or performing lengthy Microsoft salary calculations.

But it just so happens that all I am doing in fact is wasting time. Yes, we're going to add a jabberwocking loop that does absolutely nothing, then raises the Awake event. Let's code that, erm, code now.

2. Add the following method to your CDog class:

```
Public Sub Sleep()

    Dim intCount As Integer

        For intCount = 1 To 1000000
            Application.DoEvents()
        Next


    RaiseEvent Awake()

End Sub
```

This code loops around a million times, doing nothing. On my computer, the loop lasts about a minute. Yours may be faster. Or it might be slower. All depends on gravitation pull. Or processor speed. I forget. But after that short time delay, our Sleep method raises the Awake event.

So, how can we get our programs to respond to object events? With buttons, it's simple. You just enter the code window, select your button from the drop-down list, and it's hey nonny-nonny, time for a coffee break.

But, in that instance, you're working with a control, something you can see on a form. Here, we're working with pure code, an object with no visible interface. So, if we want to receive events, we need to do something a little special.

3.   In the Declarations section of Form1, add the following declaration:

```
Dim WithEvents MyDog As New CDog()
```

The code here is no different to our previous MyDog declaration, except that (a) it contains the WithEvents keyword to tell VB .NET that we want to receive any events from this object, and (b) it's in the Declarations section, where it must be to receive events. (Try, for example, declaring an object as WithEvents inside a method.)

Let's get out the Paul McKenna pendulum now and slowly, slowly, make our dog feel tired, sleepy, weary . . .

4.   Replace the code behind your Form1 button click event with:

```
MyDog.Name = "Billy"
MyDog.Bark()
MyDog.Sleep()
```

Next, let's add a little code to respond to our Awake event.

5.   In the code window behind Form1, select "MyDog" from the Class Name drop-down list and "Awake" from the Method Name drop-down.

6.   In the Awake event skeleton that appears, enter the following code:

```
Private Sub MyDog_Awake() Handles MyDog.Awake
    MessageBox.Show("Your pooch has awoken!")
End Sub
```

Excellent! Great stuff. Now let's test our application.

7.   Press F5 to run your application.

8.   Click on your button.

After a quick bark, your pup will take a quick nap (or, on my computer, an exceptionally long nap. But, then again, I *am* running a Pentium 186). So, does your pooch give you a call when he has woken? *Wizard!*

Going Further

Thought that was it for today? You should be so lucky. Instead, I'm going to leave you with a little puzzler.

Imagine that you want to add some code to run as soon as your object gets created. Perhaps you want to grab some initial data or do a little default processing. To do this, you'll need to use a method called New.

And sometimes you also need to write code to run when your object gets destroyed. When you set your object to Nothing or it goes out of scope, it gets marked to be cleared from memory when the next garbage collection runs. To run code when this collection occurs, you'll need to use a method called Finalize.

To add any of these elements to your class, simply open your class and select New or Finalize in the Method Name drop-down. (See Figure 1-4.)

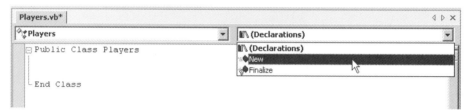

Figure 1-4. Adding a New method to our class

> **TOP TIP**   *By default, the Finalize method will already include a line of code to finalize any of its base objects:* `MyBase.Finalize`. *It's a good idea to add any of your own code before this line.*

Understand? Great. Now, of course, it's your turn. Try improving our CDog class so that it implements a New and Finalize method, even if you only simply test the feature by displaying message boxes.

> **TOP TIP**   *In the nerd world, our New method is often referred to as a con-structor, code that runs when your object is created. Our Finalize method is also commonly called the* finalizer. *You feel better for knowing that, right?*

Does the New method always run when you create your object? Also, when does the Finalize method run? It should kick in whenever the system performs garbage collection, possibly when you close your application or perhaps every few minutes. Would it be a good idea to close database connections in this method? Also, are the New and Finalize methods visible to users of your class?

Congratulations on battling it out to the end of our first "Using Objects" chapter!

Today, we started off by looking at object-oriented programming (OOP) and what advantages using objects brings us, including the popular pay raise factor. We then learned the truth of all truths: an object is really just an instance of a class.

Next up, we explored how to create our own classes, using a rather abstract Dog example. And, during that journey, we covered everything from variables to properties, methods to functions, enumerations to events, plus also found out about adding constructors and finalizers.

However, unless you actually run your own kennels, our Dog class is about as useless as Herman Munster's entry in the Mr. World competition. Still, the principles are the same, and, if we spend a few moments thinking about it, creating objects as we've done today can really help our applications.

Remember figuring out how to write to files back in Tutorial 1, "Beginning VB .NET"? It was a hassle. You had to work with FileStream objects and the like, and the code wasn't pretty. And what if you wanted to read from a file? You'd have to do it all over again. But knowing what you do now, you could just compact all that code into a few methods, all inside your own FileWork class, using the functionality as and when you wanted it. As we'll learn next week, you could even pack that class code into your own separate DLL, meaning that you can reuse the functionality among your numerous applications.

Let's continue brainstorming. Maybe you could create classes to hold all your customer details, adding the lot to your database simply by calling one little method? Sure, you'd have to write all the code to begin with, but, after that, you're just working with one easy-to-use object. We'll look at this more in the next chapter.

How about if you wrote a series of classes that went and nabbed the latest marketing response figures from your sales database, and the database they used changed servers? There's no need to go searching through reams of data access code: your centralized, bug-free class is the only place you'd need to look.

As I said before, just after objects make your life a little harder, they make it one hell of a lot easier.

Take five right now. Go grab a cup of java and think how you might be able to use objects in your own world—to help simplify, to help reuse, to help maintain.

Then take ten, and join me again soon, refreshed and raring to go for the second chapter in "Using Objects." But, until then, this is your host, Karl Moore, signing off. Toodle-pip!

CHAPTER 5.1

- *OOP* stands for *object-oriented programming* and refers to the in-demand ability to create and use objects in your applications.

- Objects are instances of a class. A class contains the actual code, whereas an object is an independent, usable instance of the class.

- Objects are useful because they allow you to simplify your programs by encapsulating complex code, providing an easy-to-understand interface. In addition, objects allow you to reuse your code by packaging the source classes into a DLL assembly, ready for consumption by other applications. Another advantage is maintainability: due to the centralized nature of objects, it's easier to locate bugs and make logic changes.

- To add a class to your Visual Studio .NET project, select Project ➢ Add Class from the menu.

- Inside your class, you can add any code you deem necessary, including variables and properties (data-holders, often referred to as *fields*), enumerations, methods, and functions (procedures, often simply referred to as just *methods*), and events.

- A property allows you greater control of what information your class stores. It consists of a Get and Set block: the Get block returns the property value, and the Set block sets the property value. It is up to you to actually implement this functionality. Here is an example property:

```
Private shtQuantity As Short

Public Property Quantity() As Short
    Get
        Return shtQuantity
    End Get
    Set(ByVal Value As Short)
        If Value > 0 And Value < 50 Then shtQuantity = Value
    End Set
End Property
```

- An enumeration allows you to provide a list of potential options. You can then declare a variable as using that enumeration, or perhaps incorporate it into your property. Here is an example of an enumeration, alongside a public variable using that enumeration:

```
Public Enum Characters As Short
    TheGood = 1
    TheBad = 2
    TheUgly = 3
End Enum

Public ActorNiche As Characters
```

- Events allow you to inform the user of your object that something has happened. You declare an event in your class like this:

```
Public Event MyEventName(ByVal EventArg1 As String, ByVal Etc As Integer)
```

- To raise an event in your code, use the RaiseEvent method, like this:

```
RaiseEvent MyEventName("Param1", 10)
```

- To respond to an event in code, you need to declare your object using the WithEvents keyword in the Declarations section of your form, module, and so on. You then need to either select the object event using the drop-down Class Name and Method boxes, or utilize the Handles statement. (See the Help index for more information.) Here is an example object declaration using WithEvents:

```
Dim WithEvents MyFiles As New FileWork()
```

- By preceding a class-level variable or method with the Private keyword in a class, that item is not made public and is only visible to the class. Using the Public keyword, however, makes it visible to users of the class.

- To run code when a new instance of your class is created, insert it behind a method called New (the constructor). To run code when the object is destroyed by the garbage collection process, add it to the Finalize method (the finalizer). To generate these methods "shells," open the class code window and select New or Finalize from the Method Name drop-down.

Objects in Real Life, Class Libraries, and More

"Before software can be reusable, it first has to be usable."—Ralph Johnson

WELCOME TO THE SECOND CHAPTER in Using Objects! And for once, I'm going to spare you a witty clip from *101 Openings for .NET Chapters*, because (a) most are about as amusing as getting an arrow in the head, then realizing there's an enormous electricity bill attached, and (b) today, we need all the space we can get for reams more object code.

In the last chapter, we got a grasp of the basics. We looked at the benefits of objects, figuring out how to create our own classes. But today, we'll really take off, learning how to create our own real-to-life Customers class, plus uncovering how we can package this into a completely separate DLL file.

We'll also talk about how you can use the techniques we learn today to save time and earn you hard cash. Plus, as this is the last chapter in Tutorial 5, "Using Objects", we'll review where you can go from here and check out a big bundle of extremely interesting frequently asked questions.

All that to come—so hold onto your lil' cotton socks. It's time to groove.

Creating a Customers Class

Sometimes it's better when certain things are kept apart. Like cats and dogs. Or me and chocolate. Or the Spice Girls.

Or your program and classes . . . *oh yes*, it's another silky smooth introduction. Bet you didn't see that one coming.

You see, in the last chapter, we learned how you can create classes inside your application and use them as objects. But, when a class is inside your application, no other programs can "see" or use its functionality. For this, you need to separate it, putting your classes somewhere completely different.

What do I mean? Good question. I'm not too sure myself, but, the way I figure it, you can slap your classes into a class library. This is a project that gets compiled into a DLL, which you can reference from any of your projects and instantly use the functionality within.

So, in brief, putting your classes into a class library enables you to *reuse* your code.

Next up, we're going to build our own class library. We're also going to be a little special with this one, adding two classes to handle our company clients: a Customer class that will hold details of an individual customer, and a Customers class that manages individual Customer objects.

Having one class maintain a *collection* of other classes like this is an incredibly common technique in the object-oriented programming world and this will serve as a great little primer.

Clear as mud? You'll understand more as we continue. And, when we pause for thought later, you'll realize what power something that seems so simple can give you. I promise.

Creating Your Class Library

Let's begin by creating our class library.

1. Create a new class library project in VS .NET, christened "MyCustomers", remembering to note the project location. (See Figure 2-1.)

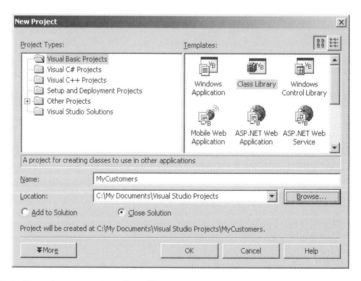

Figure 2-1. Creating our new class library project

As its name just might suggest, class libraries typically contain classes, classes, and more classes. You can add forms and modules too if you fancy, but remember this *won't* become an application you can run—it's just a DLL, a common storage place for your class code. Right now, you should be staring at a rather blank-looking Class1.

2.   Using the Solution Explorer or the Properties window, rename Class1.vb to "Customer.vb".

3.   Edit Customer.vb, changing the name of Class1 to "Customer".

To keep this sample simple, we're going to make this Customer class exceptionally easy to understand. In fact, we'll only be adding a few public variables. Ready?

4.   Add the following variable declarations to your Customer class:

```
Public CustomerID As String
Public Name As String
Public Address As String
```

Supercool! That's our first class finished already. Nope, we haven't used any of those wizzy features we talked about last week—but we've still got one big class to go.

Creating Your Customers Collection Class

Our next class will be called "Customers", and it will store a collection of individual Customer objects.

When you want to add to this collection, you might pass a Customer object to your Customers Add method. Or you may use the Remove method to zap a customer. You'll also need to be able to find and edit a customer, too.

So, our Customers class is basically a manager, minus the salary. Again, as shown in Figure 2-2, *it'll hold a collection of individual Customer objects*.

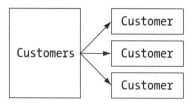

Figure 2-2. Our Customers class, handling numerous Customer objects

1. Add a new class to your project, naming it "Customers".

2. Declare the following object inside your Customers class:

```
Private mcolCustomers As New Collection()
```

You might be wondering what this is all about. Well, the Collection class is a part of the VB .NET runtime. It's a widget whose job is to simply hold a bunch of ordered items. What an exciting life.

Here, we're going to use this Collection object to internally store our individual Customer objects. We'll be telling it to store this object, store that object, find that last object, remove the other object. *Whatever.* It's our holder.

Moving on, what features will we need to add to this Customers class to deal with our Customer objects? For a start, you'll need to actually *add* a Customer object to our collection. So, an "Add" method that accepts a Customer object is a good idea.

3. Add the following code to your Customers class:

```
' Adds a customer to our collection
Public Sub Add(ByVal Customer As Customer, ByVal Key As String)
    mcolCustomers.Add(Customer, Key)
End Sub
```

Here, we're taking a Customer object as a parameter, alongside a key string. We then add that object to our internal collection, along with its key.

The Collection object uses keys to identify individual objects. A key is basically just a unique string that is paired with the object you pass in. We'll see how we can use that key later.

What else do we need to add? How about a property that returns the number of Customer objects in our collection? Sounds pretty smart to me. However, this will be a read-only property, of course (which means that we need to use that cool ReadOnly keyword, along with just a Get statement).

4. Add the following property to your Customers class:

```
' Returns the number of Customer objects in our collection
Public ReadOnly Property Count() As Integer
    Get
        Return mcolCustomers.Count
    End Get
End Property
```

> **TOP TIP** *Here, we've seen how to create a read-only property using the ReadOnly keyword and just the Get code block. If you need to create a rather more unusual write-only property, use the WriteOnly keyword and simply implement the Set block.*

Understand everything so far? Top notch. Next, we're going to add a property that gives the user access to an object from our collection. It will accept a key string (or an index number, from 1 to the Count value) and return one of our Customer objects. Let's add that now.

5. Add the following property to your Customers class:

```
' Returns a Customer object from our collection
Public ReadOnly Property Item(ByVal IndexOrKey As Object) As Customer
    Get
        Return mcolCustomers.Item(IndexOrKey)
    End Get
End Property
```

Here, we're accepting an IndexOrKey parameter as an object. An object can hold anything—including a number or a string. We use this to get the requested item from the collection, returning a reference to the original.

What else do we need to add? Well, how about a Remove method?

6. Add the following code to your Customers class:

```
' Removes a Customer object from our collection
Public Sub Remove(ByVal IndexOrKey As Object)
    mcolCustomers.Remove(IndexOrKey)
End Sub
```

This is pretty simple (at least, in comparison): we're just removing the object with the specified key string or index number from our collection.

Well, that's finished our two core classes. Next, it's time to build our project. And it's about time—my brain is starting to smoke.

7. From the menu, select Build ➢ Build MyCustomers.

This will build our class library, creating a final DLL file from our two classes. Go check it out now. How large is that DLL?

What new features might we think about adding? How about a LoadDB method or an OnUpdate event? Can you think of an instance where objects like this could be useful to you in the real world? If you can't right now, you will by the end of the chapter.

But most importantly for the moment, how can we use this DLL from another project, using some of the customer functionality we've built so far? Let's look at that next.

Adding a Test Project

What's the difference between a well-dressed man and a tired dog? One wears a suit; the other just pants. What's the difference between an optimist and a pessimist? An optimist invented the airplane; a pessimist invented the seatbelts.

Now for a teaser slightly less exciting: what's the difference between a *solution* and a *project* in Visual Studio .NET? A project can be a Windows application or class library, but a solution is a collection of one or more such projects.

Told you it wasn't as exciting. It's the punch line, I think.

Anyway, in this section, we're going to test your class library so far. How? By adding another project to our solution—this time, a standard Windows application.

1. From the menu, select File ➢ Add Project ➢ New Project.

2. Create a Windows application called "CustomerTest".

3. Right-click on CustomerTest in the Solution Explorer and select "Set As Startup Project".

Next, we need to add a reference to our actual MyCustomers.dll file, so we can use the classes we created earlier. You won't be able to view any of our original code via the DLL, but you will be able to create objects from our classes and use their functionality.

4. From the menu, select Project ➢ Add Reference.

5. Click on the Browse button and select your MyCustomers.dll file.

6. When finished, click on OK in the Add Reference dialog box.

We're going to work on our actual Windows application now. We'll create a simple customer editor to demonstrate the principle of using external objects in our code. It'll also show us how we can use the common collection class we built, and, when we pause for thought later, we'll talk about how this apparently simple program can be expanded to give you more power than the International Board of Electricity Suppliers.

7. Decorate Form1 in your CustomerTest project as appropriate, ensuring that you add the following controls per our screenshot (Figure 2-3).

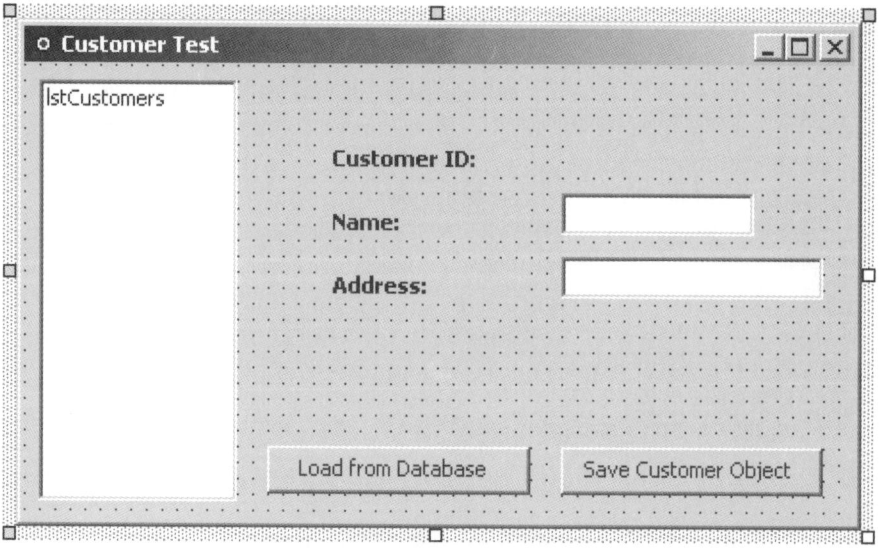

Figure 2-3. Our Customers class, handling numerous Customer objects

- *ListBox*—Name: lstCustomers

- *Button*—Name: btnLoad; Text: "Load from Database"

- *Button*—Name: btnSave; Text: "Save Customer Object"

- *Label*—Name: lblCustomerID; Text: (blank)

- *TextBox*—Name: txtCustomerName; Text: (blank)

- *TextBox*—Name: txtAddress; Text: (blank)

Here, we have two main buttons: "Load from Database" and "Save Customer Object". Each will want to access our Customers object, so we'll want to declare an instance of the object somewhere they can both see it—say, in the Declarations section of our form. Let's do that now.

8. In the Declarations section of your form, add the following declaration:

```
Dim MyCusts As New MyCustomers.Customers()
```

Talking of those two buttons, let's code the former first and the latter last.

9. Add the following code to respond to the click event of btnLoad:

```
Dim MyCust As MyCustomers.Customer, shtCount As Short

' Add Customer objects to Customers
For shtCount = 1 To 10
    MyCust = New MyCustomers.Customer()
    MyCust.CustomerID = "MYC" & shtCount
    MyCust.Name = "Customer " & shtCount
    MyCust.Address = (shtCount * 6) & " Veebee Lane, Warks"
    MyCusts.Add(MyCust, MyCust.CustomerID)
    MyCust = Nothing
Next

' Retrieve individual Customer objects
For shtCount = 1 To MyCusts.Count
    MyCust = MyCusts.Item(shtCount)
    lstCustomers.Items.Add(MyCust.CustomerID)
Next
```

Understand what's happening here? We start off by declaring MyCust, ready to hold a customer. Then we jump into a loop, which cycles around ten times. Inside that loop, we set MyCust equal to a new Customer object, then fill out a few pseudo details. After that, we add the Customer object to our Customers collection, using the CustomerID number as the key. Finally, we set our object to nothing, telling VB we've finished using MyCust to hold this Customer object.

Of course, we could be cycling through the records in some data source here, adding the data to our own customized objects. Or perhaps we could include a LoadDB method in our Customers class to do it all for us. Imagine how simple that would make our code!

Moving on, the next loop here simply cycles around from 1 to the `.Count` property of our Customers object. It uses the loop number to retrieve an individual Customer item from our Customers class, then adds its CustomerID to our list box.

What do you think? Understandable? Let's add a little code behind our list box now.

10. Add the following code to respond to your list box SelectedIndexChanged event:

```
Dim MyCust As MyCustomers.Customer
MyCust = MyCusts.Item(lstCustomers.SelectedItem)

lblCustomerID.Text = MyCust.CustomerID
txtCustomerName.Text = MyCust.Name
txtAddress.Text = MyCust.Address

MyCust = Nothing
```

You should be able to understand this beast: we're just declaring a MyCust placeholder, ready to hold a Customer object. Then, we use the SelectedItem value of the list box (the CustomerID key, remember) to retrieve a reference to the relevant Customer object from the Customers object. After that, we simply put data from our Customer object into our controls. Finally, we set our Customer object to nothing, telling VB we've finished working with it.

And, if you understand that, you should have no problem with our "Save Customer Object" button. It's exactly the same, only the other way around. Uhm, so not exactly the same, really. Let's go.

11. Add the following code to respond to the click event of btnSave:

```
Dim MyCust As MyCustomers.Customer
MyCust = MyCusts.Item(lstCustomers.SelectedItem)

MyCust.Name = txtCustomerName.Text
MyCust.Address = txtAddress.Text

MyCust = Nothing
```

Here, we're just obtaining a reference to our original Customer object, then editing its details. Make sense? Do you understand the meaning of the word *reference* here?

Let's test our application so far.

12. Press F5 and test your application. (See Figure 2-4.)

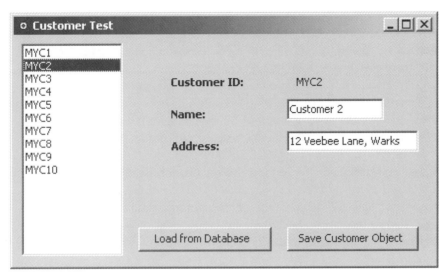

Figure 2-4. Our final application in action

What happens when you click on your "Load from Database" button? And what if you edit the information in our controls, click on the "Save Customer Object" button, move off this customer, and then back onto it? Are your changes stored?

Supercool! Now, can you imagine if you could actually build a *real-world* application using code as simple as this here?

Time to pause for thought. Please, step into my office.

Time for a Chat

Well done on coming all this way. Things are looking really good, but it's time for us to sit down and review what we've actually done so far.

Today, we've created our own class library project, holding two separate classes. We have the Customer class, which just stores individual customer details, plus the Customers class, which essentially manages an internal collection of Customer objects.

We also compiled this class library into a completely independent DLL file, which can be referenced from any external project using the Add Reference dialog box.

In the sample Windows application we designed, we learned how to create individual Customer objects and add them to our Customers collection. We also learned how to retrieve and edit individual Customer objects too.

Now, let's pause for thought and contemplate on a few little pointers that may have escaped your attention among the flurry of code.

First off, our classes are currently simple data holders. They're just a method of storing organized data in memory, but just imagine if we added a couple of extra functions here.

What if we implemented a LoadDB method in our Customers class? With just a little data access code, we could soon add all our existing customers to the collection. And, then, as a user of your object, you'd be able to easily access any details about any customer within seconds in just a couple lines of code. How about if you added an UpdateDB method too?

And we've almost forgotten the Customer class. Imagine how that could be expanded!

So, the first point is that our classes may seem relatively simple right now. But, with just the slightest amount of extra code, you can give them a whole new dimension.

There's a second point here, too: as a user of the class, you'd find your code incredibly simple and quick to write. Who ever heard of just running an `.UpdateDB` method to perform such complex database work? What happened to all your spaghetti code? *That's* the power of objects.

Back in my early programming days, I pioneered something called NESIE, an intelligent application that handled the manufacturing plants of a rather large, rather unglamorous drainage company. Alas, during the official handover, the project was thrown to the sharks: our client suddenly decided that the user interface just wasn't simple enough and one big wizard was required instead.

In an application in which most of your code is stored behind the forms, this would've caused big problems. It would probably be quicker to rewrite the entire program, rather than attempt any dramatic user interface changes. But, with NESIE, we'd actually used objects, meaning we had to rewrite only a little, simple code, thus enabling us to concentrate on changing the actual presentation layer. Erm, while still claiming overtime for "complete reprogramming".

Oh, what a life.·

> **TOP TIP**   *You may have heard programmers talk about building three-tier or n-tier applications. They're simply referring to splitting your application into multiple layers. In such situations, you'd typically have a presentation layer (your Windows or Web application), a business logic layer (your objects), and a data access layer (your database and possibly another set of interfacing objects). Such a way of working is strongly associated with object-oriented programming and is particularly useful when programming in teams or for the enterprise. For more information, look up "distributed applications, overview" in the Help index.*

My next point is that you don't actually have to create your classes like we've done here.

In the real world, many applications use collections in the manner we've demonstrated today. These types of relationships are all over the place. In fact, many have an even richer hierarchy, created in exactly the same way. For example, your Customer object might also include an Orders collection of Order objects.

However, this is still pretty complex. You don't *have* to have relationships between classes like this.

Our CDog class from last week is an ideal example of this. It doesn't rely on anything else. It stands alone. Another example: you might create a class to store all your useful file-editing functions or perhaps a Logon class to validate the user. In early 2001, I created a successful commercial product called WebZinc, which consisted of four *completely independent* Internet manipulation classes.

So, in brief, you don't need to interconnect your classes to use objects, although it's a very common way of dealing with "relational" data.

Just one more little note before I die of old age: remember that our class library actually compiles into a *separate* DLL. This is ready to be consumed by any .NET-supporting language, which means that you can use your functionality from an ASP.NET Web page, a VB .NET Windows application, or a C# class library.

And no one can see your original code either, meaning you could even take that DLL file and sell it on for hard cash. I did with WebZinc—and it's made my company more dough than a hyperactive baker.

Next, we're going to talk about distributing your DLL. But, before we do, think about how you can adopt the customer classes we created today to suit your own situation. And, if you have time . . .

- Currently, our customer browser doesn't allow you to remove an entry. How could you add that? And what about updating the list box?

- Also, you'll note that the user can't currently add a customer. How could you implement that feature yourself?

- Try adding two items with the same key to your Customers object. What happens? How can you fix that? Error-handling code?

- Would an Exists method, returning a True or False depending on whether a specified key is in our collection, be useful? If so, how could you add that? One clue: if an item doesn't exist in our collection, what is returned `Is Nothing`. Try it out.

- It may take you an extra hour, but why not try building your own SQL Server database, with a Customers table? Then, implement your own LoadDB and UpdateDB methods in your Customers class. You'll see the real power of objects start to unveil.

Distributing Your DLL

So, you've spent an absolute age creating that new class library. In your case, it's up to the usual spectacular standard. In my case, it's up to the usual spectacular substandard.

But, after you've compiled and have that oh-so-precious DLL in your digital hands, what's to do next? Well, you have a few separate options.

If you wish to distribute your actual DLL on its own, you can either simply copy it direct over to another machine, or create a setup project in just the same way as we did back in Chapter 1.5 of Tutorial 1, "Beginning VB .NET".

What if you've used your DLL in a project, such as our customer browser? It's simple. When the application using your DLL is compiled, a copy of it will be automatically placed inside its Bin folder.

So long as you keep this file alongside your compiled application, you'll have no problems. For regular Windows applications, this means keeping your DLL with your EXE file. For Web applications, this means ensuring that your DLL is kept in the Bin folder, next to your compiled Web application DLL.

Alternatively, you can create a setup project for your application just as we did back in the first tutorial. The dependency on your DLL will be automatically detected and included in your setup.

Of course, if you simply use classes directly in your project, then you just compile your application as usual. But then you don't get all those reuse benefits.

Well, that's enough for this section. Linguists tell us there are 35,000 useless words in the English language—and I'm rapidly running out. Quickly, therefore, let's look at our FAQs, then discuss where you can take your knowledge from here.

FAQ

Still scratching your head when it comes to objects? Got a couple of questions you'd like answered? Let's review our *long* list of frequently asked questions and see if we can soothe those puzzlers.

I want to add a "status flag" to my Order class that the Orders class in the same project can see, but nobody else. Is that possible?

So far, we've discussed using only the Public and Private keywords to declare something, but there's also another amazing useful prefix: Friend.

Adding "Friend" to the beginning of anything—from a variable to a function—will ensure that it's visible only to other classes in your project and not to the outside world. It's great for features like flags or initializing values in fellow DLL objects that you would rather hide from the DLL end user. Sounds like just your cup of tea.

Can I expose functionality from my modules through class libraries?

Absolutely! In older versions of Visual Basic, this was an absolute impossibility. However, with VB .NET, simply add a module to your class library, ensuring that you declare it as Public. After that, just insert your public methods and functions. You'll be able to access each of these from outside your class library without instantiating a new object.

For example, if you had the following inside a class library:

```
Public Module MyModule

    Public Function GetDate() As Date
        Return Now
    End Function

End Module
```

You could call it in an application that referenced your class library, as so:

```
Dim MyDate As Date
MyDate = MyClassLibrary.MyModule.GetDate
```

I'm using enumerations in my classes. However, how can I ensure that the programmer using my class actually selects one of my enumeration options, rather than specifying something else?

Behind the scenes, enumerations use integers to save the stored value. This, however, means that your object user can set a property that uses an enumeration to any integer—and get away with it, even though that integer might not be referring to an enumerated option at all.

However, there is a way to check. Here, our sample code uses the Enum class to verify whether the enumerated argument contains a valid CarTypes option, via the IsDefined function. If it doesn't, an error is thrown back to the code:

```
Public Enum CarTypes
    BrandNew = 1
    SecondHand = 2
    DodgyBanger = 3
End Enum

Public Sub SetCarType(ByVal NewCarType As CarTypes)
    If Not [Enum].IsDefined(GetType(CarTypes), NewCarType) Then
        Throw New ArgumentOutOfRangeException()
    End If
End Sub
```

I know I can create and use objects pretty much anywhere—in forms and modules, say. But where can I use the WithEvents keyword?

The WithEvents keyword gives you the opportunity to respond to events raised by an object. If you've used older versions of Visual Basic, you may be accustomed to only using the keyword behind forms or classes, but, with VB .NET, you can use it almost anywhere, including behind simple modules.

I've created my own subroutine that needs to run when the same event occurs in any of about five objects. Instead of using the code editor to add code behind each individual event, is there a way to get VB .NET to run my one routine to handle them all?

You're right: there is a simple way to tell VB .NET to run your routine whenever a particular event fires in any of your objects. You simply use the Handles keyword, appending each object event to the end of your subroutine.

So long as your method or function has the same "signature" (that is, arguments and types) as the event, VB .NET will run your code when it fires. Here's a chunk of example code:

```
Public Sub StoreWeatherChange(ByVal UpdateText As String) _
    Handles State1.WeatherChange, State2.WeatherChange

    MessageBox.Show("An official change has been logged: " & _
        vbNewLine & UpdateText)

End Sub
```

I have a bunch of methods in my object that write reports out to certain log files. For example, the SaveLogonInfo will automatically write out data to the USER_LOGON_DATA.TXT file. However, sometimes I want the user to be able to change this, but, if I add it as a parameter, my programmers will have to enter this name each time in code and may get it wrong. Is there any way to have an optional parameter, but with a default value?

Long question, short answer: *yes.* Just use the Optional keyword and provide a default, like this:

```
Public Sub RunProcess( _
    Optional ByVal FileName As String = "USER_LOGON_DATA.TXT")
    ' code goes here
End Sub
```

Here, if you don't provide a value for the FileName parameter, USER_LOGON_DATA.TXT is automatically used. Note that, if you have multiple parameters, you'll need to keep all your optional ones to the end.

My object holds an expensive database connection open and I'd like to close it in the Finalize method. My problem is that garbage collection may take a few minutes before it steps in and runs Finalize. What can I do?

This is a common scenario and is easily sorted with the addition of another method, typically called Dispose.

Take your case. You have all your clear-up code in the Finalize method. Now create a Dispose method that calls that Finalize method and tells garbage collection not to run the Finalize method when the object is released from memory (because we've just done so). Confused? Here's all that explained in code:

```
Implements System.IDisposable

Public Sub Dispose() Implements System.IDisposable.Dispose
    ' Call Finalize method
    Finalize()
    ' Don't run that Finalize method again
    ' when object is eventually released
    GC.SuppressFinalize(Me)
End Sub

Protected Overrides Sub Finalize()
    ' Any DB clear-up code goes here
    MyBase.Finalize()
End Sub
```

Here, we have a Finalize method that could potentially contain our clear-up code. We also have a Dispose method, which calls Finalize, then tells the Garbage Collection class to suppress the finalization (in other words, not to bother running the Finalize method when this object (Me) is eventually released from memory).

And, if the user of your class ever forgets to call Dispose, at least the connection will be closed when garbage collection finally does kick in.

It's worth noting that here we're using the line `Implements System.IDisposable`. This basically forces us to add a Dispose method, to implement the interface of `System.IDisposable`. This is a technique called *polymorphism*, the ability to have defined methods that multiple objects implement. It's like a technical way of telling the .NET Framework that our class adheres to the Dispose standard. You don't have to use it, but you're mega-cool if you do.

Oooh, polymorphism. That reminds me, a friend was telling me how all OOP languages have to abide by four key rules. Polymorphism was one of them. What are these rules?

Many moons ago, some wizzy scientist type dreamt up the four key concepts that every object-oriented programming language must adhere too. These are polymorphism, encapsulation, abstraction, and inheritance.

Polymorphism is the ability to write code that can operate on objects from more than one class, such as a Print method on Invoice and Quotation objects. Next we have encapsulation, the ability to create an "interface" completely independent of the code behind it. There's abstraction too, the ability to take a concept and create an abstract of it within our code. (A Customer object, for example, is an abstraction of a real-world customer.) But these have all existed in Visual Basic since version 4, and inheritance is the real newbie here. Inheritance is the ability to "inherit" functionality from other base classes.

Still, this is all boring theory, and, if you want more information, look up "object-oriented programming, basic concepts" in the Help index.

I know it's possible to raise events in your objects, passing back parameters. However, I hear that your user can also change those arguments in code and your object will automatically receive the new values. Is this possible? How do you do it?

Absolutely—with the use of *ByRef*.

When passing data around in VB .NET, you have two ways of doing so. The first is ByVal, *by value*, which basically just passes around the data itself. This is the default. The second method is ByRef, *by reference*, which passes a reference back to the original variable or object.

Although ByVal is great for most of our work, ByRef does have its uses. Consider an event such as:

```
Public Event OnAdd(ByVal ID As String, ByRef Cancel As Boolean)
```

This event is raised just before each record is added to the database. Here, we're passing an ID number by value and a Cancel Boolean by reference. Now, in our code, if we tried to change ID, it wouldn't affect our actual object in the slightest. However, because Cancel has been passed ByRef, if we tried to change its value, it would also affect the original variable in our object.

So, here's how we might change the value of Cancel in code:

```
Public Sub MyObject_OnAdd(ByVal ID As String, ByRef Cancel As Boolean) _
    Handles MyObject.OnAdd

    If ID = "KM4097" Then
        Cancel = True
    End If

End Sub
```

And we could then read the updated value in our class code, after raising our event, like this:

```
Dim blnCancel As Boolean   ' False, by default
RaiseEvent OnAdd("KM4097", blnCancel)

If blnCancel = True Then
    ' don't add record
End If
```

Understand? Have another read through and it should all make sense. Sorted!

Can I expose my .NET components to the world of COM?

You certainly can, by creating a COM Callable Wrapper (CCW). You can learn how to do this by checking out "Exposing .NET to the COM World" in Chapter 8.3, "Advanced Tips and Techniques".

What's the difference between a class library and a component? It all seems very different from the days of VB6.

A class library is simply a bunch of classes, functionality typically compiled into a single DLL assembly. A component, on the other hand, is basically a class with *standards*.

The .NET Framework likes to have things working a standard way. It likes having New constructors, for example—and preferably a Finalize method. If it can rely on these features being available, it can call them at just the right time.

To ensure that its components implement all the desired features, the .NET Framework includes a `System.ComponentModel.Component` class that all "components" should inherit from, as so:

```
Inherits System.ComponentModel.Component
```

This simply ensures that you stick to the standards and marks you out as a good programmer. You can automatically add these standards to your class, by selecting Project ➤ Add Component from the menu.

So, a class library is a collection of classes, and a component is a class that adheres to .NET Framework standards.

I've heard a lot about the GAC. What is it?

GAC stands for the *global assembly cache*. In the olden days of COM, your DLL was typically registered once and available to the whole machine. With .NET, your DLL is partnered by default with just one application, thus ensuring that you don't receive conflicts or experience other sticky problems. This is known as *side-by-side execution*.

However, you can still register your DLL in something called the *global assembly cache*, should you want to. This makes your DLL available to multiple programs on a computer, while still combating a number of the old DLL problems (such as compatibility and security).

For more information on registering your DLL in the GAC, look up "global assembly cache" in the Help index.

WHERE TO GO FROM HERE

A policeman out on his nightly patrol leaves his beat, running back to his home. He throws a pebble up at the bedroom window. His wife opens the window and asks the problem.

"It's freezing out here, love!" he shivers. "Pass me my thick overcoat on the bedside chair!"

She grabs the overcoat and throws it down onto the lawn. The policeman puts it on and feels much warmer. The next morning, he returns to the station and walks to the tea room.

"Blimey, George," cries a colleague. "How long have you been a sergeant?"

In my own twisted way, I'm trying to tell you that there's always something new to discover. And objects are no exception.

We've covered all the basics, but there are plenty of frills still left to discover, such as inheritance, the ability to automatically "inherit" the functionality of another class (for example), or overloading, a technique that allows you to have multiple methods of the same name that accept different arguments.

Oh yes, there's always more to learn. And here to help out is my quick and handy rundown of the top object resources:

- *Visual Basic .NET and the .NET Platform* (Apress, ISBN 1-893115-26-7): In this advanced programming guide, Andrew Troelsen looks at generating almost every possible kind of .NET application, including numerous object-based projects.

- Other books: *Teach Yourself Object-Oriented Programming with VB.NET in 21 Days* (Sams, ISBN 0-672321-49-1); *VB.NET Object and Component Handbook* (Prentice Hall, ISBN 0-130651-90-7).

- `www.fawcette.com/vsm/`: The Fawcette group produces the popular monthly magazine, *Visual Studio*, which regularly covers advanced object-centric topics. There's also a mass of free content online.

- `www.vbforums.com`: This helpful community site provides answers to Visual Basic questions from all. Includes its own OOP and .NET forums.

- `www.developersdex.com`: This is a very useful programming portal, with object-related articles, the latest Knowledge Base additions, plus news-group listings.

- `www.dotnetextreme.com`: This great site packs a bundle of small how-to guides. Includes OOP features.

- `www.nakedvariables.com`: Whether you're wanting the latest in hardcore multitier ADO.NET data access techniques or the underground scoop on how to create top-notch objects in .NET, this handy link station brings you the best of the rest, all on one page.

- `www.apress.com`: No, I'm not biased. Rather, Apress publishes the popular *About VS .NET* fortnightly newsletter, which often contains news, updates, and book releases of interest to object programmers (especially over the coming months).

- `news.devx.com`: Showcasing a bundle of active discussion groups, this site has one dedicated to object-oriented programming in Visual Basic. Worth a visit.

Don't forget that Web sites and books all have an expiration date. For all the very latest in .NET, head down to `www.apress.com`.

CONCLUSION

Well done on completing the "Using Objects" tutorial!

It's been an upward struggle, but we've finally made it, and your code, career, and bank balance will undoubtedly improve as a result.

What have we covered today? We started by looking at how we can create our own class library, compiling our code down into a separate DLL and consuming that functionality from another application.

We moved on to explore collection classes, understanding how this common way of creating relationships between classes can really help your code. After that, we talked about distributing our compiled classes, reviewed a big bundle of frequently asked questions, plus figured out where you can take your knowledge from here.

So, as we conclude this tutorial, let's ask . . . what have we learned?

We've found out that objects allow you to *simplify*; they allow for *reuse*; and they allow for *maintainability*. They make your life a little harder, before making it one hell of a lot easier.

Oh, and they ensure both a hefty salary and respected industry kudos.

But make sure that you keep playing. In this area especially, there's much more to learn, and you'll gain a real understanding only if you actually *use* the technology. And take this rule of thumb with you today: if your next application takes longer than an hour to write, you should be using objects. Good luck!

Well, that's all from me. Until the next time, this is your host, Karl Moore, signing off for tonight. Cheerio!

- A class library is a project designed to primarily hold classes. This project type compiles into a DLL, which can be referenced and used by any .NET-supporting language.

- When dealing with data-holding classes, it's common practice to split the process into two separate classes for simplicity: one class to hold actual items of data and the other to manage a collection of those data classes. For example, you may have a Cars collection class that manages individual Car data objects.

- The Collection class allows you to store multiple objects alongside a related key and is commonly used to implement collection classes. Here is an example of its use:

```
Dim MyCollection As New Collection()
Dim MySampleClass As SampleClass

' Create and add new
MySampleClass = New SampleClass()
MySampleClass.MySampleProperty = "Sample Value"
MyCollection.Add(MySampleClass, "MyKey")

' Get reference and edit
MySampleClass = MyCollection.Item("MyKey")
MySampleClass.MySampleProperty = "New Sample Value"

' Remove from collection
MyCollection.Remove("MyKey")
```

- To compile your class library DLL, select Build ➤ Build <ProjectName> from the menu.

- To add a reference to your DLL in a Visual Studio .NET project, from the menu select Project ➤ Add Reference. Under the .NET tab, click on Browse and select your DLL.

- Any projects that reference your DLL will automatically store a copy of the DLL in its Bin folder after compilation. Any derived setup projects will also include a copy of the DLL by default.

Services Rendered

Introducing the World of Web Services

"Programming today is a race between software engineers striving to build bigger and better idiot-proof programs, and the Universe trying to produce bigger and better idiots. So far, the Universe is winning."—Richard Cook

TRUTH BE KNOWN, COMPUTERS ARE highly unsociable creatures.

I mean, they won't even talk to each other unless you string a mass of cable between them. And, if you're actually looking to get them engaged in any sort of productive conversation, you'll need to tweak network settings, twist hub knobs, pray nightly to the almighty power of Bill Gates, *and* cross your fingers.

Thankfully, however, there's a cure for such typically timid devices. It's the .NET Framework, and it works like alcohol for computer chips. Install this baby and suddenly your quiet chunk of silicon seems better at schmoozing than Dale Carnegie.

Why? Because that .NET Framework includes ASP.NET. And ASP.NET includes Web services. And Web services give you the ability to write programs on different machines that can talk to each other, easily.

Your client program might ask your main computer for information about a customer, for example. Or query the government for its latest tax rates, say. Or nab late-breaking headlines straight from CNN. Or *whatever*.

It's all possible, when you get talking—via Web services.

Could be useful? Fancy learning more? Then sign up and step this way . . .

How It All Works

Sometimes you simply can't do everything on one computer. It's often best to separate the functionality, using programs that talk to and help applications on different computers. Enter stage left: *Web services*.

Now, imagine you work for Deals on Wheels, the most popular car dealership this side of the Mississippi. The whole group runs on your applications, and, with five popular sites, you're exceptionally pleased.

The problem is your users aren't. And, in stereotypical user fashion, they do nothing but moan and request new features. (Difficult to imagine, I know.) Anyway, first on their list of improvements is an automatic credit check performed on each client as soon as their details are entered into your system.

Oh, great. I mean, how on Earth can you implement something like that? Hmm, I guess you could just write the credit-checking code yourself, then update all the users with a new version of your customer database program. But surely that wouldn't be quite so comprehensive as a third-party check, and what about that "credit check free" day they were talking about? Yuck. What an administrative nightmare.

Actually, maybe it's just easier to tell the users that they should physically call your checking agency. After all, *they've* got the information, and *your* computers can't talk to *theirs*, can they?

What's that? Oh, your boss Dodgy Del has his own personal request, too? When a customer steps through his doors to trade in a rusty old motor, Sam the Salesman instantly heads to his desk and checks out the trade-in value in his pricing guide. Problem is, this is often the *1986* pricing guide—and Del guesses he's losing thousands of dollars a month due to out-of-date information.

He suggests a centralized database containing all the latest prices—and you shiver, thinking of all the different applications you'll need to update for this. Reams of data access code in three different languages flash before your eyes. But, after all, there's no easier way, is there?

Hmm, I could just say "no" to both of these questions, but then that'd make for a real short chapter. Instead, I'm going to answer "yes," and welcome you to the world of Web services, part of ASP.NET. Erm, so just what are Web services?

Web services are a way of creating programs that talk to and help applications on different computers. You have a server machine that "exposes" the service and clients that "discover" and "consume" that service.

So, your credit-checking agency may make a service available over the Internet that allows you to pass details of your customer to it in code, and the service will return the credit rating. Or you might create your own service on the main company server that looks up car prices in a database, and then simply call this one service from each of your applications. That's what Web services allow you to do: get programs on different computers talking together. They allow you to *distribute* the functionality of your application. How could something like this help you, right now?

Hmm, you still look a little suspicious. I'm guessing you think I've slipped off into my own little fantasy world once again and that this sounds all too good to be true. Well, I've had my cold shower, and can inform you that it *is* possible, right now, today, with Web services.

How? Well, you (or perhaps that credit-checking agency) start by creating a Web service project in Visual Studio .NET. This is basically just a project containing code, a little like the class library we worked with in Tutorial 5, "Using Objects". Then the development begins, and our friendly coder tells VB .NET to show certain bits of his code to the world.

So, maybe he'll tell it to expose that DoCreditCheck method or perhaps that GetCarPrice function.

When finished, the code is compiled, and that "Web service" is made available on a master computer somewhere—our network, the Internet, or wherever. And that's it for your Web service: it's up, running, and waiting to serve.

Next, it's time to develop your client, the program that will use the Web service. You start by "discovering" the Web service and its features, then use all those exposed functions exactly as you would a local piece of code, and they run, all the way over on the other machine. It all just works: you do nothing special.

The Geeky Bit

That's right: *you* do nothing special. However, our lovely .NET Framework is being smarter than da Vinci in Gucci. When you run the functions belonging to that Web service, it calls the remote machine passing any parameters, runs the Web service code, and returns any data back to your client program *automatically*. Complete doddle.

And all of this works via something called SOAP. Shower jokes aside, *SOAP* stands for the *Simple Object Access Protocol* and refers to how Web services talk. And how do they talk? Behind the scenes, everything is converted and passed about as XML, which is just plain, structured text. And this XML is transferred over HTTP, which is typically used for viewing Web pages. (See Figure 1-1.)

Why is this clever? Two reasons. First off, XML is pure text, and pure text is *speedy* and *understood by all platforms*. And, because it works via HTTP, it also bypasses any annoying firewalls that may attempt to thwart your development efforts. But, again, this is all handled automatically for you, so there's no need for concern. Again, it's just a complete doddle.

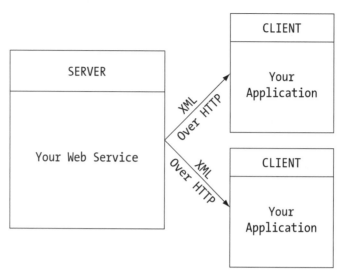

Figure 1-1. A Web service in action

And if you're coming from the old school of DCOM and all that jazz, you're in for a particularly pleasant surprise: with Web services there's no registering, no settings to fine-tune, no annoying tight-coupling. Basically, it's a complete doddle. Did I mention that?

So, Web services allow you to get computers talking. You expose certain functionality through a service, and your clients "discover" and "consume" that service, live via XML over HTTP.

Ready to start exploring Web services in real life? Let's dive into meat space and put all this fantasy into practice. Oooh, matron!

Creating a Web Service

George Bush (Sr.) once said, "I pushed the button down here and one up here with the green thing on it. And out came a command to somebody that I had written."

Uh-huh. Well, perhaps creating Web services wasn't for him. But, for us, it's time to put all this theory into action, getting our palms dirty with a little hands-on.

1. Launch Visual Studio .NET and create a new ASP.NET Web service, changing its location to `http://localhost/MyHelper`.

After a little whizzing and whirring, you should be presented with a pretty dull-looking screen. This is Service1.asmx.vb, the code file behind your actual service. However, I don't see any code right now, presumably because we're in design mode. Let's change that.

2. On the menu, select View ➢ Code to open the code window.

> **TOP TIP** *Instead of constantly using the menu to open the code window, just press F7. It'll take you straight to the code behind the object you're working with.*

You should see a small mound of code in front of you, although nothing shockingly horrid. We have a line that imports the Web service namespace, making its functionality available to use. Aside from that, it just looks like a regular class that inherits from the WebService class. It also includes a bundle of comments, currently wearing a very chic shade of green.

Now, let's add a function to this class—just a bog-standard, run-of-the-mill function.

3. Add the following function to your class:

```
Public Function Reverse(ByVal Text As String) As String
    Return StrReverse(Text)
End Function
```

Well, it beats a simple Hello World sample, but only *just*. Yes, it's a chunk of code that takes a string and reverses it, but, unless you're about as bright as a blown bulb, I guess you already figured that out.

Anyway, now it's time to reveal the real secret of Web services. It's the key to instantly exposing your data to the world, it's the backbone to the entire .NET concept, it's . . . <WebMethod()>.

Yes, I know. Profound. But just by adding this simple "attribute," we're telling VB .NET that this is a "WebMethod," a method or function that should be made available via your network, the Internet, or wherever.

4. Add the <WebMethod()> attribute to the beginning of your function, so it reads:

```
<WebMethod()> Public Function Reverse(ByVal Text As String) As String
    Return StrReverse(Text)
End Function
```

And surprise, surprise—that's our Web service finished! Let's build our solution, then see what this simple <WebMethod()> attribute has done for us.

5. From the menu, select Build ➢ Build Solution (or press `Ctrl+Shift+B`).

Accessing the Web Service from a Browser

There are two key ways to access your Web service. The first is from a Web browser. That's our cue.

1. In your application, press F5 to start your Web service.

Your default browser should fire up, directing itself to somewhere like `http://localhost/MyHelper/Service1.asmx`.

What you're looking at in Figure 1-2 is an automatically generated interface to your HTTP Web service.

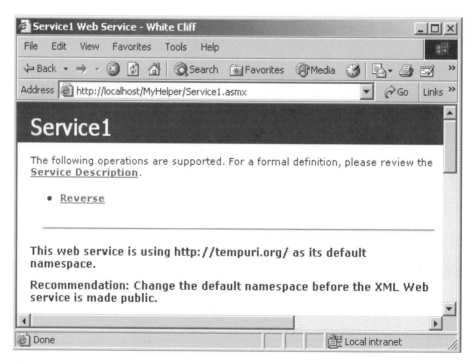

Figure 1-2. Accessing our Service from a browser

Here, we can see our Web service is very originally entitled "Service1" and that it exposes one operation called "Reverse".

2. Click on the Reverse link.

You'll be taken to a page that describes our Reverse operation. From here, you can either test it directly or check out some simply *thrilling* sample SOAP code. Think I'll just test it.

3.   Enter a value for the Text parameter, such as your name.

4.   Click on the Invoke button to run your function.

A separate window should pop open and display something like:

```
<?xml version="1.0" encoding="utf-8" ?>
<string xmlns="http://tempuri.org/">erooM lraK</string>
```

Huh? Well, this is XML, that "eXtensible Markup Language" we talked about earlier and stumbled across back in Tutorial 2, "Doing Databases". Here, this chunk of XML is telling us that our Reverse operation has returned a string saying "erooM lraK". Think I'll just stick to *Karl*.

> **TOP TIP**   *XML is the glue that holds a lot of .NET together. It's essentially a self-describing structure that can hold hierarchical data. Or at least that's the official lowdown. Personally, I just think, "Hmm, looks a bit like HTML." Simple minded, you see.*

5.   Close your browser windows and click on the Stop button in VB .NET.

So, that's a Web service. Okay, admit it: it looks about as useful as an ice machine at the North Pole. But this is only the raw Web interface. There's another, much more powerful way of accessing them, a way that completely hides all the XML from us and makes development easy.

I'm talking about using Web services . . . in your applications.

Accessing the Web Service from an Application

Next, let's throw together an application that actually "consumes" this Web service. You can create this on the same machine as your Web service if you like, or on another computer in your network. It really doesn't matter; as long as your browser can access the Web service, your program will be able to also.

1.   Create a new Windows application using Visual Studio .NET.

2.   From the menu, select Project ➢ Add Web Reference.

You should be looking at the Add Web Reference screen. If not, either your machine has contracted the Squiggle virus, or you've accidentally unplugged your monitor. Next, you need to tell VS .NET where your Web service is located.

3.   Type in your Web service ASMX address, which will be something like `http://localhost/MyHelper/Service1.asmx`, and press the Enter key.

> **TOP TIP**   *If your Web service is on the local machine, you can try clicking on the "Web References on Local Web Server" link to locate your service. If your service is on another machine in the network, replace the "localhost" portion of the sample address with the actual machine name, IP address, or Web address—basically, whatever you'd type into a Web browser to access your Web service.*

4.   When your Web service appears, click the Add Reference button. (See Figure 1-3.)

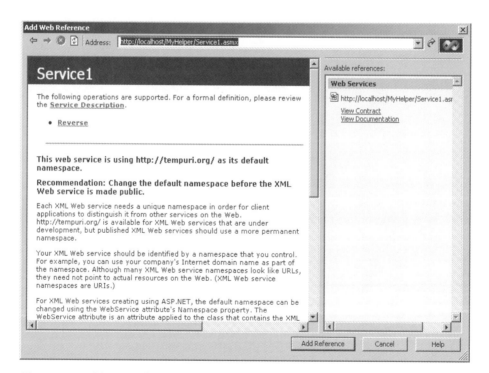

Figure 1-3. Adding a reference to our Web service

Take a glance at the Solution Explorer. You'll notice a new Web References entry there, with "localhost" or your machine name just underneath. Try expanding this node, browsing all the files underneath it. These have all been automatically generated and exist to tell VB .NET how to talk to the service on that machine.

5.   Draw a button out onto the Form designer.

6.   Behind the click event of the button, add the following code:

```
Dim objHelper As New localhost.Helper()
```

Here, we're treating our Web service just like any regular object we've seen so far in this book. Once again, you may need to change "localhost" to your machine name, as listed in the Solution Explorer.

> **TOP TIP**   *Our code here is actually working with a "helper" class that Visual Studio .NET automatically creates for you. When you use its properties and such, this "wrapper" class makes the Web service call, processes the results, and passes them back to your code. If you want to look at the Helper class code, click on "Show All Files" in the Solution Explorer, then expand the Web References folder, then localhost. For each Web reference here, you'll see two XML-based files: a DISCO file that provides details on discovering the service, and a WSDL (Web Service Discovery Language) file that provides details on the capabilities of the service. Expand that ServiceName.WSDL file and look at the ServiceName.VB file underneath it. This is the Helper class code. You can even edit it, if you're feeling particularly randy.*

That's our new objHelper object instantiated. Now we're ready to use it. Try typing objHelper and pressing the period key immediately after. What happens? (See Figure 1-4.)

Figure 1-4. Our Web service in the code window

What's that? You don't remember coding all those features? Well, you're either a Steve Jobs reincarnate who can program subconsciously (and at rather an impressive pace), or these are simply standard extras above and beyond your own simple function, extra widgets automatically added to help you use the Web service. I might be wrong, but I'd go for option two.

Let's use our Reverse function in code now. Here, we're simply going to display a message box, telling VB to display the result of Reverse on "Karl Moore". (That's me, by the way.)

7. Underneath your existing button click code, add the following code:

```
MessageBox.Show(objHelper.ReverseString("Karl Moore"))
objHelper = Nothing
```

Understand? We're just telling it to run our function with this particular string and to display the results in a message box. Finally, we just set our objHelper variable to nothing, telling it that we're no longer using it: we're just being tidy, as learned how back in Tutorial 5, "Using Objects".

8. Press F5 to test your program.

9. Click on your button.

What happens? After a short delay, you should get back "erooM lraK".

Now try clicking on the button a second time. See what happens? First time round it was about as slow as a slug. To be specific, a dead slug. Now it zaps away at the speed of light, having already made that initial connection. Just a consideration.

> **TOP TIP**   *Wondering how to discover and consume a Web service in something other than a Windows application? Perhaps you want to use the functionality from an ASP.NET Web application or maybe even another Web service? No worries: it all works in exactly the same way. Just "Add Web Reference" and start coding. There's no difference.*

If you've got a few minutes before moving on, try creating a function that returns an integer as opposed to a string. How does the XML differ? Also, can you use multiple parameters just as you can with a regular function? One more test: try adding a method or function that doesn't include that WebMethod attribute. What happens? Can you see it via your browser?

Getting bored yet? No? Oh, well, let me tell you about my Victorian stamp collection. Oh, you *are* getting bored? Right then, let's move on and imagine some of the possibilities here.

Imagining the Possibilities

What's that? The complexity of your organization slightly surpasses our Reverse sample? Oh, darn. Sorry about that. Maybe I can offer you a coupon against my next book or something.

But, you see, although we've covered only the core essentials here—and pretty quickly, too—it's still more than enough for you to get your own Web services into production. It's all about `<WebMethod()>`.

Just imagine the possibilities open to you, right now. Imagine looking up car trade-in prices from any of your applications, simply by using your one centralized function. Imagine adding new customers just by calling an Add method on your Customer Web service. Imagine being able to change any part of your application code just by editing one project on your server.

<takes deep breath>

Imagine consuming a third-party, Internet-based Web service to authorize a MasterCard transaction or to check a customer's credit. Imagine exposing your own product stock information over the Web, or making data such as weather reports and sports scores available to your service subscribers.

> **TOP TIP** *The UDDI Directory from Microsoft attempts to list many of the third-party Web services available for you to consume. You can view the directory by visiting* http://uddi.microsoft.com/visualstudio *in the Add Web Reference dialog box. Alternatively, search it by clicking the XML Web services link on the Visual Studio .NET start page. Another useful directory can be found at* http://www.xmethods.com.

At the time of going to press, among the public Web services in action were a live dictionary and thesaurus, a horoscope generator, an SMS service, an NFC headlines application, and a music teacher search engine. Diverse? Oh yes. *Just imagine.*

And you think that's all? No, sir. You see, with all these possibilities, passing about plain data is often not enough. You need to crank up the volume, with *smart data*—and we'll see at how you can do that, next.

Passing Smart Data

The problem with using Web services as we've shown here is that they're a little limiting. I mean, let's say that you've created a groovy customer management Web service on your network. Perhaps it contains an Add method that accepts details of your customer and adds them to the database. No problem. But what about actually *retrieving* your customers?

Think about it. Functions can return only one item, such as a True or False, or perhaps a string. They can't, for example, return a list of customers and their orders . . . unless, of course, you pass around *smart data*.

I'm talking about relational, multitable DataSets. I'm talking about arrays. I'm talking about classes. I'm talking about structures. I'm talking about smart data, data containing multiple portions that can be passed back through a function—even in a Web service.

To demonstrate the concept, I'd like to create a Web service that opens a database of your choice, then passes all the required data from one particular table data back to your user as an easy-to-use, typed DataSet. Okay, let's get started.

1. Create a new ASP.NET Web service at http://localhost/MyDataService.

Now, we're going to start off by using the Server Explorer to connect to your database. I'm going to leave this bit up to you; you can connect to your company database, one of the sample Access or SQL Server databases we created back in Tutorial 2, "Doing Databases", or perhaps just infamous Northwind. Your call.

Personally, I'm going to connect into the Surgery.mdb sample we created back in Tutorial 2, "Doing Databases".

2.   From the menu, select View ➤ Server Explorer.

3.   If your database is not shown under Data Connections or as an SQL Server database under the Servers entry, click on the "Connect To Database" button and enter the details. (See Figure 1-5.)

Figure 1-5. Browsing a database via the Server Explorer

4.   Expand the Tables list under your database.

5.   Drag and drop the table you want to use in this example onto your Service1.asmx.vb page (currently in design mode).

You'll find OleDbConnection1 and OleDbDataAdapter1 added to your service—or perhaps SqlConnection1 and SqlDataAdapter1 if you're using SQL Server. As you may remember from Tutorial 2, "Doing Databases" (*please* say you've read it), the Connection object here actually "calls" your database, and the DataAdapter talks through that connection to get information out or to modify existing data.

6.   Rename your Connection object to "connMyDatabase".

7.   Rename your DataAdapter object to "daMyDataAdapter".

Next, let's sort out our DataSet. Eh? A *DataSet* is basically a widget that holds the data coming back from your database. Actually, we're going to create a *Typed DataSet*, which is just a regular DataSet that runs off a template telling it about the tables and fields it will hold, thereby making our later programming much easier.

8. Right-click on your DataAdapter object and select Generate DataSet.

9. Choose the New option and enter a name of "MyData".

10. Ensure your table is checked in the list of tables to add to this DataSet.

11. Check the "Add This DataSet To The Designer" box.

12. Click on OK.

Two things just happened here. First off, MyData.xsd has been added to your project; it lists the fields that your DataSet will hold. Secondly, MyData1 has been added to your Web service. This is your typed DataSet, based on that MyData.xsd "template." (See Figure 1-6.)

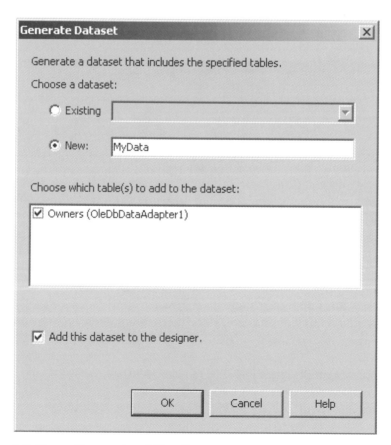

Figure 1-6. Generating our typed DataSet

13. Rename MyData1 to "dsMyDataSet".

Great! We've sorted the data access objects out. Next, we need to go add code to our Web service to retrieve information from this database and pass it back.

14. Press F7 to switch to the code mode for your Web service.

15. Add the following code to your Service1 class:

```
<WebMethod()> Public Function GetData() As MyData
    ' Passes populated Typed DataSet back to client
    daMyDataAdapter.Fill(dsMyDataSet)
    Return dsMyDataSet
End Function
```

Here we have a function called GetData that returns a DataSet of the MyData type, a DataSet that adheres to our MyData "template" class. The code simply fills our DataSet with information from our database table and returns it. Simple.

Oh, and of course we have that magical keyword `<WebMethod()>` there, too. Leave it out and this service can't strut its stuff.

However, most databases aren't read-only: you'll typically want to update them, too. Next, we're going to accept the entire DataSet back and update the backend database as required, However, in the real world, you might just want to accept individual Row objects and go from there.

16. Add the following code to your Service1 class:

```
<WebMethod()> Public Sub UpdateData(ByVal Data As MyData)
    ' Updates the backend database where needed
    daMyDataAdapter.Update(Data)
End Sub
```

Here, we're just accepting a MyData typed DataSet and using the DataAdapter object to update our backend database. No problem. Well, that's our whole Web service pretty much finished now and our cue to run a quick build.

17. Press Ctrl+Shift+B to build this solution.

Retrieving Smart Data

But what good is data without someone to use it? As Confucius once said, "It ain't." Which is why we're about to create a neat little Windows application to discover and consume the features of our new service.

1. Create a new Windows application.

2. From the menu, select Project ➢ Add Web Reference.

3. Type in your Web service address:
   `http://localhost/MyDataService/Service1.asmx`.

4. Click on "Add Reference" when the page has loaded.

Next, let's add code to test our Web service.

5. Add a button to Form1.

6. Behind the click event of your button, add the following code:

```
' Declare Service and DataSet 'template'
Dim MyWebService As New localhost.Service1()
Dim MyDataSet As localhost.MyData

' Grab data
MyDataSet = MyWebService.GetData

' Retrieve sample data -
' your fields may be different
Dim strText As String
strText = MyDataSet.Owners(0).Address
MessageBox.Show(strText)

' Update DataSet -
' again, your fields may be different
MyDataSet.Owners(0).Name = "Mr Bibbles"

' Send back to Web service
MyWebService.UpdateData(MyDataSet)
```

Okay, it might be a little more in-depth than our Reverse sample, but it's still pretty understandable. We're creating a new instance of our own local Service1 class, then using its functionality to work with our Web service—grabbing our data, displaying one particular field, changing a little data, then running an update. Top stuff.

The special thing to note here is that, when we compiled our Web service, it recognized we were exposing a typed DataSet and included details of our MyData schema alongside, allowing us to use its objects in code as we have done here. How very clever.

7. Press F5 and test your application.

Does it all work as expected? How could we improve the interface? Well done on completing this sample!

So, what have we created in under two dozen lines of code? On the server side: a Web service that exposes data direct from your database using a typed DataSet. On the client side: an application that can use all the power of your "disconnected" data in just a few lines of code—without having to worry about the data access code in the slightest.

This is smart data. It's a lot more than just a single True or False return value, and its simplicity can really help speed up your application development. And what do you know—it doesn't stop with DataSets. You can expose data-holding classes, structures, and arrays through your Web services, too. Just use them and let Visual Studio .NET do the rest.

Tsk, can you spell *clever chuff*?

The Top Five Distribution Tips

So, you've written the greatest Web service since SlicedBread.asmx, and now you want to roll it out to the world? Yes, you could just take what you've done so far and follow the deployment instructions in the next section, but five quick changes will give your service that professional touch, mini alterations that should precede the distribution of *any* Web service.

Get out that notebook. It's time to talk turkey.

1. Rename your class.

Nobody likes dealing with a Web service called Service1, so, before you redistribute, make sure that you rename your class from something like `Public Class Service1` to something like `Public Class Customer`. Or something. Ahem.

2. Christen your ASMX file.

You've renamed your Web service so it sounds all professional, but your clients are still accessing your Service via the `http://localhost/Customer/Service1.asmx` file. Eugh. To combat this, simple rename your ASMX file by right-clicking on it in the Solution Explorer and selecting Rename.

3. Add a service description.

What does your Web service do? Provide access to your customer database or allow you to send SMS messages? Well, you could just let your clients guess. However, a more user-friendly technique would be to add a description to the `<WebService()>` attribute. So, before distributing, change your class as follows:

```
<WebService(Description:="This is a class that does amazing things with data.")> _
 Public Class AmazingData
    ' ... etc ...
 End Class
```

This description is used in the automatically generated Web interface and is automatically absorbed by all clients using your service and utilized in the Visual Studio .NET programming environment.

4. Add method descriptions.

Just as your service can include a description, so can your individual methods and functions. Again, this is used by the Web interface and Visual Studio .NET. And, again, it's simple to implement: just add a description to each `<WebMethod()>` attribute, like so:

```
<WebMethod(Description:="Returns the current server date and time.")> _
 Public Function GetServerDate() As Date
     Return Now
 End Function
```

5. Change the namespace.

You've already seen the .NET Framework organizing functionality into "namespaces." They're just unique identifiers for a certain set of functionality. That's all a namespace is here, too: a unique string that identifies this Web service. By default, it's `http://www.tempuri.org/`, and you will need to change this to a unique value. The namespace you provide doesn't necessarily have to point to anything on the Web, but it's recommended that you at least own the domain you use (I mean, *purr-lease*). So, change the namespace to something unique before unveiling your service by altering the Namespace property of the `<WebService()>` attribute, as so:

```
<WebService(Description:="Yadda", _
Namespace:="http://www.amazingdata.com/query/")> _
 Public Class AmazingData
   ' ... etc ...
 End Class
```

Deploying Your Web Service

Once you've finished your Web service, you can stick it literally anywhere. And, resisting another crude Bill Gates prod, I'm talking about the Internet or your network.

How? Well, if you built your Web service on the server it will be running on, you don't actually need to do anything else. When you build your service in Visual Studio .NET, it's automatically deployed for you.

However, if you want to move it over to another machine, you'll need to use the Copy Project feature. Simply open your Web service in Visual Studio .NET and select Project ➤ Copy Project from the menu. Change the Project Destination folder to the new HTTP home of your service and ensure that the "Copy: Only files needed to run this application" option is selected. Then click on the OK button.

> **TOP TIP** *You've seen that Web services run over HTTP. In fact, they work in just the same way as regular ASP.NET Web applications, which means that you can administer them via the Internet Services Manager plug-in: to launch it, select Start ➤ Program Files ➤ Administrative Tools ➤ Internet Services Manager. Useful for deleting all those Hello World samples!*

Alternatively, if you're deploying via FTP to a .NET host, copy across your ASMX pages, Web.config and VSDISCO files. You'll also want to transfer your compiled DLL assembly from your local Bin subdirectory to a Bin subdirectory on the server. Basically, copy across anything that isn't a Visual Studio .NET project file, in the exact same way as you would with an ASP.NET Web application.

You can also upload direct to a supported .NET host by clicking the Web Hosting link on the Visual Studio .NET Start page.

And that's a rap, folks: your Web service is now exposed to the world. Let the consuming commence!

FAQ

Still got a couple of questions about Web services? Looking to learn from the mistakes of others? Let's review our list of frequently asked questions . . .

In your examples, you've worked on a Web service project with just one Service class. Can you have multiple Service classes in one Web service project?

Absolutely! Simply add another Web service to the project, by selecting Project ➢ Add Web Service from the menu. You can even add a Web service to a regular ASP.NET Web application in exactly the same way.

My code always seems to have something wrong with it. Is there any way to debug a Web service, just as you would a Web form or a regular Windows application?

Yes—literally *just* as you would a Web form or regular Windows application! Simply move to the line you wish to break on and press the F9 key to turn debugging on. Next, run your service live by pressing F5—then either run the application that uses this Web service or access its operations via the Web interface. When the line you highlighted is about to run, your code will break and you should be able to step through line by line using F8. Happy bug hunting!

What happened to all those ASP.NET objects, like Application and Session?

Well, because Web services are a part of ASP.NET, objects such as Application, Session, Server, User, and all their merry friends are still at your disposal (though admittedly not used here quite as often). Check out the Help index or Tutorial 3, "Working the Web" to find out more.

I've added a few new methods to my Web service. Have I now got to update all my clients?

Don't worry—as long as you haven't "broken" any of your existing methods, you won't have any problems. If, however, you want to use these new methods in your applications, open the client project and, using the Solution Explorer, right-click on the Web reference and select Update Web Reference. Your new methods will be discovered, and you'll be instantly able to use the new features in code.

I'm wanting to expose some pretty sensitive information via my Web service. Do these things do security?

You bet your bottom dollar, kiddo. You can either implement your own authentication by adding username and password arguments to your methods, or use one of the ASP.NET authentication options, presenting your credentials before you begin using the service. For more information, look up "Web services, security" in the Help index for the full lowdown.

I like to know my file extensions. What does ASMX stand for?

Despite many leading publications revealing that "it doesn't have any real meaning," I can tell you that *ASMX* stands for *active server methods*, with the *X* just referring to the next generation of development techniques (that is, old ASP pages are now ASPX pages).

Good news! My Wonderful Weather Web service has grown to great heights. Bad news! My code runs a powerful algorithm to correctly predict whether it rains or shines, and that takes time. Now that I'm getting requests every second or so, my servers are clogging up. What can I do?

It's a little-known fact, but you can actually "cache" what a Web service gives out and automatically serve up the same response next time. How? Simply by specifying a CacheDuration in the WebMethod attribute, like this:

```
<WebMethod(CacheDuration:=60)> _
Public Function GetWeather() As String
    ' . . . complicated code . . .
End Function
```

Here, the Web server will cache and serve up the same results for GetWeather sixty seconds after the last query. You can test this baby by returning the time. See what happens?

Our company has just created a whole bundle of Web services containing company-wide functionality. The project is proving exceptionally popular among the developer team—and, to cope with demand, we're going to have to transfer the service to more powerful servers. Won't this break the programs currently using our Web service?

If your existing clients are looking to access a Web service and it isn't there, yup, their applications will either raise an error or die a dramatic death. Either way, it ain't good.

However, it's relatively simple to change the server name of your Web service. In Visual Studio .NET, simply open your project and select your Web service under the Solution Explorer, Web References folder. You should notice a few items in the Properties window—including Web Reference URL. Change this property to point to your new Service, then recompile your application.

If your Web service often changes location, it might be worthwhile changing the URL Behavior property to Dynamic. If you're working on a Web application, this adds a line containing the URL to Web.config (or App.config for Windows applications).

If changes occur in the future, you'll no longer have to redistribute all your files again—just send out an updated .config file. Top stuff!

WHERE TO GO FROM HERE

Looking to learn more about Web services? You're not alone—and, thankfully, the world is starting to brim with resources for the new technology. Helping you wade through the rubble, here's my pick of the best:

- *Architecting Web Services* (Apress, ISBN 1-893115-58-5): If you're looking for a full-on book delivering nothing but Web service information, this is the title for you. A real work of art.

- Other books: *Professional ASP.NET Web Services* (Wrox, ISBN 1-861005-45-8).

- Visual Studio .NET Help: The Visual Studio .NET documentation provides a full walkthrough of Web services in a data-driven environment. Definitely worth a browse. On the Programs menu, select Microsoft Visual Studio .NET ➢ Microsoft Visual Studio .NET Documentation.

- www.xmethods.com: Showcasing examples of Web services in action, this site is essentially the mini *Yahoo!* of the ASMX world. Current listings include an SMS service, a dictionary, and a horoscope service.

- `www.vbws.com/newsletter/`: Want the latest news on Web services? Trainer Yasser Shohoud publishes his own newsletter giving the full lowdown, each and every month. Subscribe for free here.

- `www.dotnetjunkies.com`: Incredibly useful .NET developer site, with pages dedicated to creating Web services. Tips, tricks, code samples, and more at this site. Definitely worth a surf.

- `www.asp.net`: Only Microsoft could own such an exclusive address. Lists all the latest books, community sites, and code samples.

- `www.vbxml.com`: Your one-stop shop for learning more about XML, the markup language behind Web services. Also includes numerous .NET code snippets.

- `www.webservices.org`: Providing industry news and details on Web services implemented on *all* platforms. On the whole, a pretty drab site—but, if you're into the likes of Linux and Java, a decent resource.

- `www.dnj.com`: Homepage of the popular Microsoft-endorsed programming magazine, *Developer Network Journal*. Regularly features articles on implementing Web service technologies. Plenty of online content too, plus the option to subscribe (plug, plug).

- `microsoft.public.dotnet.framework.aspnet.webservices`: The official Microsoft newsgroup for Web services discussion. For speedier answers, try searching the archives first at `www.googlegroups.com`.

CONCLUSION

When asked exactly what .NET is, Microsoft's official answer is always ".NET is the Microsoft Web services platform."

In other words, Web services are at the heart of Microsoft's vision for a distributed computing future. Yes, there's a lot of hype—but there's no denying that Web services are cooler than a Pepsi-drinking polar bear. And, over the last twenty or so pages, you've learned how to get your own up and running in minutes.

We launched the tutorial today by creating our own mini Web service, then looked at using its operations from a Web page—plus found out how to "discover" and "consume" that functionality from within our applications. After that, we talked about its possibilities, plus went on to access exceptionally "smart data" in under twenty lines of code.

Finally, we checked out deployment and the top five things you really should do before making your service available to the world. And finally-finally, we reviewed all those frequently asked questions alongside a list of resources to take your knowledge to the next level.

Just remember: the next time you need to get your computers more talkative than a Jerry Springer audience, think Web services. They get computers exchanging data, they distribute your application, they solve problems, they're just cool.

But that's all from me—until the next time, this is Lrak Eroom signing off for tonight, wishing you a very pleasant evening, wherever you are in the world. Goodnight!

- Web services allow you to get computers talking to each other. The process is often compared to the old DCOM; however, it is loosely coupled and based on open standards.

- On the server side of a Web service, you have chunks of compiled code that are exposed to the client. On the client side, you have an application or browser making HTTP requests to those code chunks. The .NET Framework passes data between requests about in XML (eXtensible Markup Language).

- To generate your own Web service, create a new ASP.NET Web service project in Visual Studio .NET. By default, you will have a Web service called Service1.asmx added to your application. You can add new Web services to a project by selecting Project ➤ Add Web Service from the menu.

- To author the code behind your Web service, right-click on the service in the Solution Explorer and select View Code.

- By default, none of your methods, functions, or properties are exposed as part of your Web service. To expose a chunk of code, prefix it with the `<WebMethod()>` attribute, as so:

```
<WebMethod()> Public Function GetDate() As Date
    Return Now
End Function
```

- You can view your Web service in a browser by simply building the project, then visiting its dynamically generated ASMX page. Another technique is to simply press the F5 key while working on your Web service project.

- To "discover" a Web service for use in your Visual Studio .NET application, select Project ➤ Add Web Reference from the menu. Specify the address of your Web service, press the Enter key, then select Add Reference. Alternatively, browse the Microsoft UDDI Directory at http://uddi.microsoft.com/visualstudio.

- To "consume" the functionality of a Web service in your application, simply treat it as you would any regular object. The XML is all parsed out and handled for you. For example, the following demonstrates a discovered Web service in use:

```
Dim MyObject As New LocalHost.Service1()
MessageBox.Show(MyObject.GetDate)
```

- Your application doesn't care where it accesses Web services from. The data could be coming from the local computer, across a network, or from the other side of the world via the Internet. So long as that connection is available, the Web service works.

- To distribute your Web service to another server, from the menu select Project ➢ Copy Project. Alternatively, copy the ASMX, CONFIG, and VSDISCO files across to the new Web Application directory, plus create a subdirectory called Bin, copying your compiled Bin/ProjectName.DLL assembly into it.

- Web service members can accept and return more than just base data types. They can take in and pass back anything, including DataSets, data-holding classes, and user-defined types (structures).

From VB6 to .NET

All the Changes, Quickly

"They don't make bugs like Bunny anymore."—Olav Mjelde

YOU'VE READ THE ARTICLES THAT promise it'll slash hours off your development time. You've seen the promotional videos showing what a glamorous Silicon Valley lifestyle you'll live as soon as you start using it. You've had one of those "Hate Linux, Love .NET" T-shirts thrust into your hands at the last PDC.

Yes, you've heard about .NET. You get the idea that it's something to do with the next version of Visual Basic, too. But just what is it, and can you get up and running with the new system, *today?* It's possible. And, over the next chapter, I'll be showing you how.

We'll start our journey by looking at the big picture of .NET and just where Visual Basic fits in. Then we'll begin our whirlwind tour of the new .NET development environment, explaining how it differs from VB6 as we go about creating a simple application. We'll also learn about the new project types and where you can find out more about them in this book.

After that, we'll spend quality time listing exactly how our actual code will alter. From core data type changes through to new object functionality such as inheritance, it's all here. Finally, we'll take a sneak geek peek at the top .NET resources, plus talk about where you can go from here.

Ladies and gentlemen, this is your host, Karl Moore, requesting all passengers strap in tight. The train to .NET is about to depart. And it may be one slightly turbulent ride . . .

What is .NET?

Is it a single program? Is it a Web site? Is it an illiterate Cornishman's fishing implement?

Erm, no. So, what exactly is .NET?

Officially, .NET "is the Microsoft XML Web services platform, a way of working that allows you to create software as a service." At least that's what the press release says. Back here in real life, the whole .NET thing is really just a Microsoft vision based on *distributed computing*, a dream of being able to share information over the Internet regardless of operating system, device, or programming language.

The big plan supporting that .NET vision consists of five key components, not all of which have been delivered yet. In order of priority, these are (also, see Figure 1-1):

- Development products

- Server products (such as Windows 2000 and SQL Server)

- Foundation services (such as Passport and Alerts)

- Devices (such as the Pocket PC)

- Experiences (such as MSN and Office.NET)

The item at the top of this list—development products—is the cue for our favorite software giant to blast the industry with a brand spanking new set of programming tools to back up that distributed computing dream, helping boost productivity and streamline businesses throughout the globe.

How very nice. Nothing to do with Bill wanting to make another fat pile o' cash, then.

Okay, so hype aside, what exactly are these new programming tools? Well, it all comes down to just two core pieces of software: the .NET Framework and Visual Studio .NET. And we'll be focusing on both of these for the rest of today.

Behind .NET

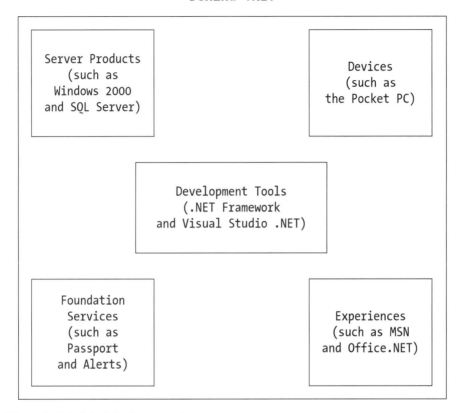

Figure 1-1. Behind the buzzwords

The free .NET Framework is really at the heart of the whole .NET idea. It's a program that sits on top of your operating system and basically runs your .NET applications (whether regular Windows applications or "distributed" applications). It handles program memory for you. It provides a store of functionality in its "base classes." It can talk to remote computers using XML. It does all the plumbing you really don't want to get involved in: it abstracts, it hides complexity, it just works. Yet, behind it all, the truth is . . . *the .NET Framework is just a Windows upgrade.*

> **TOP TIP** *You can imagine the .NET Framework as a very clever runtime for your programs. And, if you don't have it installed, you can't run any .NET applications.*

Next up, you have Visual Studio .NET. This is the next version of Visual Studio and plays home to languages such as Visual C# .NET, Visual C++ .NET, and, of course, Visual Basic .NET (VB .NET).

Of these languages, C# is the real newbie. Its syntax looks very similar to that of VB .NET, but this baby is in fact Bill Gates' .NET love child. After that, we have C++ .NET, which is essentially the old C++ with extensions to tie it in with the .NET Framework. And finally we have VB .NET: the next version of Visual Basic, the one product most important to us.

Now, before you can start using VB .NET, you need to get the .NET Framework and Visual Studio .NET onto your machine. If you haven't done that, follow the guidelines in Appendix A. When you're ready, let's move on for our first glimpse of the new development environment.

Introducing Visual Studio .NET

If you have Visual Studio .NET installed, it's time to go exploring. Ready?

1. Launch Visual Studio .NET by selecting Start ➤ Programs ➤ Microsoft Visual Studio .NET ➤ Microsoft Visual Studio .NET.

You should be looking at a colorful Start page. This replaces the rather bland New or Open pop-up of Visual Basic 6 fame. With its online links down the left side, this page is intended to turn into something of a developer portal.

2. Click on the New Project button.

This is more the sort of screen you're used to welcoming you in VB6. (See Figure 1-2.) It allows you to select a new sort of project to create. However, the options here are most certainly different to those we'd find in the old school.

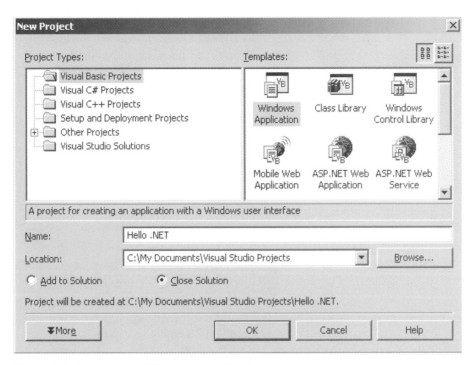

Figure 1-2. Creating our Windows application project

First off, you can create projects in any of three different languages. Naturally, we're concerned with only Visual Basic here, but, even so, the available projects still look confusing. Let's explain them away now.

You've got the Windows application here, which is the equivalent of a standard EXE. Desktop applications will never die. Next, there's the class library. Although COM has actually disappeared from .NET, this is your rough equivalent to an ActiveX DLL project. (See Tutorial 5, "Using Objects", for more information.) Moving on, a Windows control library allows you to build your own controls, a sort of ActiveX control project.

If you have the Mobile Internet Toolkit installed, your next entry will be a Mobile Web application, which allows you to create your own ASP.NET sites for wireless devices—from microwaves to mobile phones. (See Tutorial 4, "Going Mobile".)

After that, you have an ASP.NET Web application that mixes all the great Web capabilities of ASP with the Visual Basic ability to drag, drop, and code. It's a project that allows you to build fully functional Web sites in seconds. (See Tutorial 3, "Working the Web".)

An ASP.NET Web service is next on the list, a project that allows you to expose your code methods or functions over your network or the Internet. They said DCOM was COM on a longer wire. Well, Web services is an even better version of DCOM on an even longer wire. If you've ever dealt with sticky-sticky SOAP in VB6, this is the native .NET implementation. (See Tutorial 6, "Services Rendered".)

Moving on, the Web control library allows you to build "controls" to use on Web pages. These are HTML based and have absolutely nothing to do with ActiveX. A console application is next on the list and allows you to build a DOS-like console program, which was incredibly difficult in VB6 days. (been there, wrote the article, still getting the complaints.) Finally, the Windows service allows you to build your own service, which in the old days would require either a nightmarish amount of API code or the purchase of a third-party plug-in. The remaining projects are just empty placeholders.

Here, we'll be creating a Windows application whilst looking at a couple of development environment changes. More in-depth looks at each project type can be found in the individual parts of this book.

3.   Select the Windows Application icon.

4.   Change the Name to "Hello .NET".

5.   Note the Location folder and click on "OK".

You should now be staring at your new (and rather plain) Hello .NET project. Recognize anything?

In the middle window you should have your form, the screen that users see when they finally run your application. To the left, you have the toolbox, which holds controls ready to add to that form. Have an explore through the various tabs: you'll find a whole host of controls here, many more than the intrinsic bundle you had with VB6.

These are part of the core .NET Framework, which means that all your users will automatically have them installed. So, if you do use something like the OpenFileDialog control in your application, you won't need to go bundling an extra DLL to ensure that it works on the client machine. It just *will*. Well, hurrah for that!

You'll find most of your old favorites here, too—with an occasional name change thrown in to warrant the purchase. The CommandButton control became Button, for example. The Caption property of the Label command turned into a Text property. The Menu Editor turned into the MainMenu control. Still, nothing too serious.

Casting your eye over to the bottom right of your screen now, you'll find the trusty Properties window. No real difference here—some things never change. You'll find that your form has a few new interesting properties though—Opacity, for example.

Moving upward slightly, you'll see the Solution Explorer. This is exactly the same as our old Project Explorer, except it can host multiple projects as part of your solution (like a project group). The extra tabs under the Properties and Solution Explorer windows allow you to use the help, and explore classes in your application.

Let's move on.

6. Draw a button out onto your form.

7. Double-click on the button to open up the code window under a new tab, as shown in Figure 1-3.

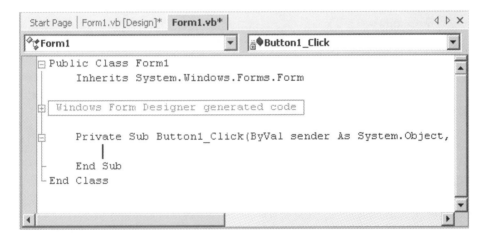

Figure 1-3. Our code window

Wow! You don't remember writing that code? Hmm, me neither, actually. So where did it all just come from? Well, this is automatically generated code that describes your form. Let's explain it away, line by line.

First off, glance across to the Solution Explorer. Your form file is called Form1.vb—there's no .frm extension here. Most Visual Basic .NET code files end in .vb. It's the content inside that describes what they are.

This explains why our form starts off with Public Class Form1 and finishes with End Class. Yes, our form is really a class: in VB6, we could treat forms as though they were classes, but they weren't *really*. In VB .NET, they are. In fact, apart from "primitive data types" such as a Boolean or Integer, everything we use in VB .NET is based on a class—even a string.

The next line, `Inherits System.Windows.Forms.Form`, tells VB .NET that this class "inherits" the functionality of a form, the functionality described in the `System.Windows.Forms.Form` part of the .NET Framework.

The following line has a gray chunk displaying the words "Windows Form Designer generated code". This is a collapsed mound of code, which you can view in full by clicking the little + symbol to its left.

After you've done that, you'll probably wish you hadn't. This is your form in the nude. It includes descriptions of what controls you have on the form, along with their positioning and initial properties. Tsk—move over, *Playboy*.

> **TOP TIP**   *You can automatically make regions of your code collapsible by adding* `#Region` *and* `#End Region` *keywords around your code.*

After this, we see our actual `Button1_Click` subroutine—finally, something you recognize. Or is it? First off, you have a couple of extra arguments here providing extra (and often useless) event information.

Also, in VB6, if you changed the name of the `Button1_Click` method, it would no longer run the code behind that method when you clicked on Button1. In VB .NET, this isn't the case: scroll to the end of the first line of `Button1_Click` here. See the Handles keyword? This is what determines which methods run when an event occurs.

Anyway, it's about time we added some code. And what simpler way to start than displaying the clichéd Hello World in a message box. Not difficult, right? Well, guess what? They changed that too. The new .NET way of displaying a message box is using the static Show function of the MessageBox class.

8.   Add the following code to respond to the click event of Button1:

```
MessageBox.Show("Hello World!")
```

Actually, I'm lying. You can still use `MsgBox` and all its related result constants, but `MessageBox` is the new and improved way of displaying messages within Windows forms like this.

> **TOP TIP** *Notice how your code is automatically formatted? Just write it and VB .NET will position it for you. It'll also complete If statements and property declarations for you. Top stuff!*

> **ANOTHER TOP TIP** *If you make a coding error in VB .NET, it doesn't wait until you compile your application to point it out: it's immediately highlighted via a Word-style squiggly underline. Hovering your mouse cursor over the region displays a description of the problem.*

Let's run our application.

9. Press the F5 button or select Start from the menu to run your application.

You'll see a bunch of information fly past an "output" window as your code is compiled. Ignore it—it just means that your final EXE file is being slapped together.

Within a few seconds, your program should pop up. Yes, it has a slightly different feel—and that Form icon definitely has to go. But, on the whole, it's not all that alien and a click of your Button control should produce the results you expect. Right? Supercool.

Well, that's our first glimpse at the Visual Studio .NET interface. A speedy exploration, yes—but it should've answered a few of the initial questions that VB6 developers always ask. (We'll be back looking at compiling and upgrading our applications using Visual Studio .NET later.)

So, let's recap: what differences have we seen so far? A whole bundle of new and exciting project types are now available. We have a host of new intrinsic controls to play with. Most development files have a .vb extension. Form .vb files are really classes and include code that describe how the form is laid out. When your code compiles, a host of useless information spurts into the Output window.

Oh, and I forgot to mention: you also have pretty pastel menus, too. (See Figure 1-4.) Now you know where all those research and development dollars went. (After all, they are *incredibly* good looking.)

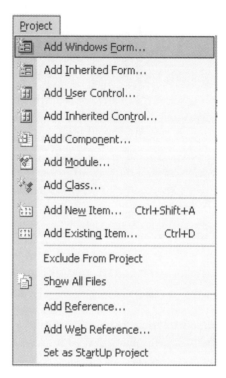

Figure 1-4. Pick a menu option. Any menu option.

And that's about it. It's a shift, yes—but mind blowing it ain't.

Well, that's our first glimpse of the development environment. Next, let's look at how the actual Visual Basic language has changed with .NET.

How Your Code Changes

So, what are the Visual Basic language differences that really matter to you? Let's run through the top changes.

Integer Upgrades

Visual Basic has changed the way it stores integers to bring it in line with other languages. Thankfully, they've all been upgraded, meaning that they can now hold greater-ranging values, so you can still get away with doing it the old way. However, just in case you're conscious of wasting those extra bytes of memory, Table 1-1 shows how it's altered.

Table 1-1. Integer Changes

VISUAL BASIC 6	VB .NET	TYPE
Byte	Byte	8-bit integer
Integer	Short	16-bit integer
Long	Integer	32-bit integer
n/a	Long	64-bit integer

Also, if you're used to converting your numeric data types to use the Windows API—*stop!* VB .NET is now on par, and you don't need any conversion. You can find a full list of VB .NET data types and what they can hold in Appendix D.

Strings

Talking about the API, if you're a heavy user, you'll be used to passing about fixed-length strings. Well, you don't have those in VB .NET. Previously, you would have declared a string like so:

```
Dim MyString As String * 100
```

But, in the VB .NET world, you'll need to add a special attribute to accommodate these, like so:

```
<VBFixedString(100)> Dim MyString As String
```

The information in <pointed brackets> is an attribute. We'll discuss these more later.

Variant and Currency

Variant and Currency . . . you *are* the Weakest Link, goodbye! Both of these aging data types have been thrown out the window. In VB .NET, the Object type can hold absolutely anything, so it's a good replacement for Variant. And the Decimal data type is a decent replacement for Currency, too.

Again, Appendix D features a full list of VB .NET data types and what they hold.

Array Alterations

Think you know arrays? Think again. In VB .NET, they've changed.

The big alteration is that arrays are now *always* zero based. That means you can't define the lower boundary yourself: it's always zero. A typical declaration will now look something like:

```
Dim MyArray(9) As String
```

Here, we have a string array containing ten elements—from zero through to nine. This also means that the LBound statement is now pretty useless because it always returns 0.

Declaring Properties

In the golden olden days, we'd create properties as separate Get, Set, and Let blocks. In VB .NET, they've been combined into one chunk, with a Get block to retrieve the property and a Set block to store it.

Here's an example property in VB .NET:

```
Dim mstrUsername As String

Public Property Username() As String
    Get
        Return mstrUsername
    End Get
    Set(ByVal Value As String)
        mstrUsername = Value
    End Set
End Property
```

This property also demonstrates the Return keyword, which passes back a value in your property or function, then immediately exits.

User-Defined Types

If you've worked with the API, you'll know it tends to call our user-defined types *structures*. Well, get used to it: the Type keyword has now been replaced with Structure. Here's an example user-defined type in VB .NET:

```
Public Structure MyStructure
    Dim Username As String
    Dim LogonCount As Integer
End Structure
```

It's also worth noting that you can now add subroutines to your structures, too (yes, code inside a defined type), effectively turning them into mini classes. Also, you can't declare fixed-length arrays inside a structure. To enforce this, you need to add another "attribute" to the beginning of your array, like so:

```
<VBFixedArray(9)> Dim MyArray() As String
```

Change the Scope

VB .NET now supports block-level scoping. If you typically declare all your variables at the top of your routine, you shouldn't run into any problems with the new feature.

But imagine this scenario: you declare a variable inside a loop and refer to it later outside the loop. In VB6, it's no problem. In VB .NET, it's outside the scope of the loop and therefore isn't available. Worth keeping in mind.

ByVal Is Default

By default, all parameters in VB .NET are passed ByVal (by value). In VB6, the default was ByRef (by reference). If you know what these keywords mean, you'll know how it might affect you, so make sure you change the ByVal keyword where needed.

Set Has Disappeared

Virtually everything you use in VB .NET is an object. And, if you continued using VB6 syntax in VB .NET, that would mean having to use the Set statement to do something as simple as changing the value of a String variable. Not very sensible, I'm sure you'll agree.

Therefore, they decided to scrap the Set statement altogether. After all, if everything *is* an object, the Set keyword only serves to annoy. You can still try using it, but VB .NET will automatically remove and attempt to spank you silly.

Also, most default properties have disappeared in VB .NET. You can no longer do something like this:

```
Dim MyString As String
MyString = TextBox1
```

Why not? Have a think about it. If you don't have the Set statement, you *can't* have defaults. It's not an obvious connection, but imagine changing the String type here to Object. Now, exactly *what* are you trying to retrieve: a reference to the TextBox or the Text property? Have a ponder.

It's worth noting, however, that there is a way to create your own special default properties—which we'll examine later.

Error-Handling Changes

You can still use those favorite "On Error Goto" statements in VB .NET. However, there's also a new way of dealing with errors, familiar to C++ and Java programmers. It's called *exception handling*, and it works by implementing a Try-Catch-Finally block.

Here's an example:

```
Try
    ' potentially problematic code goes here
Catch
    ' errors are caught here
Finally
    ' optional, runs at the end,
    ' whether an error or not
End Try
```

Here, we add our code under the Try block. Should any errors occur while running it, the code inside the Catch block kicks in. At the end, whether an error occurred or not, the code within the Finally block executes. You can see this in action in Chapter 1.5 of Tutorial 1, "Beginning VB .NET".

Also, if we want to raise an error in our code, you throw the "exception," like so:

```
Throw New System.Exception("An error has occured!")
```

Namespaces

Throughout this book, you'll find reference to various "namespaces." What are they? If you've ever worked with some of the really advanced API functions, you may already have some pretty far-out ideas. Well, forget all that and listen up.

The .NET Framework includes a core of useful functionality in its "base classes." The thing is, with 7,002 base classes, they'd get awfully difficult to browse and utilize if they weren't organized into categories. Thankfully, they are—into *namespaces*—which you can imagine as separate folders and subfolders of a digital filing cabinet.

For example, earlier we stumbled across `System.Windows.Forms.Form`. This is the Form class, which is inside the Forms namespace, inside the Windows namespace, which is inside the "mother" of the .NET Framework base classes, System.

Other useful namespaces include `System.Data`, which includes functionality to access your data stores, or `System.Xml`, which provides objects allowing you to work with XML documents. And then you have the `Microsoft.VisualBasic` namespace, which is referenced by default in any Visual Basic project, providing access to much of the VB6 functionality you're already acquainted with.

You can use the objects inside a namespace by typing out the whole namespace qualifier or by referencing a particular namespace first—either via the Imports section of the Project properties or by using the Imports keyword.

Here, for example, we're running the AppActivate method of the `Microsoft.VisualBasic` namespace directly:

```
Microsoft.VisualBasic.AppActivate("Calculator")
```

TOP TIP   *Unless your project is referencing a third-party or custom DLL, all the namespace functionality you can access in your project is available to everyone who has the .NET Framework installed. This means that you don't have to distribute extra DLLs to, say, use ADO.NET data access code.*

ANOTHER TOP TIP   *You might be wondering what happens when Microsoft changes the .NET Framework base classes. Will it simply break your applications? Yes, it could, but they have a strong responsibility for keeping it 100% compatible. It's also possible to create your application so that it runs on only a particular build of the .NET Framework, therefore ensuring complete application stability.*

So, namespaces are a way of organizing functionality and classes.

It's worth noting that such functionality doesn't necessarily have to exist within the same runtime—you might have members of the same namespace in different DLLs, for example. It's just a logical grouping, and you can create your own using the Namespace keyword.

They're Objects, Jim...

If you program using objects, you may be excited by the rumors that VB .NET is now a fully object-oriented (OO) language.

And it's true. With VB .NET, we see all of the four main principles of an OO language adhered to. There's polymorphism, the ability to write code that can operate on objects from more than one class—such as a Print method on Invoice and Quotation objects. Then we have encapsulation, the ability to create an "interface" completely independent of the code behind it. There's also abstraction, the ability to take a concept and create an abstract of it within our code. (A Customer object, for example, is an abstraction of a real-world customer.)

But we've had all of these features since Visual Basic 4. The fourth element of a true OO language, however, is inheritance—and we never *really* had that in VB6. Inheritance is the ability to "inherit" functionality from another class.

Now, I could talk theory until I die of either old age or boredom—but, really, what does this all mean? How will the objects you're used to building change and what new features are now available?

Brace yourself for a rather long, skip-it-if-it-doesn't-apply-to-you features list. And make sure you explore each new concept in code yourself. It's the only way to learn. Okay, gang—I'm going in . . .

Class Keyword

Classes and their names are now defined according to the Class keyword. For example, here we're defining a class called Class1. We'd put all our code somewhere in the middle:

```
Public Class Class1

End Class
```

This format also allows you to create multiple classes inside one file, which is useful if you're dealing with particularly small, data-holding or related classes.

Class Libraries

You can now store your classes in something called a class library project, covered in greater detail in Tutorial 5, "Using Objects". This is essentially the .NET equivalent of an ActiveX DLL project. A class library compiles down to a DLL, known as an *assembly*. (In fact, all DLLs and EXEs created in Visual Studio .NET are known as *assemblies*.)

Property Changes

You've already seen that properties are now declared differently, with the Get and Set portions enclosed in the same block of code. You can also make them read- and write-only by using the ReadOnly and WriteOnly keywords, respectively. For example:

```
Public ReadOnly Property ServerDate() As Date
    Get
        Return Now
    End Get
End Property
```

Default Properties

In VB .NET, default properties are created using the Default keyword—and only a parameterized property can be made default. Here is an example:

```
Public Class MyRestaurant

    Default Public Property TableSeated(ByVal TableNo As Short) As Boolean
        Get
            ' use TableNo parameter
            ' and return True/False
        End Get
        Set(ByVal Value As Boolean)
            ' store the passed Value,
            ' using TableNo parameter
        End Set
    End Property

End Class
```

And we could use this default property, like so:

```
Dim MyObject As New MyRestaurant()
MyObject(4) = True
```

Constructors

In VB6, we could write code to run when our class was instantiated by adding code to the `Class_Initialize` method. Erm, that's gone.

In its place we have a "constructor," a special method that is always invoked as an object is created. To create a constructor for your class, simply add a method called "New". When your class is created, the code inside that method will run. Simple!

You can also add parameters to your constructors. For example:

```
Public Class MyCustomer
    Public Sub New(ByVal Name As String, ByVal Address As String, _
        Optional ByVal Phone As String = "Unknown")
        ' initialization code goes here
    End Sub
End Class
```

Here we have a class with a constructor that accepts multiple parameters. We might then create an instance of such a class, like so:

```
Dim MyObject As New MyCustomer("Scott Bloggs", "20 Mount Street")
```

It's also possible to have multiple constructors, each accepting different arguments. This is called *overloading*, and we'll stumble across it within the next few minutes.

Termination

They changed the `Class_Initialize` event, so you're probably thinking they've changed the `Class_Terminate` event too, right? If so, you're spot on. It's disappeared, replaced by the Finalize method.

To write code for the Finalize method, select the Finalize method from the code window Method Name drop-down box. You'll be presented with a template to edit, looking something like this:

```
Protected Overrides Sub Finalize()
    ' add any finalization code here
    MyBase.Finalize()
End Sub
```

Just add your code and you're ready to run. But first let's review how objects are disposed in VB .NET. And it helps if you can completely forget how VB6 does it. COM has gone. Reference counting has gone. Circular reference problems have gone.

In VB .NET, you have something called *garbage collection*. This is a .NET Framework system process that periodically runs and physically checks for any variables that reference objects in memory. If an object isn't being used, it gets destroyed.

This means that, when you set your object variable equal to Nothing, the object isn't immediately removed from memory. It's simply marked for destruction. It may take several minutes before garbage collection kicks in and your object actually disappears.

This is called *non-deterministic finalization* and basically means that you can't control exactly when your Finalize method runs. In other words, it's not a good idea to close costly database connections here.

Two further points. Firstly, you can launch the garbage collection process yourself, by simply running System.GC.Collect(). However, due to the immediate system slowdown you'll experience, it's not a line of code you'll want to add casually.

Secondly, if you must control exactly when your Finalize code runs, you might want to implement a Dispose method, which is a rapidly emerging standard for destroying objects. The FAQ in Chapter 5.2 of Tutorial 5, "Using Objects", has a response showing you just how to do this.

Overloading

When a Java programmer first explained the concept of overloading to me, I was pretty confused. I'd never stumbled across it before and instantly damned the technique as being pointless. Now, however, I realize just how useful overloading can really be. Allow me to explain.

Overloading allows you to create multiple methods or functions with the same name, though that accept parameters of different data types. For example, you might define the following:

```
Public Overloads Sub Find()
    ' code goes here
End Sub


Public Overloads Sub Find(ByVal CustomerName As String)
    ' code goes here
End Sub


Public Overloads Sub Find(ByVal CustomerID As Integer)
    ' code goes here
End Sub
```

Here we have three completely separate methods. If we just run a .Find in our code, the first method will run. If we run a .Find passing in a string argument, the second will run. If we run a .Find passing in an integer, the third will run.

After you've created such overloaded methods, you'll notice the IntelliSense in VB .NET picks this up and offers you multiple options when using the method. Use the Up/Down keys to view the various method parameter combinations.

A simple idea—but very effective when used correctly.

Delegates

Delegates let you pass methods or functions about as actual parameters, allowing you to call the original method/function with a simple line of code.

How? It works like this. You start by declaring the "signature" of an imaginary method or function, listing its parameters and return type. This is called your *delegate*, which you can treat like a user-defined type. You then accept a parameter of this type in one of your functions.

In your application, you can then pass an actual method or function with a "signature" matching the delegate as a parameter to that function, using the AddressOf keyword. When your code needs to call the method or function you pass in, it simply needs to use the delegate's Invoke method.

It's a confusing concept to read about—and even more confusing to write—but here's a little code that should help explain it all away:

```
Public Class Form1

    . . . other code . . .

    Private Sub Button1_Click(ByVal sender As System.Object, _
        ByVal e As System.EventArgs) Handles Button1.Click

        Dim MyObject As New MyLogClass()
        MyObject.ProcessLog(AddressOf Log)

    End Sub

    Public Sub Log(ByVal Action As String)
        MessageBox.Show(Action)
    End Sub

End Class
```

```
Public Class MyLogClass

    Public Delegate Sub MyLog(ByVal LogAction As String)

    Public Sub ProcessLog(ByVal Log As MyLog)
        ' process log
        Log.Invoke("Duplicate Logon Attempt, User #68")
        Log.Invoke("Porn Restricted, Machine #46")
        Log.Invoke("Logon Denied, Machine #11")
    End Sub

End Class
```

Delegates are actually how VB .NET implements the Event, RaiseEvent, WithEvents, and Handles keywords behind the scenes—and can prove useful in certain programming situations. You can find out more about this feature by looking up "delegates, overview" in the Help index.

Shared Members

Shared members are properties and procedures in a class that are shared by all instances of that class. When using a shared member, you don't have to create a new instance of the class: you just use it, as you would code in a module. Shared members are also sometimes called *static* members.

As an example, the Show function of the MessageBox class is a shared member: you just use it, without creating a new instance of MessageBox. Shared members are particularly useful when dealing with settings that perhaps aren't specific to any one instance of a class, but need to be shared between all instances, sort of like a global variable in the object world.

You can implement a shared member simply by adding the Shared keyword after the scope. Here's an example of shared members in action:

```
Public Class SystemInfo

    Private Shared mintRamCache As Integer
    ' shared between all members

    Public Shared Property RamCache() As Integer
        ' shared between all members
        Get
            Return mintRamCache
        End Get
```

```
        Set(ByVal Value As Integer)
            mintRamCache = Value
        End Set
    End Property

End Class
```

You could set this shared property from within your application quite simply, like so:

```
SystemData.RamCache = 20
```

Attributes

Attributes allow you to provide additional information about your "assemblies" (compiled components), modules, classes, methods, properties, and variables.

For example, when you add a form to your application, it automatically generates code that includes an InitializeComponent method to lay out the controls. The first line of that method looks like:

```
<System.Diagnostics.DebuggerStepThrough()> Private Sub InitializeComponent()
```

Before the regular method declaration here, we have an attribute in <pointed brackets>. This particular attribute tells the debugger to ignore this method, to step over the code—a great example of attributes in action.

Another use is in creating Web services. By simply adding a <WebMethod()> attribute, a particular method can be exposed, DCOM-style. This is covered in more depth in Tutorial 6, "Services Rendered".

Other attribute uses include declaring fixed-length strings and arrays, as we've already seen, plus setting defaults and descriptions when creating our own component classes.

> **TOP TIP**   *The .NET Framework includes a bunch of "ready-to-use" attributes, listed when you open the pointed bracket. You can also define your own for special use in your applications. For more information on attributes in general, look up "attributes [Visual Basic], overview" in the Help index.*

So, attributes provide extra information—and, when your project is compiled, that information is often stored in your assembly "metadata." We'll learn more about this shortly.

Inheritance

Inheritance allows you to inherit the interface and functionality of another class, which is a feature new to Visual Basic.

For example, you might have a Person class that holds generic information about an individual. You might then have a couple of further classes—Customer and Employee, for example—that inherit functionality from those classes, plus add their own individual properties.

Here's an example of this in action:

```
Public Class Person
    Public Name As String
    Public Address As String
    Public Phone As String
End Class

Public Class Customer
    Inherits Person
    Public CustomerID As String
    Public LastOrderDate As Date
End Class

Public Class Employee
    Inherits Person
    Public EmployeeID As String
    Public PhotoLink As String
End Class
```

Here, we have one parent class that describes a person. Admittedly, it's incredibly small and perhaps not very life-like, but you get the picture. We then have two further classes that inherit the Person class and add their own functionality—meaning, for example, that the Customer object gets a Name, Address, and Phone property, automatically handled by the Person class. So, we could use our Customer class like so:

```
Dim MyCustomer As New Customer()
MyCustomer.Name = "John O'Groats"
```

You can also override certain elements of the class you're inheriting from. For example, if you wanted to do some special checks on the Phone field of an employee, you might override the *Person* Phone field and run your own *Employee* Phone code instead. You do this using the Overrides keyword.

VB .NET offers numerous other inheritance-related features too, including the new ability to inherit a Form class and amend the design and supporting code, a function known as *visual inheritance*. (See the "Using Visual Inheritance" section in Chapter 8.2, "Intermediate Tips and Techniques".)

Using Modules

Remember modules? In VB6 days, they were never even thought about in the object world. Well, now if you declare your module as public, you can expose its functionality via your compiled DLL. And, if you wanted to go all out, you could even add classes *inside* modules. I know. Weird.

Adding Namespaces

Remember namespaces? They're logical ways of grouping functionality and classes. Think of a digital filing cabinet. And, should you feel so inclined, you can create your own namespaces to group classes or modules, using the Namespace keyword. For more information, look up "namespaces, declaring" in the Help index.

No More DLL Hell

Most developers have taken the rough ride to DLL Hell. Only a few return. Thankfully, .NET sorts all those sticky issues. Allow me to elucidate.

By default, if you reference a DLL file in your .NET application and then compile your program, a copy of that DLL gets stored alongside your EXE (or whatever your application compiles down to). When you run that EXE, the DLL with it is used. In other words, there's no sharing anymore—it's called *side-by-side execution.*

If you really want to, you can add that DLL to something called the *global assembly cache* (*GAC*). This allows you to continue sharing your DLL between multiple clients. However, it stops the return of DLL hell due to the GAC's ability to automatically handle different versions of the same DLL.

Interfaces

You can now generate your own official interfaces using the Interface keyword. There's no longer any need to create "interface" classes with empty properties and methods.

Creating Components

Classes are reusable chunks of code. You know that. Well, in the .NET world, you also have "components"—which are essentially *classes with standards.*

Standards? In other words, they all implement a certain interface: System.ComponentModel.IComponent, which the .NET Framework can rely on and utilize. You can find out more about this in the FAQ of Tutorial 5, "Using Objects". Alternatively, look up "components, vs. classes" in the Help index.

Getting It Out

So, you've finally managed to get your head around a few of the changes and have thrown together your own sample .NET application. Now it's time to compile. What do you do?

It's relatively simple. No, really. You just open your project and select Build ➤ Build from the VS .NET menu. That's it. You'll end up with a compiled EXE or DLL in your project Bin folder. (This is known as your assembly.) Alongside that, you'll have any dependencies, such as third-party or custom DLLs you may have referenced.

Now, you may have heard some people talk about *Intermediate Language.* This is a little like the P-Code that Visual Basic used to have. When the VB compiler builds your project, it compiles your code down to Microsoft Intermediate Language (MSIL). This is stored in your final assembly, alongside something called "metadata" which provides extra information about your application and its interfaces.

When your application is run for the first time on a machine, something called the *Common Language Runtime* (*CLR*, part of the .NET Framework) optimizes this MSIL code for that computer, fully compiles it, and caches the final program.

No, you don't need to know such behind-the-scenes detail—and there's a lot more I could bore you with—but knowledge of the buzzwords helps in understanding some of those more confusing magazine articles you'll find floating about.

So, your application is compiled and you're ready to distribute. But how? Well, you could build yourself a setup package, as described in Chapter 1.5 of Tutorial 1, "Beginning VB .NET".

Or you could simply XCOPY—that's right, just copy and paste your assembly and any dependencies straight across to any machine bearing the .NET Framework—and that's it! There's no registering (unless you're using that global assembly cache), no DLL hell, nothing.

And, if you think about it, that power brings with it a mass of new opportunities. For example, it means you can now create entire applications that run directly from CD-ROM. It also resolves all those sticky, fat-client, distribution problems that made everyone turn to browser-based solutions in the first place. New, more advanced features such as the ability to download required assemblies on demand, to obtain updates as necessary, and to implement in-code security checks will also boost the attractiveness of Windows application development.

Return of the Fat Client? It might just be coming to a desktop near you.

Upgrading Your Existing Applications

So, you've seen the changes and think some of the new features are worthy of upgrading your existing application. But you fear porting your code across for the mass of compile errors you'll stumble across?

I don't blame you. I tried it with a simple copy-and-paste, and there were so many squiggly underlines, it looked as though my two-year-old niece had been trying to speed type in Word again. That's why Microsoft bundles the Upgrade wizard with Visual Studio .NET, which is waiting right now to upgrade all your existing projects.

To launch it, simply open your main VBP project file from within VS .NET and follow the wizard prompts. It's not perfect and won't catch everything, but it'll at least provide an educational overview of how your old code translates across.

WHERE TO GO FROM HERE

When I initially plotted this chapter, I never realized just how in-depth this "overview" could get. Having finished it, I realize I've only skimmed the surface—and there's still so much more I want to babble on about.

Still, it serves its purpose as a speedy introduction, yet begs the question: where now?

First off, I'd recommend that you browse through at least the Review Sheets in Tutorial 1, "Beginning VB .NET". You can read the chapters if you want, too. They won't teach you any new groundbreaking programming techniques (unless you've never used a loop before), but they do provide basic background, and plus will help acquaint you with some of the new terms and ways of working.

After that, I'd recommend that you start working through each of the tutorials in this book, one by one. From data access to Web forms, mobile applications to Web services, it's all completely new stuff, so I can guarantee you won't get bored.

And if, on your journey, you want to check out a few extra resources for assistance, here are my best picks for taking your knowledge right to the next level:

- *The .NET Languages: A Quick Translation Guide* (Apress, ISBN 1-893115-48-8): Take your VB6 knowledge and apply it straight to the .NET world, with this neat guide to translating between the VB6, VB .NET and C# languages.

- *Moving to VB .NET: Strategies, Concepts, and Code* (Apress, ISBN 1-893115-97-6): What's important in .NET? And what will affect the move across? Split into three parts—Strategies, Concepts, and Code—this book attempts to lend a helping hand.

- *Visual Basic .NET and the .NET Platform* (Apress, ISBN 1-893115-62-7): Looking to push VB .NET to its limits? Read and learn as Andrew Troelsen creates virtually every possible type of .NET application.

- *Standard VB: An Enterprise Developer's Reference for VB6 and VB .NET* (Apress, ISBN 1-893115-43-7): This reference book provides a huge wad of rules and guidelines for design, development, and quality assurance what-nots in the Visual Basic programming world.

- `http://localhost/quickstart/`: Got questions? This QuickStart tutorial from Microsoft is set up on your machine when you install Visual Studio and provides you with answers to the most-common developer questions.

- `www.dotnetjunkies.com`: It's the site that apparently puts the dot in .NET. Not sure about that, but it certainly packs a whole host of tips and tutorials for getting yourself started. A mound of ready-to-run samples are available for download, too.

- `www.dotnetextreme.com`: This well-designed site packs a lot of .NET content for those coming from VB6, with a goal of smoothing the transition.

- `www.gotdotnet.com`: It's the official Microsoft .NET learning site. Includes a very cool 3-D revamp of the old Quick Basic game, *Donkey*, created entirely in VB .NET!

- `microsoft.public.dotnet.languages.vb`: The official Microsoft newsgroup for VB language discussion. For speedier answers, try searching the archives first at `www.googlegroups.com`.

You'll also find specific site recommendations at the end of each individual tutorial in this book. Try flicking through to pick up some of the greatest .NET Web stops.

CONCLUSION

Congratulations on finishing this VB .NET tutorial!

Actually, it wasn't much of a tutorial—more an information dump. But it still provided a list of the core differences between VB6 and VB .NET, allowing you to get up and running with the new system in under an hour. Or so. Ahem.

We started with a quick explore of the development environment, then looked at how our core code changed. After that, we explored some of the new object features, plus looked at both upgrading and distributing our projects.

But this is just the beginning. *<cue drum roll>*

If you really want to get to grips with .NET—get reading the books, get surfing the sites, get participating in the newsgroups—and play, play, play. Hands-on is the only real way forward.

Yes, it's changed. Yes, it's a pretty big change. But you don't have to scrap everything you know. Rather, build on it. Explore the concepts, embrace the new features, and—if you do nothing else—look up "upgrading Visual Basic applications, overview" in the Help index. Interesting stuff.

Well, that's all for now—so, until the next time, this is Karl Moore wishing you all the very best and welcoming you to the world of .NET!

Tips and Techniques

Beginner Tips and Techniques

This section covers the following tips:

- Making Your Form Transparent

- Snapping to the Grid

- Resizing Controls at Runtime

- Adding Menus to Your Program

- Changing Your Window State

- Adding the With Keyword

- Using Visual Inheritance

- Typing the TODO: Statement

- Setting a Site Home Page

- Adding Smart Navigation to Web Forms

- Changing the Tab Order

- Generating Random Numbers

- Exiting Your Code

- Customizing the Cursor

- Using Special Code Characters

- Creating a Number-Only Text Box

- Reversing a String

- Rounding a Number

- Replacing Text the Easy Way

- Listing and Setting Fonts

- Trimming a String

- Ending Your Application

- Retrieving a Number Using Val

- Resetting the Windows

- Capitalizing Your Characters

Making Your Form Transparent

You can give your Windows form a great transparent look by altering its Opacity property. Set this anywhere between 0% (completely transparent) and 100% (regular opaque) to see the windows underneath your application.

Snapping to the Grid

When designing your Windows forms, controls snap to the form grid by default. Although sometimes helpful, this can often be a hindrance when working with controls that need to be more delicately positioned. To stop snapping to the grid, turn the SnapToGrid property of your form to False. To make the grid invisible, set the DrawGrid property to False.

Resizing Controls at Runtime

When the user resizes your Windows form at runtime, all of your controls will stay in place by default. They will not automatically resize with the form. You can change this behavior by editing the Anchor property of a control.

The Anchor property determines which of a form's sides will stretch with that control. After the default, the most common setting for this property is "Top, Bottom, Left, Right"—meaning that the control will stretch with all sides of your form, behaving like the majority of resizable Windows applications.

The Dock property of a control is also useful when positioning and resizing controls. It allows you to dock a control to a particular side of a form and stick with that side, regardless of how the form is resized. To set this, simply select a new region via the Dock property drop-down.

Adding Menus to Your Program

You can add menus to your Windows forms using the MainMenu control. Simply drag the control onto your form and enter your text into the "Type Here" boxes to visually build your menu. Using an ampersand (&) in the name will turn the letter to its right into a shortcut key. You can change the properties of each individual MenuItem entry using the Properties window, or double-click on an item to add code to its click event.

Changing Your Window State

Two main properties determine the state of your Windows form when it loads: StartPosition and WindowState. The most common StartPosition property value is CenterScreen.

The WindowState property controls whether your form is maximized, minimized, or left as in design mode. You can change this in the Property window or in code, for example:

```
Me.WindowState = FormWindowState.Maximized
```

Adding the With Keyword

The With keyword allows you to write multiple chunks of code that refer to the same item, without having to consistently type the item name. The following example best explains this concept, where we tell VB .NET we'll be working "With" ComboBox.Items, then use the individual properties and methods of that item, eventually finishing with an End With statement:

```
With ComboBox1.Items
    .Add("Single Room")
    .Add("Double Room")
    .Add("Family Room")
    Label1.Text = "Choose from the " & .Count & " room options:"
End With
```

Using Visual Inheritance

Visual inheritance allows you to create one "master" form, then have other Windows forms inherit its layout and code. For example, you might create one master form for your application wizard, then add further wizard forms that automatically inherit its appearance and functionality, customizing each as appropriate.

To use visual inheritance, first design and code your master form, then build your application (`Ctrl+Shift+B`). Next, select Project ➢ Add Inherited Form from the menu. Enter a name, click on Open, and choose the form you wish to inherit from. Then, further customize this form to meet your needs.

It's worth noting that any changes you make here will not alter your original form; rather, they will just override those original inherited settings from your master form.

Typing the `TODO:` Statement

The Task window in VB .NET is a great way of keeping track of tasks that are related to your project. For example, if you have code issues or compile errors, VB .NET will automatically list them here.

You can also add your own comments to the Task list, using the TODO keyword. To use this feature, simply add a comment to your code that starts with the TODO keyword. It will automatically be added to your existing Task list. For example:

```
' TODO: Rewrite function so works with .DOC files
```

To view the Task list, select View ➢ Other Windows ➢ Task List from the menu, or press `Ctrl+Alt+K`. The Task list often filters its contents, so it displays only certain information. To view everything, right-click on your list and select All Tasks ➢ All.

Setting a Site Homepage

If you're creating your own Web application, your start page will be called WebForm1.aspx by default. This means that, when a user visits your site, they will have to type in an address akin to `http://www.mysite.com/WebForm1.aspx`.

To get around this, right-click on WebForm1.aspx in the Solution Explorer and choose Rename. Name your form "default.aspx", which is the name of one of the files that Internet Information Services first attempts to display whenever a surfer accesses your root application folder.

The next time a visitor checks out http://www.mysite.com/, your default.aspx page will automatically load.

Adding Smart Navigation to Web Forms

Smart Navigation is a little-known Internet Explorer feature that enables the individual controls on your Web forms to maintain focus between postbacks, plus allows you to suppress that "flicker" that occurs as you load the new page.

To turn on this little-known feature, simply set the smartNavigation property of your ASPX page to True. Note that Smart Navigation only works on Internet Explorer 5 and above; however, the .NET Framework will automatically detect this and serve up the "smart" code only if the target browser supports it.

Changing the Tab Order

In Windows forms, the tab order determines which controls receive the focus and in what order as your user presses the Tab key.

To stop a control from receiving the focus when your user hits the tab key, set its TabStop property to False. To change its tab order, alter the TabIndex property to a value starting at 0, where 0 is the first control to receive the focus.

One simple way to set the tab order is to select View ➤ Tab Order from the menu, then select your controls in the proposed tab order. The TabIndex property will be automatically set for you.

Generating Random Numbers

It's often useful to generate random numbers in your applications. The System.Random class provides numerous functions to help you do this.

The most common function, however, is to pick a random number between two particular boundaries. The following function encapsulates this for you: simply call GetRandomNumber, passing in both Low and High values, and it'll return a random number between (and possibly including) those integers:

```
Dim objRandom As New System.Random(System.DateTime.Now.Ticks _
    Mod System.Int32.MaxValue)

    Public Function GetRandomNumber(Optional ByVal Low As Integer = 1, _
        Optional ByVal High As Integer = 100) As Integer
    ' Returns a random number,
    ' between the optional Low and High parameters
    Return objRandom.Next(Low, High + 1)
End Function
```

Here is an example of it in use:

```
Dim intDiceRoll As Integer
intDiceRoll = GetRandomNumber(1, 6)
```

Exiting Your Code

You can exit any method, function, or property using the Return statement. When working with a function or property, providing a value immediately after this keyword passes it back as the return value and then immediately exits your code.

Customizing the Cursor

You can change the cursor in your application a number of different ways. The simplest method of doing this is to edit the Cursor property of your Windows form. A more powerful way is to set the property in code, specifying one of the default cursors as the new value, or loading a new cursor from a file:

```
Me.Cursor = Cursors.Hand
Me.Cursor = New Cursor("c:\myapp\groove.cur")
```

Also, if you have a long operation running, you might want to temporarily set the current Cursor property to a wait cursor in code, then revert to the default afterwards, as so:

```
Cursor.Current = Cursors.WaitCursor
' do processing here
Cursor.Current = Cursors.Default
```

To create your own cursor CUR files, click Project ➢ Add New Item and select Cursor File.

Using Special Code Characters

Visual Basic includes a couple of special characters to help you write code. These are the underscore (_) and colon (:).

The underscore is used when you want to carry a line of code onto the next line, making it more easily readable. For example:

```
MessageBox.Show("To use the system, first enter your username, " & _
    "then specify a password and hit the Logon button. If you " & _
    "have problems, please call IT&T on 5917")
```

Whereby the underscore is used to trim long lines of code, the colon is typically used when working with short lines of code. It allows you to have multiple lines of code on the same physical line, which is great when dealing with short or related statements. For example:

```
Label1.Text = "Finished" : MessageBox.Show("Operation Complete!")
```

Creating a Number-Only Text Box

In some instances, you only want to allow the user to enter a numeric value in a TextBox control on your Windows form.

To do this, you need to write code to check every key press in that text box. You need to verify the typed character's ASCII key value is not less than 48 (the number 0 key) and not greater than 57 (the 9 key). If it's outside these ranges, you simply tell the TextBox control that you have "handled" that character and it doesn't get added to the box.

Here is a chunk of sample code you could add underneath a TextBox KeyPress event to do this:

```
If Asc(e.KeyChar) < 48 Or Asc(e.KeyChar) > 57 Then
    ' Cancel non-numeric characters
    e.Handled = True
End If
```

Another way to do this would be to create a list of allowable characters. Here, for example, we're allowing numbers, spaces, colons, and dashes:

```
Dim strAllowableChars As String
strAllowableChars = "0123456789-: "
' If the character they have entered isn't in our list ...
If InStr(strAllowableChars, e.KeyChar.ToString) = 0 Then
    ' Cancel the character
    e.Handled = True
End If
```

Reversing a String

You can reverse a string very easily using the StrReverse function. Simply provide a string and it'll reverse it for you. For example:

```
Dim strInput As String
strInput = InputBox("Enter your name:")

strInput = StrReverse(strInput)
MessageBox.Show(strInput)
```

Rounding a Number

When working with decimal numbers in your code, you often need to round to the nearest whole number, or two significant digits when dealing with money.

To do this, use the Round function of the System.Math class. Pass a Decimal or Double value to the function as the first argument. By default, it will round to the nearest whole number; however, you can also specify a number of significant figures as a second argument.

For example:

```
Dim MyNumber As Decimal = 58.65183
MyNumber = Math.Round(MyNumber, 1)

MessageBox.Show("Your number rounded to one " & _
    "significant figure is: " & MyNumber)
```

Replacing Text the Easy Way

There's an easy way to replace text within a string with something else: the eternally friendly Replace function.

To use it, simply pass in three arguments: your string, the text you want to find, and the text you want to replace it with. It will return the corrected text. For example:

```
Dim MyString As String
MyString = "Welcome, User - today is {day}"

MyString = Replace(MyString, "{day}", Now.DayOfWeek.ToString)
MessageBox.Show(MyString)
```

Here's another example, showing how we could use it to manipulate a TextBox control, replacing all the line feeds with spaces, turning it all into one long sentence.

```
TextBox1.Text = Replace(TextBox1.Text, vbNewLine, " ")
```

Listing and Setting Fonts

You can list all the currently installed TrueType and OpenType fonts on your system by cycling through the font families in the `System.Drawing.FontFamily.Families` namespace.

For example:

```
Dim MyFontFamily As FontFamily
For Each MyFontFamily In System.Drawing.FontFamily.Families
    ComboBox1.Items.Add(MyFontFamily.Name)
Next
```

You can set the font for a particular control in code by creating a new Font object, then setting it to the control Font property. For example:

```
Dim MyFont As Font
MyFont = New Font("Verdana", 8)
TextBox1.Font = MyFont
```

Trimming a String

When you "trim" a string, you remove any excess spaces from its far left and far right. That means a string such as " Karl " turns into "Karl".

To do this, you use the aptly named Trim function. For example:

```
Dim strData As String
strData = "   This is my data.     "
strData = Trim(strData)

MessageBox.Show(strData)
```

Ending Your Application

To quit your application, you should run the Exit method of the Application object. For example:

```
Application.Exit()
```

Retrieving a Number Using Val

The Val function returns the first identifiable parts of a number from a string. For example, it will return the number 152 from "15 2nd Street" and 50.5 from "50.5g Sodium".

It stops attempting to find a number when it stumbles across a textual character. That means "The customer is 22" returns a simple 0.

Here's an example of Val in use:

```
Dim MyNumber As Double
MyNumber = Val("1052423.94 total assets")

MessageBox.Show("Your number was: " & MyNumber)
```

Resetting the Windows

Although the Visual Studio .NET toolbars and windows are extremely customizable, they're often a little too flexible, which can lead to a messy and unproductive development environment.

To reset all windows to their default positions, launch Visual Studio .NET, select Tools ➤ Options, and click on Reset Window Layout.

You might also want to open your solution folders and delete all files with a .SUO extension. This will erase all your layout options for an individual solution, such as open windows, breakpoints, and caret position.

Capitalizing Your Characters

You can easily capitalize your strings using the UCase and LCase functions. Each converts the passed string into uppercase or lower case appropriately. For example:

```
Dim MyText As String
MyText = "this is my text"
MyText = UCase(MyText)

MessageBox.Show(MyText)
```

Intermediate Tips and Techniques

This section covers the following tips:

- Finding the Application Directory

- Formatting Dates

- Exploring the Command Window

- Creating an MDI Application

- Adding Toolbars

- Reading an XML File

- Using DataSets and XML

- Creating Your Own Icons

- Reading and Writing to Files

- Finding the Last Day of the Month

- Using the Handles Keyword

- Converting Text to Proper Case

- Storing to the Clipboard

- Working with Files

- Highlighting Form Errors

- Using the IIF Function

- Validating an E-Mail Address

- Resetting a Form

Finding the Application Directory

In Visual Basic 6, you had the `App.Path` property to find the path of your current executable file. In VB .NET, you have to uncover this yourself by stripping it from the `Application.ExecutablePath` property.

The following function does that for you. To use it, simply call GetAppPath. A string containing the current application path, with a trailing slash, will be returned.

```
Public Function GetAppPath() As String
    ' Returns the current application path,
    ' with a trailing slash
    Dim strPath As String
    strPath = StrReverse(Application.ExecutablePath)
    strPath = Mid(strPath, InStr(1, strPath, "\"))
    strPath = StrReverse(strPath)
    Return strPath
End Function
```

Here is an example of it in use:

```
MessageBox.Show(GetAppPath)
```

Formatting Dates

The `Format` function of the `Microsoft.VisualBasic` namespace allows you to format dates with ease. Simply pass it your data along with a formatting string, and it'll return the correct implementation.

For example:

```
Dim MyDateString As String
MyDateString = Format(Now(), "dd/MM/yy hh:mm:ss")
' On June 18th 2002 at 02:05:52 pm, this returns:
' 18/06/02 14:05:52
MessageBox.Show(MyDateString)
```

Other popular values to use as options in that second Style argument include:

- *Long Date or D*: Returns a long version of the date according to your system's long date format

- *Short Date or d*: Returns a compact version of the date according to your system's short date format

- *MM*: Returns the current month part of the date as a two-digit number (for example, 06)

- *M*: Returns the current month part of a date, minus any preceding zeros (for example, 6 rather than 06)

- *DD*: Returns the day number of the date (for example, 31)

- *YYYY*: Returns the year of the date (for example, 2002)

- *hh*: Returns the hour of the time (for example, 12)

- *mm*: Returns the minute of the time (for example, 55)

- *ss*: Returns the second of the time (for example, 59)

- *R*: Formats the date and time as Greenwich Mean Time (GMT)

- *The colon and slash*: The colon (:) and slash (/) characters are used to separate parts of the date and time, respectively. These may differ in some locales and may be replaced as appropriate.

- *MMM*: Displays the month abbreviation (for example, Jan)

- *MMMM*: Displays the full month name (for example, January)

- *z*: Displays the timezone offset without a leading zero (for example, -8)

- *ampm*: Returns AM or PM, depending on the time

You can also format numeric strings with the Format function. For more information, look up "Format function" in the Help index.

Exploring the Command Window

The Command window in Visual Studio .NET allows you to both access common commands as well as to evaluate statements, depending on its mode. To open the Command window, select View ➤ Other Windows ➤ Command Window from the menu, or press Ctrl+Alt+A.

The Command mode allows you to access common Visual Studio .NET commands. To enter this mode, type >cmd into the window and press the Enter key. After this, you can access the various menu commands by typing them directly into this window (for example, Window.CloseAllDocuments to close all current documents). Type alias for a full list of alias shortcuts (for example, CloseAll).

The more-useful Immediate mode is used for evaluating and executing statements while your code is paused at runtime. To enter this mode, type immed into the window and press Enter. After this, you can use the window to run commands, set variables, or read values (for example, MyVariable = "Etc").

Press the F1 key while inside the Command window for more information on the commands available.

Creating an MDI Application

MDI stands for *Multiple Document Interface*. It's where you have one "master" form and any number of "child" forms within it, as in Figure 2-1.

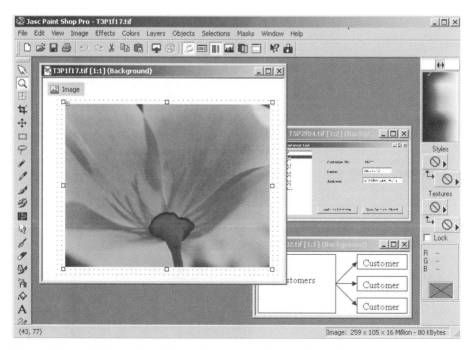

Figure 2-1. An MDI application in application (a.k.a. PaintShop Pro)

To set your "master" form, change its IsMdiContainer property to True. Then, to display a child form within your master form, run code similar to the following, setting the MdiParent to your current Form object:

```
' Code behind Form1, our master Form
Dim MyForm As New Form2()
MyForm.MdiParent = Me
MyForm.Show()
```

You can get a direct reference to the currently active MDI child form, by referencing the ActiveForm property of your master Form object. For example:

```
' Code behind Form1, our master Form
Dim MyForm As Form
MyForm = Me.ActiveForm
MessageBox.Show(MyForm.Text)
```

You can also arrange your children windows by using the LayoutMdi method of your master Form object. You can set this to cascade your child windows, tile them horizontally or vertically, or arrange them as icons. Here is an example of its usage:

```
' Code behind Form1, our master Form
Me.LayoutMdi(MdiLayout.TileHorizontal)
```

Adding Toolbars

Toolbars can appear on any form, including MDI containers. They allow you to add multiple buttons (usually containing images) and have your code respond when clicked.

To add a toolbar, first drag an ImageList control onto your form. This will store any images used in your toolbar. Use the Images property to add multiple images to its store.

Next, drag a Toolbar control onto your form. Change its ImageList property so it references your ImageList. Next, use the Buttons property to add multiple ToolBarButton items to the collection, setting the ImageIndex, Text, and ToolTipText properties as appropriate.

To add code to respond when your user clicks on a button, use the ButtonClick event of the toolbar. Behind this, you'll need to analyze the "e" parameter, which will allow you to determine which button was clicked on. For example:

```
Private Sub ToolBar1_ButtonClick(ByVal sender As System.Object, _
        ByVal e As System.Windows.Forms.ToolBarButtonClickEventArgs) _
        Handles ToolBar1.ButtonClick

Select Case e.Button.Text
    Case "Open"
            ' run open code
    Case "Close"
            ' run close code
    Case "Print"
            ' run print code
End Select

    End Sub
```

Here, we're looking at the button text and running code depending on which button the user clicked on. Another method could be to analyze the index number, running code depending on the button position. For this, you'd look at the value of `MyToolbar.Buttons.IndexOf(e.Button)`.

Reading an XML File

XML is an acronym for *eXtensible Markup Language,* and is essentially a standard for describing structured data in plain text format. Its simplicity and cross-platform abilities have made it a popular method through which to store and transfer data.

Here is a sample XML document, Simple.XML:

```
<?xml version="1.0"?>
  <books>
    <book>
    <author>Moore</author>
```

```
<title>Surviving in the Wild</title>
<price format="sterling">19.99</price>
<pubdate>20/05/2002</pubdate>
</book>
<book>
<author>Briggs</author>
<title>Making Your Money Work</title>
<price format="dollar">31.95</price>
<pubdate>17/02/2003</pubdate>
</book>
</books>
```

The simplest method of reading an XML file in your application is to use the
XmlTextReader class, inspecting each "node" of your document in turn. The
following code demonstrates this, reading a block at a time, then adding the
XmlTextReader properties for that block to an output string:

```
' Open XML for reading from file or URL
Dim MyReader As New Xml.XmlTextReader("c:\simple.xml")
Dim strOutput As String, intCount As Integer

' Read each node of the XML document
Do While MyReader.Read

    ' Check the node type
    Select Case MyReader.NodeType

        ' If the start of an element . . .
        Case Xml.XmlNodeType.Element

            strOutput += "<" & MyReader.Name
```

```
                            ' Read the attributes
                            If MyReader.HasAttributes Then
                                For intCount = 0 To MyReader.AttributeCount - 1
                                    MyReader.MoveToAttribute(intCount)
                                    strOutput += " " & MyReader.Name & "=" & MyReader.Value
                                Next
                            End If
                                  .

                            strOutput += ">"


                    ' If this is an elements' text ...
                    Case Xml.XmlNodeType.Text
                        strOutput += MyReader.Value



                    ' If this is the end of an element ...
                    Case Xml.XmlNodeType.EndElement
                        strOutput += "</" & MyReader.Name & ">"


            End Select
    Loop
```

Using DataSets and XML

Because DataSets typically hold structured data, they're an obvious target for working XML documents. To help simplify this process, two key methods are included with the DataSet component to automatically handle XML for you: WriteXml and ReadXml.

To use these, simply call the methods as so, passing in a relevant filename:

```
Dim MyDataSet As New DataSet()
' do loading and editing here
MyDataSet.WriteXml("c:\mydocument.xml")
MyDataSet.ReadXml("c:\myfile.xml")
```

Creating Your Own Icons

You can create your own icons in VB .NET by selecting Project ➢ Add New Item from the menu, then choosing Icon File and clicking Open. From here, use the drawing tools to create your perfect ICO file.

To change a Windows form to use this icon, click the ellipsis next to its Icon property in the Properties window. Then, navigate to your project folder and select the ICO file you just created.

Reading and Writing to Files

Reading and writing to simple text files is perhaps one of the most common tasks in the programming world. The old VB6 way of doing this is now defunct, and a new .NET method is here, involving objects within the System.IO namespace.

The following functions help simplify the process of reading and writing to files. The first is called ReadTextFromFile and accepts a filename as a parameter. It returns the text from the specified file:

```
Public Function ReadTextFromFile(ByVal Filename As String) As String
    ' Returns text from the specified file

    On Error Resume Next

    Dim strFileText As String

    ' Open the file and launch StreamReader object
    Dim MyReader As System.IO.StreamReader = System.IO.File.OpenText(Filename)
    ' Read all text through to the end
    strFileText = MyReader.ReadToEnd
```

```
' Close the stream
MyReader.Close()

' Return data
Return strFileText
```

```
End Function
```

The second code snippet is a method called WriteTextToFile, and accepts a filename and the text to write as parameters:

```
Public Sub WriteTextToFile(ByVal Filename As String, ByVal Text As String)
    ' Writes the passed Text into the specified file

    ' Create file and StreamWriter object
    Dim MyWriter As System.IO.StreamWriter = System.IO.File.CreateText(Filename)
    ' Write text to the stream
    MyWriter.Write(Text)
    ' Close the stream
    MyWriter.Close()

End Sub
```

Here is an example of each of these code snippets in action:

```
WriteTextToFile("c:\myfile.txt", TextBox1.Text)
MessageBox.Show(ReadTextFromFile("c:\myfile.txt"))
```

Finding the Last Day of the Month

When creating business applications, it's often useful to find out the last day of a particular month. The following function enables you to do this: simply pass in a month and year, and it will return the number of days in that month:

```
Public Function LastDayOfMonth(ByVal MonthYear As String) As Integer

    ' Returns the number of days in the specified month,
    ' MonthYear parameter should be in the format MM/YYYY

    Return DatePart("d", DateAdd("d", -1, DateAdd("m", 1, _
            DateAdd("d", -DatePart("d", MonthYear) + 1, MonthYear))))

End Function
```

This function works by essentially adding one month to your existing date, then moving back one day and returning the day number. Here's an example of its usage:

```
Dim intLastDay As Integer = LastDayOfMonth("2/2004")
MessageBox.Show("The last day of February 2004 is: " & intLastDay)
```

Using the Handles Keyword

The Handles keyword can be used to make a method run whenever a particular event occurs, provided that the method arguments exactly match those of your event.

For example, this UpdateScreen method handles the MyCustomerObject Change event, which contains no arguments:

```
Public Sub UpdateScreen() Handles MyCustomerObject.Change
    ' code goes here
End Sub
```

Another popular example of the Handles keyword is in reacting to button click events, like so:

```
Private Sub Button1_Click(ByVal sender As System.Object, _
        ByVal e As System.EventArgs) Handles Button1.Click
    ' code goes here
End Sub
```

Most of the time, this Handles code is generated for you. However, knowing you can add it yourself opens new avenues; for example, you could add multiple methods that react to one event, or perhaps one method that handles multiple events.

This also means you can change the name of methods such as Button1_Click to, perhaps, "OK" or "CancelEntry". Its name doesn't matter; the Handles keyword does.

Converting Text to Proper Case

You have the UCase and LCase functions to appropriately case all the characters in a string. However, often you need to just capitalize the first letter of every word in your string. You do this using the StrConv function, instructing it to *Conv*ert your *Str*ing to "ProperCase".

The following sample demonstrates it in action:

```
Dim MyString As String
MyString = "tHis iS my POORLy casEd STrInG!"
MyString = StrConv(MyString, VbStrConv.ProperCase)

MessageBox.Show(MyString)
' returns: This Is My Poorly Cased String!
```

Storing to the Clipboard

We've all worked with the Windows clipboard before, whether to copy a picture from Adobe PhotoShop over to PowerPoint, or simply cut and paste a bundle of text in Microsoft Word.

And adding clipboard integration to your own application isn't as difficult as it sounds. You simply need to use the Clipboard object. To set data to the clipboard, simply pass it as a parameter to the SetDataObject method, like so:

```
Clipboard.SetDataObject(TextBox1.Text)
```

You can also retrieve data from the clipboard, using the GetDataObject.GetData function. Here, we're retrieving simple text from the clipboard, but you could use the GetDataObject.GetDataPresent function to find out what's on the clipboard, then retrieve and manipulate anything from sound files to bitmaps:

```
TextBox1.Text = Clipboard.GetDataObject.GetData(DataFormats.Text)
```

Working with Files

If you're looking to manipulate files using the .NET Framework base classes, you should be heading to the System.IO.File class, where you'll find functions to delete files, copy files, check file attributes, and much more.

Here is a commented example demonstrating the most common uses of the File class:

```
Dim objFile As System.IO.File

' Check for existence of a file
Dim blnExists As Boolean
blnExists = objFile.Exists("c:\unlikely.txt")

' Delete a file
objFile.Delete("c:\goodbye.txt")

' Copy a file
objFile.Copy("c:\source.txt", "e:\destination.txt")

' Move a file
objFile.Move("c:\oldlocation.txt", "e:\newlocation.txt")

' Check whether a file is read-only
Dim blnReadOnly As Boolean
blnReadOnly = objFile.GetAttributes("c:\readonly.txt").ReadOnly

' Check whether a file is hidden
Dim blnHidden As Boolean
blnHidden = objFile.GetAttributes("c:\hidden.txt").Hidden

' Check a file creation date
Dim datCreated As Date
datCreated = objFile.GetCreationTime("c:\created.txt")
```

It's worth noting that you don't have to create a new File object to use this functionality. The File class consists of what are known as shared methods, meaning that you can call them directly without having to instantiate a new object. This means you can delete a file with one direct line of code, like this:

```
System.IO.File.Delete("c:\goodbye.txt")
```

Highlighting Form Errors

The ErrorProvider control provides a great way of providing visual user feedback. If a problem occurs—perhaps your user has entered an incorrect customer number into a text box—you can use the ErrorProvider to add a flashing error icon next to the control, along with a Tool Tip describing the error.

The following code demonstrates use of the ErrorProvider in its simplest form. (The code assumes that you have a Windows form containing an instance of the ErrorProvider control, called ErrorProvider1 and a TextBox control called TextBox1.)

```
' Set an error on a control
ErrorProvider1.SetError(TextBox1, "Invalid Phone Number - Try Again")

' Remove the error
ErrorProvider1.SetError(TextBox1, "")
```

The first line here sets the error. This results in a blinking error icon to the right of the control, which displays the error as its Tool Tip. (By default, the blinking stops as soon as you view the error message.) The second line here removes the error flag.

It's worth noting that each of these settings—icon, blink style and rate, alignment—are completely customizable. Simply edit the ErrorProvider control via the Properties window. Also, the ErrorProvider does a particularly good job working with data bound forms. Check out "ErrorProvider component, overview" in the Help index for more information on this feature.

Using the IIF Function

IIF is a function that enables you to essentially compress mini If-Then statements into just a single line of code, thereby reducing clutter in the code window.

The IIF function requires three parameters to work properly: first, an expression; second, an object to return if the expression evaluates to True; and, third, an object to return if the expression evaluates to False.

Here's a demonstration of the IIF function in action, returning an "OVERNIGHT SHIPPING" string if the order amount is greater than 500:

```
Dim intOrderAmount As Integer = 10000
Dim strOrderPriority As String

strOrderPriority = IIf(intOrderAmount > 500, _
            "OVERNIGHT SHIPPING", "REGULAR DELIVERY")
```

Validating an Email Address

When creating Web and mobile applications, the RegularExpressionValidator control can help you validate whether a particular email address is correct. However, this provides you with only a simple Yes or No. If you want to give your user more information, as is common practice on many sites, you need to write a custom function to handle the situation.

The following code is just that function. It's called IsEmailAddress and accepts an email address as a string, plus an optional string by reference. If the email address is valid, a True is returned by the function. If it's invalid, however, a False is returned and the string variable passed in by reference is set to an appropriate descriptive error message (saying, for example, that the email address contains too many "@" symbols):

```
Public Function IsEmailAddress(ByVal EmailAddress As String, _
        Optional ByRef RejectReason As String = "") As Boolean

    ' Returns a True if the passed EmailAddress is valid,
    ' otherwise returns a False plus passes the reject
    ' reason back to the RejectReason argument

    Dim strPrefix As String
    Dim strSuffix As String
    Dim strMiddle As String
    Dim intCharCount As Integer
    Dim strBuffer As String

    ' Trim excess spacing
    EmailAddress = Trim(EmailAddress)

    ' Reject short addresses
    If Len(EmailAddress) < 8 Then
        RejectReason = "Your address is too short"
        Return False
    End If

    ' Reject addresses with no @ sign
    If InStr(EmailAddress, "@") = 0 Then
        RejectReason = "Your address doesn't contain the @ sign"
        Return False
    End If

    ' Reject addresses with too many @ signs
    If InStr(InStr(EmailAddress, "@") + 1, EmailAddress, "@") <> 0 Then
        RejectReason = "Your address contains too many @ signs"
        Return False
    End If
```

```vb
' Reject addresses without a period
If InStr(EmailAddress, ".") = 0 Then
    RejectReason = "Your address doesn't contain a period"
    Return False
End If


' Check ordering and length formatting
If InStr(EmailAddress, "@") = 1 Or InStr(EmailAddress, "@") = _
    Len(EmailAddress) Or InStr(EmailAddress, ".") = 1 Or _
    InStr(EmailAddress, ".") = Len(EmailAddress) Then
    RejectReason = "Your address is badly formatted"
    Return False
End If


' Check for invalid characters
For intCharCount = 1 To Len(EmailAddress)
    strBuffer = Mid(EmailAddress, intCharCount, 1)
    If Not (LCase(strBuffer) Like "[a-z]" Or strBuffer = "@" Or _
            strBuffer = "." Or strBuffer = "-" Or strBuffer = "_" Or _
            IsNumeric(strBuffer)) Then
        RejectReason = "Your address contains invalid characters"
        Return False
    End If
Next


' Check length of suffix
strBuffer = Microsoft.VisualBasic.Right(EmailAddress, 4)
If InStr(strBuffer, ".") = 0 Then
    If Len(strBuffer) > 4 Then
        RejectReason = "Your address suffix is too long"
        Return False
    Else
        RejectReason = Nothing
        Return True
    End If
End If


' Retrieve and check length of suffix
If Microsoft.VisualBasic.Left(strBuffer, 1) = "." Then _
        strBuffer = Microsoft.VisualBasic.Right(strBuffer, 3)
If Microsoft.VisualBasic.Left(Microsoft.VisualBasic.Right( _
        strBuffer, 3), 1) = "." Then strBuffer = _
        Microsoft.VisualBasic.Right(strBuffer, 2)
```

```
If Microsoft.VisualBasic.Left(Microsoft.VisualBasic.Right( _
        strBuffer, 2), 1) = "." Then strBuffer = _
        Microsoft.VisualBasic.Right(strBuffer, 1)


If Len(strBuffer) < 2 Then
    RejectReason = "Your address suffix is too short"
    Return False
End If


' Otherwise, success!
RejectReason = Nothing
Return True
```

```
End Function
```

You might use this function like so:

```
Dim strAddress As String, blnValid As Boolean, strRejectReason As String
strAddress = InputBox("Enter your e-mail address:")
blnValid = IsEmailAddress(strAddress, strRejectReason)

MessageBox.Show("Is Valid? " & blnValid & " - " & strRejectReason)
```

Resetting a Form

If you've created a data entry style Windows form that needs "resetting" with each addition, the code to clear the TextBox controls, uncheck the CheckBox controls (and so on) can all get a little repetitive—particularly if you have to write it for multiple forms.

That's where the following method could prove useful. Simply pass in a form as a parameter, and it'll reset the main data entry controls: TextBox, CheckBox, and ComboBox. You could also easily extend it to cater for RadioButton, ListBox, CheckedListBox, DomainUpDown, NumericUpDown, MonthCalendar, and DateTimePicker controls, too. To ensure flexibility, this subroutine automatically bypasses all controls with "skip" somewhere in the Tag property.

Here's the code:

```
Public Sub ResetForm(ByVal FormToReset As Form)

    ' Resets the main data entry controls on the passed FormToReset

    Dim objControl As Control

    ' Loop round every control on the form
    For Each objControl In FormToReset.Controls

        ' Check we don't need to skip this control
        If InStr(objControl.Tag, "skip", CompareMethod.Text) = 0 Then

            If TypeOf (objControl) Is System.Windows.Forms.TextBox Then
                objControl.Text = ""   ' Clear TextBox
            ElseIf TypeOf (objControl) Is System.Windows.Forms.CheckBox Then
                Dim objCheckBox As System.Windows.Forms.CheckBox = objControl
                objCheckBox.Checked = False ' Uncheck CheckBox
            ElseIf TypeOf (objControl) Is System.Windows.Forms.ComboBox Then
                Dim objComboBox As System.Windows.Forms.ComboBox = objControl
                objComboBox.SelectedIndex = -1 ' Deselect any ComboBox entry
            End If

        End If
    Next
End Sub
```

You could use this function like so:

```
ResetForm(Me)
```

Advanced Tips and Techniques

This section covers the following tips:

- Introducing the VS .NET Command Prompt

- Using Keywords in Your Code

- Declaring Static Variables

- Checking for a Leap Year

- Creating a GUID

- Generating OLE DB Strings with Ease

- Checking for a Whole Number

- Read the Command Line Parameters

- Getting Special Folder Locations

- Checking for a Previous Instance

- Saving to the Registry

- Using COM Objects

- Turning a Recordset into a DataSet

- Exposing .NET to the COM World

- Storing Often-Used Code

- Saving Time with Macros

- Using Simple Encryption

- Encrypting a File

- Generating Memorable Passwords

- Printing from Your Program

- Creating and Sorting Arrays

- Using the Special Array Functions

- Collections in .NET

- Finding MTS and MSMQ

- Fine-Tuning Your ASP.NET Applications

Introducing the VS .NET Command Prompt

As you work through the Visual Studio .NET documentation, you'll start to realize just how many tools require you to run them from the command line for full control.

However, setting the proper directory and locating the exact EXE file required via the command prompt can prove troublesome. Thankfully, Visual Studio .NET comes with a feature that automatically sets up a command prompt with all the correct environment variables ready for you to use.

To access this, select Start ➤ Programs ➤ Microsoft Visual Studio .NET ➤ Visual Studio .NET Tools ➤ Visual Studio .NET Command Prompt.

Using Keywords in Your Code

You can use keywords as variable names in your code by enclosing them in square brackets, as so:

```
Dim [Loop] As Boolean
[Loop] = True
```

Alternatively, you can refer to a keyword-named variable without the need for square brackets by preceding it with its full, qualifying namespace.

Declaring Static Variables

VB .NET programmers often overlook static variables. They allow you to declare a variable in a subroutine and manipulate its value; when the subroutine exits, the variable disappears from scope, but its value isn't lost. Rather, it's preserved for the next time you enter the subroutine.

To use this functionality, simply use the Static keyword when declaring your subroutine variable. For example:

```
Private Sub Button1_Click( ... ) Handles Button1.Click

    ' Declare static variable
    Static intClickCount As Integer
    ' Increment counter
    intClickCount += 1
    ' Display current value
    MessageBox.Show("You've clicked me " & intClickCount & " time(s)!")

End Sub
```

Checking for a Leap Year

In the past, you'd have to write your own complex routines to check whether it was a leap year. However, the System.DateTime namespace now contains its own IsLeapYear function. Simply pass it a four-digit year and it'll return a True or False as appropriate.

For example:

```
Dim blnIsLeapYear As Boolean
blnIsLeapYear = System.DateTime.IsLeapYear(2004)

MessageBox.Show("Is 2004 a leap year? " & blnIsLeapYear)
```

Creating a GUID

A GUID is a globally unique identifier, a 128-bit integer typically used when you need to ensure you have a completely unique value. A GUID is generated based on numerous varying factors, and the likelihood of two matching GUIDs ever being generated is phenomenally low.

To generate a GUID using the .NET Framework, you need to use the NewGuid function of the `System.Guid` namespace. The following GetGUID function does this for you, returning the GUID as a string:

```
Public Function GetGUID() As String
    ' Returns a new GUID
    Return System.Guid.NewGuid.ToString
End Function
```

You can use this function like so:

```
Dim MyGUID As String
MyGUID = GetGUID()
```

Generating OLE DB Strings with Ease

You're often required to generate OLE DB connection strings for use in your code; however, it's never an easy task. You can either rummage through the documentation and attempt to piece together your own, or use the VS .NET Server Explorer to make a connection and then inspect its properties.

One handy alternative, however, is to type out the following code into Notepad, saving the file with a .VBS extension. Whenever you need a connection string in the future, simply launch the file. It'll run your VBScript, visually prompt you for the database details, and then offer the final connection string for you to copy from an InputBox:

```
Dim objDataLinks, strRetVal
Set objDataLinks = CreateObject("DataLinks")

On Error Resume Next ' ignore cancel

strRetVal = objDataLinks.PromptNew

On Error Goto 0

If Not IsEmpty(strRetVal) Then

InputBox "Your Connection String is listed below.", _
    "OLE DB Connection String", strRetVal

End If

Set objDataLinks = Nothing
```

Checking for a Whole Number

It's often useful to check whether a number your user has entered is a whole number (such as 16) or a decimal (such as 5.2 or 182.302).

The following function determines this for you. It's called IsWholeNumber and accepts an object as the Number argument, returning a True if it is whole:

```
Public Function IsWholeNumber(ByVal Number As Object) As Boolean

    ' Accepts a number and returns True or False

    ' Raise error is Number is not number
    If Not IsNumeric(Number) Then Throw New System.ArgumentOutOfRangeException()

    ' Return a True if Number minus integer version of number equals zero
    Return (Number - CInt(Number)) = 0

End Function
```

This function could be used like so:

```
Dim blnWhole As Boolean
blnWhole = IsWholeNumber(4.5)
blnWhole = IsWholeNumber(17)
```

Read the Command Line Parameters

Command line parameters can be incredibly useful. They allow users or other applications to pass startup information to your program. For example, if your program was called myapp.exe, they might run the following:

```
myapp.exe /nodialogs
```

Here, we have one command line parameter, "/nodialogs". In VB6, we could read this using the Command property. In VB .NET, this has been replaced with the `System.Environment.GetCommandLineArgs` function, which returns an array of the passed parameters.

You can read these parameters like so:

```
Dim MyStartupArguments() As String, intCount As Integer
MyStartupArguments = System.Environment.GetCommandLineArgs

For intCount = 0 To UBound(MyStartupArguments)
    MessageBox.Show(MyStartupArguments(intCount).ToString)
Next
```

Getting Special Folder Locations

It's often useful to know the location of a particular folder. For example, you
might want to know where the Favorites folder is, so you can add a link to your
company Web site. Or you may need to know where the Desktop directory is, so
you can save a file directly to it.

For this, the .NET Framework provides the
`System.Environment.GetFolderPath` function. Simply call this, passing in
a SpecialFolder enumeration. This will then return a string containing the appropriate path.

For example:

```
Dim MyFolderPath As String
MyFolderPath = System.Environment.GetFolderPath( _
            Environment.SpecialFolder.Favorites)
MessageBox.Show(MyFolderPath)
```

Checking for a Previous Instance

There are times when it's useful to check whether another instance of your application is running. For example, when starting up your program, you may want to
check whether another version is already running in the background and, if it is,
give that instance the focus.

In Visual Basic 6, you had the `App.PrevInstance` property to do this. In
VB .NET, we need to check whether the current process is running more than
once. That's what our code does here, encapsulated in the PrevInstance function.
It returns a True if your application is already running on the same machine:

```
Public Function PrevInstance() As Boolean
    If UBound(Diagnostics.Process.GetProcessesByName _
        (Diagnostics.Process.GetCurrentProcess.ProcessName)) > 0 Then
        Return True
    Else
        Return False
    End If
End Function
```

You might use this code like so:

```
If PrevInstance() = True Then
    ' Get all previous instances
    Dim Processes() As Process
    Processes = Diagnostics.Process.GetProcessesByName( _
        Diagnostics.Process.GetCurrentProcess.ProcessName)
    ' Activate the first instance
    AppActivate(Processes(0).Id)
    ' Exit the current instance
    Application.Exit()
End If
```

Saving to the Registry

The registry is a great place to store your application settings. It's used by almost every Windows application and you can view its entire contents by selecting Start ➤ Run and launching REGEDIT.EXE.

To manipulate the registry in your code, you need to use objects inside the `Microsoft.Win32` namespace. To simplify this process, the following functions encapsulate all the required code for you, allowing you to read from or write to the registry in just a line of code.

The first function is called ReadFromRegistry and accepts a location and a name of the key to retrieve:

```
Public Function ReadFromRegistry(ByVal Location As String, ByVal Name As String)

    ' Returns a value from the registry

    Dim MyKey As Microsoft.Win32.RegistryKey
    MyKey = Microsoft.Win32.Registry.CurrentUser.OpenSubKey(Location)
    ReadFromRegistry = MyKey.GetValue(Name)
    MyKey.Close()

End Function
```

The second block of code is a method called WriteToRegistry. It accepts a location, key name, and the actual data to store with the key, as parameters:

```
Public Sub WriteToRegistry(ByVal Location As String, _
    ByVal Name As String, ByVal Data As String)

    ' Writes a value to the registry

    Dim MyKey As Microsoft.Win32.RegistryKey
    MyKey = Microsoft.Win32.Registry.CurrentUser.CreateSubKey(Location)
    MyKey.SetValue(Name, Data)
    MyKey.Close()

End Sub
```

You could use the preceding functions as follows:

```
WriteToRegistry("Software\White Cliff\MyApp", "Username", "John")
MessageBox.Show(ReadFromRegistry("Software\White Cliff\MyApp", "Username"))
```

Using COM Objects

Although .NET doesn't use COM internally, that doesn't mean you have to throw out all those third-party components or handy business objects you built back in the VB6 days. You can still use them all, easily, in the .NET environment.

To add a COM reference to your Visual Studio project, select Project ➢ Add Reference from the menu. Choose the COM tab, highlight a component, and then click on Select. After you click on OK, Visual Studio .NET will run the TLBIMP.EXE (Type Library Importer) tool, which creates a .NET DLL from your COM DLL Type Library and references it in your project. This .NET DLL uses a service called COM Interop (System.Runtime.Interop) to call your old COM objects.

After this, you can use that COM component just as you would a regular .NET object. For example, after referencing the Microsoft Word 10.0 Object Library, the following code could be run to use the component:

```
Dim MyWord As New Word.Application(), MyDoc As Word.Document
MyWord.Visible = True
MyDoc = MyWord.Documents.Add()
MyDoc.SaveAs("c:\hello.doc")
```

You can also utilize ActiveX controls in your .NET applications by right-clicking on the toolbox, selecting "Customize Toolbox" and then selecting a COM component. This works in much the same way as referencing a COM DLL.

However, be aware that, due to the extra processing going on here, using COM objects in .NET may result in a slight performance dip.

Turning a Recordset into a DataSet

Looking to use some of those frilly ADO.NET DataSet features, but don't quite fancy recoding your entire ADO-based application at this stage? Thankfully, it's easy to move your Recordset data into an ADO.NET DataSet, with a little help from the DataAdapter class.

For this to work, you'll need to already have your ADO code working in .NET. Whether you've upgraded an existing VB6 project or copied and pasted your old code, it should all run without problems, and you should have a reference to the Microsoft ActiveX Data Objects (ADO) COM component (if not, see the "Using COM Objects" section).

Next, to turn your Recordset into a table in the DataSet, simply create a DataAdapter object and run the Fill method, passing in your DataSet, Recordset, and a table name as arguments.

Here's a function that performs the conversion for you, demonstrating the exact process:

```
Public Sub FillDataSetFromRecordset(ByVal SourceRecordset As ADODB.Recordset, _
    ByVal DataSetToFill As System.Data.DataSet, ByVal TableName As String)

    ' Takes an ADO RecordSet and places its data
    ' into an ADO.NET DataSet, as TableName

    Dim dapDA As System.Data.OleDb.OleDbDataAdapter
    dapDA.Fill(DataSetToFill, SourceRecordset, TableName)

End Sub
```

Exposing .NET to the COM World

Just as you can utilize your COM objects in the .NET world, you can also do the reverse: use .NET objects in the COM world.

Why would you want to do this? Good question, although it's not unimaginable to think of applications that can't be immediately migrated—perhaps due to sheer volume or obscure incompatibilities—though which could still benefit from the new technology.

To do this, you'll need to use RegAsm.exe, the Assembly Registration Tool. It's a command line application that takes your DLL as an argument and registers or deregisters it for use under COM. A further parameter of `/tlb:myname.tlb` to RegAsm.exe will also generate a type library, enabling you to early bind in applications such as Visual Basic 6.

To learn more about exposing your .NET components to COM, look up "exposing .NET Framework components to COM" under the "Visual Basic and Related" Help index.

Storing Often-Used Code

There's an easy way to store often-used code and templates in VS .NET. Simply drag the code from your code window over to the General tab of the toolbox. When you need to use it again, simply drag and drop back into your code window. And, best of all, these snippets persist from project to project, saving even more development time.

Saving Time with Macros

If you have a repetitive task that you often perform in the Visual Studio .NET development environment, you might want to consider creating it as a macro and running it when you require that functionality once more.

For example, you might create a macro to print all the open documents, add customized revision markers, change project properties to standardize your development, or insert common routines.

You can get highly in-depth with macros, writing code to perform almost any task. However, the simplest method is to simply "record" your activities and have Visual Studio .NET write the code for you. You can do this by selecting Tools ➤ Macros ➤ Record TemporaryMacro. To play it back, select Run TemporaryMacro, or press Ctrl+Shift+P.

For more information on recording macros, look up "macros, recording" in the Help index. For more information on macros in general, look up "macros, Visual Studio .NET" in the Help index.

Using Simple Encryption

There are times when you want to very simply encrypt a small piece of text to store in the registry, a database, or file, but you don't want the overhead or complexity of a Government-standard encryption technique.

A much simpler encryption method is required, and the following function provides just that. It's called Crypt: pass it your plain text and it'll encrypt it into a completely unrecognizable string; pass it your encrypted text and it'll decrypt it. Just the ticket, and all in fewer than fifteen lines of code:

```
Public Function Crypt(ByVal Text As String) As String

    ' Encrypts or decrypts the passed Text

    Dim strTempChar As String, i As Integer

    For i = 1 To Len(Text)
        If Asc(Mid(Text, i, 1)) < 128 Then
            strTempChar = Asc(Mid(Text, i, 1)) + 128
        ElseIf Asc(Mid(Text, i, 1)) > 128 Then
            strTempChar = Asc(Mid(Text, i, 1)) - 128
        End If
        Mid(Text, i, 1) = Chr(strTempChar)
    Next

    Return Text

End Function
```

You could use this function like so:

```
Dim MyText As String

' Encrypt
MyText = "Karl Moore"
MyText = Crypt(MyText)
MessageBox.Show(MyText)

' Decrypt
MyText = Crypt(MyText)
MessageBox.Show(MyText)
```

Encrypting a File

Simple encryption is useful for storing settings and usernames. But, if you're dealing with particularly sensitive information, such as passwords or credit card details, you need to take further steps.

The System.Security.Cryptography namespace includes a number of classes designed to help you securely encrypt and decrypt your data. Here, you'll be able to use objects that are designed to work with everything from MD5 to RC2, Rijndael to SHA1.

One of the most popular cryptography algorithms, however, is DES (the Data Encryption Standard). The following functions help simplify some of the functionality in the DES-related classes, allowing you to perform one of the most common tasks: encrypting and decrypting a file.

Some pointers before you get started. To encrypt a file using a symmetric algorithm such as DES, you need two things: a secret key and an initialization vector (IV). These are the two elements that, combined, both "lock" and "unlock" your data. They're stored as sixteen-bit byte arrays and can be automatically generated for you.

To generate a random key, use the GenerateKey function. It'll return a byte array. To generate a random IV, use the GenerateIV function. This will also return a byte array.

To encrypt data to a file, call the SaveEncryptedFile method. It accepts four parameters: the key byte array, the IV byte array, your data as a string, and the final filename.

To decrypt a file, use the LoadEncryptedFile function. It takes three parameters: the key byte array, the IV byte array, and your filename. The function returns the file contents as a string.

Here are the core encryption functions you'll want to use:

```
Imports System.Security.Cryptography
' You must first 'import' the System.Security.Cryptography
' namespace, either via the Project Properties
' or by placing this Imports statement above your class/module

    Public Function GenerateKey() As Byte()
        ' Returns a random key to use
        Dim objDES As New System.Security.Cryptography.DESCryptoServiceProvider()
        objDES.GenerateKey()
        Return objDES.Key
    End Function
```

```
Public Function GenerateIV() As Byte()
    ' Returns a random IV to use
    Dim objDES As New System.Security.Cryptography.DESCryptoServiceProvider()
    objDES.GenerateIV()
    Return objDES.IV
End Function

Public Sub SaveEncryptedFile(ByVal Key() As Byte, ByVal IV() As Byte, _
    ByVal Data As String, ByVal Filename As String)

    ' Create new file stream
    Dim objFileStream As New System.IO.FileStream(Filename, _
        System.IO.FileMode.Create, System.IO.FileAccess.Write)

    ' Convert data to byte array
    Dim bytInput As Byte() = New _
        System.Text.UnicodeEncoding().GetBytes(Data)

    ' Create new DES instance
    Dim objDES As New DESCryptoServiceProvider()
    ' Sets Key and Initialization Vector
    objDES.Key = Key
    objDES.IV = IV

    ' Create a DES encrypter from this object
    Dim objDESEncrypt As ICryptoTransform = objDES.CreateEncryptor()

    ' Create a CryptoStream object that encrypts stream using DES
    Dim objCryptStream As New CryptoStream(objFileStream, _
        objDESEncrypt, CryptoStreamMode.Write)

    ' Write to DES-encrypted file
    objCryptStream.Write(bytInput, 0, bytInput.Length)

    ' Close streams
    objCryptStream.Close()
    objFileStream.Close()

End Sub

Public Function LoadEncryptedFile(ByVal Key() As Byte, _
    ByVal IV() As Byte, ByVal Filename As String) As String
```

```
                      ' Create new file stream
                      Dim objFileStream As New System.IO.FileStream(Filename, _
                          System.IO.FileMode.Open, System.IO.FileAccess.Read)

                      ' Create DES decryptor
                      Dim objDES As New DESCryptoServiceProvider()
                      ' Sets Key and Initialization Vector
                      objDES.Key = Key
                      objDES.IV = IV

                      ' Create a DES decryptor from this object
                      Dim objDESDecrypt As ICryptoTransform = objDES.CreateDecryptor()

                      ' Create a CryptoStream object to read and DES decrypt incoming bytes
                      Dim objCryptStream As New CryptoStream(objFileStream, objDESDecrypt, _
                          CryptoStreamMode.Read)

                      ' Return decrypted results
                      LoadEncryptedFile = New System.IO.StreamReader(objCryptStream, _
                          New System.Text.UnicodeEncoding()).ReadToEnd()

                      ' Close streams
                      objCryptStream.Close()
                      objFileStream.Close()

                  End Function
```

Here's how you might use these functions from within your application:

```
' Generate keys and IVs
Dim bytKey() As Byte = GenerateKey()
Dim bytIV() As Byte = GenerateIV()

' Save encrypted data
SaveEncryptedFile(bytKey, bytIV, "Hello World!", "c:\encrypted.txt")

' Read encrypted data
Dim strData As String
strData = LoadEncryptedFile(bytKey, bytIV, "c:\encrypted.txt")
MessageBox.Show(strData)
```

```
' Store keys and IVs as strings,
' perhaps for saving to a binary file or DB
Dim strKey As String, strIV As String
strKey = New System.Text.UnicodeEncoding().GetString(bytKey)
strIV = New System.Text.UnicodeEncoding().GetString(bytIV)


' Convert back to bytes
bytKey = New System.Text.UnicodeEncoding().GetBytes(strKey)
bytIV = New System.Text.UnicodeEncoding().GetBytes(strIV)
```

Generating Memorable Passwords

Generating automatic passwords for your users is a common programming scenario. However, due to the techniques typically employed, most autogenerated passwords end up looking like *YPSWW9441*—which although highly secure, is also completely unmemorable.

The following function generates a password using friendly alternating consonants and vowels, making for much more memorable passwords. Asking the function to generate a five-character password, for example, may result in *BONES* or *LAMOT*.

To use this function, call GeneratePassword, passing in the length of your desired password. The final password will be returned as a string:

```
Dim objRandom As New System.Random(System.DateTime.Now.Ticks _
    Mod System.Int32.MaxValue)


Public Function GeneratePassword(ByVal Length As Integer) As String

    ' Creates a memorable password of the specified Length

    Dim blnOnVowel As Boolean
    Dim strTempLetter As String
    Dim strPassword As String
    Dim intCount As Integer

    For intCount = 1 To Length

        If blnOnVowel = False Then

            ' Choose a nice consonant - no C, X, Z, or Q
            strTempLetter = Choose(GetRandomNumber(1, 17), _
                "B", "D", "F", "G", "H", "J", "K", "L", "M", _
                "N", "P", "R", "S", "T", "V", "W", "Y")
```

519

```
                ' Append it to the password string
                strPassword += strTempLetter

                ' Swich to vowel mode
                blnOnVowel = True

            Else

                ' Choose a vowel
                strTempLetter = Choose(GetRandomNumber(1, 5), _
                    "A", "E", "I", "O", "U")

                ' Append it to the password string
                strPassword += strTempLetter

                ' Switch back again, ready for next loop round
                blnOnVowel = False

            End If
        Next

        Return strPassword

End Function

Public Function GetRandomNumber(Optional ByVal Low As Integer = 1, _
    Optional ByVal High As Integer = 100) As Integer
    ' Returns a random number,
    ' between the optional Low and High parameters
    Return objRandom.Next(Low, High + 1)
End Function
```

You could use the GeneratePassword function like so:

```
Dim MyPassword As String
MyPassword = GeneratePassword(5)
MessageBox.Show(MyPassword)
```

Printing from Your Program

You can print from your program in a number of ways. One option, for example, is to automate Microsoft Word, edit a document in code, then programmatically print it out.

However, if you're looking to print directly from your application, the .NET Framework provides a number of classes to help you in the `System.Drawing.Printing` namespace.

The core class here is `PrintDocument`. At its simplest, printing involves instantiating a `PrintDocument` object, setting its properties, and calling the `Print` method. With each page to be printed, the PrintDocument raises a PrintPage event, to which you need to add your own printing logic. Other key classes in the same `Printing` namespace include `PrinterSettings`, `PageSettings`, and `PrintPreviewControl`.

As you can imagine, this is a large area and can get relatively complex. The following class attempts to simplify one of the most common uses: the printing of a simple text file. Simply add the following class code to your project and use as directed.

It's worth noting that this class actually *works,* as opposed to the less-functional TextFilePrintDocument class bundled by Microsoft in the Windows Forms QuickStart tutorials, which cuts out as soon as a blank line is encountered in the passed text file.

```
Public Class TextFilePrint

    ' Inherits all the functionality of a PrintDocument
    Inherits Printing.PrintDocument

    ' Private variables to hold default font and stream
    Private fntPrintFont As Font

    Private objStream As IO.StreamReader

    Public Sub New(ByVal FileStream As IO.StreamReader)
        ' Sets the file stream
        MyBase.New()
        Me.objStream = FileStream
    End Sub

    Protected Overrides Sub OnBeginPrint(ByVal ev As Printing.PrintEventArgs)
        ' Sets the default font
        MyBase.OnBeginPrint(ev)
        fntPrintFont = New Font("Times New Roman", 12)
    End Sub
```

```
Public Property Font() As Font
    ' Allows the user to override the default font
    Get
        Return fntPrintFont
    End Get
    Set(ByVal Value As Font)
        fntPrintFont = Value
    End Set
End Property

Protected Overrides Sub OnPrintPage(ByVal ev As Printing.PrintPageEventArgs)
    ' Provides the print logic for our document

    MyBase.OnPrintPage(ev)

    Dim sngLinesPerPage As Single = 0
    Dim yPos As Single = 0
    Dim intCount As Integer = 0
    Dim sglLeftMargin As Single = ev.MarginBounds.Left
    Dim sglTopMargin As Single = ev.MarginBounds.Top
    Dim strLine As String

    ' Calculate number of lines per page, using MarginBounds
    sngLinesPerPage = ev.MarginBounds.Height / _
        fntPrintFont.GetHeight(ev.Graphics)

    ' Read a line from our file stream
    strLine = objStream.ReadLine()

    ' Loop around while we have data in our line
    ' and our counter is less than the number of lines per page
    While (intCount < sngLinesPerPage And Not (strLine Is Nothing))

        ' Position our line
        yPos = sglTopMargin + (intCount * fntPrintFont.GetHeight(ev.Graphics))

        ' Draw our text onto the print document
        ev.Graphics.DrawString(strLine, fntPrintFont, _
            Brushes.Black, sglLeftMargin, yPos, New StringFormat())

        ' Increment the counter
        intCount += 1
```

```
            ' If the counter is less than the number of lines per page,
            '  read in another line from our file stream
            If (intCount < sngLinesPerPage) Then
                strLine = objStream.ReadLine()
            End If

        End While

        ' If we still have data remaining, go print another page
        If Not (strLine Is Nothing) Then
            ev.HasMorePages = True
        Else
            ev.HasMorePages = False
        End If

    End Sub

End Class
```

We could use this class as follows:

```
' Create new StreamReader object

Dim MyReader As System.IO.StreamReader = System.IO.File.OpenText("c:\readme.txt")

' Create object, set document name and print
Dim MyPrintObject As New TextFilePrint(MyReader)
MyPrintObject.Print()

' Close object
MyReader.Close()
```

Creating and Sorting Arrays

An array is essentially a collection of items, accessible through one variable name. You can size an array so it holds many "elements" and perhaps even multiple "dimensions."

Arrays can prove highly useful in many different programming scenarios. Here is how we could declare an empty array in VB .NET:

```
Dim MyArray() As String
```

Here is a more in-depth code sample demonstrating creating an array and storing data within it:

```
Dim MyArray(9) As String
' Creates ten string elements, 0 to 9

Dim intCount As Integer

' Fills the individual elements, from 0 to 9
For intCount = 0 To 9
    MyArray(intCount) = "Element Number " & intCount
Next
```

All arrays in VB .NET are zero-based, meaning that, if we declared our array with the number nine, it would hold ten elements, numbered from zero to nine. To add new elements to an array—whether it already contains elements or is currently empty—resize it using the ReDim statement:

```
Dim MyArray(9) As String
' Creates ten string elements

ReDim MyArray(11)
' Change to twelve elements
```

By default, the ReDim statement automatically erases any existing data in your array. To keep any existing data, use it with the Preserve keyword:

```
Dim MyArray(9) As String
' Creates ten string elements

ReDim Preserve MyArray(11)
' Change to twelve elements
```

You can find out the "upper boundary" of your array using the UBound statement:

```
Dim MyArray(9) As String
' Creates ten string elements

Dim intUpperBoundary As Integer
intUpperBoundary = UBound(MyArray)
' Returns the number 9,
' signifying you have elements from 0 to 9
```

To erase your entire array, use the Erase statement:

```
Dim MyArray(9) As String
' Creates ten string elements

Erase MyArray
' Erase everything from the array
```

You can sort your arrays, using the Sort method of System.Array, as so:

```
Dim MyAlphabet(4) As String, intCount As Integer

' Populate array
MyAlphabet(0) = "F"
MyAlphabet(1) = "W"
MyAlphabet(2) = "A"
MyAlphabet(3) = "Z"
MyAlphabet(4) = "I"

' Sort array
Array.Sort(MyAlphabet)

' Cycle through individual elements
For intCount = 0 To UBound(MyAlphabet)
    MessageBox.Show("Element " & intCount & " is: " & MyAlphabet(intCount))
Next
```

Note that your array doesn't merely have to hold a string. It can literally be an array of *anything*. You can find out more about arrays by looking up "arrays, Visual Basic" in the Help index.

Using the Special Array Functions

A number of special array functions are designed to help ease your work with arrays. These are Split, Join, and Filter.

The Split function takes a string and a delimiter. It then divides your string into individual array elements, depending on where it finds the delimiter. This is best shown by example:

```
Dim MyCustomerFile() As String, intCount As Integer

' Split string up using the delimiter
MyCustomerFile = Split("YO4928;SJ1482;OW4891;DI1325", ";")

' Cycle through the individual elements
For intCount = 0 To UBound(MyCustomerFile)
    MessageBox.Show("Element " & intCount & " is: " & MyCustomerFile(intCount))
Next
```

This Split function can prove incredibly useful, especially when parsing text or reading from files.

The Join function does exactly the reverse. It takes a bunch of array elements and adds them together, placing a delimiter between each element in the string. For example:

```
Dim MyWords(4) As String, MyFinalSentence As String

' Populate individual elements
MyWords(0) = "This"
MyWords(1) = "is"
MyWords(2) = "my"
MyWords(3) = "great"
MyWords(4) = "sentence."

' Compose final string,
' with a space between each element
MyFinalSentence = Join(MyWords, " ")
MessageBox.Show(MyFinalSentence)
```

Again, this is an incredibly useful timesaver when processing text.

The final useful function is Filter, which will filter out or "filter in" certain array elements. It accepts your array as a parameter, plus a string to match. It also sports a third Include argument. This defaults to True, signifying that any array element containing your match text is "filtered into" the final array. If you set this to False, any array element containing your match text is filtered out of the final array.

For example:

```
Dim Addresses(4) As String
Addresses(0) = "Weddington Lane, Caldecote"
Addresses(1) = "Eastbourne Road, Caldecote"
Addresses(2) = "High Street, Nuneaton"
Addresses(3) = "Edinburgh Road, Nuneaton"
Addresses(4) = "Nine Mews, Stratford"

Addresses = Filter(Addresses, "Nuneaton")
' Returns all elements of our array containing 'Nuneaton'

Addresses = Filter(Addresses, "Nuneaton", False)
' Returns all elements of our array not containing 'Nuneaton'
```

Collections in .NET

Collections are objects that have a life ambition of managing other objects. You can add, retrieve, or remove individual objects from the collection, with each object typically holding an associated key. All this functionality was demonstrated in Chapter 5.2 of Tutorial 5, "Using Objects".

Here is a demonstration of Collection object functionality that works with an imaginary Customer object:

```
Dim MyCustomer As New Customer(), MyCustomerCollection As Collection

With MyCustomer
    .Name = "John Brown"
    .Address = "17 Thistle Way"
    .Postcode = "CV10 9SQ"
End With
```

```
' Adding a customer
MyCustomerCollection.Add(MyCustomer, "MyKey")

' Retrieving a customer
MyCustomer = MyCustomerCollection.Item("MyKey")

' Removing a customer
MyCustomerCollection.Remove("MyKey")

' Counting the number of items in the collection
Dim intCount As Integer
intcount = MyCustomerCollection.Count
```

The Collection object exists in the `Microsoft.VisualBasic` namespace and was available in previous versions of VB. With .NET, we also find a new host of Collection-style objects available to us in the `System.Collections` namespace, including ArrayList, BitArray, HashTable Queue, SortedList, and Stack. Check out the Help index for more information on each of these.

Finding MTS and MSMQ

The .NET Framework contains support for all those big boys' toys you may have used in previous versions of Visual Basic (plus, in many cases, it allows you more control and easier-to-write code).

The feature once known as *MTS*, then later integrated into COM+, for example, is now bundled as part of Enterprise Services, accessible via the `System.EnterpriseServices` namespace. If you previously used object pooling or distributed transactions, these features are now all easily implemented via attributes.

For more information on Enterprise Services, look up "EnterpriseServices namespace" under the "Visual Basic and Related" Help index.

If you're used to writing transactional components that work with MSMQ (Microsoft Message Queuing), you might wonder how you can continue working with the technology. Thankfully, things are now slightly easier, and the `System.Messaging` namespace holds all the functionality you need to create queues, store messages, and more.

For more information on MSMQ, look up "message queues, overview" in the Help index.

It's worth noting that, although the functionality of both preceding namespaces is logically stored under the System namespace, it's physically stored in a separate DLL. To use this functionality, you need to first add a reference to the particular DLL by clicking on Project ➤ Add Reference and selecting the appropriate file (such as System.Messaging.dll).

Fine-Tuning Your ASP.NET Applications

You can fine-tune your programs in many different ways, but, in the world of high-demand ASP.NET Web applications, it's more important than ever. The following bundle of tuning tips are recommended for especially busy sites.

- Use the Caching feature where possible, with everything from regular pages to searches.

- Store large, frequently accessed DataSets in the Application object. Look up "cache, datasets" in the Help index for more information.

- When building strings, use the more efficient StringBuilder class, as opposed to the "&" concatenation character.

- Use the client to do as much work as possible, such as in the validation process, as opposed to requiring a postback.

- Don't use server-side controls where static HTML will suffice.

- Implement stored procedures for common database operations.

- Design your application with server farms in mind, ensuring that you utilize ViewState where possible.

- Where possible, try not to call old COM components.

- When using collection classes, such as Hashtable, try to initialize them with an item count to avoid unnecessary memory reallocation later.

These aren't required (and may even be disadvantageous) for most small to medium Web applications. However, if your site counter is on overload, this list is certainly worth reviewing.

Appendixes

This section includes the following appendixes:

- Appendix A: Installing Visual Studio .NET

- Appendix B: Project Defaults

- Appendix C: Standard Naming Conventions

- Appendix D: Windows Form Controls

- Appendix E: VB .NET Data Types

- Appendix F: SQL Server Data Types

Installing Visual Studio .NET

So, you've decided Visual Basic .NET is the programming language for you and need to slap it on your machine?

First off, you need to buy it. And that means making our first decision. You see, Visual Studio .NET comes in four separate flavors: Professional, Enterprise Developer, Enterprise Architect, and Academic.

If you're the penny-pinching type, the Professional version of Visual Studio .NET is the cheapest of the range and is bundled with Visual Basic .NET, Visual C++ .NET, and Visual C# .NET. It allows you to do everything we cover in this book, including build and run Windows applications, Web applications, and Web services.

If you're feeling a little more affluent, however, Enterprise Developer is most probably your best bet. It includes all the features of the Professional version, plus comes with Visual SourceSafe and developer editions of .NET server products such as SQL Server and Windows 2000.

The third option, Enterprise Architect, features all the above, plus a few system modeling features used by manager folk. And, finally, the Academic version is similar to the Professional version, plus it includes a number of extra wizards specific to the academic community and a particularly attractive price tag too—but it's available only to student types. D'oh!

In reality, it doesn't really matter which version you pick—even the basic product contains everything you need to get started. My best bet for most programmers? Go for Enterprise Developer: it contains everything you need, without going overboard. (It'll still take a bite out of your wallet, however.)

So, you've reviewed the options and chosen an appropriate version of Visual Studio .NET. Now, can your machine handle it?

To run the software, you'll need at least a PC with a Pentium II-class processor capable of 450MHz or higher. It's also recommended that you have 500MB of disk space available on your system drive, along with a potential 3GB handy for the actual installation.

In terms of operating system and RAM, Visual Studio .NET will install on Windows 2000 Professional (with 96MB of RAM), Windows 2000 Server (with 192MB of RAM), Windows NT 4.0 Workstation (with 64MB of RAM), and Windows XP Professional (160MB of RAM).

Of course, the rule of thumb here is more is better. And less? Oh, that's just disastrous.

A quick word of advice here: you won't want to install Visual Studio .NET on an NT 4.0 machine. Why? Windows NT doesn't support ASP.NET, one of the biggest areas of .NET, and it also doesn't allow for COM+ or multiprocessor garbage collection. The rest of this installation guide presumes you *didn't* choose NT 4.0.

So, your machine is capable of running your version of Visual Studio .NET. Next, you need to ensure that you have the right software already on the machine. What does this mean? First off, you need to set up Internet Information Services (IIS) on your computer if you don't already have it. You can check whether this is already installed by seeing whether the Internet Services Manager program (in Windows 2000) or Internet Information Services (in Windows XP) exists on your computer. To check, browse the Programs ➢ Administrative Tools menu.

To set up IIS on Windows 2000 or Windows XP, open the control panel, select the Add/Remove Programs applet, and choose Add/Remove Windows Components. In the Windows Components wizard, select Internet Information Services (IIS) from the Components list and click on Next to begin the installation.

> **TOP TIP** *If you install IIS after setting up Visual Studio .NET, you'll need to take a few extra steps. If you do not have a FAT16 or FAT32 file system, you'll need to install IIS and then repair Visual Studio .NET via the Add/Remove Programs applet. If, however, you do have a FAT16 or FAT32 file system, you'll need to install IIS, manually set up FrontPage extensions, and then repair VS.NET.*

Next up, if you plan to compile code related to Microsoft Messaging Queue (MSMQ), you'll need to install Message Queuing Services. To do this, follow the same procedure as installing Internet Information Services as above, except this time selecting the Message Queuing Services option.

So, you've purchased your version of Visual Studio .NET, found a machine capable of running it, and installed all the necessary software prerequisites? Great stuff. Now you're ready to rumble.

First off, make sure that you're logged in with administrative permissions. Why? Some features such as the debugger create their own system accounts and require such privileges to set them up. Note, however, that after the installation your VS .NET user doesn't necessarily need administrative privileges to run the application.

Right then: it's time for the actual installation. Take your Setup CD-ROM or DVD and insert it into your computer. The setup should automatically start; if not, open the drive via My Computer and double-click on the Setup.exe file.

You'll be guided through the entire installation process. This typically involves entering your serial number, selecting an installation directory, copying files, and configuring your machine. The whole process will last at least an hour, so get that kettle boiling.

> **TOP TIP**   *If you experience problems during the Visual Studio .NET setup, refer to Readme.htm in the root directory of your installation CD-ROM. It often provides useful information on known issues or last-minute workarounds.*

After the installation has finished, you'll want to perform just a couple of actions to fine-tune your copy of Visual Studio .NET.

First off, launch it. To do this, select Start ➢ Programs ➢ Microsoft Visual Studio .NET ➢ Microsoft Visual Studio .NET. In later revisions of the program, you may be prompted with a screen asking you to register online or via telephone using a special key. You can skip this initially; however, the program will run only a set number of times before you're forced to spill the beans to Microsoft.

In Visual Studio .NET, let's first set up your preferences. On the Start Page, click on the My Profile link down the left side. From the Profile drop-down list, select Visual Basic Developer. This will set Visual Basic as the default language, plus apply a set of typical keyboard shortcuts, as taught in this book and used in VB6.

Next up, you might consider checking for any updates, such as service releases or, more likely, bug fixes. To do this, select Help ➢ Check for Updates from the menu. You'll need an Internet connection to download the latest files.

And that's it! You've successfully installed Visual Studio .NET on your development machine.

One quick note for when you start creating projects in Visual Studio .NET: the Option Strict setting is turned off by default. You can set this value either in code or by right-clicking on your project in the Solution Explorer, selecting Properties, and choosing the Build item.

This value dictates that all object types must be explicitly declared, and any nonexact matches will prevent your application from compiling. For example, with Option Strict turned on, you could not create a string and set an Integer value to it. Instead, you would have to physically convert this value. (Look up "type conversion" in the Help index for more information.) With Option Strict turned off, Visual Basic handles all this automatically for you.

This Option Strict addition was added to help build enterprise projects that are more bug free, although it can prove inflexible and hinder learning Visual Basic. All samples in this book are based on this default setting of Option Strict turned off.

Project Defaults

WHEN YOU CREATE A NEW VB project in Visual Studio .NET, you'll notice numerous files and references added by default, creating a starting point for your application.

Translating these additions back to the real world can often be a confusing task. Therefore, the following sections detail the most-common project types and related template settings.

Windows Application

When creating a Windows application, the following is automatically added to your project:

- *AssemblyInfo.vb*: Used to describe your assembly plus contains versioning information. Edit this file to alter such data.

- *Form1.vb*: Standard Windows form, ready for you to manipulate.

- *Default references to*:

  - *System*: The mother of the .NET Framework base classes. Includes commonly used value and reference data types, plus defines events and event handlers, interfaces, attributes, and processing exceptions.

  - *System.Data*: Contains classes to handle ADO.NET data access.

  - *System.Drawing*: Contains classes to handle GDI+ graphics functionality.

  - *System.Windows.Forms*: Contains classes for creating Windows-based form applications.

  - *System.Xml*: Contains classes that provide standards-based support for processing XML.

- *Default namespace imports (Project, Imports)*:

  - Microsoft.VisualBasic

  - System

  - System.Collections

  - System.Data

  - System.Diagnostics

  - System.Drawing

  - System.Windows.Forms

Class Library

When creating a class library, the following is automatically added to your project:

- *AssemblyInfo.vb*: Used to describe your assembly, plus contains versioning information. Edit this file to alter such data.

- *Class1.vb*: Standard class template, ready for you to manipulate.

- *Default references to*:

  - *System*: The mother of the .NET Framework base classes. Includes commonly used value and reference data types, plus defines events and event handlers, interfaces, attributes and processing exceptions.

  - *System.Data*: Contains classes to handle ADO.NET data access.

  - *System.Xml*: Contains classes that provide standards-based support for processing XML.

- *Default namespace imports (Project, Imports)*:

  - Microsoft.VisualBasic

  - System

- System.Collections

- System.Data

- System.Diagnostics

Web Application

When creating a Web Application, the following is automatically added to your project:

- *AssemblyInfo.vb*: Used to describe your assembly, plus contains versioning information. Edit this file to alter such data.

- *Global.asax*: Contains template code for responding to application-level events raised by ASP.NET, such as Application_Start.

- *Styles.css*: Contains the default HTML style settings.

- *Web.config*: Contains your ASP.NET application settings, such as authentication and session settings.

- *<ProjectName>.vsdisco*: XML-based file used by ASP.NET when discovering Web Services on the server, only required if you add a Web Service to your application.

- *WebForm1.aspx*: Blank Web Form, ready for you to manipulate.

- *WebForm1.aspx.vb*: Underneath WebForm1.aspx in the Solution Explorer hierarchy (click Show All Files to open direct), this file contains a class file for the default WebForm1.aspx page, containing system generated and user code.

- *Default References to*:

  - *System*: The mother of the .NET Framework base classes. Includes commonly used value and reference data types, plus defines events and event handlers, interfaces, attributes, and processing exceptions.

  - *System.Data*: Contains classes to handle ADO.NET data access.

- *System.Drawing*: Contains classes to handle GDI+ graphics functionality.

- *System.Web*: Contains classes for browser/server communication.

- *System.Xml*: Contains classes that provide standards-based support for processing XML.

- *Default namespace imports (Project, Imports)*:

  - Microsoft.VisualBasic

  - System

  - System.Collections

  - System.Configuration

  - System.Data

  - System.Drawing

  - System.Web

  - System.Web.UI

  - System.Web.UI.HtmlControls

  - System.Web.UI.WebControls

Web Service

When creating a Web service, the following is automatically added to your project:

- *AssemblyInfo.vb*: Used to describe your assembly, plus contains versioning information. Edit this file to alter such data.

- *Global.asax*: Contains template code for responding to application-level events raised by ASP.NET, such as Application_Start.

- *Web.config*: Contains your ASP.NET application settings, such as authentication and session settings.

- *<ProjectName>.vsdisco*: XML-based file used by ASP.NET when discovering Web services on the server.

- *Service1.asmx*: The actual Web service file, which references the underlying assembly (your code compiled into a DLL).

- *Service1.asmx.vb*: Underneath service1.asmx in the Solution Explorer hierarchy (click on "Show All Files" to open directly), this file contains a class file for the default Web service page, holding system-generated and user code.

- *Default References to:*

  - *System*: The mother of the .NET Framework base classes. Includes commonly used value and reference data types, plus defines events and event handlers, interfaces, attributes and processing exceptions.

  - *System.Data*: Contains classes to handle ADO.NET data access.

  - *System.Web.Services*: Contains classes enabling you to build and consume XML Web services.

  - *System.Web*: Contains classes for browser/server communication.

  - *System.Xml*: Contains classes that provide standards-based support for processing XML.

- *Default namespace imports (Project, Imports)*:

  - Microsoft.VisualBasic

  - System

  - System.Collections

  - System.Configuration

  - System.Data

  - System.Drawing

  - System.Web

  - System.Web.UI

  - System.Web.UI.HtmlControls

  - System.Web.UI.WebControls

Standard Naming Conventions

It's good programming practice to use standard prefixes with your controls and variables. This ensures your code remains clear and understandable. The following list provides an overview of popular conventions:

ITEM	PREFIX	EXAMPLE
Form	frm	frmMain
Class	cls / C	clsOrder
Module	mod	modGeneric
Label	lbl	lblUsername
LinkLabel	lnk	lnkVisitSite
Button	btn	btnOK
TextBox	txt	txtPassword
CheckBox	chk	chkRemember
RadioButton	rad	radMale
GroupBox	grp	grpOptions
PictureBox	pic	picAuthor
DataGrid	grd	grdOrders
ListBox	lst	lstSubscribed
CheckedListBox	clst	clstExtras
ComboBox	cbo	cboRoomNumber
TreeView	tvw	tvwFolders
ListView	lvw	lvwFiles
TabControl	tab	tabSettings
DateTimePicker	dtp	dtpAppointment

ITEM	PREFIX	EXAMPLE
Timer	tmr	tmrCheck
Splitter	spl	splGeneral
ProgressBar	pbar	pbarTimeLeft
RichTextBox	rtf	rtfDocument
ImageList	imgl	imglToolbar
ToolBar	tlb	tlbMain
MenuItem	mnu	mnuFileExit
String	str	strAnalysis
Date	dat	datLastVisit
Boolean	bln	blnFlag
Short	sht	shtCurrent
Decimal	dec	decRate
Long	lng	lngSystemID
Integer	int	intCount
Byte	byt	bytAge
Char	chr	chrFirst
Single	sgl	sglRemaining
Double	dbl	dblTotalBalance
Structure (User-Defined Type)	udt	udtCustomer
Object	obj	objRandom
DataSet	ds	dsmembers
DataRow	dr	drEntry
OleDbConnection or SqlConnection	conn	connLuxor
OleDbCommand or SqlCommand	cmd	cmdDelete
OleDbDataAdapter or SqlDataAdapter	da	daUserList
OleDbDataReader or SqlDataReader	rdr	rdrItems
Crystal Report	rpt	rptSales

It is also common practice to prefix module-level variable declarations with "m" and global declarations with "g"—although, as ever, this is not enforced and simply serves as a suggestion to help assist your development.

You can also find a full list of recommended code styling guidelines for your Visual Basic program, by looking up "naming conventions, Visual Basic" in the Help index.

Windows Form Controls

When working with Windows Forms, you have 46 default controls available for use. The following alphabetically sorted list provides a simple description of each to help you choose which is best for the task at hand.

All items noted as components have no form-visible interface, and their actions must be manipulated in code. Here goes *<breathe in>*:

1. *Button:* Standard button the user can click to perform actions.

2. *CheckBox:* Allows the user to check an On or Off option.

3. *CheckedListBox:* Displays a list of items with a checkbox next to each.

4. *ColorDialog:* Component, allows the user to select a color from a dialog box.

5. *ComboBox:* Displays a list of options in a drop-down box.

6. *ContextMenu:* Component, allows you to create a pop-up menu.

7. *CrystalReportViewer:* Executes and displays a Crystal Report document.

8. *DataGrid:* Displays tabular data from a DataSet, plus allows for updates.

9. *DateTimePicker:* Allows the user to select a single date from a list of dates or times.

10. *DomainUpDown:* Displays strings that a user can browse through and select from.

11. *ErrorProvider:* Component, highlights errors in a user-friendly manner.

12. *FontDialog:* Component, allows the user to select a font via a dialog box.

13. *GroupBox:* Acts as a visible container for other controls.

14. *HelpProvider:* Component, associates a HTML help file with a Windows application.

15. *HScrollBar* and *VScrollBar*: Horizontal and vertical scroll bars, to allow for programmatic scrolling through a list of items.

16. *ImageList*: Component, stores images for use on other controls, such as the ToolBar and TreeView.

17. *Label:* Displays read-only text.

18. *LinkLabel:* Displays a Web-style link with a click event.

19. *ListBox:* Allows the user to select one or more items from a list.

20. *ListView:* Displays a list of items with icons, Windows Explorer-style.

21. *MainMenu:* Displays application menus.

22. *MonthCalendar:* Allows the user to select a date or range of dates from a month-by-month calendar.

23. *NotifyIcon:* Allows you to add icons to the system taskbar.

24. *NumericUpDown*: Displays a predetermined set of numbers that the user can browse through and select from.

25. *OpenFileDialog:* Component, allows users to select files to open via a standard dialog box.

26. *PageSetupDialog*: Component, displays a dialog box allowing the user to change page setup details for printing.

27. *Panel:* Provides grouping of controls, such as RadioButton controls.

28. *PictureBox:* Displays graphics in BMP, GIF, JPEG, WMF, and ICO format.

29. *PrintDialog:* Component, allows user to select a printer, the number of pages to print, and other settings via a standard dialog box.

30. *PrintDocument*: Component, allows user to set properties that describe what to print and then to actually print it.

31. *PrintPreviewControl*: Allows you to display a PrintDocument as it will appear when printed, without any user interface extras.

32. *PrintPreviewDialog*: Component, displays a PrintDocument in a dialog box, as it will appear when printed, alongside options to print, zoom, and move between pages.

33. *ProgressBar:* Indicates the progress of an operation graphically.

34. *RadioButton*: Allows the user to select an option from two or more exclusive buttons.

35. *RichTextBox*: Allows users to enter, display, and manipulate text with formatting.

36. *SaveFileDialog*: Component, allows the user to specify a save filename via a standard dialog box.

37. *Splitter*: Allows the user to resize a docked control, typically used for splitting forms into two components.

38. *StatusBar*: Displays status information, typically at the bottom of a form.

39. *TabControl*: Displays multiple tabbed pages, each containing their own controls.

40. *TextBox*: Allows editable, multiline input from the user.

41. *Timer*: Component, raises an event to run your code at specified intervals.

42. *ToolBar*: Displays menus and picture buttons that activate commands.

43. *ToolTip*: Component, displays text when the user hovers the mouse over controls.

44. *TrackBar*: Displays a bar for the user to position, perhaps for setting a numeric value or navigating through a large amount of information.

45. *TreeView*: Displays a hierarchy of items that can be expanded and collapsed, Windows Explorer–style.

<breathe out>

VB .NET Data Types

The following table lists the data types that are available in VB.NET, listed alongside their Common Language Runtime (CLR) base type.

VB DATA TYPE NAME	CAN HOLD	SIZE IN MEMORY	CORRESPONDING CLR TYPE
Boolean	True or False	2 bytes	System.Boolean
Byte	0 to 255	1 byte	System.Byte
Char	One single character	2 bytes	System.Char
Date	January 1, 0001 00:00:00 through to December 31, 9999 11:59:59 PM	8 bytes	System.DateTime
Decimal	0 through to +/- 79,228,162,514,264,337, 593,543,950,335 with no decimal point; 0 through +/-7.922816251 4264337593543950335	16 bytes	System.Decimal
Double (double-precision floating-point)	-1.79769313486231570E+ 308 through to -4.9406564 5841246544E-324 for negative values; 4.9406564 5841246544E-324 through to 1.79769313486231570E+ 308 for positive values	8 bytes	System.Double
Integer	-2,147,483,648 through to 2,147,483,647	4 bytes	System.Int32
Long (long integer)	-9,223,372,036,854,775,808 through to 9,223,372,036, 854,775,807	8 bytes	System.Int64

VB DATA TYPE NAME	CAN HOLD	SIZE IN MEMORY	CORRESPONDING CLR TYPE
Object	Any type can be stored in an Object variable	4 bytes	System.Object (class)
Short	-32,768 through to 32,767	2 bytes	System.Int16
Single (single-precision floating-point)	-3.4028235E+38 through to -1.401298E-45 for negative values; 1.401298E-45 through 3.4028235E+38 for positive values	4 bytes	System.Single
String	0 to approximately 2 billion Unicode characters	Depends on platform	System.String (class)
User-Defined Types	Each member of the structure is determined by its data type	Depends on platform	System.ValueType (inherits from)

In the .NET world, you officially have two different "types": value types and reference types. Value types simply contain core values and are stored on the application stack. Sample value types include Boolean, Integer, and Date.

Reference types are stored on the runtime heap, pointing to a particular object in memory. All objects derived from classes are reference types, including the String type, all arrays, forms, and so on.

In the real world, this behind-the-scenes difference has no or little impact on our programming. With powerful, highly requested applications, however, take the following two details into account:

- All reference types are handled by the .NET Framework garbage collection process. This means that unused objects are marked for deletion and destroyed, say, every few minutes. At busy times, this can result in a lot of objects just consuming memory, waiting to be destroyed. So, where possible, use the more efficient value types.

- Strings are more efficiently concatenated using the StringBuilder class. Using the simple & concatenation command can result in wasted memory strings that require garbage collection.

SQL Server Data Types

The following table lists the data types that are available in SQL Server.

DATA TYPE NAME	CAN HOLD
bigint	Whole number from -9223372036854775808 to 9223372036854775807
int	Whole number from -2,147,483,648 to 2,147,483,647
smallint	Whole number from -32,768 to 32,767
tinyint	Whole number from 0 to 255
bit	Either a 0 or 1
decimal	Fixed precision and scale numeric data from $-10^{38}+1$ to $10^{38}-1$
numeric	Same as decimal
money	Money values from -922,337,203,685,477.5808 to 922,337,203,685,477.5807
smallmoney	Money values from -214,748.3648 to 214,748.3647
float	Floating precision number from $-1.79E+308$ to $1.79E+308$
real	Floating precision number from $3.40E+38$ to $3.40E+38$
datetime	Date and time from January 1, 1753, to December 31, 9999, with an accuracy of 3.33 milliseconds
smalldatetime	Date and time from January 1, 1900 to June 6, 2079, with an accuracy of one minute

char	Fixed-length non-Unicode string with a maximum length of 8,000 characters
varchar	Variable-length non-Unicode string with a maximum of 8,000 characters
text	Variable-length non-Unicode string with a maximum of 2,147,483,647 characters
nchar	Fixed-length Unicode string with a maximum of 4,000 characters
nvarchar	Variable-length Unicode string with a maximum length of 4,000 characters
ntext	Variable-length Unicode string with a maximum length of 1,073,741,823 characters
binary	Fixed-length binary data with a maximum of 8,000 bytes
varbinary	Variable-length binary data with a maximum length of 8,000 bytes
image	Variable-length binary data with a maximum length of 2,147,483,647
sql_variant	Generic data type, can hold all SQL Server data types, except text, ntext, and timestamp
timestamp	Database-wide unique number that gets updated automatically whenever a row is updated
uniqueidentifier	Globally Unique Identifier (GUID)

Index

Apress Titles

ISBN	PRICE	AUTHOR	TITLE
1-893115-73-9	$34.95	Abbott	Voice Enabling Web Applications: VoiceXML and Beyond
1-893115-01-1	$39.95	Appleman	Dan Appleman's Win32 API Puzzle Book and Tutorial for Visual Basic Programmers
1-893115-23-2	$29.95	Appleman	How Computer Programming Works
1-893115-97-6	$39.95	Appleman	Moving to VB. NET: Strategies, Concepts, and Code
1-59059-023-6	$39.95	Baker	Adobe Acrobat 5: The Professional User's Guide
1-893115-09-7	$29.95	Baum	Dave Baum's Definitive Guide to LEGO MINDSTORMS
1-893115-84-4	$29.95	Baum, Gasperi, Hempel, and Villa	Extreme MINDSTORMS: An Advanced Guide to LEGO MINDSTORMS
1-893115-82-8	$59.95	Ben-Gan/Moreau	Advanced Transact-SQL for SQL Server 2000
1-893115-91-7	$39.95	Birmingham/Perry	Software Development on a Leash
1-893115-48-8	$29.95	Bischof	The .NET Languages: A Quick Translation Guide
1-893115-67-4	$49.95	Borge	Managing Enterprise Systems with the Windows Script Host
1-893115-28-3	$44.95	Challa/Laksberg	Essential Guide to Managed Extensions for C++
1-893115-39-9	$44.95	Chand	A Programmer's Guide to ADO.NET in C#
1-893115-44-5	$29.95	Cook	Robot Building for Beginners
1-893115-99-2	$39.95	Cornell/Morrison	Programming VB .NET: A Guide for Experienced Programmers
1-893115-72-0	$39.95	Curtin	Developing Trust: Online Privacy and Security
1-59059-008-2	$29.95	Duncan	The Career Programmer: Guerilla Tactics for an Imperfect World
1-893115-71-2	$39.95	Ferguson	Mobile .NET
1-893115-90-9	$49.95	Finsel	The Handbook for Reluctant Database Administrators
1-59059-024-4	$49.95	Fraser	Real World ASP.NET: Building a Content Management System
1-893115-42-9	$44.95	Foo/Lee	XML Programming Using the Microsoft XML Parser
1-893115-55-0	$34.95	Frenz	Visual Basic and Visual Basic .NET for Scientists and Engineers
1-893115-85-2	$34.95	Gilmore	A Programmer's Introduction to PHP 4.0
1-893115-36-4	$34.95	Goodwill	Apache Jakarta-Tomcat
1-893115-17-8	$59.95	Gross	A Programmer's Introduction to Windows DNA
1-893115-62-3	$39.95	Gunnerson	A Programmer's Introduction to C#, Second Edition
1-59059-009-0	$49.95	Harris/Macdonald	Moving to ASP.NET: Web Development with VB .NET
1-893115-30-5	$49.95	Harkins/Reid	SQL: Access to SQL Server
1-893115-10-0	$34.95	Holub	Taming Java Threads
1-893115-04-6	$34.95	Hyman/Vaddadi	Mike and Phani's Essential C++ Techniques
1-893115-96-8	$59.95	Jorelid	J2EE FrontEnd Technologies: A Programmer's Guide to Servlets, JavaServer Pages, and Enterprise JavaBeans
1-893115-49-6	$39.95	Kilburn	Palm Programming in Basic
1-893115-50-X	$34.95	Knudsen	Wireless Java: Developing with Java 2, Micro Edition
1-893115-79-8	$49.95	Kofler	Definitive Guide to Excel VBA
1-893115-57-7	$39.95	Kofler	MySQL
1-893115-87-9	$39.95	Kurata	Doing Web Development: Client-Side Techniques
1-893115-75-5	$44.95	Kurniawan	Internet Programming with VB

ISBN	PRICE	AUTHOR	TITLE
1-893115-38-0	$24.95	Lafler	Power AOL: A Survival Guide
1-893115-46-1	$36.95	Lathrop	Linux in Small Business: A Practical User's Guide
1-893115-19-4	$49.95	Macdonald	Serious ADO: Universal Data Access with Visual Basic
1-893115-06-2	$39.95	Marquis/Smith	A Visual Basic 6.0 Programmer's Toolkit
1-893115-22-4	$27.95	McCarter	David McCarter's VB Tips and Techniques
1-59059-021-X	$34.95	Moore	Karl Moore's Visual Basic .NET: The Tutorials
1-893115-76-3	$49.95	Morrison	C++ For VB Programmers
1-893115-80-1	$39.95	Newmarch	A Programmer's Guide to Jini Technology
1-893115-58-5	$49.95	Oellermann	Architecting Web Services
1-59059-020-1	$44.95	Patzer	JSP Examples and Best Practices
1-893115-81-X	$39.95	Pike	SQL Server: Common Problems, Tested Solutions
1-59059-017-1	$34.95	Rainwater	Herding Cats: A Primer for Programmers Who Lead Programmers
1-59059-025-2	$49.95	Rammer	Advanced .NET Remoting
1-893115-20-8	$34.95	Rischpater	Wireless Web Development
1-893115-93-3	$34.95	Rischpater	Wireless Web Development with PHP and WAP
1-893115-89-5	$59.95	Shemitz	Kylix: The Professional Developer's Guide and Reference
1-893115-40-2	$39.95	Sill	The qmail Handbook
1-893115-24-0	$49.95	Sinclair	From Access to SQL Server
1-893115-94-1	$29.95	Spolsky	User Interface Design for Programmers
1-893115-53-4	$44.95	Sweeney	Visual Basic for Testers
1-59059-002-3	$44.95	Symmonds	Internationalization and Localization Using Microsoft .NET
1-59059-010-4	$54.95	Thomsen	Database Programming with C#
1-893115-29-1	$44.95	Thomsen	Database Programming with Visual Basic .NET
1-893115-65-8	$39.95	Tiffany	Pocket PC Database Development with eMbedded Visual Basic
1-893115-59-3	$59.95	Troelsen	C# and the .NET Platform
1-59059-011-2	$59.95	Troelsen	COM and .NET Interoperability
1-893115-26-7	$59.95	Troelsen	Visual Basic .NET and the .NET Platform
1-893115-54-2	$49.95	Trueblood/Lovett	Data Mining and Statistical Analysis Using SQL
1-893115-68-2	$54.95	Vaughn	ADO.NET and ADO Examples and Best Practices for VB Programmers, Second Edition
1-59059-012-0	$49.95	Vaughn/Blackburn	ADO.NET Examples and Best Practices for C# Programmers
1-893115-83-6	$44.95	Wells	Code Centric: T-SQL Programming with Stored Procedures and Triggers
1-893115-95-X	$49.95	Welschenbach	Cryptography in C and C++
1-893115-05-4	$39.95	Williamson	Writing Cross-Browser Dynamic HTML
1-893115-78-X	$49.95	Zukowski	Definitive Guide to Swing for Java 2, Second Edition
1-893115-92-5	$49.95	Zukowski	Java Collections
1-893115-98-4	$54.95	Zukowski	Learn Java with JBuilder 6

Apress Titles Publishing SOON!

ISBN	AUTHOR	TITLE
1-59059-022-8	Alapati	Expert Oracle 9i Database Administration
1-59059-039-2	Barnaby	Distributed .NET Programming
1-59059-019-8	Cagle	The Graphical Web
1-59059-015-5	Clark	An Introduction to Object Oriented Programming with Visual Basic .NET
1-59059-000-7	Cornell	Programming C#
1-59059-014-7	Drol	Object-Oriented Flash MX
1-59059-033-3	Fraser	Managed C++ and .NET Development
1-59059-038-4	Gibbons	Java Development to .NET Development
1-59059-030-9	Habibi/Camerlengo/Patterson	Java 1.4 and the Sun Certified Developer Exam
1-59059-006-6	Hetland	Practical Python
1-59059-003-1	Nakhimovsky/Meyers	XML Programming: Web Applications and Web Services with JSP and ASP
1-59059-001-5	McMahon	Serious ASP.NET
1-893115-27-5	Morrill	Tuning and Customizing a Linux System
1-59059-028-7	Rischpater	Wireless Web Development, 2nd Edition
1-59059-026-0	Smith	Writing Add-Ins for .NET
1-893115-43-7	Stephenson	Standard VB: An Enterprise Developer's Reference for VB 6 and VB .NET
1-59059-032-5	Thomsen	Database Programming with Visual Basic .NET, 2nd Edition
1-59059-007-4	Thomsen	Building Web Services with VB .NET
1-59059-027-9	Torkelson/Petersen/Torkelson	Programming the Web with Visual Basic .NET
1-59059-018-X	Tregar	Writing Perl Modules for CPAN
1-59059-004-X	Valiaveedu	SQL Server 2000 and Business Intelligence in an XML/.NET World

Available at bookstores nationwide or from Springer Verlag New York, Inc. at 1-800-777-4643; fax 1-212-533-3503. Contact us for more information at sales@apress.com.

books for professionals by professionals™

Apress™

About Apress

Apress, located in Berkeley, CA, is a fast-growing, innovative publishing company devoted to meeting the needs of existing and potential programming professionals. Simply put, the "A" in Apress stands for *"The Author's Press™"* and its books have *"The Expert's Voice™."* Apress' unique approach to publishing grew out of conversations between its founders Gary Cornell and Dan Appleman, authors of numerous best-selling, highly regarded books for programming professionals. In 1998 they set out to create a publishing company that emphasized quality above all else. Gary and Dan's vision has resulted in the publication of over 50 titles by leading software professionals, all of which have *The Expert's Voice™*.

Do You Have What It Takes to Write for Apress?

Apress is rapidly expanding its publishing program. If you can write and refuse to compromise on the quality of your work, if you believe in doing more than rehashing existing documentation, and if you're looking for opportunities and rewards that go far beyond those offered by traditional publishing houses, we want to hear from you!

Consider these innovations that we offer all of our authors:

- **Top royalties with *no* hidden switch statements**
  Authors typically only receive half of their normal royalty rate on foreign sales. In contrast, Apress' royalty rate remains the same for both foreign and domestic sales.

- **A mechanism for authors to obtain equity in Apress**
  Unlike the software industry, where stock options are essential to motivate and retain software professionals, the publishing industry has adhered to an outdated compensation model based on royalties alone. In the spirit of most software companies, Apress reserves a significant portion of its equity for authors.

- **Serious treatment of the technical review process**
  Each Apress book has a technical reviewing team whose remuneration depends in part on the success of the book since they too receive royalties.

Moreover, through a partnership with Springer-Verlag, New York, Inc., one of the world's major publishing houses, Apress has significant venture capital behind it. Thus, we have the resources to produce the highest quality books *and* market them aggressively.

If you fit the model of the Apress author who can write a book that gives the "professional what he or she needs to know™," then please contact one of our Editorial Directors, Gary Cornell (gary_cornell@apress.com), Dan Appleman (dan_appleman@apress.com), Peter Blackburn (peter_blackburn@apress.com), Jason Gilmore (jason_gilmore@apress.com), Karen Watterson (karen_watterson@apress.com), or John Zukowski (john_zukowski@apress.com) for more information.